Indian Miniature Paintings and Drawings

THE CLEVELAND MUSEUM OF ART

CATALOGUE OF ORIENTAL ART

PART ONE

By Linda York Leach

Published by The Cleveland Museum of Art : 1986
In cooperation with Indiana University Press

The Cleveland Museum of Art
Catalogue Series

Catalogue of Oriental Art

Part One   *Indian Miniature Paintings and Drawings* (published 1986)
Part Two   *Japanese Prints*
Eight Dynasties of Chinese Painting: The Collections of the Nelson Gallery-Atkins Museum, Kansas City, and the Cleveland Museum of Art (published 1980)

Catalogue of Paintings

Part One   *European Paintings before 1500* (published 1974)
Part Two   *Illuminated Manuscripts*
Part Three *European Paintings of the 16th, 17th, and 18th Centuries* (published 1982)
Part Four   *European Paintings of the 19th Century*
Part Five   *American Paintings to 1900*
Part Six   *Modern Paintings*

Copyright 1986 by The Cleveland Museum of Art
11150 East Boulevard, Cleveland, Ohio 44106
All rights reserved
Printed in the United States of America
Design by Merald E. Wrolstad
Editing by Sally W. Goodfellow
Composition by Beacon Graphics, Ashland, Ohio 44805
Printing by Eastern Press, Inc., New Haven, Connecticut 06507

Distributed by Indiana University Press, Bloomington, Indiana 47405

Library of Congress Cataloging-in-Publication Data

Cleveland Museum of Art.
   Indian miniature paintings and drawings.

   (The Cleveland Museum of Art catalogue of
Oriental art; pt. 1)
   Bibliography: p. 319.
   1. Miniature painting, Indic — Catalogs.
2. Drawing, Indic — Catalogs. 3. Cleveland Museum of
Art — Catalogs. I. Leach, Linda York, 1942–
II. Title. III. Series.
ND1337.I5C56   1986   751.7′7′0954074017132   85-7740
ISBN 0-910386-78-1

Contents

Acknowledgements

I would like to thank numerous people who helped me with the catalogue and made the research enjoyable. The atmosphere promoted in the Cleveland Museum by former director Sherman E. Lee always stimulated scholarly inquiry. His interest, patience, and willingness to listen to ideas were invaluable as my work on the catalogue took shape in the early 1980s. Dr. Stanislaw J. Czuma, the Museum's curator of Indian and Southeast Asian art, has not only become a close friend but has provided guidance in acquiring background material on various Indian subjects.

The preparation of this catalogue was my introduction into Indian art, and many others outside the Museum were indeed kind in initiating me into the field. Cary Welch shared both his time and his characteristic zest for paintings generously. Catherine Benkaim introduced me to many people and allowed me to use her extensive slide collection. She and her husband, Ralph, provided encouragement and valuable suggestions in addition to making me feel welcome among museum staffs, collectors, and dealers. Robert Skelton helped me, as he has many others, with inexhaustible energy and painstaking care. His gentle sense of enthusiasm for his work turned what could have been drudgery into a really adventurous experience. My friend Jerry Losty kindly assisted with the identification of early Jain material, for which I am most grateful. Sven Gahlin, Toby Falk, Betty Tyres, and the staff of the India Office Library in London were also most helpful.

Finally, I wish to thank those who have done a great deal in producing this book. Sally W. Goodfellow has worked long hours editing, sorting out confusing material, organizing the bibliography and the photographs, and compiling captions. Judith DeVere patiently and expertly typed and retyped much of the manuscript. Merald E. Wrolstad was responsible for the design of the book, and Jo Zuppan helped in the early stages of manuscript editing. Georgina Toth lent assistance with bibliographical research and queries, and Eleanor Scheifele, with securing photographs of comparative material. These and many others contributed their particular talents in bringing the catalogue to its final realization.

Formation of the Collection

The collection of Indian paintings in the Cleveland Museum began in 1925—a relatively early date for an American museum—when Ananda K. Coomaraswamy sold some paintings from his own collection to the institution. Up to that time, a few purchases of Mughal miniatures had been made and a few gifts accepted; however, the quality of these miniatures varied and little was known about them by the staff or, in all probability, by their donors. The purchases from Coomaraswamy therefore represent the first deliberate acquisition and the first acknowledgement of the Museum's commitment toward familiarizing the public with this area of non-Western art.

In the United States, the Museum of Fine Arts, Boston, under its early curators Kakuzō Okakura and Coomaraswamy, provided leadership in collecting Asian art. Many of the Indian miniatures Coomaraswamy chose for his private collection were portions of sets, and he sold examples from these series to several museums in the eastern United States as a means of educating others to his taste. The Cleveland Museum owns miniatures from the three areas—Malwa, Jammu, and Kangra—favored by this scholar because of their pure Rajput style. Coomaraswamy's ideas paralleled those of the English art philosophers like Roger Fry who were beginning to look at exotic art on the basis of universal values. Color, abstract shape, linear rhythm, and so on, were seen as principles that animated the art of all cultures. The door to this approach had been opened by French post-Impressionist painters like Cézanne, Gauguin, and Matisse, whose paintings Fry interpreted to the public from about 1909, several years before Coomaraswamy's two-volume *Rajput Painting* was published. In his writings Coomaraswamy stressed the neglected Rajput schools in preference to Mughal painting, which, with its Renaissance and Baroque influences, had found greater acceptance in the West. Abstraction rather than naturalism prevailed in the works he championed. His defense of Rajput works succeeded in part because the Malwa miniatures he valued, for example, were viewed by people who were familiar with the works of Gauguin.

Through his sales, his writings, and his personality, Coomaraswamy greatly influenced the development of the Cleveland Museum collection. Although the perimeters of the taste he promulgated have since changed, the individual paintings he dispersed retain their interest. Formulated in simple terms with basic abstract elements, these works have a classic quality.

From the 1930s through the 1960s the Museum collection continued to grow, with purchases from the well-known dealer Nasli Heeramaneck. In general, he reflected Coomaraswamy's ideals, as demonstrated by his selections of Central Indian paintings, with their clear colors, flat planes, and freedom from Mughal influence (see [81], for example).

Western awareness of the diversity in Rajput painting developed slowly as collections from an increasing number of Indian states came to light. Pictures from the state of Kota were relatively unknown until the early 1950s, when their energy and freshness quickly became admired. An article in *The Bulletin of The Cleveland Museum of Art* (Lee, 1957, pp. 180–83) that compared a Malwa painting representing Coomaraswamy's aesthetic to a newly acquired Kota picture [77] was an early venture into a different kind of evaluation for Indian miniatures. The Kota hunting scene, in the context of this article, was indeed startingly novel and demanded careful attention. Broader critical standards thus evolved in Indian painting, and the diversity of Indian miniatures became a major source of interest.

Mughal paintings were acquired by the Museum from various sources; several can be traced back to the French dealer Demotte who had obtained many of the most significant Mughal albums, which he broke up prior to their sale (see [11]). The largest group of Mughal paintings was purchased in 1971 from the collection of John Mac-Donald. Shortly before that time, the Museum had acquired the *Tuti Nama* manuscript, which was subsequently reproduced in facsimile, in 1976 (see below). Since it incorporates various Sultanate and pre-Mughal Rajasthani styles with the evolving idiom of the Mughal court, this manuscript has significantly altered the study of Mughal painting. Some background, therefore, seems appropriate to include here.

THE CLEVELAND *TUTI NAMA*

The *Tuti Nama,* or *Tales of a Parrot,* is undoubtedly one of the most important acquisitions to have been made by an American museum in the field of Indian painting. The manuscript, illustrating fifty-two stories told by a parrot to entertain his flighty mistress, was done in the very earliest part of Akbar's reign.

The book, which was thought to be eighteenth-century Persian, was for many years in a private library in Baltimore, Maryland. It was acquired from this estate by a dealer who also assumed the volume to be Persian. Recognizing it to be a much more significant, Indian work, Sherman E. Lee succeeded in purchasing the majority of the folios for The Cleveland Museum of Art.

The illustrations are delightful in their own right, but they are highly important from an art-historical standpoint for several reasons. They demonstrate the character of the young emperor Akbar's studio at its inception, showing how his painters were taken from many differing provincial ateliers. Because aspects of Rajput painting are quite recognizable, the leaves demonstrate that Hindu illustration was indeed fairly well developed before the advent of the Mughals and was not an inspiration of the imperial court. Finally, since some of the *Tuti Nama* folios are inscribed with artists' names, the early work of particular painters can be documented; the most important are the two Hindus Basawan and Daswanth, described by Akbar's biographer Abu'l Fazl as being foremost in the studio after its Persian founders. Daswanth committed suicide in the 1580s, and his paintings are relatively rare. Basawan was the genius who set the style of painting throughout the Akbari period, and the *Tuti Nama* shows that he was a leader from the beginning of his career, adapting European ideas more boldly than his contemporaries.

The *Tuti Nama* has been employed in this catalogue in the discussion of several works because it is a crucial landmark for Rajasthani, Sultanate, and early Mughal painting. Its 211 miniatures provide the best evidence of types of painting existing side by side in the mid-sixteenth century. It is, however, a complex work that required extensive stylistic analysis and merited thorough coverage in several publications. For this reason, a decision was made shortly after its acquisition to produce a detailed analysis, a translation, and a facsimile of the folios, together with a small exhibition catalogue. The *Tuti Nama* is thus outside the scope of the present catalogue, but the information contained in the publications listed below provides a scholarly appraisal of this work that may be of interest to the reader:

The Cleveland Museum of Art's Tuti-Nama [*Tales of a Parrot*], by Ziya'u'd-din Nakhshabi. Translated and edited by Muhammed A. Simsar. Cleveland: Cleveland Museum of Art; Graz, Austria: Akademische Druck, 1978. First complete translation to appear in any Western language; 48 color plates.

The Cleveland Tuti-Nama Manuscript and the Origins of Mughal Painting. Chicago: University of Chicago, The David and Alfred Smart Gallery, 1976. Catalogue of the exhibition held at The Cleveland Museum of Art November 9–December 19, 1976, and at The David and Alfred Smart Gallery January 12–February 27, 1977. Introduction by Sherman E. Lee; essay by Pramod Chandra; catalogue by Daniel Ehnbom; 28 black and white plates.

Tuti-Nama [facsimile]. Vol. 55 in Codices Selecti series. Graz, Austria; Akademische Druck, 1976. Complete color facsimile-edition in the original size of the manuscript in The Cleveland Museum of Art and of separate folios from private collections. Casebound in leather; 211 color plates.

Tuti-Nama [commentary]. Vol. 55* in Codices Selecti series. Graz, Austria: Akademische Druck, 1976. Commentarium by Pramod Chandra. 120 black and white plates.

L.Y.L.

PUNJAB
HILLS

RAJASTHAN

Jammu

- Jammu
- Mankot
Chamba
- Basohli

Chamba

Nurpur
Guler
- Kangra
- Guler

Kulu
- Bilaspur
Kangra
Mandi
Kulu

Bilaspur

Jaswan

Garhwal

Bikaner

- Bikaner

Jaipur

Jaisalmer

- Amber/Jaipur

- Kishangarh

- Jodhpur

Amber

- Ajmer (Sawar)

Marwar

Ajmer

Bundi

- Bundi

Mewar

Sirohi
- Sirohi
Abu
- Udaipur
Chitor

- Kota

Kota

- Chawand

Explanatory Notes

Sanskrit terms may, in some cases, vary in form — that is, because diacritical marks have not been used. Numerous past variations in romanized spellings of some of the terms may also account for occasional inconsistencies.

Numbers in brackets refer to catalogue entries.

Letters in parentheses [e.g., (A) or (B-E)] refer to works cited in the "Comparative Material" section at the beginning of a catalogue entry.

The number that follows the title of a work (e.g., 44.501) at the beginning of each catalogue entry is the accession number assigned by the Cleveland Museum.

References cited more than once are given in abbreviated form; the full citations are provided in the *Select Bibliography*. When cited only once, however, a reference is given in full form in the appropriate footnote or under "Published" in the preliminary material in a catalogue entry, if applicable.

The *Glossary* is not intended to be exhaustive: proper nouns have been omitted, and whenever a definition is provided within the text itself, the term has not been included in the glossary.

I. Early Painting: The Jain, Sultanate, and Early Rajput Schools

The Jain Tradition

The strongest, most continuous miniature-painting tradition in India prior to the Mughal conquest was that of the Jains, whose scriptures were illustrated in many north Indian areas, particularly the western state of Gujerat. Jainism, based upon the teachings of Mahavira, who lived in the sixth century BC, emerged at approximately the same time as Buddhism and developed certain beliefs and practices similar to those of Buddhism. Monks of both religions commissioned cave paintings such as those in Jain caves at Udayagiri (first century BC), where remnants of color still adorn a few walls. The exact relationship between vestigial wall paintings and the book-painting tradition is conjectural, given the contrast between the two media and the fact that designs were presumably done by different craftsmen. However, there seems to have been some stylistic correlation: although the Jain wall paintings at Sittanavasal in southern India have little relation to the earliest-preserved scriptural illustrations, a Hindu ceiling painting at Ellora—geographically nearer to Gujerat—reveals characteristics similar to the Jain illustrations.

Over the centuries the Jains have cultivated values of discipline, individualism, and conservatism—all of which have contributed to their survival. While the conservative nature of Jainism eventually led to stagnation for its painters, this same quality probably saved the religion from extinction when like Buddhism it was faced by a seemingly all-pervasive Hindu faith. During the years when ancient Indian beliefs were being codified into an organized Hindu religious system, the Jains were carefully maintaining their traditions, developing libraries as scriptural depositories, and training monks according to a strict standard. Thus they maintained their unique identity and have made, and continue to make, important contributions to Indian culture.

Both Buddhism and Jainism were minority religions that rebelled against the destiny of suffering for sins of other lives (karma) and maintained that liberation from continual rebirth was possible. Such liberation has always been the aim of stoical Jains, and indeed most of Jain painting or sculpture portrays how freedom from rebirth is won. Although scriptural illustrations have served as a reminder of truth rather than as art that existed for its own sake, the Jain painters have clearly lavished care and attention in creating scenes that depict the ideal world of Jain saints.

The twenty-four *tirthankaras* ("ford-makers," or those who have found a path through the maze of birth and rebirth) are the most important subjects of painted illustration. Mahavira, the twenty-fourth *tirthankara*, is considered to have been an historical person. Through self-denial and indifference to transitory phenomena, he, like the legendary *jinas* (saints) before him, achieved freedom from rebirth and left an example to his followers. An early schism between two Jain sects—the naked Digambaras and the more worldly Svetambaras—may have prompted the writing down of precepts and *tirthankara* biographies. Although the date of the earliest illustrations of the various scriptures are unknown, examples have survived from the eleventh century. The faithful acquired merit by donating scriptures, which proliferated in libraries because so many Jains were wealthy and generous banker- or merchant-patrons.

The most usual text illustrated was the *Kalpa Sutra*, dealing generally with the *tirthankaras* but centering around the life of Mahavira [3]. The *Kalpa Sutra* has always conveyed a sense of dignity to the Jain laity, and gave organization and purpose to monks by holding before them the eventual goal of becoming a *siddha*, or soul freed from the trammels of reincarnation, as Mahavira was. Mahavira's actions of wordly renunciation, the plucking out of his hair, and meditating either seated in a lotus posture or standing erectly (*kayotsarga*) all provide an ennobling model for the activities that monks have followed through the centuries and still carry on.

While one of the achievements of modern scholarship has been to document the widespread nature of the painting style associated with Jainism, the original development of the style clearly occurred within western India. Gujerat seems always to have been an exceptional center of crafts, and its people are notably design conscious; certainly the creativity of its miniature painters on a two-dimensional field owes much to Indian fabric design of the period and its ornamental stylization. Because of its location and its enterprising, cosmopolitan people, Gujerat has been molded in a distinct manner, and its regional "personality" has had a pronounced effect on arts such as Jain manuscript illustration. With the disruption of a relatively unified political organization after the fall of the Gupta dynasty, most of

India returned to being a society dominated by village life and agriculture. Gujerat, however, was at the time rising as a bustling center of textile production and trade. By the eighth century it had attracted Arab traders and its ports were renowned for the number and variety of goods flowing through them. The Jains living in its many cities and towns spent heavily on temples, libraries, manuscripts, and so forth, thereby providing evidence of the cultural expressiveness of the religion.

Gujerat was raided by Mahmud of Ghazni in the early eleventh century, but the real impact of Islamic destruction was not felt until the end of the thirteenth century when Alauddin Khalji destroyed dozens of culturally significant sites, including various Jain monuments. The combination of material wealth with energy and cultural sophistication in Gujerat, however, provided the basis for a renaissance in the early fifteenth century when a Muslim dynasty began to beautify its new capital, Ahmedabad, with many exquisite mosques and tombs. Their architecture combined the lacey decoration characteristic of Jainism with Muslim forms—one indication that the new rulers consciously appreciated the past heritage of Gujerat. In manuscript painting this tolerant atmosphere promoted a style that became progressively richer and more crowded with detail but remained surprisingly independent of Islamic influence.

The earliest Jain manuscripts were done on palm leaves, which were superseded by paper during the fourteenth century. Simple and straightforward, the palm-leaf scenes preserve some of the formal qualities and the monumentality of the wall-painting tradition. The Cleveland Museum owns examples of the uncluttered early style dating from the late thirteenth century that are drawn vividly and powerfully when compared with later manuscripts that could be considered more gracefully calligraphic.

Given the conservative nature of the Jain tradition, compositional arrangements and forms tended to remain much the same over the years, but decorative flourishes multiplied and the entire drawing style changed gradually to one that was much more contrived and ornamental. Artists had attempted to express a buoyant life quality by means of repeated curling lines, which increasingly strained the fixed limits of their paintings. For a time they succeeded in producing small compositions electrically charged with a great deal of vitality, but after about 1500 their work appears constricted and rather mechanical.

As Jain miniatures had become more florid, artists concentrated even more on the fabrics actually depicted in the scenes, along with such patterned items as the architectural tiles introduced to India by Muslims. Tilework, hangings, and other decorative arts provided a symbolic indication of settings, but the structural framework of houses or palaces was omitted in the anti-spatial miniature designs usually placed on a red background. In landscape scenes a single tree indicating a grove, or a deer suggesting a herd would be placed near a stream defined by abstract ripples in a textilelike pattern, also against a red ground, which symbolized fertility or renewal. Figures were arranged in angular poses that emphasized the virtuosity of linework and, as was usual in Indian tradition, their bodies were associated with natural elements—hands, for example, were commonly bent back to the wrist with fingers widely splayed, much like open flower blossoms. Facial features conformed to a convention, of which the most characteristic element was a projecting, further eye.

For several hundred years Jain artists produced shorthand versions of dramatic episodes: they omitted any pictorialization of emotion and telescoped time as well as space in their lively two-dimensional symbolic scenes. Ultimately linked to the ascetic goals of the religion, the conventions of Jain painting often require a kind of translation. Although the objects of the natural world are done as symbols, primarily because of pictorial limitations, many concepts—such as that of Mahavira as a liberated soul, or of his universal preaching—are inherently abstract and are therefore depicted with a mathematical purity and precision. While symbols in Jain painting that have emotional connotations (as, for example, the use of red ground to denote vitality) in time also became part of the Rajput visual tradition, the stoicism of the Jain is far removed from the understated but smoldering passions expressed in Hindu literature that provide a clue to understanding this latter heritage.

The Development of Rajput Painting

The Rajputs were latecomers to Indian society, arriving in about the sixth century AD as one of the invading forces that destroyed the golden age of the imperial Guptas, the last rulers of a unified India until the coming of the Mughals, and plunged the subcontinent into disunity for a millennium. This culturally inferior group of Hunnic descent secured a high caste status because of their forcefulness; ultimately they developed a rough chivalric code akin to that of medieval Europe. In the deserts and scrub forests of Rajasthan as well as in the cool Himalayan foothills, this Rajput caste took over the defense and kingship of states ranging in size from several hundred square miles to only a few. The Rajputs' chief pleasure lay in fighting, and they exaggerated every opportunity to wage bloody battles among themselves that generally resulted in little territorial gain but preserved their status as warriors.

Both in Rajasthan and the Himalayas the clans made some kind of oral record of their histories in the medieval period. Certain clans trace their origins to supernatural ancestors such as the sun (Mewar in Rajasthan) or Rama (Chamba in the Himalayas). In most states historical notations were kept with varying degrees of accuracy about migrations, rulers, and clan relationships—as when subgroups split off and formed separate states. Despite the fact that the Rajput groups settled in numerous disparate environments, they preserved many of the same attitudes and customs—so that whether a ruler was situated in a rocky desert fortress or in a fertile Himalayan valley, he probably felt it good to expend much of his time in riding, hawking, or other kinds of hunting.

Distinctive clan activities seem to have been modified in part by the effects of Hinduism on the groups. Many rajas were devoutly interested in one or more Hindu deities, but the brahmins also must have influenced the development of worship as expressed in art. For example, beginning in about the eleventh century, long ballads of heroism became very popular with the Rajput clans and are still illustrated by folk painters today. Such ballads, however, bear little relation to the works illustrated by Rajput court painters in the late fifteenth and early sixteenth centuries. These court texts were mainly the great religious writings concerning the god Vishnu's incarnation, Krishna, whose personality was celebrated with increasing fervor and ceremony through the medieval period.

Rajput poets also composed related secular verses (in a much more sophisticated style than the chivalric ballads) that communicate an unfulfilled romantic passion akin to worship. While the bardic tales are rambling, episodic stories, the more polished religious or secular poetry condensed extremely intense descriptions into electric, tension-filled verse. This frequently used type of verse-symbolism originating in literature also became characteristic of Rajput painting and provides the key to its power. Although the basic techniques for creating poetic scenes developed out of the wire-line drawing used by the austere Jain artists, impassioned literary sentiment determined the emotional breadth of this Rajput art. The type of description equating man with nature was based on the writings of the Gupta period, but it had a new tightness and tension that mirrored the changes taking place in Indian society.

Below the sublimated emotion in both painting and love poetry lay the Rajputs' ambivalent attitude towards women. Such social regulations as those controlling early arranged marriages resulted in not only a progressive loss of feminine freedom from the Gupta era but also a simultaneous idealization and degradation of women that was accentuated by the medieval Muslim invasions. The defeats of the Hindu warrior caste and the threats posed to their homes by Muslim males were in part compensated for by the Rajputs' possessiveness of women. In addition, as Muslim rules of seclusion (*purdah*) brought about restrictions by Hindus, the women became ever more tantalizingly unapproachable. Thus much of the ardor and suppressed emotion of Rajput poetry or painting arose from the barriers erected between the sexes. The relaxed, loving gestures common in Gupta sculpture and painting were clearly foreign to the later period, when despite the depiction of erotic passion there is little open warmth or stable affection linking male and female figures. The arts, however, reflected a fascination with sexuality and sexual psychology that continued from the earlier medieval period when analyses of types of loves became popular.

Among the most gripping and personal of the Rajput poetic verses are those by the lover Bilhana evoking memories of his mistress; they were probably illustrated about 1525. These illustrations of Bilhana's *Chaurapanchasika* epitomize early Rajput symbolism. The poem's title, therefore, is often used to classify other similarly illustrated texts of the period (see [8i]). The architecture and the rudimentary landscapes of the early Hindu manuscripts are distinctive, but it is the style of figure drawing that best defines the group and is most emphatically portrayed in the *Chaurapanchasika*.

While the term "*Chaurapanchasika* style" is an imprecise one, often less appropriate than the classification "early Rajput," it seems acceptable as a reminder that a particular figure type is crucial in the development of Indian painting and that this type had its origins in an intense romantic idealism like that of Bilhana's love lyrics. The symbolically treated scenes of the poet's mistress, with her huge eyes, pendulous breasts, small waist, and delicately gesturing hands encompassing both passion and composure, are entirely worthy of the descriptive encomiums in the verses.[1] The *Chaurapanchasika* figure not only is characteristic of the early Hindu manuscripts (see [8iii]) but also carried over into Rajput and popular Mughal paintings of the early seventeenth century.

The passionate idealization of love had become the subject of devotional as well as secular literature. Radha's yearning for Krishna, mirroring the soul's quest for union with the divine, was perhaps most compellingly expressed in the erotic verse-drama of lovers' quarrels and reconciliations—the often-illustrated *Gita Govinda*. Jayadeva, the twelfth-century Bengali court poet who made this major venture into impassioned sacred verse, created the personalities of Krishna and his mistress so vividly that later writers then elaborated upon his concepts for several centuries. Jayadeva's own source for his vibrant creation was apparently the scriptural account of Krishna's life found in Book 10 of the *Bhagavata Purana* (see [8i–8iii]). This detailed account loosely weaves together the several separate themes of Krishna's endangered youth, his valiant deeds as a young cowherd, his love exploits, and his altered life as a prince in Mathura.

The god's biography commences with the threats of Krishna's wicked uncle, the ruler Kansa, who knows that one of his relative's children will overthrow him. Despite the fact that Kansa has imprisoned Krishna's parents, the infant's father, by divine intervention, is able to remove the child to a pastoral site. Krishna then grows up in the herding village of Gokula as the foster child of the headman Nanda and his wife Yasoda, who dotes on the mischievous boy. Although the young Krishna easily annihilates the various demons Kansa sends to destroy him, the cowherds believe it wise to move to the more remote village of Brindaban to avoid the mysterious plague of disasters threatening their children. Krishna grows up in the midst of these cheerful herders, who are irresistibly drawn by his charming personality but who are never fully allowed to realize his divine powers. The village girls are quickly and fatally swayed by his beauty, his irreverent pranks, and his masterful authority. Although the rule of the age was that women were carefully constrained by husbands and female relatives, literature discusses love for the *parakiya* ("one belonging to another"). In Krishna's case he calls the *gopis* (cowherding girls) from their husbands, and they willingly assent. Radha's position as Krishna's ultimate beloved is variously treated by different writers, since in certain cases she too is someone else's wife. Such themes, very important in the devotional paintings of the Sultanate era, continued throughout the Mughal period.

The hereditary artist-craftsman portraying the symbolic yearning of Radha for Krishna surrendered his own will in a parallel fashion when picturing the mythic world. Creativity occurred not through the inflation of personality but through the discovery of egolessness, which has always been at the core of Indian religious idealism. When the artist subordinated himself to the enormous power of Hindu traditionalism, he unlocked his own vitality and originality, but only in relation to this stable body of belief. Creativity without this underlying religious purpose would have been functionless, whereas the idea of devotional submission and union with perfect order appealed to the artist on his deepest motivational level.

Much of the power of Rajput miniatures arises from the fact that the painter was always reacting to what had been expressed by the body of his fellow artists in the past. His own work thus lay in heightening the intensity of already-developed symbols—for example, the women drawn in *Chaurapanchasika* style by such painters radiate power and passionate vitality because they are long-pondered symbols that have been given a personal emphasis. This response to collective thought demonstrates the tremendous strength of Hinduism's social appeal—a force that in many ways remained completely unaltered by the Muslim invasions of the Sultanate period.

The Courts of the Muslim Sultanate

The Muslim Sultanate rulers who established themselves in northern and central India from the beginning of the thirteenth century were perpetually contending against an alien and hostile environment. Although no determined armies opposed their conquests, these Muslims, who were contemptuous of infidels, often found themselves more alarmingly ostracized by native Hindus. The newcomers, effectively isolated by difficult geographic or climatic conditions as well as strange social conditions, must have felt that tenure was uncertain. The times demanded strong men, and contenders for power rose and fell. Although neither Jain nor Hindu artists were much affected by the constant political upheavals of the Sultanate period, such

unstable conditions understandably had a pronounced effect on Muslim painters by forestalling—if not altogether eliminating—the development of either a continuous or widespread tradition. When viewed in comparison with the long, conservative history of Jain painting, the lack of continuity or cohesive style in the works sponsored by Muslim sultans is particularly striking.

The Muslim rulers were ambitious patrons of architecture and threw their energies into erecting massive, structurally exciting buildings that harmonized well with the harsh, brooding Indian landscape. Because a monument to the glory of one's own career in this turbulent era seemed a noble, practical desire, architecture fared much better than the more frivolous art of miniature painting. The Sultanate rulers who were of Turkish and Afghan origin had no inherited tradition of patronage, in contrast to the Timurid princes of Persia for whom cultivated refinements were part of privilege. In addition, few Indian Sultanate rulers were sufficiently aware of aesthetic enjoyment to challenge the religious prohibitions of figural representation that still surrounded the art of miniature painting.

Since Islamic immigrants from Turkey, central Asia, Afghanistan, Persia, and Arabia mingled and contributed to Indian society at this time, it is natural that their presence should be reflected in the arts. Architecture, for instance, reveals central Asian or Arabic strains in addition to Persian ones. So few miniature paintings are preserved from this period and so little is known of their history, however, that it is difficult to estimate the amount of inspiration coming from countries other than Persia. One of the few examples of an apparent exotic influence is provided by an early series that illustrates tales of the mid-thirteenth-century Delhi writer Amir Khusrau. This series resembles manuscripts of Mamluk Egypt, which had trading connections with the subcontinent (see [1]).

Because miniature painting was exceptionally well developed in Persia, painters and probably manuscripts flowed into India from various Persian locations. The imported styles were usually those of Shiraz or Bukhara; however, no one manner of painting had a truly creative impact on India. Persian works were idealized and precious, while the developing Hindu style was warm, bold, and earthy. The transition between the two idioms was therefore difficult, and in only a few cases did painters escape being suspended uneasily between Indian and foreign traditions.

The process of creating Indianized styles of Islamic painting was an evolutionary one that went through various preliminary stages before the rapid development of the Mughal school in the Akbari period. Throughout the Sultanate era poor painters continued to migrate from Persia, and because they could not deal with the challenges of their new environment, they simply executed inferior Persian pictures for the Muslim ruling class. Such men functioned on an artisan level and would not have been competitive in their home areas, but relied on the novelty of their idiom in a foreign land for survival. Since they were forced by their limitations to cling to old techniques, they were incapable of sharing much with one another or participating in the development of a cohesive style. Certain native painters attempted to please Muslim patrons by being adaptive, but they reached dead ends aesthetically: for example, several Islamic manuscripts executed in the wire-line drawing style of the Jains indicate the pervasiveness of the Jain idiom at this time, but most are limited in expression. The genuinely creative works coming at the end of the period are few but significant because they show that social interchanges had taken place between the Hindu and Muslim communities. Like the Persian artist and his Indian assistants who seem to have worked on the *Nimat Nama* cookery book done in Mandu, the capital of Malwa, successful painters were perhaps innovative because cooperation stimulated them. The *Nimat Nama* is well organized in a Persian fashion but infused with Hindu warmth and filled with details that reflect observation of Indian life.

Since Sultanate paintings are often indistinguishable from other provincial Persian works, they have been difficult to attribute; no evidence remains that any were done in the first centuries of the Muslim conquest. Although by the fourteenth century wall paintings and probably some manuscripts were being illustrated in Delhi, the art was treated with disapproval by austere sultans.[2] The continually shifting governments of Delhi were generally fighting difficult battles on several fronts, and sultans struggled for ascendancy over their own nobles. The city was thus an environment for iron-willed men who exercised considerable determination in order to govern. It is not known what types of painting flourished in this atmosphere, since the city's culture was irrevocably destroyed by Timur's massacre in 1398. The Mongol conqueror not only slew Delhi's inhabitants but carried off anyone valuable to him, such as craftsmen. While the bereft heartland slowly recovered, the provincial areas governed by independent Islamic dynasties developed various art and architectural styles. Because Gujerat, Jaunpur, Malwa, or Bengal seemed to permit a more informal integration of cultures and a more flexible lifestyle than Delhi, the evolution of Indo-Islamic styles was hastened in these areas.

The central Indian state of Malwa had an ancient Hindu literary history that was overlaid with traditions introduced by its Muslim rulers. As was characteristic of the mixed standards during the period, both the *Nimat Nama* (ca. 1500–1505) and a *Bustan* in Herat style with little Indian influence dated to 1502/3 were produced in the Mandu court. The former, detailing the favorite recipes of Ghiyas-ud-din of Mandu (r. 1469–1501), was not completed until shortly after his death but is nevertheless a lively record of the palace environment he created. This eccentric, hedonistic ruler surrounded himself with female attendants who served as bodyguards and worked in his *karkhanas* (possibly including the painting studio). Although unsophisticated by Persian standards, Ghiyas-ud-din's painters created spirited arrangements of color and pattern that are partially Indian. The ruler testing favorite recipes is shown with his female attendants, who often wear Indian printed textiles or have Indian features. Despite the fact that elements are naively presented, the manuscript demonstrates a new level of Indo-Islamic assimilation that is both charming and vital.[3]

From the diversity of styles in the Cleveland *Tuti Nama*, it is evident that by the sixteenth century there were numerous regional variations in painting occasioned by the independence of Sultanate principalities. The division and extent of many of these artistic areas is, however, imperfectly understood as yet. The most prominent style (from a still-unspecified location) appearing in the *Tuti Nama* is that used for the Cleveland Museum's early sixteenth-century *Laur Chanda* leaf [7]. The artists who worked in this style had managed to assimilate Muslim and Rajput characteristics quite effectively. Persian pastel colors, curling clouds, and other motifs create a pleasing setting for Indianized figures attired in costumes with Rajput features.

Artists schooled in this style, who were taken to Akbar's studio after his accession in 1556 and who worked on the *Tuti Nama*, proved that they were well trained technically and also had a facility for developing the graceful architectural and natural features of this style in more mature ways. The variety of artists at Akbar's disposal demonstrates that by the end of the Sultanate period painting was of great interest to many patrons. Although these overlords had not created unified schools, they had attained more leisure and freedom in their new environments and gradually had become more discerning in their patronage. Without the pool of talent represented by his many Muslim Sultanate and Rajput artists, Akbar clearly would not have been able to demand so much from his studio. The quick development of the Mughal style and the rapid completion of so many large projects really depended upon this corps of willing workers who had already been trained in attractive but less naturalistic styles to please the rulers and princes of various courts from western Gujerat to eastern Gaur in Bengal.

1. L. Shiveshwarkar, *The Pictures of the Chaurapanchasika* (New Delhi: National Museum, 1967).

2. Firoz Shah Tughluq (r. 1351–88) is known to have spoken out against wall painting; see K. S. Lal, *Twilight of the Sultanate* (London: Asia Publishing House, 1963), p. 241.

3. R. Skelton, "The Ni'mat Nama: A Landmark in Malwa Painting," *Marg* 12 (1958): 44–50.

Figure 1*v*.

Figure 1*xi*.

Figure 1*xii*.

1 *Fourteen Palm-Leaf Pages*   71.118–71.131

Jain, western India, Gujerat, ca. 1280, each painting approx.
5 × 5 cm, each page approx. 5 × 31 cm.
Purchase from the J. H. Wade Fund

Acquired as a group, these palm-leaf pages (two broken leaves retain only the text—71.118 and 71.121) are done in much the same style but come from several different manuscripts. Two colophons dated 1278 and 1279 verify that many of the pages were produced at the same time, and the remainder must be judged nearly contemporary on stylistic grounds.

Because Jain palm pages are virtually unknown in collections outside India, these fragile thirteenth-century examples are highly significant acquisitions.[1] The largest group (five pages) comes from a *Kalpa Sutra* with a colophon stating that it was done in 1279 for the ruler Sarangadeva in Anahillapura. The city of Anahillapura, in Gujerat, was the capital of the Solanki dynasty and a major center of manuscript production, since many of its rulers either were Jains or patronized the religion. In the mid-twelfth century the Solanki line died out and rule was assumed by the vassal Vaghelas. Although they were less powerful, this dynasty remained in power until the Islamic conquest of Gujerat in 1297. Sarangadeva (r. 1274–94) was the last of these kings to have a long, relatively successful reign. The size of his territory had decreased considerably and he was unable to mount large, effective military campaigns. Nevertheless, life in Gujerat continued to be comfortable, and the influence of the Jains had increased, so that artistic commissions were still frequent.[2]

Gujerat had tempted Islamic adventurers from the beginning of their entrance into India; for example, Mahmud of Ghazni, who was attracted by stories of fabulous wealth, plundered Somnath and other sites in 1026.[3] In 1197 a major Islamic incursion was ultimately repulsed, and conquest was postponed for a century.

The Gujeratis were renowned for the production of both cotton and silks, and since they were also extraordinarily adept traders, interested in seafaring, their cities prospered greatly. At the height of Solanki power Anahillapura was India's richest city, with luxurious palaces, flourishing markets, and large religious schools.[4] At the time the *Kalpa Sutra* was done (from which the Cleveland pages derive), it was still wealthy though less influential; but in the Islamic period its elegant stone buildings were plundered for the construction of other centers.[5]

Like other thirteenth-century leaves, these are done in a relatively basic style with few details and rough but decisive calligraphic strokes. Their simplicity is perhaps due to the transitional state of the art (which was altering from an imitation of wall painting) as much as to the confusion of Gujerati politics. Since the pages acquired by the Museum are from several manuscripts, their classification was initially difficult. However, they have been divided by such features as texts, formation of the *Devanagari* letters, and

ornamentation around the central holes used to thread the books together. As an example of the last feature, which was uniform for each manuscript, one central perforation is ornamented with a flower enclosed in a square [1*xii*], whereas many of the others are decorated with different types of dashes. The size of the palm leaves, although varying slightly within a manuscript, has also proven to be crucial in analyzing this group.

The pages are organized as follows:

Manuscript A   *Kalpa Sutra*.

This is a fairly small, narrow manuscript with only three to five lines per page, and bears the inscription and data given under 1*v* (below).

1*i*   A monk preaching (71.119).
1*ii*   A seated monk holding a flower (71.120).
1*iii*   Sakra with his elephant goad and a parasol (71.122).
1*iv*   Gautama seated in *pravachanda mudra* (71.123).
1*v*   Mahavira preaching to a kneeling woman (71.124).
Inscription: "SRI ANAHILLAPURE MAHARAJADHIRAJA SRI SARANGADEVASYA VIJAYARAJYE LIKHITAM on the fifth day of the bright half of Jyestha, Samvat 1336" (AD 1279).[6]
1*vi*   A Jain monk (possibly Kalaka) with a layman (71.127). This page is from the end of a *Kalacharyakatha;* the story of Kalaka (the monk who fought a king over the abduction of his sister and corrected the time of an important Jain festival) was regularly attached to the *Kalpa Sutra*. Because the leaf appears to be the same in size and painting and writing style as the leaves in the *Kalpa Sutra* described above, it was probably appended. (Examples from this group of leaves are reproduced in Nawab, 1956, pl. III figs. 8–11, and pl. X fig. 48; also in W. N. Brown, 1933, figs. 7–9. Other leaves from this manuscript are in W. N. Brown, 1933, fig. 10, and in Nawab, 1956, pl. III fig. 7.)

Manuscript B   *Kalacharyakatha*.

1*vii*   The single Cleveland leaf (71.126) from this manuscript has two illustrations and bears a colophon dated "Samvat 1335" (AD 1278) and naming an unknown city—[A?]lhadanapura—as the site of production. The illustrations, slightly more detailed than those of the Anahillapura pictures, show two monks holding their face cloths while two laywomen make gestures of respect. (Repr. in W. N. Brown, 1933, figs. 7 and 8.)

Manuscript C

Two leaves from a work on yoga. This text is in Sanskrit, unlike the *Kalpa Sutra* written in Prakrit, but one of the illustrations [1*viii*] is a standard type also employed in *Kalpa Sutras*. Both illustrations are quite detailed, and the leaves are in a precise hand with seven lines to the page.

1*viii* Mahavira(?) in heaven seated in *padma asana* (71.129).

1*ix* Mahavira(?) preaching to another monk, with a row of two monks, two nuns, and a laywoman along the bottom (71.128). Like the previous page, this composition is a standard one (see also 1*xii*); it commonly appears near the end of manuscripts.

Manuscript D

Two leaves from an unidentified work on or by Hemachandra. Hemachandra, the twelfth-century Jain pundit who was powerful in influencing the policy of the Solanki kings and soliciting funds for building temples, is revered for his teachings and for several important treatises he wrote that were copied and preserved in Jain *bhandars*. The pages here are vividly colored in reds, yellows, and greens, and are more heavily outlined in black than the other Cleveland leaves.

1*x* A *tirthankara* in heaven (71.130).

1*xi* A monk (Hemachandra?) expounding to a layman (71.131).

Manuscript E

Single leaf of an unidentified work. This leaf is extremely wide (written with nine lines to the page), and appears to be the final page of a manuscript.

1*xii* Mahavira preaching to a monk, with a row of two small laymen and two laywomen below (71.125).

1. Six palm leaves from a manuscript dated AD 1260 are owned by the Museum of Fine Arts, Boston; W. N. Brown, 1933, figs. 5 and 6.

2. Majmudar, 1965, p. 105.

3. Majmudar, 1968, p. 98.

4. Majmudar, 1965, p. 101.

5. Majmudar, 1968, p. 30.

6. J. P. Losty of The British Library translated the inscriptions and assisted in clarifying the texts of the palm-leaf pages.

2 *Rsabhanatha's Birth* 76.27

Folio 40 from a *Kalpa Sutra* manuscript, Jain, western India, Gujerat, ca. 1400, 9.4 × 28.4 cm.
Gift of Dr. Norman W. Zaworski
Comparative Material: (A) *Birth of Neminatha*, Jain, western India, Gujerat, ca. 1400; Nawab, 1959, pl. 30, fig. 37.
(B) *Birth of Mahavira*, Jain, western India, Gujerat, 1370; M. Chandra, 1949, fig. 56.

The first *tirthankara*, Rsabhanatha, is endowed by the Jain sect with an heroic personality like that of primal figures in many early civilizations; he is, in other words, considered responsible for the origin of the crafts and for various inventions as well as being credited with becoming the first monk. His history in the *Kalpa Sutra* follows the more detailed account of Mahavira, with significant sacred events such as his tonsure described in the same conventionalized way.

This leaf depicts Rsabhanatha's birth in a standard manner, though only in more ornate manuscripts is Queen Maru attended by two maids rather than one. The drawing, combining sophistication and spirited freshness, is of exceptional quality superior to that of certain contemporary examples, such as the illustrations of a *Kalpa Sutra* dated 1404 in the Royal Asiatic Society.[1] The queen lies on a swing with the hanging ropes that have been attempted in a naturalistic manner (although humorously confused by the bodies of the attendants). Geometric forms like those of the roof are rendered precisely, while curves are buoyant and lively like those of the queen's reclining figure depicted with elegant calligraphic strokes. Although such confident drawing occurs in earlier palm manuscripts—as, for example, in a text dated 1370 (B)—the setting here has been made more ornate as well as more descriptive without any of the stiffness that results from the repetition of prescribed Jain compositions.

A close parallel both stylistically and in details of composition among the many superficially similar versions of a birth scene is an equally calligraphic depiction of the blue *tirthankara* Neminatha (A).

1. Topsfield, 1981, fig. 170.

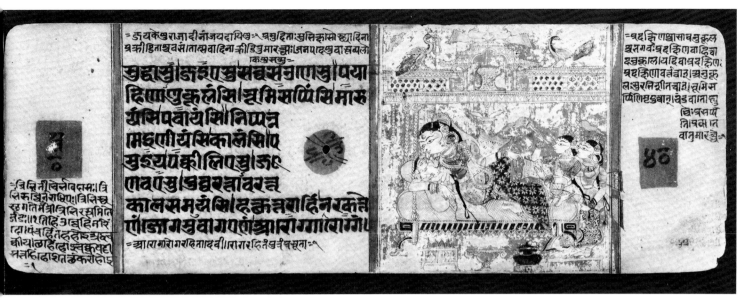

Figure 2.

Figure 2, detail.

3 Twenty-Four Miniatures from a Kalpa Sutra Manuscript

32.119/1-24

Jain, western India, Gujerat, 3rd quarter 15th century, each page approx. 12.5 × 25.7 cm.
Purchase, Edward L. Whittemore Fund
Ex collection: Heeramaneck.
Published: W. N. Brown, 1934, figs. 41, 71, 98.

This manuscript of the *Kalpa Sutra* now has seventy folios, of which the last but not final page is numbered seventy-six; since it is nearly complete, it provides a good example of the manuscripts presented to Jain *bhandars* in the latter part of the Sultanate period (Brown lists missing folios in the sequence). Its twenty-four miniatures are refined drawings with characteristically rococo details whose subjects and general compositions follow the type prescribed during the era. The artist, for instance, invariably depicts the events that in Jain ritual are considered particularly crucial in the life of a *jina*, or conqueror of the phenomenal world (heavenly descent and conception, birth, renunciation and initiation, enlightenment, nirvana) and treats them much like other fifteenth-century scenes of the same subjects. Mahavira, the twenty-fourth and probably historical *tirthankara*, is used in the sutra as the primary model for the righteous ascetic life and victory over the material world.

At the beginning of the manuscript Mahavira is shown in heaven, where he waits through aeons in a state of perfection and bliss until his time to be born as a *tirthankara*. In a pointed slight of brahminism, he first enters the womb of the brahmin wife Devananda, who has had auspicious dreams signalling a special birth. Sakra (Indra), however, the old Vedic figure of the king of the gods, decides that the fetus must be transferred to the womb of a member of the ruling *ksatriya* caste—a duty he assigns to his ram- or horse-headed general, Harinegamesin. Queen Trisala then has the fourteen auspicious symbols (which include an elephant, bull, lion, banner, garlands, the sun and moon) appear in her dreams as Harinegamesin successfully makes the transfer. Surprised by her dreams, she awakens her husband, King Siddhartha, who interprets the omens as meaning that the queen will give birth to either a world emperor or a savior. In the morning Siddhartha rises and bathes before having an audience with his astrologers, who confirm his prognostications. Trisala is then frightened because the sober and saintly embryo does not move in her womb, but when this intuitive child perceives the reason for her concern, he stirs slightly and she rushes to communicate her relief.

When Mahavira is born he is ceremonially bathed and anointed, and while Sakra puts Trisala into a deep sleep, he is taken to heaven to be blessed by the gods. A few events in Mahavira's youth are then described. The saint had vowed not to enter the religious life until after the death of his parents, which occurs when he is thirty. Sakra then comes to remind him of his obligations, and Mahavira gives away all his possessions before plucking out his hair

to symbolize his renunciation and dedication—a ceremony still performed in public by Jain monks every four months. Mahavira then meditates, living an austere life and surviving attacks by hostile villagers, dogs, and serpents without reaction, after which he obtains omniscience by perceiving universal truth as distinct from such phenomena. At death he attains the state of a *siddha*, or liberated soul.

The sutra follows with the histories of Neminatha and Parsvanatha, the twenty-second and twenty-third *tirthankaras*. Neminatha bested his cousin Krishna three times in tests of strength: he breaks the string of his unbendable bow and frustrates him in a wrestling match that both symbolizes the *jina's* superiority to Hindu heroes and pokes sly fun at the dominant religion. Parsvanatha is shown with open-hooded *nagas* surrounding his head; this symbolizes the extraordinary protection afforded a personality with supernatural potentialities and recalls the time when he saved the lives of these snakes.

Illustrations of the first *tirthankara*, Rsabhanatha, show him as the first king and an inventor of certain crafts. The other *jinas* are mentioned more briefly in the text, which then details the heads of the sect after Mahavira's death. One of these monks is Sthulabhadra, who lived with a beautiful courtesan named Kosa; on becoming a monk, Sthulabhadra continued to stay with her in a celibate state as a penance, rejecting all her approaches until she finally became a nun in admiration of his strength of character. Sthulabhadra's sisters, also nuns, are sometimes shown with him to illustrate an incident in which he transformed himself into a lion to exhibit his powers, frightening them, and nearly ending his progress in the order because of the conceit the deed demonstrated [3xxiv].

The miniatures and their subjects are as follows:

3i *Mahavira in the Puspottara Heaven* (32.119/1). This composition conforms in almost every detail to the standard of the later fifteenth century (W. N. Brown, 1934, fig. 2; throughout the sequence of illustrations the Cleveland manuscript is close to this manuscript in the Freer Gallery of Art, Washington): Mahavira sits in *padma asana*, crowned and heavily bejeweled. The configuration is somewhat the same as that customary for the goddess Laksmi (since both personages are emblems of auspiciousness), with two small elephants lustrating the figure and lotuses as symbols of fertility. Celestial musicians play flutes in small pavilions above Mahavira's throne, and attendants with *chauris* stand on either side of him.

3ii *The Brahmin Wife Devananda Has the Fourteen Lucky Dreams* (32.119/2). The auspicious objects are an elephant, a bull, a lion, garlands, a vision of Laksmi, a banner, a full jar, an ocean of milk, a lotus lake, a heavenly palace, a heap of jewels, a brilliant smokeless fire, and the sun and moon.

Figure 3*viii*.

3*iii* *Sakra Reverencing Mahavira's Embryo* (32.119/3). The king of the gods is in heaven with an honorific parasol over him. Surrounded by all the rich trappings of his celestial office, he reverences the embryo of Mahavira, which he realizes is just descending to earth.

3*iv* *Sakra Summons Harinegamesin* (32.119/4). Sakra on his throne bids his *yaksa* general (in this case, ram-headed) to transfer the embryo to the womb of a *ksatriya* woman.

3*v* *Harinegamesin Moves the Embryo* (32.119/5). The general removes the fetus from Devananda, above, to Queen Trisala, below.

3*vi* *Trisala Dreams* (32.119/6). The queen has the fourteen lucky dreams pictured in the same order as in 3*ii*, except that the sun and moon are shown before the lotus lake.

3*vii* *King Siddhartha Rises and Bathes* (32.119/7). The king kneels in an elaborate pavilion surmounted by peacocks while having his hair dressed by an attendant who has (mistakenly?) been given a crown and halo (see also W. N. Brown, 1934, fig. 41).

3*viii* *Siddhartha Hears the Recitation of Trisala's Dreams* (32.119/8). Siddhartha and Trisala are seated in the palace on the same level, although Siddhartha is on a more elegant throne.

3*ix* *Siddhartha Explains the Dream to Trisala* (32.119/9). The scene is abbreviated in the artistic composition as Siddhartha, after hearing the dreams, for the sake of propriety takes Trisala behind an ornamented veil before the arrival of the two interpreters shown seated in the lower register. When they conclude their opinion, the king goes and tells it to his wife.

3*x* *Trisala's Grief* (32.119/10). In the upper register the queen, who appears in larger proportions because of her social status and importance in the tale, sits dejectedly before her attendants fearing that the embryo is not alive. In the lower register she communicates her relief after Mahavira's movement.

3*xi* *The Birth of Mahavira* (32.119/11). Trisala, lying on a typical couch-bed, holds the baby in her arm as a maid approaches with flowers (?).

3*xii* *Mahavira's Lustration* (32.119/12). Sakra holds Mahavira on his lap beneath a canopy while two of his sixty-three other personalities hold water vessels. Symbols of universal order showing Mahavira's importance include two of the bulls representing the four directions and the peaks of Mt. Meru, which had bowed in reverence at the arrival of the savior.

3*xiii* *The Vigil on the Sixth Night* (32.119/13). The scene shows four female attendants celebrating this auspicious period after Mahavira's birth.

3xiv *Mahavira Gives Away His Possessions* (32.119/14). Mahavira sits on a throne attended by two monks (?) under a canopy decorated with *hamsas*. At his side is a stand that appears to be heaped with jewels, from which he gives a jewel (or similar gift) to a bearded old man.

3xv *Mahavira's Initiation* (32.119/15). Mahavira is carried in the *diksa* (initiation) palanquin still fully jeweled and dressed; above him female attendants and celestial musicians signify the universal rejoicing on the commencement of his liberating mission.

3xvi *Mahavira's Tonsure* (32.119/16). Mahavira kneels beneath the *asoka* tree above a group of mountain peaks and plucks out his hair as Sakra, with his characteristic symbol of the elephant goad, reverently waits to receive the five handfuls that he will carry in a cup of diamond to the Ocean of Milk.

3xvii *Mahavira's Samavasarana* (32.119/17). After Mahavira has attained complete knowledge, the gods cleanse and ornament earth before listening to him preach. Three walls of jewels, gold, and silver with gateways to the four directions are erected, with the waiting gods, men, and animals symbolically represented at the outer limits. Mahavira is now once more fully ornamented as befits a *siddha*.

3xviii *Mahavira as a Siddha* (32.119/18). Mahavira is shown after death in the heaven for perfected beings, represented by the white crescent boundary before him. He is seated on a throne surrounded by lotuses; the crown is backed by curling leaves, as it was prior to his birth.

3xix *Neminatha's Samavasarana* (lower register) and *Transformation as a Siddha* (upper register; 32.119/19).

3xx *The Birth of Parsvanatha to Queen Vama* (32.119/20).

3xxi *Parsvanatha in the Storm* (32.119/21). Parsvanatha, who had saved a family of snakes, is protected by this snake king and his queen shown in human form on either side of the *jina* as well as encircling his head during a flood sent by the same *asura* who would have killed the snakes. The stream is shown behind the hero and a supporting *yaksa* below.

3xxii *Birth of Rsabhanatha* (32.119/22).

3xxiii *The Eleven Ganadharas of Mahavira* (32.119/23). Mahavira's chief disciples who founded the schools of Jainism are seated in rows. The open space is filled by an abstraction of the sacred syllable *om*.

3xxiv *Sthulabhadra as a Lion* (32.119/24). Sthulabhadra appears in a pavilion in his transformed state as a lion (but with an elephant's head) frightening his two sisters, who run back to his preceptor below.

FURTHER READING: W. N. Brown, 1934; Jain and Fischer; Losty.

Figure 3*xiv*.

Figure 3*xxiv*.

4 Two Miniatures from a Kalpa Sutra Manuscript

25.1339, 25.1340

Jain, western India, Gujerat, early 16th century, each painting approx. 9.5 × 6.8 cm, each page approx. 22.2 × 16.5 cm. Eighteenth-century gold-flecked paper borders.

Gift from J. H. Wade

Ex collection: Coomaraswamy.

Comparative Material: (A) *Sakra Reverencing Mahavira's Embryo*, page from a *Kalpa Sutra* manuscript, Jain, western India, Gujerat, late 15th century or early 16th century; W. N. Brown, 1934, fig. 9.

These leaves, which are coarser and place less emphasis on rhythmic detail than those of an earlier period (see [2]), show the breakup of the minute, idealized world that had been created by Jain painters after about 1500. The type of careful drawing associated with the religion reached its climax and then came to a dead end, partly because the religious purpose of the art did not promote change and was not in itself sufficient to maintain inspired quality. Although the spheres of Jain and Hindu artists were not obviously competitive, it is almost as if Jain painters had long filled a vacuum but collapsed as a reaction when Hindu artists seized initiative, expanded the Jain sense of space, and broke down Jain abstractions.

Here, both leaves have standard compositions:

4i *Sakra Reverencing Mahavira's Embryo* (25.1339). The painting depicts Sakra kneeling before his heavenly throne in reverence as Mahavira's embryo descends to earth (cf. A).

4ii *The Birth of Mahavira* (25.1340). This scene shows the confinement of Mahavira's mother, Queen Trisala, who is lying on a couch; an attendant stands nearby.

Figure 4*i*.

Figure 4*ii*.

5 *Folio with Dancing Women* 79.23

Jain, western India, Gujerat, early 16th century,
11.5 × 29.3 cm overall.

Gift in Memory of Herbert F. Leisy

This page is probably one of a series from a manuscript. Texts were sometimes decorated throughout with narrow panels showing women in different poses from the standard repertoire of devotional dance.[1] The most beautiful and elaborate of these manuscripts now known is the combined *Kalpa Sutra* and *Kalacharyakatha* in the Devasano Pado Bhandar, Ahmedabad.[2] The sixteenth-century Cleveland page seems to have been based on the style used in this very decorative fifteenth-century sutra, since both floral scrolls and dance figures are somewhat similar. The loose, imprecise execution of the Cleveland leaf contrasts, however, with the crisp calligraphy of the fifteenth century and shows the deterioration of Jain craftsmanship at the end of the

Sultanate period. A closely related page is in the Metropolitan Museum of Art, New York (1977.41).

1. Such a manuscript is shown in V. S. Nawab, *419 Illustrations of Indian Music and Dance in Western Indian Style* (Ahmedabad, 1964).
2. Nawab, 1956, figs. 358–66.

Figure 5.

6   A King Receiving Three Men   63.261

Page from the *Khamsa* of Amir Khusrau Dihlavi, Sultanate, 2nd half 15th century, 28.6 × 21.6 cm overall. Badly damaged, creased, torn and rubbed.

Purchase, John L. Severance Fund

Amir Khusrau, the mid-thirteenth-century poet of Delhi, was a man of broad interests who held important positions under several Delhi sultans and became one of the most influential public figures of his city and era. His greatest literary contribution is considered to be the development of a more sophisticated and modern vocabulary, combining Persian words with Braj Bhasha, the language used by the Krishna poets of Mathura. Despite the handicaps of a still-evolving linguistic structure, the emotions that this poet communicated in his writings were complex, and he thus achieved a considerable reputation internationally.

A prolific writer, Amir Khusrau appealed to Islamic literati in various cultures through his lyric verses and Sufi sentiments. To Persians, he is one of the only Indian poets whose work could be that of a native Persian—although he was born in Sultanate India of a Turkish father.[1] During his lifetime, Delhi was a thriving center of learning, but since India had not achieved any cultural distinction in the Islamic world, Amir Khusrau's success was tremendously important to his countrymen. To a certain extent, the Delhi poet's life mirrors the quest for identity and the creative borrowing taking place in architecture, literature, and philosophy throughout the Sultanate era. Miniature painting was by contrast a much less developed art. As this *Khamsa* manuscript demonstrates, patrons willingly employed artists of varying backgrounds to fill a cultural vacuum, but the ability of these painters to amalgamate several styles or to develop a native idiom was extremely limited.

Amir Khusrau's international acceptance explains how this manuscript could first reasonably have been attributed to Persia rather than to the poet's homeland. The illustrations belong to a loose group of miniatures lacking Indian stylistic traits that can still be ascribed to the Sultanate period, in this case because the vessels and a few costume or furnishing details are indicative.[2] But Amir Khusrau's *Khamsa* is singular in that most of the other Sultanate or possibly Sultanate manuscripts are derived from Timurid models. The *Khamsa* pages instead relate to the old-fashioned Mesopotamian style of painting that was common in the Islamic world during the thirteenth century;[3] characteristics that can still be seen in the Sultanate *Khamsa* pages include the simple geometric settings and the ornamentally shaded textiles. While this stiff but lively style was radically altered by the Mongol invasion of Persia, it was retained in Mamluk Egypt into the fourteenth century.[4] Persian artists of the fourteenth-century Inju school also preserved certain Mesopotamian traits, but their miniatures are much less geometric than either the Egyptian or Sultanate examples.[5] If this *Khamsa* can be associated with the Mamluk style, the relationship is due to the flourishing textile trade between India and Egypt that brought contacts on various cultural levels. Because of this sea traffic, Gujerat may be the most logical Sultanate center for the manuscript's production; but since the miniatures have no localized traits, their provenance cannot be verified.

More than twenty-five leaves of this *Khamsa* are scattered in various collections.[6] The Cleveland scene of a king meeting three men is typical of all the folios, which are energetically drawn but rarely depict action successfully; as in this instance, many of the scenes have simple red grounds and are statically organized on one plane with forms in a straight line. The text of this miniature discusses wars in North Africa, both in Zang (Ethiopia) and Morocco; the illustration may portray the king of Zang receiving three envoys. The mid-fifteenth-century date assigned to this series was based upon the type of *nasta'liq* script employed, and has been questioned.[7] Although the painting style is that of a century or more before, its retention is not unprecedented in India, since in certain instances Mongol traits were apparently preserved by Indian artists long after their general disappearance.[8]

1. R. C. Majumdar, 1960, p. 534.
2. Ettinghausen, 1961*a*, text for pl. 1.
3. R. Ettinghausen, *Arab Painting* (Lausanne: Skira, 1962), p. 87.
4. D. Haldane, *Mamluk Painting* (Warminster: Aris & Phillips, 1978), pl. 17.
5. B. Robinson, *Descriptive Catalogue of the Persian Paintings in the Bodleian Library* (Oxford: Clarendon Press, 1958), fig. 76.
6. List given in Beach, 1981, p. 46.
7. Ettinghausen, 1961*a*, p. 6.
8. I. L. Fraad and R. Ettinghausen, "Sultanate Painting in Persian Style," in *Chhavi*, Golden Jubilee Volume (Benares: Bharat Kala Bhavan, 1970), fig. 134.

FURTHER READING: Beach, 1981, pp. 42–46; A. S. M. Chirvani, "L'école de Shiraz et les Origines de la Miniature Moghole," in *Paintings from Islamic Lands*, ed. R. Pinder-Wilson (Oxford: Bruno Cassirer, 1969), pp. 124–41.

Figure 6.

Figure 7, obverse.

7 *Page from the "Romance of Laurik*   81.55
and Lady Chandaini"

From the Prince of Wales Museum *Laur Chanda*
manuscript, Sultanate, ca. 1525, 19.7 × 14 cm,
25.5 × 20 cm overall. Text on reverse (illus.). Somewhat
rubbed and worn; paint missing in a few places. Border of
thin, beige paper.
Gifts of D. J. R. Ushikubo, The John Huntington Art
and Polytechnic Trust, and Bequest of James Parmelee
by exchange

The majority of leaves known from this manuscript of the
Laur Chanda romance are in the Prince of Wales Museum,
Bombay.[1] The *Laur Chanda*, a folk story with Hindu pro-
tagonists, was adapted by a Muslim poet in the late fourteenth century for his patron, a prime minister of the Delhi
Sultanate. The story concerns the hero Laurik and his exploits as well as his arranged marriage to Maina and his
obsession with Chandaini, whom he takes as a second wife.
The love between Laurik and Chandaini was refashioned by
the Muslim poet from a typical picaresque romance into a
tale with symbolic overtones of unity with the divine. This
alteration is indicative of the mysticism characteristic of
both Muslim Sufis and Hindus that was an important development of the Sultanate period and seemed for a while to be
creating a common ground between the two religions. The
Laur Chanda was very popular and was illustrated several
times in the Sultanate era; however, with the arrival of
the fast-moving, historically minded Mughals, the tale lost
its appeal, like others such as the sometimes-illustrated
Mrigavat mystic romance, and sank into oblivion.

The mixture of Hindu/Muslim influences is striking from
a literary point of view but is also artistically significant in
this particular copy of the work. Islamic motifs such as
curling Persian clouds, key-shaped hillocks, or pale, flowery backgrounds have been transformed by Indian taste so
that the forms are much looser and more freely drawn than
those in the Provincial Persian type of scene found in such
manuscripts as the *Bustan* produced at Mandu in 1502/3.[2]
The *Laur Chanda* figures are also Indianized, although the
women have been altered more radically than the men.
Their features and proportions are much like those of the
entirely Indian *Chaurapanchasika* group and are completely dissimilar to illustrations of the Indo-Persian *Bustan*
done at Mandu. The slight, square-headed woman in the
Cleveland miniature with her *odhni, choli,* and tassel ornaments is clearly related to *Chaurapanchasika*-type females,
and the *Laur Chanda* miniatures generally look as if the
artists had readily assimilated elements of both Muslim and
native traditions. The men in the Cleveland scene have
features similar to males in the *Bustan* but by contrast are
dressed in thin muslin *jamas* tied with *patkas* rather than
in Persian costume.

Although the illustrations of the Bombay *Laur Chanda*
are the only extant ones done precisely in this style, the
type is prominent in the Cleveland *Tuti Nama*, indicating

Figure 7, reverse.

that this manner of painting was influential in the earlier
part of the sixteenth century. A *Laur Chanda* in the Ry-
lands Library, Manchester, is the closest comparison,[3] but
it is done with a more emphatic kind of drawing related to
that of Jain illustrations. The refined and delicate scenes of
the Bombay manuscript were clearly produced at a major
center with excellent cultural resources, but neither the
style nor anything else gives sufficient grounds for attribution to a specific locality at the present time.

The Avadhi text used for this *Laur Chanda* that was
characteristic of a restricted area of northeastern India is an
important clue to identification, but it needs to be analyzed
along with other elements to provide a definite provenance.
Several other Sultanate manuscripts also in this language
are illustrated in quite different styles, thus confusing attempts at attribution. The eastern city of Jaunpur, capital of
the Sharqi dynasty, which successfully challenged the domi-
nation of Delhi and was culturally developed enough to
foster an original type of architecture, is the most probable
city for the illustration of Avadhi manuscripts; whether this
particular text was one produced there is not ascertainable
from present evidence. The manuscript has also been pos-

19

tulated to come from Mandu,[4] the important cultural center and capital of Malwa; but its pastel colors and small, round figures have no real relation to the more colorful *Nimat Nama* cookery book definitely known to have come from the city.

The colors and forms in the miniatures of the *Laur Chanda* in the Prince of Wales Museum are gentle and the compositions slightly static in comparison with the animation and vitality shown by the painters of the Mandu *Nimat Nama*. Although the plot of the love story twists adventurously throughout, the quiet illustrations fail to indicate much about the bizarre catastrophes endured by the lovers. Often the artists chose to portray the simplest aspects of narration, since these could be fitted into already-known design formulas. Many of the compositions were re-used a number of times. Like this leaf, many others are formally organized, showing different conversations being held above and below, which accentuates court etiquette rather than action. The manuscript is a product of late Sultanate chivalry stressing an elaborate code of manners that affected relations between the sexes, as here. Like this miniature, many of the leaves are arranged in horizontal registers—an Indian type of composition that contrasts with the typical Persian manner of showing a flat landscape background rising in a sharp vertical that is used for settings on other pages of the series.

Possibly the most outstanding ability of the *Laur Chanda* artists was in creating delicate, varied ornamental details. The miniatures have very beautiful architectural and textile patterns imaginatively colored and often touched with gold. The striped towers rising from decorated battlements and the scrolled canopy in the Cleveland leaf are typical forms that occur in other *Laur Chanda* scenes and later were re-employed in the Cleveland *Tuti Nama*; they demonstrate the refinement and minuteness of the painters' brushstrokes.

1. The Prince of Wales Museum acquired sixty-eight leaves of this manuscript in 1957. Another five (all in damaged condition) were added to the collection in 1974. The source of these latter miniatures is probably the same as that of the Cleveland painting and other scattered leaves that are from the manuscript.

2. Ettinghausen, 1959, pp. 39–41.

3. Losty, p. 69.

4. Ibid.

FURTHER READING: P. Chandra, 1976; Khandalavala and M. Chandra, 1969; Losty.

8 Three Leaves from a Bhagavata Purana Manuscript

Pre-Mughal, ca. 1525–50

The leaves of this extensively illustrated *Bhagavata Purana* are widely scattered, but together they form what is probably the most significant illustrated work now known from the pre-Mughal period. The remarkable spontaneity, freedom, and earthiness expressed in this type of miniature provide a basis for almost all the imaginative concepts of later Rajput painting. The unconscious expression of vitality without pretentious or intellectualized stylization is the same as that in some of the greatest early Indian works and shows the maintenance of the mainstream tradition. The manuscript also gives the most complete idea that we have of the devotional sincerity of Sultanate Hindu patrons, the wealth of their cultural environment, and the talents of the painters that they employed. The fact that the text was so lavishly and carefully illustrated indicates the importance of both painting and Krishna worship in medieval life more cogently than most other preserved artifacts.

By comparison with works done after the Mughal conquest, it appears that the cultural life in independent Hindu areas during the Sultanate era was surprisingly rich and actually more vibrant than that of the seventeenth century. The information on Hindu life in the Sultanate era is far from adequate, and while this *Bhagavata Purana* and other manuscripts raise many questions about Hindu culture, they are also among the best clues as to its nature. Perceptions of an ideal world as well as artists' unconscious observations of contemporary life are recorded through a kind of symbolic shorthand. Cities and forests are depicted in an abbreviated fashion that may appear naive but which in fact is a fairly complex kind of coding. Medieval warfare, baronial castle life, and social customs are very clearly portrayed. The immediate stylistic sources for this manuscript are found in Jain painting, but this *Bhagavat* is also like the early sculptural relief carvings at Bharhut or Sanchi, suggesting that Indian rural life had not changed very much over the centuries. Not only is the way of conceptualizing narration similar, but the spirit of the paintings is also close to that of the stupa sculptures; the open and fresh spirit of the scenes, which demonstrates the painters' unqualified acceptance of the mythic world, exactly parallels the powerful expression of faith at the early Buddhist sites and is an amazing affirmation of a persistent strain in Indian thought.

The illustrations give no hint of oppression and virtually none of foreign influence. The Islamic invasions had had considerable impact in urban or trading centers, but the vivacious innocence of these paintings suggests that Hindus still had a great deal of independence in many areas as well as the resources to sponsor extensive projects. Since the evolution of Hindu art seems to have been surprisingly unaffected by the numerous political upheavals of the period, the implication is that painters were linked with devotional culture and somewhat removed from contested political centers. This was the time when the first real flowering of Krishna worship occurred in the middle of North India after inspiration from both the southern and eastern regions of the subcontinent, and the excitement aroused by poets and saints worshipping the boyish god in this era is evident throughout the manuscript.

The first Hindu miniatures, like the ones from this manuscript, have often been termed *Chaurapanchasika*-style works, since the motifs that characterize such early miniatures appear very prominently in the illustrations of the poetic love text called the *Chaurapanchasika*. This provisional classification indicates that the stylistic relationship between miniatures of this group has been the central factor of agreement between critics. The provenance of miniatures, their precise dating, and even relative chronological order still continue to be disputed after several decades. When early Hindu miniatures began coming to light, the stylistic similarities between examples seemed remarkable. Such obvious elements as bright red background patches and large-eyed, buxom female figures appear consistently in the group and also persist in seventeenth-century Rajasthani works because of earlier inspiration. In the 1950s and 1960s these easily discernible features were emphasized because they provided common ground for discussion, but as the style has become better understood, a more balanced view of similarities and differences among manuscripts has evolved.

The *Chaurapanchasika* itself is a flamboyant, polished manuscript that must come from a courtly environment and is far more provocative and intense than other works. By contrast, this earthy *Bhagavata Purana* series, which is simple and lively, is the product of another social stratum illustrating something quite different about the lifestyle and concepts of the medieval period. It seems reasonable to assume that the early style was used extensively not only for the ruling class but perhaps was even more commonly at the command of brahmins or pious wealthy patrons across much of North and Central India.

The provenance of this particular manuscript has been judged to be either the Mewar or the Delhi/Agra area. Mewar has been suggested because of its leading position in Rajasthan, the legendary reputation of artistic patronage that is supposed to have developed under the powerful Rana Kumbha (r. 1433–68), and the similarity of later manuscripts such as the 1605 set done in the Mewar provisional capital of Chawand. Delhi has been postulated because it was a center of Sultanate wealth, and there is evidence that other early Hindu manuscripts were done in this vicinity, as, for example, at Palam. Mathura near Agra was of course the area traditionally associated with Krishna's childhood and youthful maturity, and it had become the center of the Vallabha devotion that included artistic expressions as part of Krishna worship. Unfortunately, the characteristics of this *Bhagavat* are not sufficiently particularized to attribute it specifically to any one of these locations—which probably all produced Hindu religious manuscripts at this

time—although the absence of Muslim influence makes it difficult to see this text as a product of the area immediately around Delhi. By contrast, the slightly later Isarda *Bhagavata Purana* (see [9]) has been considered here as coming from the Delhi/Agra region because of Mughal traits added to its essentially *Chaurapanchasika* style, implying a proximity to the Mughal imperial model developed at Delhi.

Although ateliers varied a great deal in their sophistication, early Rajput painting seems to have been in a fluid, formative stage without divisions into local schools; a certain stylistic unity exists between paintings whose provenances are known but which have proven to be vastly separated geographically. The production of *Chaurapanchasika*-type pages has recently been extended into the Punjab Hills by the discovery of an inscribed *Devi Mahatmya* manuscript done at a town named Jaisinghnagar.[1] Other manuscripts can perhaps be linked with eastern sites such as Jaunpur.[2] The style therefore seems to have been more widespread than originally believed and to have been determined more by the pervasive nature of Hinduism itself than by governments or even Hindu clans. Judging from present evidence, there appear to have been broader, more general stylistic distinctions in this era than in the seventeenth century when Rajput painting had pronounced local traits and was almost exclusively at the service of the Hindu courts. Although the *Chaurapanchasika* style was preserved in the early seventeenth century by raja patrons in such states as Mewar or Malwa, this class cannot necessarily be credited with its origination. Despite the fact that a clear picture of patronage in the pre-Mughal era cannot yet be assembled, it is incorrect to imagine that conditions that governed the Mughal era when courts were attempting to rival the patronage of the emperors should be assumed parallel in the previous centuries. Paintings of the religious *Devi Mahatmya*, *Gita Govinda*, *Bhagavata Purana*, and other manuscripts may well have been done without court patronage for devotional reasons and thus have had a stylistic unity that was broken in the later period. The strength of the Hindu community is shown by the spirited religious faith depicted in pre-Mughal manuscripts and also by the independent evolution of the style, which can be contrasted with the pervasive Mughal influence on Rajputs during the later period.

The dates of the early Rajput manuscripts are unresolved partially because they depend on the sophistication of each specific atelier. This *Bhagavata Purana* was done by artists who were working in a deft, practiced fashion with an inherited tradition and who were confidently familiar with their idiom but at the same time still experimented with it. Since the freshness of their work is outstanding, it seems that this manuscript must have been done just as the style reached its height but before it stopped developing freely. The best comparative evidence for a date between 1525 and 1550 is provided by an illustrated section of the *Mahabharata*, dated 1516, which is bold but much more naive and must have preceded this *Bhagavata Purana* by several years.[3] A terminus ad quem is provided by the Cleveland *Tuti Nama*, illustrated in Akbar's atelier about 1560, which has several miniatures showing buxom women of a *Chaurapanchasika*-type that is clearly later but has a close relation to this *Bhagavata Purana*.

All the men in the Cleveland scene of *Nanda and the Elders* [8i] are in the *kuladhar* turbans with caplike centers that are characteristic of the *Chaurapanchasika* group of miniatures but whose origin and geographical spread still remains unknown. Thus while it was once hoped that this turban style would provide more exact information about the dating and provenance of the early Rajput group, documentation has been insufficient to do so.

Because the three miniatures owned by the Cleveland Museum are quite diverse, they appear to be by different craftsmen. Although some simple distinctions of style can be made, when the more than two hundred scattered pages of the *Bhagavata Purana* text are considered, it is very difficult to sort the paintings according to artist or to ascertain how many men in toto may have worked on the scenes. The main painters were probably heads of painting families with relatives who acted as secondary artists or as assistants. Many of the leaves bear inscriptions of either "Sa Nana" or "Sa Mitharam," often interpreted as referring to artists named Nana and Mitharam. Unfortunately, it is difficult to use style to substantiate this hypothesis as the scenes are not divisible into distinct types that correspond to the inscriptions. This failure does not necessarily negate the supposition, however, because the conditions of the age mitigated against distinct personal styles. Painting was a devotional act in which unity was emphasized, and though painters might learn certain mannerisms if they came from studios in different geographical areas, their individualistic creative personalities as such were unregarded. The main style of the manuscript is a delicate, lacy one often used for miniatures with fairly complex settings.[4] Another contrasting style of drawing is the vigorous but plain manner epitomized by the Cleveland miniature of *Nanda and the Elders* [8i]. Conceivably the same artist doing a simple scene might have used large, robust forms, while for something complex he might have found it easier to record details sketchily with many flourishes. Neither mannerism can be associated exclusively with the names of either Mitharam or Nana.[5] Other idioms of the manuscript, including figure drawing, appear to be common to scenes labeled Mitharam or Nana.

In religious manuscripts done for traditionally minded Hindu patrons, such as those produced in Mewar during the mid-seventeenth century, if the artist was credited at all, it was in a colophon at the end of the book. During the Sultanate era, when there was even less awareness of the artist-personality, inscriptions of painters' names on individual leaves is surprising. (These are not signatures but later notations on borders by someone whose writing ability shows him to have been well educated.) The hypothesis has also been presented that Nana and Mitharam represent

families of collectors who divided the manuscript and marked it to indicate the leaves in the possession of each (the prefix *sa* is interpreted as having a possessive connotation); this suggestion, however, has no precedent in Rajput painting and the problem has not been conclusively resolved.

The Cleveland miniature of the *gopis* cavorting in the Jumna [8ii] is one of a number from the pre-Mughal *Bhagavat* group with the feminine name Hirabai inscribed in a light scrawl. Often this name appears with the inscriptions of either "Sa Nana" or "Sa Mitharam" in heavy *Devanagari* characters: the scene of *Nanda and the Elders*, for example, has in addition to "Sa Mitharam," an almost obliterated inscription to Hirabai on the right side of the upper border. Since Hirabai appears as a duplicate name or afterthought on many leaves, the inscription cannot refer to an artist. The fact that it seems to have been put on casually at a date somewhat after the execution of the paintings then calls into question whether Nana and Mitharam can have been artists, because it seems as if the two types of inscriptions—both markedly unusual—should have had related purposes. The rationale behind the inscriptions remains enigmatic, and the manuscript must be considered as a special case; but because this *Bhagavat* is so important and because it is necessary to understand the Sultanate period better, the problem of Nana, Mitharam, and Hirabai remains a significant matter for speculation.

1. Losty, p. 51.
2. Ibid., pp. 50–51.
3. Khandalavala and M. Chandra, 1974.
4. For one of the many examples of this spritely style see Beach, 1966, no. 146.
5. The similarity of miniatures labeled Mitharam and Nana can be seen in many examples — among them, Archer and Binney, pl. 1c labeled "Sa Nana," compares with Hutchins, no. 18, or Khandalavala, Chandra, and Chandra, 1960, no. 12a labeled "Sa Mitharam." For a partial list of leaves belonging to this set see Beach, 1981, pp. 49–55.

8i *Nanda and the Elders*   60.53

Approx. 16.3 × 21.5 cm. Text on reverse (*Bhagavata Purana*, Bk. 10, Chap. 11, verses 21–30; illus.). Paint loss (especially white), rubbing, staining, and border damage. Inscription: "Sa Mitharam, Hirabai."

Purchase, Mr. and Mrs. William H. Marlatt Fund

Ex collection: Heeramaneck.

Published: Lee, 1960, no. 3A, and 1973, color pl. 17.

This miniature, previously considered as a scene from another portion of the *Bhagavata Purana*,[1] has now been correctly identified to accord with the text on the reverse side of the miniature that discusses the village cowherds' move to Brindaban. In these verses the simple *gopas* in whose care Krishna has been placed marvel that no child has been hurt by the accidents that have suddenly begun to occur in their midst. Unaware that Krishna's wicked uncle

सा धाणिराम

Figure 8*i*, obverse.

Kansa has been sending his demonic minions in the hope of killing his young nephew, they discern that some mysterious evil power is in the ascendancy and they determine to move without delay to the more remote Brindaban (described as being lush with grass and plants and having tall mountains that later figure in the story of Krishna lifting Mr. Govardhan).

The episode as portrayed here by the Rajput painter is formalized; because of the static composition, it may appear at first glance to be a very rudimentary effort at communicating narration. In fact, however, the scene has small subtleties that reveal something about Indian rural life, which in many ways had remained unchanged since the writing of the *Bhagavata Purana*. For example, it is inter-esting that the decision to move is being made in the traditional manner by a village council discussion and that those figures nearest the center who are clearly meant to have the significant opinions are the elders with white beards, while by contrast the few younger men are confined to the fringes of the group.

Nanda, Krishna's foster father and the village headman, because of his social position and important role in the drama is alone attired in a rich printed costume that is similar to many others in paintings of the period and therefore must represent a contemporary textile. Although Nanda and the others are stock representations of village elders and their figures are conventionalized, the painters have carefully portrayed the stout, white-haired Nanda in a consistent fashion throughout this *Bhagavata Purana* series, indicating that they wished to create believable, lifelike characters insofar as possible.

The artist's manner of depicting narration preserves features from several kinds of older Indian art and reflects a precise concern with signs and symbols that is typically Indian. The enumeration of men in a straight line to indicate a group seems typical of Jain painting, and the use of four different types of trees to signify a grove or forest goes back not only to Jain painting but also to the art of the early Buddhist stupas. While the artist has not depicted emotions on the faces of the villagers nor shown their mouths open in discussion, he has gone out of his way to portray elaborate hand gestures that loosely evoke Buddhist *mudras*. Clearly the importance of gesture and formal communication by signs had been preserved over the centuries as being essential to interaction in the society. The artist has also communicated something less specific about the ideal world of the Krishna story through his traditional expressionistic use of color. The vivid black and red used non-naturalistically are appropriate to the painter's conception of the perfect mythological world in which Krishna developed as a young man.

1. This miniature in previous publications (see list under entry heading) had been thought to be the scene of Raja Parikshit hearing his ancestors' deeds recited as the *Bhagavata Purana* prior to his death on the riverbank; the correct identification of the subject was given to the Museum by Mr. Daniel Ehnbom.

8ii *Krishna Sporting with the Gopis in the Jumna* 71.171

Approx. 16.5 × 22.2 cm. Text on reverse (illus.). Paint loss, rubbing, staining, and border damage. Inscription: "Hirabai."

Gift of Mr. and Mrs. Alvin N. Haas

Published: P. Chandra, 1976, pl. 79.

Comparative Material: (A) *Krishna and the Gopis Sporting in the Junma*, leaf from the Isarda *Bhagavata Purana*, probably Delhi/Agra area, ca. 1560–70; Welch, 1973, no. 7; Spink, fig. 117; P. Chandra, 1976, pl. 85. (B) *Gopis in the River*, leaf from a *Bhagavata Purana*, possibly Delhi/Agra area, ca. 1570; R. Parimoo, "A New Set of Early Rajasthani Paintings," *LK*, no. 17 (1974): fig. 6; P. Chandra, 1976, pl. 87.

This miniature of Krishna and the *gopis* sporting in the Jumna while musicians and girls with garlands laud them from above is done in a very spontaneous style; though the painting is considerably damaged, the *gopis* can be seen splashing each other and leaping in the water. Krishna himself is shown boldly grasping the breast of one as he splashes her—a very skillful depiction of action that perfectly characterizes the audacious violation of propriety used to describe him throughout the *Bhagavata Purana*. While the pre-Mughal style is a conceptual one, the treatment here is unusually natural and free; the poses seem to be based on observation and they express the balance of real bodies in motion. The rhythmic whorls of water that give an illusion of animation are typical of pre-Mughal Rajput handling in the *Chaurapanchasika* and other manuscripts. Inter-

Figure 8*i*, reverse.

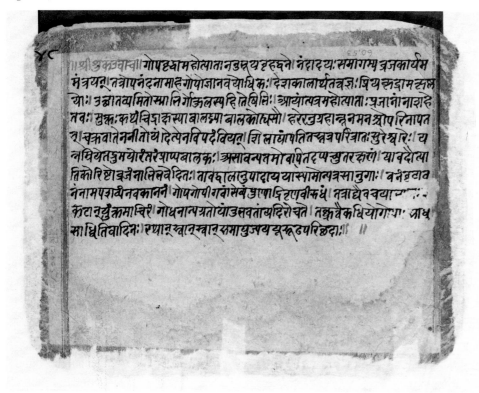

Figure 8*ii*, obverse.

estingly, this stylization is rather different from that used in two miniatures of the same scene (A, illus.; B) done only a few years later, postdating the formation of the Mughal atelier.

In both comparative miniatures, the water flows across the page on a diagonal—a concept of space apparently introduced by Mughal painters. Such parallels with the style of the early Mughal *Hamza Nama* manuscript have provided evidence for dating the Isarda *Bhagavata Purana* series (see A) later than this manuscript. If the two comparative works have innovative features, however, they are not livelier than this early scene. The figures in the second comparative example (B) are stilted and show none of the inventiveness revealed by the artist of the Cleveland miniature. Thus this leaf demonstrates that pre-Mughal conventions provided an adequate framework for the vitality the artist wished to express. Although the river itself is arranged in a simple horizontal band in this miniature, the fluid, rhythmic line along the horizon and the curves of churning water are far from static.

The painter's concept of the world is at one with his mythic theme. It is this important visionary quality that is consistently challenged by the factual reporting of the Mughal painters in the late sixteenth century. Such apparently small details as the introduction of diagonal perspective for the rendering of the Jumna actually herald a fundamental attack on the Hindu view of time and space. This manuscript is one of the last great achievements by artists completely unacquainted with the ambition of mirroring a physical universe. The scene takes place at night when Krishna has called the *gopis* away from their husbands to cavort with him. The expression is of perfect

25

time: the sky is pale blue and night is portrayed only by the symbols of stars and a full moon radiating light in the center of the composition. Heaven and earth are united as the celestials rain praise on Krishna from floating, almost swinglike, platforms backed with bright red. As the musicians festoon earth with garlands, the *gopis*—symbolizing the escape of the soul from the cloying round of everyday existence—exult in the water and in the giant lotuses that reflect a sensuous loveliness similar to that in early sculpture.

Figure 8*ii*(A). *Krishna and the Gopis Sporting in the Jumna*, from the Isarda *Bhagavata Purana*. Edwin Binney 3rd Collection.

Figure 8*ii*, reverse.

8*iii* *The Marriage of Pradyumna and Rukmavati* 76.26

Approx. 16.3 × 21.5 cm. Text on reverse (*Bhagavata Purana*, Bk. 10, Chap. 61, verses 20–24). Paint loss, staining, and edges battered. Fragmentary yellow border. Inscription in lower left damaged, replaced with: "Pradyumna ko vivahu" (the marriage of Pradyumna) in center.

Gift of Dr. Norman W. Zaworski

This miniature, arranged in two sequential narrative bands, pictures the resolution of complex circumstances surrounding the marriage of Krishna and Rukmini's son Pradyumna. This scene illustrates that a quarrel begun in one generation is expeditiously solved in the next. Krishna himself had stolen Rukmini away from her family against the will of her brother Rukmi just prior to the marriage that had been arranged for her. Rukmi desired to revenge himself against Krishna, yet the text on the back of this miniature explains that for his sister's sake he allowed his daughter Rukmavati to marry Pradyumna, whom she had chosen in a *svayamvara* (self-choice ceremony for high-born women).[1] (Pradyumna was already married to Maya; see [106iv].) The upper portion of the miniature shows the blessing of the couple. Pradyumna's face is auspiciously marked and a marriage headdress adorns his head; Rukmavati's head is decorated with flowers. The two then depart in their animal-headed chariot for Krishna's city of Dwarka, where they are shown arriving in the lower portion.

Many of the scenes in this *Bhagavat* as well as in other manuscripts use the same sequential type of composition with characters appearing two or three times and with completely different times or places juxtaposed. This scene illustrates well the transition from the narrow registers used in Jain painting to slightly larger compartments, like those of strip cartoons, which the 1516 *Aranyakaparvan* manuscript and this *Bhagavata Purana* have in common.

1. Identification provided by K. V. Krishnamachari.

Figure 8*iii*.

27

अंकनायाौ

श्रीरामेवंसदंतनोर्ज्ञितस बितयर्येप्य। प्रक्रूर बोधयामास सतोरे गोंदिल

Figure 9.

Figure 9, detail.

9 *Akrura Drives Krishna*   71.234
and Balarama to Mathura

Leaf from the Isarda *Bhagavata Purana*, probably
Delhi/Agra area, ca. 1560–70, 19.3 × 25.7 cm. Slight flaking
of paint; some rubbing. Fragmentary yellow border.
Translated inscriptions, *recto*: "Akrura having left the women
weeping, rose up and drove the chariot"; *verso*, "Fol. 38,
Akrura goes to Mathura."
Purchase, John L. Severance Fund

Comparative Material: (A) *The Departure for Mathura*, leaf
from a *Bhagavata Purana*, pre-Mughal, ca. 1525–50;
T. McInerney, *Indian Paintings from the Polsky Collections*
(Princeton: Art Museum, Princeton Univ., 1982), no. 1.

The Isarda *Bhagavata Purana*, so named because it was
discovered in the collection of the *thikana* of Isarda, is a
manuscript in the style of the *Chaurapanchasika* group
with additional Mughal influences, showing that it post-
dates the establishment of the Akbari studio.[1] The basic
elements of this Cleveland miniature all appear frequently
in the *Chaurapanchasika* itself or in associated manuscripts. The figure types and costumes are all derived from
earlier illustrations. The tasseled banner, the animal-
headed chariot drawn by a small horse, and the textile
pattern of dots and circles in the Cleveland miniature are
standard features of the *Chaurapanchasika* group and
especially of the related pre-Mughal *Bhagavata Purana* of
catalogue number 8.

In this episode of the tenth book of the *Bhagavata Purana*
as described in the line of text on the reverse, Krishna and
Balarama are being driven to Mathura by their relative,
Akrura, to confront their wicked uncle, King Kansa. The
two uncles, Akrura and Kansa, are characterized as op-
posites throughout the *Bhagavata Purana* text, since Akrura, unlike Kansa, believes in Krishna's divinity and serves
him loyally. On this occasion, Kansa has ordered Akrura to
fetch the young men for a festival, but his intention is to kill
them during contests of strength. Akrura has been forced to
perform the errand, but with the hope that Krishna will not
accompany him carelessly to death and further will not
connect him with Kansa's intrigue. To his delight, Akrura is
received with honor and questioned shrewdly about Kansa,
after which he replies straightforwardly with the history of
the king's wrong-doing.

This scene depicts the *gopis* calling after Krishna tear-
fully when he is ready to depart, stricken at being separated
from their hero, whom they rightly assume will not return
to live in Brindaban. Akrura is shown once with the women
and again in the chariot behind Krishna and Balarama
driving away in the type of successive time frame very
common in the early Hindu manuscripts. Also usual is the
fact that despite the text immediately above that describes
the women weeping, the two buxom *gopis* are portrayed
pointing at the chariot and apparently following the party
cheerfully. In most early Rajput manuscripts, specific emotion is inadequately depicted or left undefined (A), although
passion is conveyed through both color and shape in a so-

phisticated manner. In this case, a further narrative detail
betrays the artist's ignorance of the specific literary text,
since Krishna and his brother are described as being *kisora*
(boys between eleven and fifteen years of age) when they
leave for Mathura.[2] Here the two have been shown as men,
and because of their significance, they are much larger than
their uncle Akrura.

When compared with other manuscripts of the early Rajput group, the Isarda *Bhagavat* stands out, along with the
Chaurapanchasika, for its polished and tightly organized
appearance. In comparison with the previously discussed
Bhagavata Purana set [8], and A, for example, the Isarda
series gives the impression of formality and precision. As
this scene demonstrates, the series is meticulously although
very gracefully detailed. The precise wavelike scroll patterns
of the textiles and the chariot bed are very characteristic
of the manuscript's decorative quality. While some of the
colors employed are more delicate than in other early
Rajput manuscripts, background tones are strong and clear.
The Cleveland painting has a red color block setting off
Krishna and Balarama, while the remainder of the background is an intense dark blue.

In comparison with certain chariot scenes of the earlier
Bhagavata Purana manuscript, it can be noted that this
illustration is organized in a simple, purely rational manner
(cf. [8*iii*], which is in stylized registers). Few of the Isarda
scenes have elements dispersed freely across the painting
field as does the pre-Mughal *Bhagavata* manuscript; figures
are instead positioned along base lines as they are in this
example. Although specific features derived from Mughal
painting are not employed by this artist as they are in some
Isarda leaves, the general appearance is more natural than
in the earlier *Chaurapanchasika* illustrations. Idiosyn-
cratic elements of the pre-Mughal style like the arbitrarily
projecting shawls of the men or skirts of the women are less
emphasized and more stress is placed on human action.
Since the manuscript has passages proving that it was done
shortly after the formation of the Mughal studio, it was
probably produced somewhere in the nearby Delhi/Agra
area. The series has now been dispersed and leaves are
scattered in various collections.[3]

1. The most obvious evidence of Mughal influence in the Isarda
manuscript has been mentioned in catalogue number 8*ii*; the
water in a scene of *gopis* in the Jumna is patterned in a fashion that
could only have originated in the Mughal *Hamza Nama* (see [8*ii*,
comparison A]). Other intrusions from Mughal painting are more
subtle because they have been better adsorbed into the native
Indian style.
2. G. V. Tagare, *The Bhagavata Purana*, vol. 10, pt. 4, of *Ancient
Indian Tradition and Mythology* (Delhi: Vanarasi, Patna, Motilal
Banarsidass, 1978), 1489.
3. Leaves of this manuscript are published in Khandalavala and
Mittal, figs. 1–4 (fig. 2 also P. Chandra, 1976, pl. 86); Spink,
figs. 11 and 117 (also P. Chandra, 1976, pl. 85; Welch, 1973, no. 7);
M. Lerner, *Miniatures from the Jeffrey Paley Collection* (New
York: Metropolitan Museum of Art, 1974), no. 1; Hutchins,
figs. 4, 25, 26, 31.

FURTHER READING: P. Chandra, 1976, pp. 37–42; Khandalavala and Mittal, pp. 28–32.

II. Mughal Painting from Akbar through Shah Jahan

The Patronage of Akbar

The early Mughal period was one in which the Indian artist gradually came to be recognized as an individual. Under the Mughal bureaucratic system he began to get more credit for his talent than he appears to have received in the Sultanate period, when he was probably considered more or less a slave of the ruler. The artist's name may have been inscribed by librarians on miniatures of the Akbari era partly to record that he was producing his studio quota but also as an indication of increasing respect. Akbar's chronicler, Abu'l Fazl, makes it clear in his short biographies of artists that the new court was anxious to eulogize the skills of those it had trained. Despite his improved status, however, the Indian painter devoted himself to the ruler's wishes. Overt self-expression did not occur to him, in contrast to his European contemporaries who were beginning to assert their personal choices. He seemed to produce most creatively with strong, supportive patronage and direction from a dominant figure who knew his own desires, like the impatient Akbar or the aesthetic Jahangir.

The first three Mughal emperors to rule most of the subcontinent—Akbar (r. 1556–1605), Jahangir (r. 1605–27), and Shah Jahan (r. 1627–58)—were extremely good patrons: Akbar and Jahangir were actively interested in painting, while under the more formal Shah Jahan, art continued to be an important aspect of princely status. In addition, the court system set up by Akbar that included the imperial studio was maintained satisfactorily in these years despite Jahangir's willful excesses and Shah Jahan's extravagant building programs.

In 1556 it must have seemed that all material odds were against the survival of a dynasty that controlled a little territory around Delhi and had barely come through a long period of defeat and exile, but historians have rightly tended to attribute Mughal success to Akbar's acumen and superhuman drive. When the thirteen-year-old boy was notified of his father's death and was crowned, he was serving precociously as governor of the Punjab but was able to survive India's bewildering and rapacious political games during the next few years mainly by relying on the wise supervision of his tutor-guardian. Psychologically, the mature Akbar, who threw off his earlier dependency, held a dominant

position—both because he was a visionary and because his unsuperstitious mind worked on a compellingly logical level. In battle he commanded admiration and loyalty because his physical prowess drove others to do what they considered impossible. When he led his followers on rapid marches under terrible conditions, he won victories not only against surprised foes but also against the apathy and disbelief of his own army. This of course earned him a reputation that allowed him to proceed to further, greater achievements.

Akbar used such tactics to advantage in his governmental policy as well—each victory over conservatism was quickly followed by increased demands on his officials. He had an invaluable ability to channel the best energies of others by convincing them to accept his perceptions, and he never introduced controversial projects without preparatory education. The vehicle of painted illustration was one he considered significant, probably because he had been unable to achieve literacy. He thus used painting mainly as a tool to communicate his important programs of religious tolerance and his ideas about dynastic power.

When Akbar began his rule, he adopted a philosophy already promoted by Muslim Sufis and Hindu *bhaktas* in India. Both groups practiced their worship through personal acts of love and ecstasy, thereby developing a common ground between two apparently irreconcilable religions. This Hindu-Muslim ideal had had adherents like the mystic poet Kabir, whose ideas of the universal, spiritual nature of God swept India—obviously because they expressed popular sentiments.

Akbar's reign was, therefore, in accord with already-developing trends, and he became the embodiment of cultural accommodation. Much of what he achieved as a patron of art was directed at Muslim assimilation rather than primarily toward creativity for its own sake. Illustrations of the Hindu epics promoted Akbar's vision of cultural integration, providing a way for Muslims to understand the Indian past while giving Hindus the feeling that their tradition was accorded respect.

Cultural assimilation of the immigrants who gathered around Akbar was also necessary for stabilizing the Mughal position in India, since Akbar's courtiers almost instinctively compared themselves and the new dynasty unfavorably with other groups having a sophisticated traditional heritage. Akbar's father, Humayun (r. 1530–56), as an exile at the Persian court of Shah Tahmasp from 1544–45, undoubtedly felt disadvantaged and, in hiring painters of the contemporary Safavid dynasty, showed his desire to learn from the Persians. In general, the Persian court was luxurious and frivolous, but Akbar's artistic policies were more sober. His patronage centered on encouraging artists to develop objectivity and mastery of skills, for which he generated great excitement among his courtiers.

In the field of literature, the court was renowned for serious prose-writing on such topics as history or morality and for translations from other cultures on scientific or historical subjects, rather than for the romantic ballads and poems that had been composed at Sultanate centers. A corresponding situation existed in painting, since historical and religious manuscripts had high priority.

While his predecessors and those around him visualized themselves as competing with Persia (which they esteemed as the fountainhead of culture), Akbar urged something much bolder than a pale imitation of Persian refinement. He championed a new civilization with a novel set of standards. He attempted to blend the Hindu-Muslim traditions of architecture, music, and literature in a deliberate, conscious manner—unlike the assimilation that occurred counter to the intentions of the two groups during the Sultanate era. In painting, European influences provided the catalyst that transformed diverse Hindu-Muslim traits into mutually enhancing features of a new style. The introduction of European prints in particular had much to do with the way miniature painting developed. Because these models rendered the physical world in a more detailed, incisive manner than Muslim prototypes, they gave direction to Akbar's ideas. The emperor visualized utopia not through the earthly ignorance that Muslim theologians advocated but through a more realistic, pragmatic acquaintance with the possibilities inherent in both man and nature. In painting, this led to modeled, rounded depictions of human beings and greatly expanded, well-rendered natural vistas. Hindu artists—like the renowned Basawan who brought a warm, earthy view of life to imperial painting—found that their tradition gained scope and variety by contact with that of Europe.

The Organization of the Akbari Studio

Since the two experienced masters who organized Akbar's studio—Mir Sayyid Ali and Abd al-Samad—were familiar with conditions under Shah Tahmasp, they must have drawn upon their pasts to create a new environment suitable for the training of native Indian artists with diverse abilities, styles, and work habits. The Cleveland *Tuti Nama*, a collection of bawdy tales supposedly recounted by a parrot, is a work that shows the surprising number of native Indian painters who were taken into the studio at its inception. It also reveals that these painters arrived at court with varying degrees of training in an incredibly wide range of pre-Mughal styles. During the years immediately succeeding, about fifty artists (including Muslim immigrants as well as native recruits) illustrated the adventure story, generally termed the *Hamza Nama*, concerning the prophet Muhammad's uncle. This manuscript was in production throughout a fifteen-year period.

Although the *Tuti Nama* pages reveal amazing achievements by budding painters, the *Hamza Nama* was their real initiation into Akbar's requirements for imperial artists. The large size of the *Hamza Nama* pages as well as the number of illustrations made work tremendously difficult for the inexperienced. It became evident that the artists, unpracticed by comparison with those of Shah Tahmasp's atelier, needed a systematic approach to compensate for their naiveté as well as for their lack of cohesion as a studio group. The assignment of miniatures to separate designers and colorists was typical of the devices that promoted studio efficiency and uniform production during the middle of Akbar's reign. That Akbar himself was partially responsible for studio procedures is indicated by his management in other administrative areas; in addition, Abu'l Fazl's statement in his description of court practices that artistic work was examined weekly by the emperor shows Akbar's desire to maintain some personal control. From the literary evidence, Mir Sayyid Ali probably possessed a more artistic temperament, but because Abd al-Samad was given the task of teaching others (including Akbar) and was promoted to administration of the mint, he must have been a better organizer and more adept in human relations. It is the latter artist who is credited with speeding up completion of the *Hamza Nama*.

The series of three histories done during the middle of Akbar's reign devoted to Timur, Akbar, and Genghis Khan have a certain stylistic unity largely determined by the now-streamlined painting procedures. Inscriptions of names on the manuscripts of this era show that the same artists tended to cooperate throughout the period. Certain outliners were often responsible for fairly large numbers of designs; in the Victoria and Albert Museum's *Akbar Nama*, for example, the artist La'l produced nineteen compositions, Miskin seventeen, Kesu Kalan fifteen, and Basawan eleven.[1] These same men, particularly La'l, handled much of the work on other projects as well.

Individual colorists generally produced from one to three pictures in the large manuscripts, which often numbered about 150 paintings. Coloring was based on craft knowledge, as it was in Sienese tempera painting. The colorist's job was a time-consuming one involving progressive color layering and burnishing of the mineral pigments. Success therefore depended on a foundation of technical training and on the quality of materials as well as on artistic sensitivity. The improvement of raw materials, probably at about the time the *Akbar Nama* was painted, was mentioned by

Abu'l Fazl as one of the most significant developments in the period.[2]

In general, the less able artists seem to have been inspired and possibly trained by working with master outliners. Unfortunately, one of the major problems of Akbari painting is that colorists could obscure designs if they did not cooperate effectively with the busy draftsman. Often the division of labor made it tempting for the colorist to create a two-dimensional surface of bright patches of color independent of the designer's intentions. Good colorists, however, not only performed a technical labor but could take much credit for the artistic effect of the miniature. Dharm Das was one artist who selected colors skillfully and was promoted to do important pages alone. A Cleveland miniature from the Chester Beatty Library's *Akbar Nama* attributed to this painter [18i] has original pastel colors played against striking darks. Of all the pages in the Museum collection, it best illustrates the density of Akbari pigments and the resultant luster of the carefully polished surfaces.

If in Akbar's era there were painters who were primarily artisans grinding colors and doing rudimentary work, there were also artists who faced creative challenges in the same bold manner as their emperor faced political ones. Akbar's foremost artist—Basawan—stands out as an epitome of the Akbari spirit throughout a long career that almost exactly spans the reign. Although he sometimes suffered from having his talents misused (as when he was given average commissions such as a *Chingiz Nama* page that he produced with the colorist Sur Das Gujerati [16]), he readily responded to the demands of a sovereign who was liberal, dynamic, and objective—unparalleled qualities of mind that created a unique opportunity for any painter whose creative ability lay in a naturalistic direction.

Basawan's picture of a Jain monk [17], which seems to have been a psychological subject personally preferred by the artist, reveals his ease at handling impressions of European art after long familiarity. Basawan in as early a manuscript as the Cleveland *Tuti Nama* (1560–65) showed that he had a unique understanding of European artistic values, which he imparted to other artists by example. His own response was innovative, as is revealed, for example, in his ability to convey both the softness and the solidity of the Jain monk's flesh in a manner inspired by European art but which remains individual. Indeed, Basawan set the tone for the court: landscapes in a Flemish manner, carefully modeled figures, and objects hazy with aerial perspective all appear in the Akbari poetry manuscripts of the 1590s.

The Patronage of Jahangir

During Akbar's late reign, Prince Salim, who was to become the Emperor Jahangir, began to exercise his taste as a patron. The scope of the prince's early influence is, however, conjectural because, while it is evident that he had aesthetic interests, the amount of power he wielded is uncertain. The fact that the Persian-born painter Aqa Riza worked exclusively for him and did not contribute to any of the productions of Akbar's atelier may indicate that the prince had only limited access to his father's artists. But Salim may have developed gradually his hereditary right to patronage, so that by the time of his second rebellion against Akbar in 1603 he was able to attract painters to his retreat at the fort of Allahabad.

The father and son's incompatible personalities seriously affected Akbar's later reign. The prince, who seemed to fear combat, had refused twice to take the field against the Mughal's last, most implacable Rajasthani enemy, the Rana of Mewar, and in order to cover his lapse rebelled and went to Allahabad after both incidents. When he finally succeeded to the throne in 1605, in his middle thirties, Jahangir began a twenty-two-year reign that could hardly have been more contrastive with that of his father. Jahangir demonstrated no desire for administrative responsibility, merely ruling by virtue of ceremony and precedent. His interests lay primarily in the field of natural history and secondarily in painting. If it was typical of Akbar that he had set in motion an entire cultural system, it was characteristic of Jahangir to promote mainly the art of miniature painting, making selective requests to satisfy only himself.

Jahangir, engrossed by the beauty of the painted surface, inspired experiments among his artists. It is to the credit of his lively intelligence that in spite of the cloying luxuries of his position and his own intemperate appetites for drugs and alcohol, he never proffered superficial commissions. Surrounded by nobles who specialized in manipulative flattery, Jahangir could well have been devoured by his office had he not maintained the very human interests in science and art. His diary shows that his sincere enthusiasm for the development of both areas was the only stimulus that roused him from an enveloping torpor associated with the ceremonies and wealth of his position. The paintings of his reign are elegant, yet simple in contrast to those of the next generation, which are often weakened by excess detail of costumes or architecture paralleling the materialism that burdened the court.

The British Library/Chester Beatty Library's *Akbar Nama* is the only extensively illustrated work spanning the transitional era between the reigns of Akbar and Jahangir (see [18]). Since its paintings are inscribed, the manuscript is a major source of information on changes within the painting studio (for example, artists like Govardhan or Payag, who were to have careers as innovative as Basawan's, began their service on this book). The manuscript is additionally intriguing because it is a biography of Akbar, toward whom Jahangir displayed such ambivalent emotions. While the prince could not have commissioned the manuscript, it could hardly have been completed before the time of his assuming power. Despite the fact that this was a type of manuscript in which he later showed no interest, the new emperor apparently carried on the project at the beginning of his reign.

Jahangir elevated certain painters during his reign but dispensed with the services of many average ones by about 1610. His actions altered the character of the atelier to coincide with his desire for single masterpiece-illustrations produced by a few brilliant experimental artists. Certain changes in the rigid organization of the studio had already taken place by about 1600, though whether at Jahangir's instigation is unknown; most significantly, scenes had ceased to be divided between a designer and a colorist.

Much of the alteration in the make-up of the studio was due to attrition rather than to Jahangir's intervention, since numerous painters had worked through the greater part of Akbar's reign. The last of the old Akbari artists like La'l, Madhu, Sanwlah, Mukund, and Narsingh seem to have died or retired by about 1610.

Jahangir had previously begun to single out a few artists who were mainly sons of Akbari painters and thus had considerable early experience because of their backgrounds: these included Basawan's son Manohar; Aqa Riza's son Abu'l Hasan; and Govardhan, the son of the average Akbari painter Bhawani Das. Govardhan, represented in the Cleveland collection by three works [19, 26, 28i], is one of the artists who typifies Jahangir's reign, as had Basawan for the previous generation.

Like Jahangir, Govardhan, who painted in diverse styles, was a changeable man with many emotional facets. In addition, the luminosity of his carefully prepared surfaces leads to the conclusion that of Jahangir's painters, his nature best paralleled the sensuality of his patron. Jahangir and Govardhan were equally fascinated by psychology—especially the psychological states of *yogis*, who combined a social freedom and ascetic stringency that could generate intense mental experiences (see [28i]).

Two of Govardhan's miniatures now in Cleveland [26, 28i] were done in Shah Jahan's era and, as is characteristic, they continue the traditions of painting established in the late Jahangiri period when artists confidently set down their impressions in European-derived styles. Jahangir's intellectual curiosity as well as his fascination with psychology and natural history predisposed him toward European painting. By about 1615 his artists had seen a variety of styles; works, chiefly engravings, of the Northern and Southern Renaissance and finally of the Baroque styles had given them greater facility in dealing with light, movement, distance, and texture. Unfortunately, however, the alteration in mores during Jahangir's era had produced a loss in naturalism as it related to objective depiction. Inspired by their scientifically minded patron, Jahangir's group of favorite young artists—his boldest painters—had done careful but informal portrait studies; but, by about 1615, worn out and wearied by his addictions, the emperor was merely a figurehead managed increasingly by his powerful wife. The painters could hardly afford to depict such truths, nor could they avoid Jahangir's requests to record his dreams or visions as if they were heroic deeds that he had in fact accomplished. The atmosphere of the court thus became increasingly unreal, and Jahangir's painters became accustomed to subterfuge, flattery, and hypocritical elegance— all of which killed the spontaneity apparent in their earlier depictions.

The Patronage of Shah Jahan

During Jahangir's reign the Mughal reputation for success in battle was maintained solely by Prince Khurram who, though only a third son, was preferred by his father and given the title Shah Jahan following a victory in the Deccan. It was entirely due to Shah Jahan that the weaknesses of Jahangir's government were so little apparent. Courageous, conscientious, and temperate, he received many honors from his grateful father until he was frightened into rebellion by the apparent elevation of his younger brother Shahriyar.

If Shah Jahan was not as erratic a leader as his father, he was also without some of the interests Jahangir possessed because of his emotional temperament. The album of paintings and calligraphy assembled for him in 1611–12 seems to have been a dutiful exercise, since Shah Jahan displayed no particular passion for miniatures when he came to the throne. An ambitious builder and a collector of jewels, the new emperor saw miniatures as accessories of court ceremonial life rather than as enhancements for personal delight.

The artists who continued to paint for Shah Jahan in many cases showed considerable originality, perhaps because the talents and perceptions developed under Jahangir could, for a while at least, be expressed more fully for the new sovereign than for the physically drained and emotionally hardened Jahangir, who suffered severely in his later years from paranoia. Jahangir deserves credit, however, for inspiring many of the pictures done in his son's early reign that are responses to the intelligent taste and discretion blurred at the end of his own life by the effects of drugs, alcohol, and dislike of governmental responsibility. After the initial unleashing of their talents under a new sovereign, artists gradually felt Shah Jahan's lack of interest or creative patronage, with the result that their miniatures became somewhat dry.

The opulence of the Jahangiri court had been the result of Jahangir's theatricality and his desire to stress his own importance, but by Shah Jahan's time it had become an accepted standard that could not be sacrificed without loss of face. Shah Jahan doubtless took the grandeur of the court for granted and apparently wished to improve upon this show of wealth in order to demonstrate the continuing vitality of the dynasty.

After Akbar, the Mughal emperors had become so isolated in their palatial surroundings that they lived unaware of the court's complete material dependence on the productivity of the countryside. By failing to perceive the need to generate wealth by crop development or trade, the emperors continued to allow officials to secure more funds from the reluctant peasantry. Although the resultant depletion of the countryside was inevitable, given this lack of innovative leadership, its effects did not become apparent until the latter part of the seventeenth century, following the end of Shah Jahan's reign.

If lavish display was callously extravagant, it also served practical political purposes because it made the dynasty appear unassailable. Who would dare to revolt against figures that seemed almost like immortals in their bejeweled world? The fact that certain magnificent court customs were maintained for security or were consciously used as social tools to obtain subordination was adroitly masked—as was the case, for example, with daily assemblies of nobles (*durbars*) that tested loyalty. The biographical *Shah Jahan Nama* is full of scenes illustrating *durbars* far more rigidly controlled than those of Akbar's time but commemorated as ceremonies of the greatest privilege.

Since luxury was one of the major businesses of the court, it was natural that by Shah Jahan's period the value of the arts tended to be measured in ornamental terms. Because of Jahangir's scientific curiosity, the miniatures produced by his artists have substantial intellectual content, whereas in Shah Jahan's era decorative qualities gradually became paramount. Technical virtuosity in rendering complex surface patterns of decorative items in miniatures also became increasingly significant. An added dimension was the unity that evolved within the arts: architecture, miniature albums and borders, and textiles all shared the same patterns. The standard of decoration was high—as is shown by the flowered *vaslis* of various Shah Jahani folios, such as the one of small animals delicately positioned among flowering plants [28iii]. While there was much repetition of design, artists were also capable of great inventiveness and demonstrated the importance of their work by occasionally inscribing their border drawings.

Among the portraits and *durbar* scenes of Shah Jahan's era are many penetrating examples by his foremost artists, who were growing ever more practiced at utilizing European illusionism to produce extraordinary spectacles. Throughout the reigns of Akbar, Jahangir, and Shah Jahan, the most talented artists created stunning impacts by exaggerating naturalistic techniques, and in Shah Jahan's era they excelled particularly in evoking grandeur. In the *Shah Jahan Nama*, for example, many artists achieved an exactitude beyond life by rendering details of costume or architecture as if under a magnifying glass. Inlaid marble walls, sumptuous carpets, and bejeweled weapons all glow with an unearthly perfection; and ranks of massed courtiers in brilliant textiles are rendered with uncanny veracity.

By contrast, however, there are many quite plain miniatures emanating from Shah Jahan's era that demonstrate how necessary portraiture had become purely as a status symbol. The depictions of courtiers wearing elegant *jamas* and posed in stiff attitudes with swords or shields are innumerable, and the fact that many were repeated with slight costume variations probably indicates that their portraits were ordered for other officials. Like the thousands of robes of honor that the court steward had to order from *karkhanas* annually for imperial presentation to nobles, the portrait became a recognized mark of official privilege. (It is interesting that the Mughal word for "studio" [*karkhana*] was the same for "factory"—providing an indication that many miniatures were created through mass production.)

Inscriptional evidence discloses that Shah Jahan retained certain royal albums when imprisoned in 1658 by his son Aurangzeb and that until his death in 1666 he apparently perused these, associating them with events of the previous thirty years. Although wonderful miniatures were done in the first twenty years of Aurangzeb's reign, these sumptuous albums represented the end of an era of royal pomp and luxury whose type continued to be recalled nostalgically by the Mughals in subsequent, less affluent years as high points of the imperial tradition.

1. List courtesy of the Victoria and Albert Museum, London.
2. P. Chandra, 1976, p. 183.

10 Alam Shah Closing the Dam 76.74
at Shishan Pass

From the *Dastan-i-Amir Hamza*, Mughal, ca. 1570, on
cotton, 69 × 52.2 cm, 83.7 × 67 cm overall. Text on
reverse. Late remounting with gold-flecked pinkish border
paper.

Gift of George P. Bickford

Ex collections: Tabbagh, Bickford.

Published: E. Blochet, *Musulman Painting* (London:
Metheuen, 1929), pl. 189; Welch, 1973, no. 45; Czuma,
1975, no. 53.

Comparative Material: (A) *Battle at Shishan Pass*, from the
Dastan-i-Amir Hamza, Arnold and Wilkinson, pl. 2.

The early Mughal painting project, the *Dastan-i-Amir
Hamza* (*Romance of Amir Hamza*), seems to have been
unique in the Indian tradition because it is described in
special terms by Abu'l Fazl and others. Although the series
of large paintings on cotton elicited comment because such
a set was unprecedented, there is evidence that big paintings in the same style were also commissioned by Persian
patrons (large pages of a slightly later *Fal Nama* are
known).[1] A few other Indian works on cotton have been
preserved as well.[2]

The ambitious nature of launching a style with a manuscript of some 1,400 illustrations was typical of Akbar, who
was never satisfied with small-scale ventures.[3] The Cleveland *Tuti Nama* can be viewed as a preparation for the
Hamza Nama and as a formative stage in the careers of
many native Indian painters. Yet it is in the *Hamza* itself
that a more unified imperial style evolved — largely due to
the Mughals' mixed admiration of the Persians with a competitive drive for individual distinction. Akbar's confident
leadership, in addition to the inspiration provided by examples of European art and the skill of Hindu painters meant
that eventually Abu'l Fazl could boast of surpassing the
Persian masters. The great debt owed to Persia itself is
revealed in the Safavid training of the two *Hamza Nama*
directors, Mir Sayyid Ali and Abd al-Samad. Complete
Hamza Nama examples and isolated motifs such as dragons
or demons recall the spectacular *Shah Nama* of the Persian
ruler Shah Tahmasp.[4]

Perhaps the greatest difference between the Safavid and
Mughal artists lies in the fact that Shah Tahmasp's record of
legendary kings is treated as elegant fantasy, while the exaggerated adventures of Amir Hamza are immensely believable illustrations. The Safavids seem to have felt little of the
kinship that previous generations had with the tragedies
and twists of human fate running throughout the *Shah
Nama*. Contrastively, establishing themselves in a new
country had made the Mughals extremely aware of the reali-
ties of experience, and (as in many other cultures) they
employed a mythical hero to express their own triumphs
and anxieties. If on a certain level Amir Hamza appears to
represent a simplistic victory of good (or Islam) over evil,
the Mughal illustrations make it clear that the challenges

Hamza faced from the elements, hostile peoples, and a fear
of the unknown were only too real. As immigrants, such
obstacles had proved formidable; and although this early
manuscript went beyond prosaic fact into a kind of wild
allegory of struggle, it was ultimately a naturalistic description. Because a national identity was being forged, it was
logical for contemporary events to emerge symbolically in
artistic expression even though such vigor was anathema to
Persian traditions. When Akbar began to request history
subjects, the visual structure for illustrating such scenes had
already been created by *Hamza Nama* artists.

Both the Cleveland leaf and the preceding illustration,
now in the Chester Beatty Library (A, illus.), are excellent
examples of the Mughal intention to create powerfully convincing scenes. The event pictured in both scenes is the
inundation of a valley in which Amir Hamza's army is
trapped. Solomon had engaged a giant to build a dam over-
seen by his descendants, one of whom was the infidel leader
Tayhur, who set an ambush for Hamza. Although it required
four hundred men to turn the dam wheel, during this skir-
mish the enormous Tayhur accomplished it himself. As is
shown in the Cleveland miniature, a strong hero named
Alam Shah was finally able to reach the wheel and cut the
chain, stopping the water. Since the Mughal *Hamza Nama*
apparently does not follow the earlier texts that are known
in their entirety, and the writing on the back of miniatures
is obscured or difficult, details of the story line followed by
the Mughals are unclear. It has been ascertained that the
narration the Mughals relied on was probably a storyteller's
oral one that was written down at Akbar's request and thus
was different in detail from other accounts.[5] In this sequence the Beatty miniature is puzzling because it shows
the foot of a giant, presumably Tayhur, projecting from the
water. The identity of the dead infidel who had been guard-
ing the dam then becomes uncertain in the Cleveland
scene. The complete story of this particular controversy
between fire-worshippers and Muslims is contained in
several other extant scenes, which deal with unrelated
aspects of the struggle. The close association between the
Beatty and Cleveland paintings, however, shows that the
manuscript as it originally existed had been meticulously
planned to stress progression of the narrative.

Because Amir Hamza traveled across much of the then-
known world by sea, many of the Mughal illustrations depict gales or marine disasters. The real subject of each of the
two Shishan Pass scenes is therefore the flood itself, which
has been turned into an abstract essay on natural force
involving some very advanced concepts. It is interesting to
note that even at this early stage of stylistic development
Mughal painters had almost totally eliminated the age-old
Persian conventions of decoratively patterned water from
their repertoire. In most scenes large curling waves capture
the Mughal view of a raw, energetic universe. The two
paintings of the Shishan Pass deluge are among the most
exciting in the new style. The Beatty composition shows
people and animals caught in the flood's first surge, with

Figure 10.

several persons on the banks extending their arms in rescue efforts to those caught in very naturalistically portrayed waves. The Cleveland scene, close in composition and style, shows the relief of those watching from the banks as they realize that Alam Shah will close the dam.

In the Cleveland leaf much of the viewer's attention is directed to the dead man dramatically suspended in a wild and gory (typically Mughal) pose prior to his fall from the rocks. The watchers below, with fingers on mouths or arms raised in conventional Islamic gestures of amazement, seem to reflect the artist's own delight in his creation of this unprecedentedly realistic death scene. Over-concentration on individual elements or separate vignettes is characteristic of the *Hamza Nama* stage of naturalism and is retained to an extent in later Akbari painting. The artist's excitement over experimental effects often outweighs concern for compositional unity.

In addition to the bleeding man, a red drapery floating upon the waves catches the eye. The billowing contours of cloth, which allowed great freedom for modeling, became a sort of trademark of the Mughal fascination with European art, being used even earlier than the *Hamza Nama* in the well-known Cleveland *Tuti Nama* scene of the parrot brought to court.[6] The exaggerated, reversed garment folds at the waist of the dead man—bright red like the floating cloth (cloak?)—are treated in a similar manner. The fact that two points of emphasis in this picture are modeled in European fashion indicates the association of Western art with startling and spectacular effects.

Figure 10(A). *Battle at Shishan Pass*, from the *Dastan-i-Amir Hamza*. Chester Beatty Library, Dublin.

Figure 10, detail.

Although many naturalistic characteristics such as modeling in Mughal painting can be attributed to European inspiration, artists also created realistic effects from their own experience. Because the subject of this leaf poses unusual problems, the page gives a good indication of the way in which the early Mughals chose to use perspective and compositional devices. The scene, which is a close-up of the flood and lacks a horizon-line, violates both Persian and European aesthetic sensibilities. The lack of symmetry and the radical cropping are among the features that contradict Persian custom and confirm the great independent energy of the new culture. In contrast to the elaborate lavender and rose rocks found in Safavid painting, the landscape forms here are awkwardly colored, and the space created for the tents and figures differs from the conventional upward tilt of the Persian picture plane that could be considered a more graceful resolution of design problems. This artist has clearly struggled to create a stage for powerful naturalistic action, meanwhile ignoring refinement. Though some parts of the picture stress three-dimensionality, there is much inconsistency in registering distance or space; for example, the red cloth appears unattached to the water surface, and two figures at the back of the picture are large in accordance with their importance.

The figure type seen in the Cleveland leaf is common in the manuscript; many faces are done with a dropped lower jaw and jutting teeth. Poses are somewhat awkward, and limbs are depicted at totally wrong angles. The *Hamza Nama* artists apparently hoped that exaggeration would convey movement—with the result that figures make large gestures. The manner in which knees and elbows are overly flexed and actions correspondingly jerky is an almost-universal characteristic of early painting.

The artists of most pages can be spoken of only in general terms. Though a few paintings have been specifically attributed to the major artists Mir Sayyid Ali, Abd al-Samad, Daswanth, and Basawan, these attributions are tentative.[7] Shahnawaz Khan says over fifty artists worked on the *Hamza Nama*,[8] though the majority of these would have been entrusted with the coloring only. The Cleveland leaf, with its bravado brand of naturalism, is representative of one of the mainstreams of the *Hamza* style.

The Cleveland and Beatty leaves—both executed in the same bold manner—look as though they may have been produced by one artist. Because it was sometimes considered economical for related designs to be drawn by one person, the episodes may indeed have been done by the same hand.

Completing the *Hamza Nama* is supposed to have taken fifteen years, according to the contemporary account of Badauni, a chronicler who sometimes presented distorted or secondhand information. It is thus possible that the task may have required thirteen or fourteen years, though scholars have overlooked Badauni's possible inaccuracy and have attempted to plot different fifteen-year time spans for the *Hamza's* production. The key factor in dating seems to be

that Akbar and his officers were delighted by the oral recitation of the story during a campaign in Malwa in 1564. However, if this date marks the commencement of the task that should then have been completed in 1579, there is a slight contradiction with the transfer of the supervisor Abd al-Samad to the imperial mint in 1578. According to the contemporary sources, Abd al-Samad worked hard at encouraging artists to produce at a fast pace, and it seems unlikely that he would have been transferred just before the conclusion of this immense undertaking. Despite an apparent contradiction with Badauni, it seems most logical that the epic must have been completed between 1564 and 1578.[9]

No one has attempted a systematic analysis of the remaining *Hamza Nama* scenes in a stylistic order. While the early pages with text on the front tend to be stilted and timidly follow Persian conventions, those that must have been done at the end of the period are extremely advanced. The Beatty and Cleveland figures, which are the standard type, probably could not have been done before the project was well under way, given the bold handling of the flood and the European influences assimilated by the artist.

1. In the Metropolitan Museum of Art, New York, and the Musée d'Art et d'Histoire, Geneva; see also British Arts Council, *The Arts of Islam* (London, 1976), nos. 612a–b.

2. T. McInerney, *Indian Paintings from the Polsky Collections* (Princeton: Art Museum, Princeton Univ., 1982), pp. 15–16.

3. For the best presentation of known *Hamza Nama* pages see G. Egger, *Hamza Nama (Facsimile)*, 3 vols. (Graz: Akademische Druck, 1974–).

4. The earliest *Hamza Nama* paintings with text across the upper portion of the picture are close to Persian works in their flatness, figure style, etc. (see Egger, nos. V1–V4, V11; Skelton, 1976, nos. V2, V3, and his further references). Other paintings interspersed throughout the manuscript continue to express an overall Persian feeling (Egger, no. V55; Barrett and Gray, p. 76). For a comparison of a Safavid with a Mughal motif see Welch, 1972, p. 121, and Egger, no. V8.

5. James, p. 36; see Glück, pp. 67–71 for the full account of Hamza's adventures in Shishan Pass.

6. Lee and Chandra, fig. 34; until recently, it was assumed that European influence could not have affected Mughal painting until after the 1580 presentation of Plantin's *Polyglot Bible* (see B. Gray, "Review of S. C. Welch, *The Art of Mughal India*," AA 28 [1966], 99–101). Now, however, it has been acknowledged in several sources that Akbar had contact with the Portuguese by 1572 (Beach, 1976, p. 180; P. Chandra, 1976, p. 52, fn. 310). Beach (1976, p. 185) has suggested even earlier knowledge through unofficial distribution of single prints.

7. Different assumptions have been made about the *Hamza's* production. Ettinghausen has written (in *Encyclopedia of World Art* 1:18) that Mir Sayyid Ali and Abd al-Samad are credited with the directorship, but their active participation is unmentioned. Welch has made the opposite statement (1973, p. 91), attributing the drawing of designs to the directors, the coloring being left to the other artists. If fifty people were involved in the long project, it seems reasonable to expect that a greater percentage drew designs in accord with what is known of the later historical manuscripts. Several authors have ascribed paintings to such artists as Basawan, but these are merely contemporary attributions (Staude, in *Ency-*

clopedia of World Art 2: 386; Beach, 1976, p. 185; P. Chandra, 1976, p. 89).

8. Farooqi, p. 36.

9. Mistaken interpretation of a reference by the Akbari writer Qazvini has caused some scholars to accept Humayun, in certain cases against their own judgment, as the original patron of the *Hamza Nama*. The translation has now been corrected in accord with Qazvini's preface stating that the term "Imperial Majesty" refers only to Akbar (see Farooqi, pp. 35–37, and P. Chandra, 1976, p. 65).

The relative position of the *Hamza* as the first large production of the Mughal school is unquestioned despite various estimations of its exact date, and Badauni's mention that the manuscript took fifteen years to complete has generally been accepted by scholars (see Badauni, 2: 329). Among the several calculations of this fifteen-year period, the following are most recent: (a) 1558–1573 (Farooqi, p. 37), founded on an estimation of Qazvini's arrival in India and his statement that the work on the *Hamza* had been in progress seven years; (b) 1562–77 (P. Chandra, 1976, p. 66), based on several factors including Abd al-Samad's transfer to the mint in 1578; (c) 1564–79 (R. Skelton, "Mughal," *Art and Artists* [June 1979], p. 16), based on the oral recitation of the *Hamza Nama* recorded in the *Akbar Nama*; (d) 1567–82 (Pinder-Wilson, 1976, pls. 5–14), based on Badauni's statement that the *Hamza* was complete by 1582 (see P. Chandra, 1976, p. 66, for discussion of Badauni's date).

The middle positions appear most logical. The latest set of dates misses Badauni's implication that the manuscript was finished *before* 1582 and also causes a domino reaction, pushing other manuscripts into improbable later dates. The early dates presume both Qazvini's move to the capital immediately following a 1565 stay in Lahore and the rapid commencement of his historical account. In addition, Akbar would have been only fifteen in 1558, though it is impossible to assess either his maturity or power. The two dated works of the period, the 1568 *Deval Rani Khizr Khan* and the 1570 SOAS (School of Oriental and African Studies, London Univ.) *Anwari Suhaili*, fall into years covered by each of the three time spans. The early assessment is not only set without accounting for the artistic development expressed in the Cleveland *Tuti Nama* but also does not correlate with the styles of the two dated works cited above, which appear to have been done toward the beginning of the *Hamza* project (the 1568 miniatures in particular resemble the earliest *Hamza* leaves with text appearing on the front).

FURTHER READING: Beach, 1976, pp. 180–88; P. Chandra, 1976; Clarke, 1921; Egger; Farooqi; Glück; G. Meredith-Owens, "Hamza b. 'Abd-Muttalib," in *Encyclopedia of Islam* 3: 132–34; Staude, 1955.

11 *Princes Hunting in a Rocky Landscape*   40.1197

Tinted drawing, Mughal, ca. 1580–85, 26.4 × 15.8 cm, 40.5 × 26 cm with border. Several folds across paper; two partially effaced seals (unidentified). Late eighteenth-century border with gold brush drawings of birds and foliage.

Purchase, Edward L. Whittemore Fund

Ex collection: Heeramaneck.

Comparative Material: (A) *Jahangir Killing a Lion*, attributed to Farrukh Chela, Mughal, ca. 1607–10; Falk, 1978, no. 16. (B) *Hunt Scene with Jahangir*, Mughal, ca. 1620–30; *Christie*, 18 Dec. 1968, lot 76. (C) *Hunt Scene with Jahangir*, Mughal, ca. 1650; Skelton, 1969, p. 41. (D) *Hunt Scene with Rhinoceros*, Mughal, 1st half 18th century; *Sotheby*, 13 April 1976, lot 25. (E) *Zal and Rudaba*, from royal *Shah Nama*, ca. 1580; Skelton, 1976, no. V6, color pl. 31.

This very fine, early brush drawing has many compositional parallels but few stylistic comparisons because of the rarity of uncolored works from the 1580s with a similar emphasis on modeling. Here, for example, delicate repeating lines or shorter stippling strokes are utilized extensively to create textural illusions. Other works, by contrast, tend to display only firm boundary lines, without similar elasticity or potential for indicating three-dimensional form. In spite of the complexity of this drawing, the free applications of wash seem to indicate that it was intended to be fully colored. This is further borne out by the confusing and sketchy nature of the terrain: the bush in the lower center overlaps strokes of the ground plane, and the brook is vaguely defined.

About two decades after this drawing was made, the design was recast. Jahangir, who hunted constantly, was inordinately proud of his skill in the field—a proof of dynastic and personal virility, as in earlier eras. The composition of the Cleveland leaf is an obviously exciting one and is most likely to have been altered purely to eulogize the emperor. But because one of the extant versions identifies the main figures by inscription, there is some possibility that the restructuring was done to illustrate the mauling of a servant or courtier in one of the tragedies that occurred fairly frequently. The incident is not recorded by the emperor in his diary, but if it did occur, it took place before 1607, since the first preserved version showing Jahangir (A, illus.) was done by the artist Farrukh Chela around the time he completed pictures for the Chester Beatty *Akbar Nama*.

Although Farrukh Chela has reused the earlier figures, little of the previous subtler, more naturalistic, style remains; instead, the scene has been treated in a stiffer manner as conventional flattery. It was repeated several times in this way during the first half of the seventeenth century (B and C, illus.).[1] To suit the imperial theme, all the later compositions have additional figures intended to enhance the formality and significance of Jahangir's hunting party.

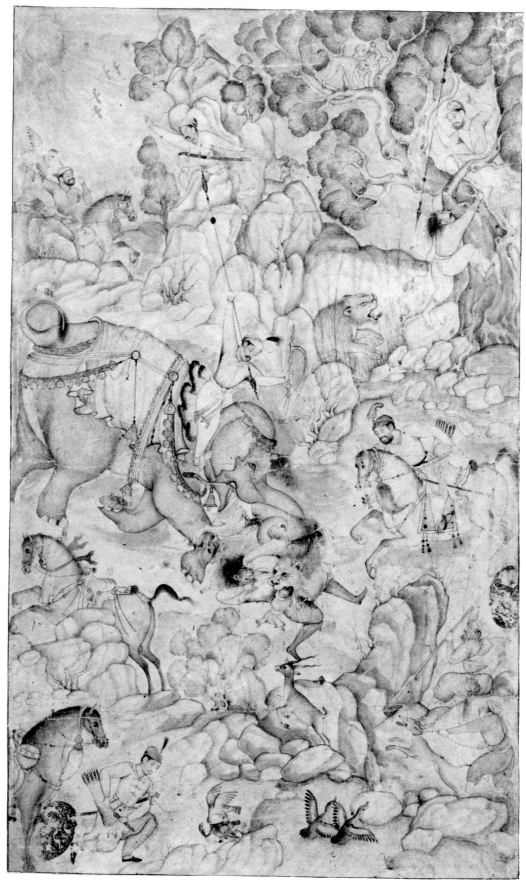

Figure 11.

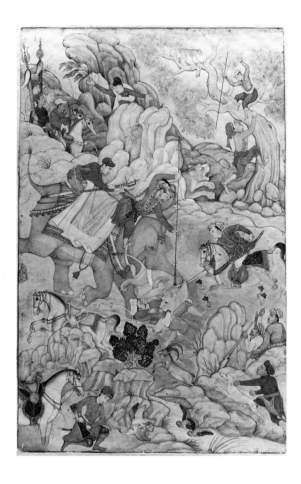

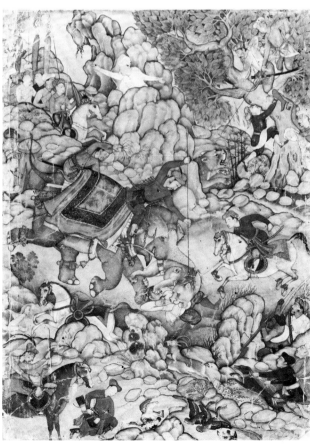

Left

Figure 11(A). *Jahangir Killing a Lion*, attr. to Farrukh Chela. Private collection. Photograph courtesy of Colnaghi Oriental, London.

Left below

Figure 11(B). *Hunt Scene with Jahangir*. Photograph courtesy of Christie's, London.

Below

Figure 11(C). *Hunt Scene with Jahangir*. Bodleian Library, Oxford, MS. Douce Or. a. 1, fol. 33r. Reproduced by permission of the Curators of the Bodleian Library.

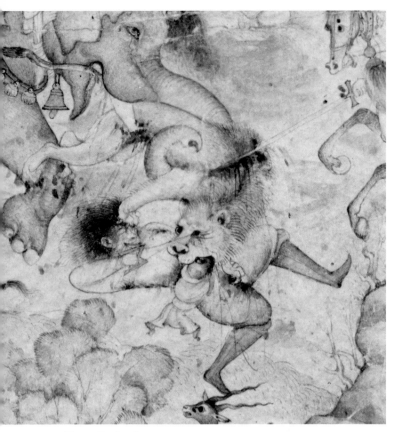

Figure 11, detail.

Figure 11, detail.

Except for the officer identified as Suhrab Khan attending Jahangir on the back of the elephant, however, the added men appear on the fringes of the scene as ciphers merely filling the design. While Farrukh Chela has employed five extra figures, one of the later artists went so far as to widen the composition to include thirteen extra people in a rather cramped, unnatural manner (B).[2]

In the later compositions Jahangir has obviously been made the focus of attention; he is large in proportion to the other figures, and effects have been slightly manipulated so that he has become the hub of a less complicated design. His heroic gesture of leaning forward to spear the lion is stressed to show the emperor's prowess, whereas in the Cleveland drawing, the smaller, anonymous figure waits with spear balanced in the air. As is demonstrated by details that emphasize the emperor and alter the drama of the interlocked elephant, man, and lion, the later theme is more banal, with less attention given to the lion's unfortunate victim.

Contrastively, the theme of the earlier Cleveland drawing is a sophisticated, philosophical one depicting a chain of antagonists bound in a struggle of killing as they are being killed. The fact that falcon hunting is shown in the air and water, while various other types of pursuit occur on land, indicates that the artist's message is a generalized one on hunting and survival; ironic or fatalistic undertones are provided by the central battle between beasts and man. This generalization is distinctive because Akbari painting is usually tied to specific portrayal of a prose or poetic story if not an historical incident. Related compositions suggest that at one time there existed a series of pictures devoted to various types of hunting in rocky landscapes, possibly with a central group of a man being gored by an animal. An eighteenth-century picture, which certainly copies or paraphrases an Akbari composition (D), is similar in theme and details.

In the Cleveland miniature, attention is divided fairly evenly among several princes (identified by the aigrettes on their turbans) intended to be viewed as ideal figures. The princes, casually dispersed in the rocky landscape, each create a small center of interest in the design. The fact that the prince in the foreground has no attendants is typical of the informality of this scene and distinguishes it from those picturing Jahangir. In contrast to the sterile effect obtained by subordinating the later compositions to Jahangir's figure, the Cleveland hunt scene exhibits rhythmic, energetic curves that animate the several separate vignettes. The man ramming his gun, the prince pulling out his dagger, the boy with the dog, and so on, though present in the later works, have much more individuality in the original. In addition, figural poses more aptly characterize actions, as can be seen by comparing the lion rushing from the reeds toward the man leaping up the tree trunk with the same passage in the other compositions.

In evaluating the artist's considerable originality, it should be noted that he has boldly attempted to handle difficult problems throughout his composition. Nevertheless, in his desire for animation he has allowed the single, twisting rhythm going through the elephant, the lion, and his victim to become slightly confused. Farrukh Chela clarified the design but lost the ferocity and tension apparent in the earlier version. Most figures in the Cleveland miniature are confidently drawn; the few traces of awkwardness have no relevance to quality but do help to resolve the problem of dating. The foreground prince, for example, with his knee positioned too far under him and his torso drawn frontally, follows the early Persian-influenced figural style adapted by the Mughals.

Dating the work depends mainly on figure treatment and costuming. The proportions of the figures and the artist's skill at showing them in action appear a little later than 1580. In comparison with figures in a leaf judged to be from Akbar's *Shah Nama* finished sometime shortly before 1582, for example, those of the Cleveland miniature are more compact, solid, and substantial (E). Flat turbans, especially those tied with ribbons, and pointed *chakdar jamas* are both characteristic of Akbar's early reign. These fashions continue to appear in paintings but are not common after the early 1580s (in the present example the *chakdar jama* is worn by four out of ten people).[3] The artist of this leaf is straightforward in his treatment, and costume is not, therefore, a nostalgic element.

Unfortunately, it is difficult to associate this hunt scene with a particular artist. Nevertheless, certain aspects of the work, such as its balanced nature, give an impression of a personality. Both action and fury are part of the scene but are well-controlled. The artist has carefully constructed lines of diagonal movement across the page, and the objects are clearly spaced in a planned manner so that the picture surface has an importance beyond the subject matter itself. Such interest in abstract pattern may reflect a Persian background, though the figures, with the exception of the prince in the left foreground, are completely Mughal. The artist may also have assimilated some knowledge of European art, as shown by the modeling and pose of the man with the gun. In total, his style is lively and individual but free of affectation, and it is tantalizing to speculate on the presence of such mature talent in the young Akbari studio.

1. The nearest approximation to the Cleveland composition was formerly in the Heeramaneck collection. It preserves the original theme and arrangement, but one man and a building have been added in the background. From a small photograph of this miniature, it appears that the Cleveland leaf is much more freely drawn and is the earlier version. Also see Goetz, 1930, pl. 11, fig. 36.

2. Proceeding clockwise from the upper right these figures are: an extra man in the tree, another behind the tree, one with a gun, one with a dog, one behind the horse in the extreme lower left, one in front of the running horse in the lower left, one sitting on the back of the elephant, two extra men behind the elephant, and four extra in the upper right.

3. The *chakdar jama* does not disappear altogether in paintings after the early 1580s but becomes much less common. Some examples of the costume appearing from around 1585–95, when placed in context with other works of the same era, give an idea of the infrequency of this fashion: Bankipur *Timur Nama*, ca. 1584–85, P. Brown, 1924, pl. XXXIV (a pointed coat); *Divan of Anwari*, dated 1588, Welch, 1963, pl. 4A; *Divan of Hafiz*, ca. 1595, *Marg* 11 (June 1958): 58; *Prince under a Tree*, by Abd al-Samad, ca. 1585–90, Welch, 1976, no. 10; *Bridge of Boats*, by Basawan, from the Victoria and Albert *Akbar Nama*, ca. 1590–95, Pinder-Wilson, 1976, p. 43 (among others in this manuscript showing *chakdar jamas*); hunt scene, *Khamsa of Nizami*, by Abd al-Samad, dated 1595; Martin, 2: pl. 179; *Chingiz Nama*, ca. 1596, see Knizkova and Marek, p. 19, for references. Nostalgia in style and costuming can be seen in the two works by Abd al-Samad, who not only used the early Akbari costume in 1595, but in both works employed figural conventions brought from Persia in the mid-sixteenth century (e.g., long waists and spidery legs). If the artist of the Cleveland hunt scene were attempting to re-create the past by the use of costume, he might use figural mannerisms as well.

12 *Babur Meeting with Sultan Ali Mirza* 71.85
at the Kohik River

Leaf from the British Library *Babur Nama*, Mughal,
ca. 1590, 28 × 16.5 cm, 41 × 27.1 cm with border. Text
panel painted over in upper right. Eighteenth-century dark
blue inner border, floral outer border.

Purchase, Andrew R. and Martha Holden Jennings Fund
Ex collection: MacDonald.

Comparative Material: (A) *Babur and Ali Mirza*, leaf from
the dispersed *Babur Nama*, Mughal, ca. 1589; *Sotheby*,
6 Dec. 1967, lot 112 (now Metropolitan Museum of Art,
67.266.3). (B) *Babur and Ali Mirza*, leaf from the
Moscow/Walters *Babur Nama*, Mughal, ca. 1593;
Tyulayev, 1960, pl. 8.

This scene illustrates a boyish adventure recorded in the
diary of the first Mughal emperor, Babur. The four successive Akbari copies illustrating the autobiographical work
afford an opportunity to compare narrative as well as stylistic developments during the period. The earliest *Babur
Nama* manuscript—considered to be the original royal volume presented to Akbar in 1589—is termed the "dispersed"
version since its leaves are scattered. Because of the early
date of the work, a few of the miniatures are rudimentary,
but the garden and plant or animal scenes in particular are
sensitively colored and the drawing style is delicate.

The second *Babur Nama* manuscript, done soon after, is
now mainly in The British Library.[1] Miniatures removed
from it early in the nineteenth century, including this one,
were chosen from various parts of the book and their absence disguised by a slight rearrangement of the remaining
pages. The text of the extracted pages was eliminated and all
were mounted on floral borders (the Cleveland leaf clearly
shows the repainted text area running through the tree in
the upper right).[2] The third manuscript, done about 1593,
is mainly divided between the State Museum of Eastern
Cultures in Moscow and the Walters Art Gallery in Baltimore. The final copy with a dated page of 1598 is in the
National Museum, New Delhi.

The *Babur Nama* is the only history manuscript besides
the *Akbar Nama* covering subjects familiar to the artists, as
is evident from the freedom and variety of their compositions. Babur had died in 1526, having lived only a few
years in India, yet his memoirs were not totally removed
from the contemporary experiences of the artists. The
founder of the dynasty had stamped his personal traits upon
the latter sixteenth century; Akbar has been said to have
resembled Babur in his objectivity, adventuresomeness,
and other characteristics, thus making Babur a comprehensible personality to these painters. In addition, although
most of Babur's experiences are set outside India, his observations on the Indian landscape are an important aspect of
the diary. Artists—often native Indians—obviously enjoyed
illustrating Babur's detailed classification of Indian flora and
fauna, lavishing equal care and attention on their settings.
Babur's writing is fresh, informal, and free-spirited; for

his age, he was an extremely tolerant person, filled with a
desire to observe and learn. The artists of the first two
*Babur Nama*s seem to mirror some of the feelings he expressed. The second manuscript, for example, from which
the Cleveland miniature is taken, is spicy and adventurous,
echoing Babur's own curiosity in such genre scenes as that
of almond-sellers surrounded by heaps of nuts they are
weighing. Strangely, although the Moscow/Walters *Babur
Nama* was done only two or three years later, the mood
changes completely in that the scenes are far more formal.
And the last *Babur Nama*, done toward the end of the
period, seems somewhat static.

The intrepid Babur, like his grandson Akbar, began his
adventures at an early age. In 1494, when his father was
killed in an accident, Babur assumed control of the small
kingdom of Ferghana at the age of eleven and a half. The
Cleveland episode occurred in 1496 and is therefore near
the beginning of each of the three successive *Babur Nama*
manuscripts compared here. Civil war in Samarkand—the
richest, most cosmopolitan center known to Babur—had
resulted in confusion. The situation aroused visions of conquest; as Babur later wrote, because "we . . . coveted Samarkand, we got our men to horse." Thus in 1496, approaching
fourteen years of age, Babur set off on his mission, joined
later by some young cousins, to capture this rich city where
power was rapidly changing hands. Ali Mirza, whose inter-
view with Babur is the subject of these miniatures, was
supposed to have been blinded during political machina-
tions, but Babur says, "When the fire-pencil was drawn
across his eyes, whether by the surgeon's choice or by his
inadvertence, no harm was done." At the time the incident
in this painting occurred, Ali Mirza had emerged at the top
of the power struggle and was briefly hailed as the *padshah*
of Samarkand. He then met with Babur and his cousins, for
although they were not formidable enemies, they could not
simply be dismissed as harmless children. It was arranged
that Babur would withdraw from Samarkand and then proceed to the meeting on the nearby Kohik River. Each party
was to bring only four or five men, and according to one
translation, the two groups may have met on an island,
though this is not illustrated in the miniatures. Babur related, "We just saw one another, . . . asked each the other's
welfare and went, he his way, I mine."[3] Despite the veiled
nature of any threat, Babur decided that winter was coming
and postponed his siege. The following year, however, after
Ali Mirza had been murdered, the young noble returned to
the city and occupied it for three months.[4]

In the first version of the meeting, now owned by the
Metropolitan Museum of Art (A, illus.), the story is accurately depicted, with the city in the background and the
two leaders surrounded by their few companions in the
foreground. Babur is correctly shown as a young man,
and the artist has given his impression of period costumes
(the hats of Turkic tribesmen being important distinguishing features).

Figure 12.

The Cleveland page is more removed from the event described in Babur's diary. Since the city of Samarkand has been eliminated, the setting is less clear. Babur is still shown as a young man, but now approaches Ali Mirza with a sizable group of attendants and some well-laden camels. Attention is diffused between the various horsemen, whereas in the earlier miniature the two leaders were clearly set apart in the central area. The artist thus appears to have less knowledge of the biography and has modified the scene to

make it more eye-catching. It is the liveliness of these added elements that characterizes the British Library *Babur Nama* as a whole.

There are thirteen figures in this scene, and the artist has depicted almost all of them in some individual action. The painter has emphasized the idea of thirst: the man drawing a container of water, for example, is a phrase borrowed from the earlier painting that the artist apparently admired for its genre qualities. Attendants behind Babur hold his wrapped

45

Figure 12(A). *Babur and Ali Mirza*, from the dispersed *Babur Nama*. The Metropolitan Museum of Art, New York; Purchase, 1967, Louis V. Bell and Joseph Pulitzer Bequest.

sword and bow. The baggage carried by the mule and two camels is rendered in detailed fashion, and the painter has even playfully drawn a pet monkey atop the lead camel headed toward the water with his tongue hanging out. The camel-tender, who lifts his arms in thanksgiving, rushes forward holding the rein of the beast, while his companion, who has already waded in, scoops water with his hands.

In the third version of the scene, from Moscow (B, illus.), the composition has been thoroughly reorganized. The design is much stronger, but all the attractive, informal elements have been purged. The continuous line of followers signifies political power, and the brotherly embrace of Babur, now a bearded man, with Sultan Ali Mirza makes them look like two important heads of state, whereas, according to Babur's memoirs, one was an ambitious, star-struck boy and the other an opportunist in a precarious position. Even the bridge across the Kohik changes the connotation of the scene to one of order and regimentation; by contrast, the two earlier miniatures portray Babur as a head of a roving, gypsylike band of adventurers. While the Moscow *Babur Nama* is not as forceful as the explosive Victoria and Albert *Akbar Nama*, its compositions include similar design devices. Careful linear organization by Basawan and other sophisticated artists of the 1590s changed the tone of Akbari manuscripts; dynamism and imperial grandeur were conveyed by the strong rhythms of deliberately arranged figural or architectural lines. The Metropolitan (A) and the Cleveland *Babur Nama* miniatures are milder in character as well as being more faithful to the spirit of Babur's account.

1. Of 183 paintings, 152 are in The British Library; see Smart, 1973, p. 56, and Pinder-Wilson, 1976, p. 37, for location of other leaves. Dr. Smart has also discovered sixteen miniatures from another *Babur Nama* in Istanbul (probably the second copy), but since it is fragmentary and otherwise unknown, it is not being used for comparison here.

2. Smart, 1977, pp. 68–69; two pages in the Morgan Library and a few in private collections have floral borders like those of the Cleveland miniature. The only published examples of the borders are in M. C. Beach, *Reflections of India: Paintings from the 16th to the 19th Century* (Toronto: Royal Ontario Museum, 1979), nos. 18 and 19.

3. Babur, pp. 63–64, 94.

4. Gascoigne, p. 19.

FURTHER READING: Babur; Randhawa, 1972; Smart, 1973, 1977, and 1978; Suleiman; Tyulayev, 1955, 1958, and 1960.

Figure 12(B). *Babur and Ali Mirza*, from the Moscow/Walters *Babur Nama*. After *Miniatures of Babur Namah* (Moscow: State Fine Arts Publishing House, 1960), pl. 8.

13 *Humayun Defeating the Afghans before Reconquering India*   71.77

Leaf from the Victoria and Albert *Akbar Nama*, Mughal, ca. 1590, 31.2 × 18.6 cm, 36.5 × 23.7 cm with border. Text on reverse. Artists' names cropped at bottom of border. Inscription below bottom edge of painting in *nasta'liq* script: "Jang karden-e lashgar-e hazrat jannat ashiyani ba afghanan va fath nomudan daer hanye ke urduye zafar qarin mutawajjih fath hindustan bud." ("The warring of the army of His Majesty 'Nestling in Paradise' [i.e., the deceased Humayun] with the Afghans, and their defeat [of them] at the time when the Camp of Victory [Mughal dominion] was being established in Hindustan.")[1]

Purchase, Andrew R. and Martha Holden Jennings Fund

Ex collection: MacDonald.

Published: Levine, 1976, pp. 89–95.

Comparative Material: (A) *Humayun Receiving the Head of Qaracha Khan*, leaf from the Victoria and Albert *Akbar Nama*, ca. 1590; Philadelphia Museum of Art, 47-49-1, unpublished.

This is one of the miniatures separated from the copy of *Akbar Nama* that was the original illustrated version of this biography designed for the emperor as it was being written by his closest friend, Abu'l Fazl. The major preserved part of this illustrated history now in the Victoria and Albert Museum commences with the year 1560, the fourth year of Akbar's reign, and ends with the year 1578 and a description of events recorded near the end of Abu'l Fazl's second volume of text.[2] Only a few leaves are known that are scattered remnants of the lost first volume in which Abu'l Fazl deals with the astrological predictions at Akbar's birth, the emperor's genealogy from Adam, and especially events in the life of his father, Humayun. The first volume of a later *Akbar Nama* (ca. 1604–7), now in The British Library, gives an idea of scenes now missing from the Victoria and Albert copy. Most of the seventeenth-century illustrations, deal with Humayun, as must have been the case with the original copy, since five of the scattered miniatures (including the one in the Cleveland collection) illustrate Humayun's activities.[3]

The Victoria and Albert *Akbar Nama* is one of the Mughal series of three histories that have similar formats and a clear, dynastic purpose. The Bankipur *Timur Nama* of ca. 1584–85, the *Akbar Nama*, and the *Chingiz Nama* dated 1596 were each intended to affirm Akbar's claim of leading a great Muslim dynasty. In the 1580s and 1590s it was still astonishing that this upstart family could hold a unified India and wield an influence rivaling that of the Timurids and Mongols. From the manuscript sequence, it is evident that Babur's paternal ancestor Timur was considered the most important of the Mughal predecessors who, though by this time a remote legendary figure, could be used to enhance Akbar's own status as conqueror. The *Chingiz Nama*, last in the series, records the deeds of the Mongol Il-Khans, Babur's maternal ancestors.

Abu'l Fazl, who was introduced to Akbar in 1574 by other members of his family and went on to become the emperor's closest friend, adviser, and biographer, may have promoted the illustration of the history manuscripts. In discussing his compilation of the *Akbar Nama*, Abu'l Fazl says that he did not care for stories of *divs* (possibly referring to the large project of producing the fantastical *Hamza Nama*) but was discontented that "the palace of history was in ruins."[4] In 1574, the year he acquired status, the imperial Record Office, which documented everything in court connected with the sovereign, was begun, and it is conjectured that Abu'l Fazl may have organized this bureau.[5] Abu'l Fazl's enthusiastic research for the biographical *Akbar Nama* and his interest in genealogy—which would relate to the *Timur* and *Chingiz Namas*—also support the hypothesis that he promoted the history-manuscript series, perhaps even originally suggesting it to Akbar.

An accepted, unified manner of composing historical scenes evolved with the *Timur Nama*. The artists subsequently used the vocabulary and techniques developed in this earlier manuscript to cope with the challenges of portraying Akbar's life. Akbar's spirit, the tumultuous events of his reign, and the painters' own stylistic confidence resulted in some of the period's most vital compositions. Akbar's awareness that he was changing the history of the entire subcontinent is an integral part of the manuscript. His artists seem to have felt a special excitement in the knowledge that a phenomenal personality was sweeping across India achieving unprecedented victories. It is obvious from the illustrations that the remote conquests of Timur or Genghis Khan evoked less response than those of Akbar, which are enlivened by numerous dramatic anecdotes. The *Akbar Nama* is also unusual in the historical cycle for its inclusion of so many genre events whose import would have disappeared in a few decades (only the *Babur Nama* compares in the artists' sympathy with their subject matter).

The Cleveland leaf dealing with Humayun is somewhat impersonal compared to scenes depicting Akbar himself. Humayun was neither a leader nor an heroic fighter, and the artists' identification with him in scenes of the first *Akbar Nama* volume seems slight. The inscription on the Cleveland leaf in Abu'l Fazl's metaphorical style refers to Humayun's victory over the Afgans as he was moving down to reconquer India, in 1555, after years of exile. Although the text on the reverse discusses an important battle in the reconquest, the artist had included nothing accurate according to the literary details, and it is probable that other illustrations of the first *Akbar Nama* volume are equally generalized. Humayun was not present during most of the encounters with Afghans, and the organizer of the campaign to reinstate him was the general Bairam Khan, later the young Akbar's counselor, who commanded the central portion of Humayun's small band of followers. It is impossible to read the *Akbar Nama* without realizing that both in Humayun's reign and during Akbar's rule as a child king, the Mughal dynasty could not have survived without this

جنگ کردن لشکر حضرت آسیانی با افغانان و فتح نمودن در حینی کار دوی ظفر قرین متوجه فتح هندوستان ا

۳۲

Figure 13.

Color Plate I. Akrura Drives Krishna and Balarama to Mathura [9].

Color Plate III. Jain Ascetic Walking Along a Riverban

lor Plate VI. A Feast in a

Color Plate VII. Portrait of Raja Bikramajit [24].

18 Two Leaves from the Chester Beatty Akbar Nama

Mughal, 1605–7

A later *Akbar Nama* than that in the Victoria and Albert Museum is divided between The British Library, which has thirty-nine miniatures from the first volume of text, and the A. Chester Beatty Library. The Beatty section encompasses volume 2, part of volume 3 of the text, and sixty-one miniatures. The first seven of these Beatty miniatures are unnumbered, but the numbering on the remainder indicates that fifty-four miniatures, or roughly half the total, have been removed from the manuscript at regularly spaced intervals.[1] The British Library *Akbar Nama* volume has eleven missing miniatures—four of these had disappeared when the manuscript was renumbered before it arrived in Europe, but the remaining seven were removed subsequently.[2] Both miniatures owned by the Cleveland Museum are from the Beatty portion of the manuscript, although [18i] resembles many pages of the British Library volume.

The British Library/Beatty Library *Akbar Nama* has been overshadowed by the earlier Victoria and Albert *Akbar Nama* and has been judged by its characteristics. The later version is often described as being "less" in some way than the Victoria and Albert manuscript. Reversing the standpoint of comparison, however, it is possible to assert that the fully colored pages of the later *Akbar Nama* are more aristocratically stylized than those of other history manuscripts. Artists of this manuscript avoided the previous muscularity, headstrong epic action, or spilled blood, and adapted courtly mannerisms instead. In the later *Akbar Nama*, action is more purely aesthetic or rhythmically abstract, and color is better modulated. Since the text was written by Akbar's most praised calligrapher, the renowned Zarrin Qalam, or "Golden Pen," it is clear that the manuscript was intended to be one of the best quality.[3] Because the British Library/Beatty version in general is not based compositionally upon the first *Akbar Nama*, specific comparisons between illustrations are imprecise. Unlike the four *Babur Nama* manuscripts whose scenes become progressively more complex but are often dependent on each other [12], illustrations of the two *Akbar Namas* are usually little related by the treatment of subject matter.

One reason that the later *Akbar Nama* has proved hard to describe is that it is the least uniform of the history productions. Several diverse stylistic groups are loosely arranged in the manuscript, and because the quality varies with stylistic difference, it therefore makes evaluation of the total work difficult. Replacement of the missing illustrations in their correct sequence would enable stylistic patterns to be more clearly seen. However, with exceptions, at the present time it appears generally true that the British Library and first portion of the Beatty manuscript are made up of highly colored paintings with rather small figures. Many of these leaves, including the Cleveland one attributed to Dharm Das [18i], have subtle, luminous color schemes and

elegantly stylized settings. Such miniatures are more like the Akbari poetry volumes of the *Khamsa* of Nizami or *Khamsa* of Dihlavi than they are reminiscent of other history manuscripts. The comparison of an Akbari poetry leaf, ca. 1597–98, by Dharm Das [18i, comparison D] with the Cleveland *Akbar Nama* scene attributable to the same artist not only shows the consistency of Das's work but also brings out the relation of the refined poetry leaf and the history-manuscript illustration. Akbari poetry miniatures were completed by a single artist, as are the great majority of miniatures in this second *Akbar Nama*; out of the sixty-one paintings in the Beatty Library only two record a second artist. The British Library/Beatty pages are small, which makes them akin to the poetry leaves, and many have comparable formats.

A large number of *nim qalam* (partially colored) pages, unparalleled in other Akbari manuscripts, occur in a block from the end of the British Library portion through the middle of the Beatty text but are less frequent in other sections [18ii]. The *nim qalam* pages tend to be harshly and perfunctorily drawn, employing compositional formulae long since stereotyped. Since few outstanding British Library/Beatty pages have been published in color, the inferior pages have made a greater impression. Leaves with strikingly rich coloring, which represent the latest stylistic evolution within the Beatty *Akbar Nama*, are comparable to Jahangir's early poetry volumes and are of very high quality.[4] These leaves are intermingled with others but are not characteristic of the early section.

The British Library/Beatty *Akbar Nama* is an important transitional work that reflects the atmosphere of the court prior to Akbar's death and during Jahangir's assumption of power. Little is actually known about this period when the Mughal painting studio underwent changes and certain artists were dropped while others rose in favor. The British Library section of the *Akbar Nama* has one miniature dated 25 January 1604, which occurs well along in the volume (fol. 145v).[5] While this miniature helps to clarify dating, it simultaneously raises questions about patronage and the period of the manuscript's completion. Since about 120 miniatures occur after the dated example, production must have extended into the reign of Jahangir. Akbari manuscripts that can be documented were finished within differing time spans, and because various factors always affected production, it is difficult to find any means of measurement. The stylistic inconsistencies of the British Library/Beatty *Akbar Nama* suggest that illustrations were spread over several years. The manuscript was begun when the rebellious Prince Salim was in Allahabad, where he remained from 1603 until November 1604.[6] It seems most logical that the British Museum and early portion of the Beatty volume were finished prior to Akbar's death in 1605, after which the work was continued by Jahangir.

Manuscript pages apportioned to individual painters would not have been finished in sequence, but presumably there was a rough order. The perfunctory *nim qalam* pages may represent Jahangir's initial disinterest followed by others showing greater commitment. In spite of his previous rebellion, Jahangir revered Akbar after his death and honored him in various ways during the early part of his reign; for example, he ordered the striking of a gold coin to commemorate his father's religious ideas.[7] Thus, continuation of the *Akbar Nama* seems consistent with other actions. Some studio production must have proceeded without radical change for a few years of the reign. The dissolution of the highly organized, regulated Akbari studio, whose artists were accustomed to producing manuscripts, seems to have been gradual. However, the British Library/Beatty manuscript already marks a change from cooperative artistic projects like the *Chingiz Nama*.

Ironically, many of the separated *Akbar Nama* pages have been placed by sheer chance in borders contemporary with the manuscript. The Cleveland scene attributed to Dharm Das [18*i*] is an example of such a page superimposed over the *Fahrang-i-Jahangiri*, or dictionary of Jahangir—one of this emperor's early commissions. Dated 1607/8, the dictionary borders continue traditions of Akbari poetry manuscripts, since the small figures ensconced in flowers compare well with those from the border of Jami's *Baharistan* done in 1595.[8] Many of the *Fahrang-i-Jahangiri* pages have animal or *waq-waq* motifs, but of those with human figures, some portray hunters, other *yogis* or various foreigners.

The verso of the Cleveland page [18*i*], decorated with men in Elizabethan costume, shows the original appearance of the dictionary text banded by a brightly colored inner floral border. This remounting project can be traced to the French dealer Demotte, who published eleven *Fahrang-i-Jahangiri* borders surrounding a variety of Mughal paintings and drawings in his 1930 catalog.[9] The removal of *Akbar Nama* leaves must have been accomplished sometime previously, as the British Library section of the manuscript belonged to Quaritch by 1912; the second portion was then acquired from the same firm by A. Chester Beatty in 1923.[10] Since so many miniatures are missing from the Beatty section of text, most of the paintings in dictionary borders came from this group; however, a miniature from the British Library section of the *Akbar Nama* (now Freer Gallery of Art, 39–57) was published with a dictionary border while still in the collection of Demotte.[11] This fact helps to establish that the dealer did indeed own and dismember both parts of the manuscript. One other published leaf in a dictionary border is also from the British Library portion of the text.[12]

1. Arnold and Wilkinson, 1: 4–5.
2. Conversation with R. Skelton; also see British Museum Trustees Report (1966/67), p. 69, and Titley, 1977, pp. 4–5.
3. British Museum Trustees Report (1966/67), p. 69.
4. See, for example, Arnold and Wilkinson, pls. 27, 28.
5. Titley, 1977, p. 5.
6. Srivastava, 2: 478.

7. J. Allan, "A Portrait Mohur of Akbar," *BMQ* 5 (1930/31): 56.
8. Bodleian Library, *Mughal Miniatures of the Earlier Periods* (Oxford: Oxford University Press, 1953), pls. 10, 11.
9. Ibid., nos. 166–74, 222, 223; this dealer has also been implicted in other recombinations of art work and in cases of outright forgery—see F. Arnau, *Three Thousand Years of Deception in Art and Antiquities* (London: J. Cape, 1961), pp. 314–15.
10. See H. Glück and E. Diez, *Die Kunst des Islam* (Berlin: Proplaen-Verlag, 1925), no. 517, which shows that Quaritch owned the British Library volume by 1925; see also Arnold and Wilkinson 1: 4.
11. Strzygowski, pl. 65, fig. 187.
12. T. Falk, "Rothschild Collection of Mughal Miniatures," *Persian and Mughal Art* (London: Lund Humphries, 1976), no. 86(i).

FURTHER READING: Arnold and Wilkinson, 1: 4–12; Beach, 1978, pp. 44–59, and 1981, pp. 102–23; Losty, pp. 93–94; Meredith-Owens; Pinder-Wilson, R. "History and Romance in Mughal India," *OA* 13 (1967): 62–64; Titley, 1977, pp. 4–5.

18*i* *Circumcision Ceremony for Akbar's Sons* 71.76

Attributed to Dharm Das, ca. 1605; placed in *Fahrang-i-Jahangiri* leaf, 1607–8; 22.9 × 12.1 cm, 34.7 × 22.5 cm with borders. Emperor's face has been damaged. Obverse: red inner border with gold-flecked design, outer border with gold brush drawing of princes discoursing. Reverse: purple inner border with gold floral design, outer border with gold brush drawing of Europeans (detail illus.).

Purchase, Andrew R. and Martha Holden Jennings Fund

Ex collections: Demotte, Kelekian, MacDonald.

Published: Welch, 1959, fig. 12.

Comparative Material: (A) *Circumcision Ceremony for Akbar's Sons*, attributed to Dharm Das, leaf from the Chester Beatty *Akbar Nama*, Mughal, ca. 1605; Skelton, 1976, no. V51, color pl. 36. (B) *Bridge of Boats Broken by an Elephant*, by Dharm Das, leaf from the British Library *Akbar Nama*, Mughal, 1603–4; *OA* 13, no. 1 (1967): 63. (C) *Babur Defeating Rana Sanga*, by Dharm Das, Mughal, 1603–4; *OA* 13, no. 1 (1967): 63. (D) *Religious Mendicants at a Garden Pavilion*, by Dharm Das, leaf from a *Khamsa* of Dihlavi (?), Mughal, ca. 1597–98; *Cincinnati Art Museum Handbook* (Cincinnati, 1975), p. 54.

This miniature attributable to Dharm Das[1] is the left half of a scene showing the circumcision of Akbar's three sons on October 22, 1573, not long after the baby Daniyal's birth. The complete double page was arranged to show contrasting views of the male and female quarters in Akbar's city of Fatehpur Sikri (though the artist's rendering of this environment is generalized). On the right in a miniature now in a private collection in England, Dharm Das has depicted the three small boys being cared for by their mothers and other harem women while gifts are received from messengers in the foreground (A, illus.). At the left in the Cleveland miniature the wall of the women's quarters projects along the edge of the composition. Akbar sits on his

Figure 18*i.*

Figure 18*i*(A). *Circumcision Ceremony for Akbar's Sons*, attr. to Dharm Das; from the Chester Beatty *Akbar Nama*. Edmund R. A. De Unger Collection, Richmond, England.

Figure 18*i*, detail of border on reverse.

Figure 18*i*, detail.

throne surrounded by well-wishers as two women dance to clapping and the beat of a tambourine by two others. Musicians with kettledrums and long horns celebrate the event in the foreground, while a servant with a tray of coins is importuned by beggars.

In 1934 both halves of the page (although not known to be related) were in the same private collection along with three other Beatty *Akbar Nama* miniatures.[2] The subjects of all these paintings were only vaguely identified. Although the depiction of festivities for male children varies somewhat when all the Akbari examples are compared, certain features are commonly included: a view into the woman's quarters, figures of musicians and dancers, and donations to the poor.[3] The identification of such motifs led to recombination of the Cleveland leaf with comparison A.[4]

In this composition the dancers and other women wearing high *chaghtai* hats are the most distinctive element. The hats were associated with the Mongol clan of Jaghatai Khan, from which Babur's mother was descended. *Babur Nama* miniatures or scenes showing Humayun with his family often include the *chaghtai* hats, which continued to be worn by women in the Mughal court.[5] However, Akbar's marriages to Hindu women also brought diverse Rajput costumes into the harem. There are several differing opinions concerning the preservation of the *chaghtai* style into Akbar's era. The most logical are that the hat and the long dress worn with it were connected either with Mongol lineage or with a professional function in the harem.[6] Although there are many miniatures of *chaghtai* dancers, the majority of *Akbar Nama* birth and festival scenes portray women in Hindu costume.

The painter has developed his own idea of the circumcision festivities, apparently putting in appropriate elements rather than consulting Abu'l Fazl's specific description in the text. Here the author states that Akbar wished to make the event one of general rejoicing, probably because during this period he and his officers were almost continuously involved in distant battle campaigns. There was a feast, a large bazaar in the court, and Akbar himself was weighed against precious substances that were then distributed.[7] As conceived by the artist, the scene is perhaps centered more on the intimate life of the harem than on any outside festivities.

The painter Dharm Das, to whom the circumcision festival scene is attributed, joined Akbar's atelier early, contributing to manuscripts like the ca.–1585 *Darab Nama*.[8] A prolific artist, he began to excel at the end of Akbar's era in the poetry volumes and in the British Library/Beatty *Akbar Nama* (see B, C, D).[9] Much of his talent lies in rendering decorative passages (D, illus.). He seems to have been a master of genteel effects rather than raw action; for example, in his *Akbar Nama* battle scenes movement is elegantly arranged. Nothing is allowed to ruin the ballet of tangled limbs across the painting surface. Color is an important part of Dharm Das's later work, and he apparently delighted in the shades and nuances that were by then available to court

Figure 18*i*(D). *Religious Mendicants at a Garden Pavilion*, by Dharm Das. Cincinnati Art Museum, Cincinnati, Ohio; Gift of John J. Emery, 1950. 288.

Figure 18*i*, detail.

painters. He adapted the plump, rather stylized figures that came into fashion in the late Akbari era. Despite the popular conventionalization, his individuality is discernible in the way he shapes oval faces with bulging cheeks and renders facial features (note the musicians and beggars in the foreground of the Cleveland miniature). His mannered shading of figures accentuates their rounded contours and stylized appearance. Backgrounds also are unnaturally shaded and very luminous. Das's skill at miniaturization really emerges in his later work: the figures in the Cleveland painting are Lilliputians moving through a bright, enameled environment. The petite dancers, eager beggars, and other figures convey the delicacy of this type of painting.

This leaf is one of many mounted on a dictionary page dating to 1607/8. Here the remounting is discernible because some of the inner border at top and bottom has been covered by the miniature. The theme of princes conversing with each other or with a *mullah* is used on many of the other pages.[10] On the reverse, the border depicts men in European costume fairly accurately with large feathered hats, ruffs or high collars, and belted tunics.

1. Welch originally made this attribution, 1959, p. 140.
2. R. M. Riefstahl, *Catalog of an Exhibition of Persian and Indian Miniature Paintings Forming the Private Collection of Dikran Khan Kelekian* (New York: Gotchnag Press, 1933), no. 94, is now Keir collection; no. 96, now CMA; nos. 93, 95, 97 are now in the Freer Gallery of Art, Washington.
3. Birth scenes containing these elements plus others such as horoscope casting are featured in both *Akbar Namas;* see Wellesz, pls. 22, 23, and Arnold and Wilkinson, pl. 21.
4. I wish to thank Ellen Smart and Robert Skelton for their help in this process.
5. See British Library *Akbar Nama* leaves picturing Humayun in Martin, 2: pl. 183; Strzygowski, pl. 65, fig. 187.
6. Kuhnel and Goetz, p. 39, say female harem guards and some ladies' maids wore this costume; Knizkova, p. 21, says it was worn by dancers and unmarried girls, but it may have been worn as originally intended only by descendants of Jaghatai's clan.
7. Abu'l Fazl, *Akbar-Nama,* III: 102–3.
8. Welch, 1960, p. 96, fn. 14.
9. For other published miniatures by Dharm Das working alone, see Welch, 1960, fig. 4; Grube, 1968, no. 99; Bodleian Library, fig. 7; Krishnadasa, 1966, pp. 36–37; Martin, 2: pl. 180; Pinder-Wilson, 1976, no. 21, right half; Beach, 1966, no. 201, and 1981, no. 12b; Arnold and Wilkinson, pls. 22, 23, 32, 35; Wilkinson, 1929, pl. XXVI.
10. Binney, 1973, no. 20.

FURTHER READING: Ansari, 1957, pp. 255–67, and 1960, pp. 107–24.

18*ii* *Akbar Mounting His Horse* 39.65

Nim qalam drawing, here attributed to Sur Das Gujerati, ca. 1605–7, 23 × 12.4 cm, 43.2 × 28.2 cm with border. Late eighteenth- or early nineteenth-century border of beasts (in gold) hunting gazelles. Inscription in Persian, upper right: "wa zahi daulatmandi" (and what good fortune!).

Purchase, Dudley P. Allen Fund

Ex collection: Demotte (?).

Comparative Material: (A) *Akbar Receiving Homage from the Nobles of Gujerat*, by Sur Das Gujerati, leaf from the Beatty *Akbar Nama* (fol. 157b, half of double page), Mughal, ca. 1605–7; Arnold and Wilkinson, pl. 26.
(B) *Defeat of Husayn Mirza in 1573*, by Sur Das Gujerati, leaf from the Beatty *Akbar Nama* (fol. 188, half of double page), Mughal, ca. 1605–7; Arnold and Wilkinson, pl. 29.

This second miniature from the Chester Beatty *Akbar Nama* is radically different from the first [18*i*] and gives an idea of the diversity within the total manuscript. It is done in the *nim qalam* manner found frequently at the end of the British Library *Akbar Nama* and through the beginning section of the Beatty *Akbar Nama.*[1] In these *nim qalam* leaves, though the greater portion of the picture is left uncolored, a few objects are either tinted or strongly colored.[2] In the example here, the color is bright and is concentrated around the figure of Akbar, who wears yellow boots, a gold robe, and a lime green turban. These vivid hues emphasize the steely sharpness of the drawing and the mannerist quality of the pictorial style. The painter has silhouetted his harsh outline drawing by stippling around the outside of the contour lines, a habit peculiar to him and a few other artists.

The scene can be attributed to Sur Das Gujerati by comparison with pages still in the Beatty manuscript that have inscriptions to the artist who frequently employed the *nim qalam* technique with heavy outlines and selective spots of color. As in the Cleveland miniature, the artist employed dark shading and cold, bright color to emphasize Akbar's face in a *durbar* scene (A), and an illustration of Akbar's victory over the rebel Husayn Mirza (B, illus.) depicts men in the upper left in a manner similar to the group in the upper right of the Cleveland picture. As these pages indicate, Sur Das was a conservative artist who had some ability to draw accurately but often did not infuse his work with emotion.

The period from 1600 until about 1610 was one during which artists commonly manifested confusion or indirection as the Akbari manuscript style was superseded. The more limited painters held to old motifs or mannerisms until these had been emphasized to an unnatural extent. In the Cleveland miniature Akbar's face surrounded by color in the center of the composition stands out in a striking way, and the contrast between this portrait, which resembles an engraving, and the stereotyped depiction of the attendants is marked. Certain artists in the Victoria and Albert *Akbar Nama* had previously used the emperor's precise depiction

Figure 18*ii*.

to single him out, but the disparity created was not so great.[3] Here the artist has used this device in order to create an effect so spectacular that it has become mannered, especially in comparison with his rendering of the stock group in the background.

Sur Das had begun his career working on a number of Akbari manuscripts as a colorist.[4] Late in the period, he began to work alone on poetic illustrations that made him one of the major contributors to the *Akbar Nama*.[5] This manuscript, however, which is the only one with an exten-

Figure 18*ii*(B). *Defeat of Husayn Mirza in 1573*, by Sur Das Gujerati; from the Chester Beatty *Akbar Nama*, fol. 188. Chester Beatty Library, Dublin (titled: *Battle of Ahmadabad*).

sive sample of his work, seems to be the painter's final court project. While many of the painter's *Akbar Nama* illustrations are impersonal, some scenes are animated and very pleasing, such as the one showing nobles of Gujerat meeting Akbar (the left half of comparison A). The emperor's campaign to conquer Gujerat had been a critical one, and the large Western Indian state later rebelled several times. Thus there were numerous scenes in the *Akbar Nama* devoted to events in the native regions of this painter whose name characterizes him as a provincial. Sur Das, selected to do a large percentage of the Gujerati illustrations, painted the thorny desert scrub or the distinctive costumes of his home region knowledgeably.

Regrettably, despite the short quotation from the *Akbar Nama* text in the upper right corner of this page, the scene is too general to be positively identified. The illustration may well be the right half of a double page that when reconstructed would reveal the narrative clearly. Since the terrain in this miniature is much like that in Sur Das's

pictures of Gujerat, it seems likely that the happening took place in western India. However, an episode that has been equated with this illustration is Akbar's mounting of the horse Hairan in the north near Lahore.[6] Akbar often rode this difficult animal into the wilderness to meditate. One day, lost in thought, he let the horse disappear, but it later almost miraculously returned and allowed him to ride it to his camp.[7] Because this incident occurred when Akbar was alone and in quite a different type of landscape from the desert illustrated here, the association with this text is imprecise and must remain tentative. Many of the *Akbar Nama* scenes imperfectly fit textual descriptions and thus such a subject cannot be discounted; however, there are also other likely identifications of this illustration, which appears to be the start of a hunt.[8]

This miniature is unlike the majority of separate leaves that have been mounted on the pages of Jahangir's 1607/8 dictionary. After being extracted from the text in the early twentieth century, this Cleveland leaf was put into a much later and less finely decorated nineteenth-century border, the same as one surrounding an *Akbar Nama* miniature owned by the Freer Galley of Art.[9] A comprehensive list of the scattered leaves from this *Akbar Nama* is provided in a forthcoming catalogue of Indian miniatures in the Chester Beatty Library (to be published by Sotheby Parke Bernet), by Leach and Skelton.

1. The British Library *Akbar Nama* contains a few *nim qalam* pages at the end; see, e.g., Martin, 2, pl. 182 and fols. 69r, 125v, 129r, 136r, 137v, 139r, 142v; in the Beatty *Akbar Nama* the majority of the first twenty paintings are *nim qalam* scenes, but only a few are found in the latter part of the manuscript.
2. Skelton, 1969, p. 41, defines *nim qalam* as "a technique in which the pigment is built up into an opaque coating over parts of the picture only, and much of the surface is left uncolored or only lightly tinted or stippled."
3. Pinder-Wilson, 1976, no. 36.
4. For a list of Sur Das's works see [16], fn. 4.
5. For a list of British Library *Akbar Nama* folios (Or. 12988) see Titley, 1977, pp. 4–5; for those in the Chester Beatty Library see Arnold and Wilkinson, 1: 7–10.
6. Beach, 1981, p. 120.
7. Abu'l Fazl, *Akbar Nama*, II: 92–93.
8. There are other possibilities for the identification of the leaf. The shield of leaves held by one of Akbar's attendants suggests a hunt, as do the small bucks—a common quarry. These animals were the subject of an incident in August of 1573 that was recounted at a gap in the illustration of the Beatty manuscript. The rebel Husain Mirza had begun a campaign in Gujerat after learning that Akbar was well-occupied. Akbar determined to foil him, and he commenced a rapid march west that exhausted many of his followers. In this section of the text, Akbar's mounting of a horse is mentioned several times as being auspicious because of his rapid progress toward the unsuspecting foe. One day he stated lightheartedly that if one of his cheetahs could catch a certain buck, he would consider it a sign that Husain Mirza would be captured (the buck was soon brought down). The running buck and the cheetah might possibly be shown on the other half of a double page. The incident falls between paintings numbered 118 and 122 and is described in the *Akbar Nama*, III: 59–65.
9. Beach, 1981, no. 12b.

19 *Antelope and Deer Hunt* 39.66

By Govardhan, Mughal, ca. 1607–8, 20 × 11.8 cm,
37 × 25.3 cm with border. Slightly damaged, stained, and
rubbed; slight tear repaired near female antelope's head.
Late eighteenth- or early nineteenth-century aqua and gold
border with white cartouches. Painting signed "Govardhan"
in lower right by feet of deer in foreground.

Purchase, Dudley P. Allen Fund

Comparative Material: (A) *Salim in the Hunting Field*,
Mughal, Allahabad, ca. 1602–4; Binney, 1973, no. 45.
(B) *Abu'l Fazl Presenting a Volume of the Akbar Nama to
Akbar*, by Govardhan, leaf from the Chester Beatty *Akbar
Nama*, ca. 1605–7; Arnold and Wilkinson, 2: frontispiece.
(C) *Border of Artist Portraits*, by Daulat, Teheran/Berlin
album, Mughal, dated 1608; Godard, 1936, pp. 18–23.
(D) *Border*, by Govardhan, Mughal, dated 1609–10,
Teheran/Berlin album; Kuhnel and Goetz, pl. 38.
(E) *Border*, attributed to Govardhan, Teheran/Berlin
album, Mughal, ca. 1610; Beach, 1966, no. 198 recto.

This scene of deer and antelope hunting is one of the earliest extant pictures by Jahangir's major artist, Govardhan,
as well as one of the most complex early Jahangiri animal
studies. Not only is the miniature expressive for a young
painter, but the artist's skill in handling the subject is un-
expected because, except for a small sketch of a lion bearing
an inscribed attribution, no pictures of animals by Govardhan are known.[1] The antelopes and deer moving with heavy
dreamlike leaps across the page are, however, elegantly
formed and seem to have engaged the painter in genuinely
sympathetic observations of animal life. The miniature was
done at the beginning of the era when such studies multiplied because of Jahangir's interests. Some hunt scenes
from Allahabad as well single animal or bird portraits
demonstrate the types of works being produced in this
genre from 1600–1610. As more becomes known, it is increasingly clear that numerous young artists like Payag,
Haribans, Inayat, and Padarath were involved in doing
animal paintings around this date and that only later in
Jahangir's reign did nature painting become a talent exclusive to a few artists.[2]

Govardhan's spotted axis deer, the two graceful nilgai
(large Indian antelopes), and the goat exemplify the best
qualities of the Jahangiri animal-portrait tradition, but like
many Mughal studies of animals this composition has dis-
continuous elements. The nilgai and the spotted deer, for
example, appear to have weight and volume created by
shading, yet they are paradoxically suspended on the page
with no clear relation to the ground plane or to one another.
As is typical of the Jahangiri era, the artist has captured the
individual animals in exquisite detail but compared to later
Rajasthani painters has ignored their habitats. Jahangir, the
amateur naturalist, was largely responsible for this tendency, since he required his artists only to observe animal
physique accurately. The strengths and weaknesses of
Govardhan's composition are common to most Jahangiri
natural-history paintings.

The color scheme of this miniature is restricted, but the
shades of plum and various greens are muted and combined
with the brownish hues of the animals in an exceptionally
sensitive way. Govardhan has applied the paint decoratively
in a manner that not only makes the landscape appear soft
and lush but also creates shadowy textural effects on the
animals' fur. Despite the intrusion of the hunt, the har-
monious purples, greens, and neutrals emphasize that the
miniature is meant to recall natural beauty rather than to
describe violent action. The attacking cheetah and the little
black buck who has been brought down as his mate makes
her escape are often-used, conventionalized motifs that

Figure 19, detail.

Figure 19.

signify hunting without actually depicting it. These two animals of minor interest have been somewhat artificially positioned in the picture, since the rear claws of the attacking cat do not grip anything as they should. The composition is somewhat stilted, but the artist has boldly attempted to render the characteristic movement of the ungulates. Studies of running animals done at close range are rare, and it appears that Govardhan used the hunting theme merely to provide a logical reason for the picture.

Govardhan's scene is related by subject matter and composition to the series of hunt illustrations apparently done in Allahabad as a record of Jahangir's princely shoots. Painters of the early seventeenth century were striving to build a new type of picture by arranging larger forms in the fore- and middle-grounds while retaining the impression of space given in Akbari miniatures. In attempting to alter pictorial space, they sometimes placed foreground action in an Akbari panorama meant to extend far into the distance. Along

Figure 19(A). *Salim in the Hunting Field*. Edwin Binney 3rd Collection. Photograph courtesy of the Portland (Oregon) Art Museum.

with his colleagues, Govardhan has glimpsed a new objective but has not found an adequate structure for his ideas. The dark tree in the upper left of his picture—a traditional Akbari signal of distance—is dwarfed by the figures near it, and the three men are unusually large to occupy the upper section of a miniature. A rather similar distribution of space occurs in one of the Allahabad hunt scenes (A, illus.) that shows Jahangir (Salim) examining two dead nilgai (and again includes the attacking-cheetah motif found in the Cleveland picture). Much of this page is allotted to foreground action, and the old-fashioned spatial device of placing figures in back of a land mass is used, as in Govardhan's miniature.

Govardhan's scene is not, however, part of the Allahabad series, since the artist has used thick, creamy paint in contrast to the thin, bright tints of these Allahabad works.[3] What is apparently Govardhan's first miniature for an imperial manuscript was done in 1604 for the volume of the *Akbar Nama* now in the British Library.[4] The artist seems to have come into prominence, because he was chosen to do several more miniatures for the second part of this text, now in the Beatty Library. These bear little resemblance to the Cleveland miniature but are probably contemporary with it since, despite a difference in figure style, the artist seems to be struggling with similar technical problems (B). By comparison with Govardhan's work after 1610, all the early miniatures show the artist striving to develop figural movement and physique as well as to create original compositions. Such early pictures are appealing because of Govardhan's ability to coordinate lush colors, and—despite the unusual subject of the Cleveland picture—all reveal his desire to create the beautiful, almost tactile surfaces so apparent in the miniatures of his later career.

From their output it is evident that the more advanced artists of the early seventeenth century were working together and borrowing from each other to develop a fresh idiom in the atmosphere of optimism fostered by their new patron, Jahangir. Govardhan had less experience than others, but about the time the Cleveland miniature was painted, his talent seems to have put him into the company of painters who broadened his artistic views.

On a page-border from the Jahangiri album divided between Teheran and Berlin, Govardhan is pictured with four other artists, including the portraitist himself—Daulat

Figure 19(C), detail. *Border of Artist Portraits*, by Daulat. After *Athar-e Iran*, I (Haarlem: Enschedé, 1936), fig. 9.

(C, detail illus.). By this time the studio had a fixed tradition, so that three of the men—Manohar, Abu'l Hasan, and Govardhan—were sons of imperial artists, while Bishndas was the nephew of one. The fact that Govardhan, Manohar, and Bishndas were Hindus is indicative of the mix of religions in the atelier. The five painters were united by their court positions, relative ages, and willingness to develop their abilities.

Usually figural borders show several men grouped together, either along the top or bottom sections. Of the five artists, Govardhan was selected to be the only man seated between two others (lower center). Their mutual closeness and Govardhan's turning pose, which balances his interest between Bishndas and Daulat, certainly points to a sympathetic association. Daulat—a bold experimental colorist—and Bishndas—an incisive portraitist—had greater experience than Govardhan and from their portraits were probably a few years older. Both were interested in figural plasticity (see, for example, the *Yog Vashisht* of 1602 or the *Nafahat al-Uns* of 1604),[5] and it seems likely, therefore, that Govardhan's association with the two men may have given his early work needed direction.

The Cleveland hunt scene fits stylistically between Govardhan's *Akbar Nama* pages in the Beatty Library and his own border drawings for the Teheran/Berlin album, one of which is dated 1609/10 and specifies Govardhan's filial relation to Bhawani Das, a fairly prolific Akbari painter.[6] These border compositions (D, E) include the fully modeled figures characteristic of the painter's maturity, which make the figures of the Cleveland scene appear somewhat ungainly in comparison. Despite its tentative quality, the miniature is, however, one of the finest natural studies of this period that was dominated by increasing realism as well as by the emperor's fascination with animal life.

1. Pinder-Wilson, 1976, no. 123, (not illus.); Alvi and Rahman, 1968, pl. VIII (a later painting with a bear in it, inscribed to Govardhan, cannot really be considered an animal study).

2. The Allahabad hunt scenes, which appear to be a record of Prince Salim's animal kills, include (in addition to comparison A): Chester Beatty Ms. 50.1; a picture in the Victoria Memorial, Calcutta; *Pantheon* 8 (July-Dec. 1931): 387; *Sotheby*, 10 Oct. 1977, lot 28; Blochet, 1930, no. 177.

   Payag signed a painting of a bull, ca. 1605–10 (McInerney, no. 12); two other animal miniatures of a yak and a buck from the same source can possibly be attributed to him also. One of the Allahabad scenes (*Sotheby*, 10 Oct. 1977, lot 28) can be attributed to Haribans on the basis of an inscribed painting in Chester Beatty Ms. 5, fol. 58b. Inayat and Padarath both did animal studies that are mounted in the Minto album.

3. The characteristics of Allahabad painting are best demonstrated by the *Yog Vashisht* and *Raj Kunwar* in the Chester Beatty Library and by the Walters Art Gallery manuscript of 1602. See Beach, 1978, pp. 33–40; see also Skelton, 1969, p. 44.

4. The *Akbar Nama* illustration by Govardhan of *Bairam Khan Teaching Akbar to Shoot* is reproduced in Schulberg, p. 168.

5. *Yog Vashisht*, Chester Beatty Ms. 5, fol. 249; *Nafahat al-Uns*, British Library, Or. 1362, fols. 135b, 142a.

6. Kuhnel and Goetz, p. 9.

20 *Seated Scholar*   71.306

Nim qalam drawing, border fragment from the Teheran/Berlin album, Mughal, ca. 1605–10, 10.3 × 7.5 cm, 21.5 × 15.6 cm overall. Mounted in two eighteenth-century borders of turquoise paper with gold flecks.

Gift of Mr. and Mrs. John D. MacDonald

Ex collections: Nemes, MacDonald.

Published: Kuhnel, no. 115 (untrimmed).

Comparative Material: (A) *Scholar*, border fragment from the Teheran/Berlin album, Mughal, ca. 1605–10; Sarre and Martin, no. 922. (B) *Scholars*, three border fragments from the Teheran/Berlin album, Mughal, ca. 1605–10; Marteau and Vever, pl. 238.

This fragment from the border of a Jahangiri album depicts a serious middle-aged scholar in Persian dress who is making a point with his outstretched hand and finger. Although the figure is only partially colored so that the elegant drawing shows through, a few details are vividly painted. The scholar wears a *kuladhar* turban with a bright maroon *kullah* (cap) around which his gold and white turban cloth is wound. While his coat is tinted pale pink rather than being solidly painted, his robe is dark brown and is tied with a gold, red, and blue *patka*.

It is probable that two groups of album leaves—one now in Berlin, the other in Teheran—that include figural borders of this type, were originally sections of the same manuscript. Subject matter, size, and complimentary dating make it likely that the leaves were once together.[1] As dated examples attest, Jahangir's album was begun by 1600, when he was still a prince, and was continued into the latter part of his reign without significant change.[2] Double pages of miniatures framed by borders with gold scrolls and birds alternate with double pages of calligraphy surrounded by figural compositions. That the figural borders were at first some of Jahangir's most valued works is indicated by the signature of favorite artists.[3] However, although there was never any lapse in quality, these small, unpretentious drawings may have been eclipsed by more spectacular works as the emperor's reign progressed.

While these *muraqqa* panels continue the formats that were employed for borders in the 1590s, the figures themselves have evolved significantly. They are much more naturalistic, for example, than the generalized, doll-like images from the borders of the 1595 *Baharistan* of Jami. That the emperor desired his artists to make this particular album especially naturalistic and to plan each border as an individual creative project is evident in the contrast of leaves from the contemporary 1607/8 *Fahrang-i-Jahangiri* that are much more decorative [18i].

This *muraqqa*, or album combining miniatures and calligraphic passages, is one of the major pieces of evidence that can be used to analyze Jahangir's patronage. Though the emperor showed a strange lack of discrimination in randomly grouping excellent and indifferent Persian paint-

Figure 20.

ings, European engravings, and Indian paraphrases of European art, the figural borders framing the calligraphic passages are done with sensitivity and are carefully organized according to themes that range from the portrayal of Deccani swordsmen to northern nomads, and from sherbet-making to acrobatics.[4] These borders balance unity with variety, elegance with simplicity. The unpretentious nature of decorations, which at the same time receive such detailed attention, epitomizes the emperor's exquisite taste.

The Cleveland fragment is from a page that can be partially reconstructed because of the care taken to make each of these leaves distinctive. This fragment was once in the Nemes collection in Budapest, as was comparison A (illus.) belonging to the same page. Three further sections (B, illus.) have been published from a series of five formerly in collection. Since the borders of this manuscript normally involve seven or eight figures, the number of fragments is not unusual. The figures are all scholars pictured with their books and writing instruments. As here, Muslim scholars were commonly depicted in long coats and with accessories of dress such as the *kuladhar* turbans that had Persian associations; it was also traditional for pictures of scholars to be done in conservative styles, thus accounting for the fact

Figure 20(A). *Scholar,* border fragment from the Teheran/Berlin album. After Sarre and Martin, *Meisterwerken Muhammedanischer Kunst* (Munich: F. Bruckman, 1912), no. 922.

Figure 20(B). *Scholar,* border fragment from the Teheran/Berlin album. After Marteau and Vever, *Miniatures persanes . . .exposées au Musée des Arts Décoratifs 1912* (Paris: Bibliothèque d'art et d'archéologie, 1913), pl. 238.

that these fragments have a slight resemblance to Persian paintings, unlike the borders that informally picture Indian craftsmen.

After being cut apart, the fragments of this page were combined with small additional sections of the gold-flowered ground to make them uniformly rectangular. The Cleveland piece was originally published with the background extending downward on the left; it was later trimmed and an extra section of leaves and flowers was pasted onto the lower right to complete a rectangle. The irregular shape suggests that the scholarly figure was once kneeling in the upper left corner of the border. His position and pointing finger would relate him to a figure facing the opposite direction and perhaps discussing a text (B, no. 240). Many of the album borders include portraits, whereas others are exacting depictions of crafts or occupations that reflect the scientific observation characteristic of the emperor himself. Although very refined, the border of scholars is a traditional subject done in a more conventionalized fashion than borders picturing craftsmen, and so unfortunately cannot be attributed to any of the artists known to have worked on the *muraqqa* project.

1. See Wilkinson and Gray, p. 173, for a discussion of the Teheran/Berlin sections. Beach (1965, p. 66) and Godard (1936, p. 11) state that the albums are separate entities. See also Beach, 1978, p. 43, and 1981, p. 156. Ninety-two folios are in Teheran, twenty-five in Germany.

2. In addition to figural borders pictured in sources listed under *Further Reading*, see Gray, 1950, no. 704; Beach, 1966, no. 198; *Cincinnati Art Museum Handbook* (1975), p. 54; Khandalavala and M. Chandra, 1965, fig. 14; Welch, 1963, no. 27; Welch, 1976, no. 13; *Perzische Miniatuur uit de Keizerlije Collecties te Teheran* (Teheran, 1957), no. 49. See Welch, 1963, p. 226, fn. 24 for list of museums owning leaves from this *muraqqa*.

FURTHER READING: Beach, 1965 (pp. 63–91), 1978 (pp. 43–51), and 1981 (cat. no. 16); Devapriam; Godard, 1936; Goetz, 1958 (article of same title in *East and West* 8, no. 2 [July 1957]); Hajek; Kuhnel and Goetz; Wilkinson and Gray, 1935a.

21 *Battle between Feridun and Minuchir* 45.171

By Dhanraj, leaf from a *Shah Nama* ms., Mughal, ca. 1610, 12.4 × 11 cm, 34.6 × 22.9 with outer border. Large inner border of buff with pale gold foliage and birds; outer border of pinkish tan with gold floral scrolls.

Purchase, Edward L. Whittemore Fund

Ex collection: Heeramaneck.

Comparative Material: (A) *Feridun Striking down Zahhak*, by Bishndas and Inayat, leaf from a *Shah Nama* ms., Mughal, ca. 1610; Strzygowski, pl. 84, fig. 225 (published as belonging to Demotte, now Los Angeles County Museum of Art). (B) *The Birth of Rustam*, here attributed to Aqa Riza, leaf from a *Shah Nama* ms., Mughal, ca. 1610; Falk, 1976, no. 88(i). (C) *Storming of a Town*, by Govardhan, leaf from a *Shah Nama* ms., Mughal, ca. 1610; *Sotheby*, 7 Dec. 1971, lot 188A. (D) *Akbar Receiving His Mother*, by Dhanraj, leaf from the Chester Beatty *Akbar Nama*, Mughal, ca. 1605–7; Arnold and Wilkinson, pl. 13. (E) *Shah Nama*, text page, Mughal, ca. 1610; *Sotheby*, 12 April 1976, lot 7.

This miniature shows a legendary battle organized much like that of the earlier historical *Akbar Nama* scenes. Fully armored, opposing troops fight in close hand-to-hand combat, while musicians in the rear urge on their respective sides. The British Library/Chester Beatty *Akbar Nama* has the same sort of decorative emphasis as this slightly later mythical scene. By the 1590s artists were progressively moving away from depicting action for its own sake and were growing self-consciously aesthetic. Impetus for developing more ornamental styles came particularly from Jahangir, who was inspired by his Persian-born artist Aqa Riza both when a prince and in the period immediately following his accession. The height of the fashion for Persian-influenced works was around 1610, just about the time this miniature was painted.

One contrast between Persian and Akbari painting occurs in the choice of colors, which are much more subtle in Safavid manuscripts. Soft, muted coloration denoted urbanity and culture to the Persians but did not reflect the mood of strong action in most Akbari paintings. However, Jahangir's interest in Persian art was one of the factors that brought about a change to more delicate and atonal color schemes in the late sixteenth century. Colorists began to refrain from utilizing raw, unmodulated hues or the combination of primary red and blue that was so traditional in Jain or Hindu ateliers and had been characteristic of much Akbari painting.

The *Shah Nama* manuscript group of about 1610, to which this battle scene belongs, clearly exemplifies the new refinement.[1] In the Cleveland painting, although there are areas of clear red, the main warm tones are pink, orange, and wine, conforming to Persian standards. Other leaves of the group have pastel color schemes balancing several related hues in Persian fashion (see B). The objects in the paintings are very small in scale, with deft emphasis on

Figure 21.

minutiae such as textiles and architectural patterns. In this battle between Feridun and Minuchir, gold is employed extensively, as it is in the entire manuscript group, to bring out details—in this case, of the arms and armor. The legendary battle, unexciting as an event, stresses design rather than vitality or furor (cf. C, another *Shah Nama* battle scene). The slight, long-waisted figures in this scene, fighting and dying very tastefully, further relate to Persian tradition.

The borders of each *Shah Nama*, elaborately drawn and painted in gold are close to those of Jahangir's dictionary of 1607–8 (see [18*i*]), thus providing an indication of the date

Figure 21(A). *Feridun Striking down Zahhak*, from a *Shah Nama* manuscript. Los Angeles County Museum of Art, from the Nasli and Alice Heeramaneck Collection, Museum Associates Purchase, M. 78.9.5.

of the manuscripts.[2] *Feridun Striking Down Zahhak* (A, illus.) is a larger miniature than B, C, or the Cleveland miniature, with a more elegant, ornate border than these leaves. It most probably belongs to a royal version from which two smaller copies in the same style were made by court artists. Painting B, C, and text-page E are banded by ribbonlike inner floral borders in bright colors like those of Jahangir's dictionary. The Cleveland page simply has a linear border separating the painting and text from the two large outer borders, one of which is off-white and the other amber. This difference of the inner border is enough evidence to predicate two sets, though all pages are the same in size, in arrangement of text, and in other vital details.[3]

The painter Dhanraj, who did this battle scene, was an artist of average skill who had worked on several Akbari manuscripts.[4] A painting from the Chester Beatty *Akbar Nama* (D, illus.), done by Dhanraj a few years before in a different style, illustrates through contrast the Persian influences affecting the production of the *Shah Nama* manuscripts.

1. See Wilkinson, 1929, pp. 10–11, for some of the characteristics of similar manuscripts.
2. At least one page of this group was owned by Demotte and may have given him the idea of using the similar dictionary borders he had acquired as mounts for other paintings, especially the British Library/Chester Beatty *Akbar Nama*, which has some comparable stylistic elements. Strzygowski, pl. 84, fig. 225, which links A with

Figure 21, detail.

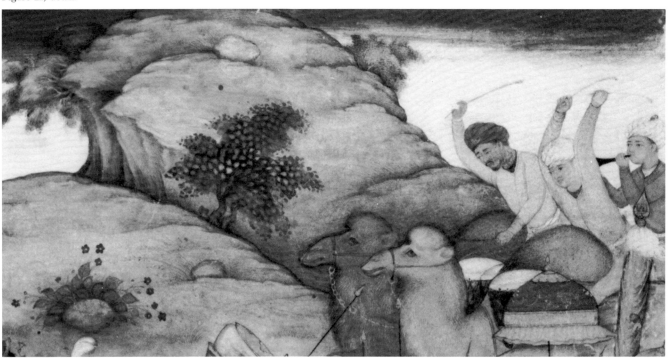

Figure 21(D). *Akbar Receiving His Mother*, from the Chester Beatty *Akbar Nama*, fol. 25. Chester Beatty Library, Dublin.

Demotte's collection, was published long after the Beatty *Akbar Nama* leaves were extracted and affixed to the dictionary pages, but Demotte could have had the page in his possession for many years.

3. In addition to B, C, and text-page E, no. 88(ii) in Falk, 1976, also belongs to this *Shah Nama*. Sizes of the pages including outer borders are as follows: *Sotheby*, 12 April 1976: 34.7 × 23.1 cm; *Sotheby*, 7 Dec. 1971: 34.3 × 23 cm; Falk, 1976, 88(i): 34.6 × 22.5 cm, and 88(ii): 34.5 × 23 cm; Cleveland miniature: 34.6 × 23 cm; comparison A from the Los Angeles County Museum of Art is much larger (53.3 × 40.6 cm), though stylistically it is similar and has been recorded previously as being from the same set as B and C (see Falk, 1976, p. 174).

4. Dhanraj is named in several Akbari manuscript productions; he did three pages for the British Library *Babur Nama* (fols. 204v, 305v, 478r); was colorist for two pages of the *Chingiz Nama*; did one page for the New Delhi *Babur Nama* (fol. 40v); one page for the Beatty *Akbar Nama* (D); a page for the Keir Nizami (fol. 203r—see Skelton, 1976, p. 243); a page for Nasiri's *Ethics* (*Sotheby*, 27 Nov. 1974, lot 684); outlined one page for the 1595 *Khamsa* of Nizami (B.L. Or. 12208, fol. 65r); a genealogy for Jahangir (Falk, 1976, no. 90); and two miniatures for Sir Cowasji Jehangir's *Iyar-i-Danish* (nos. 18 and 19).

FURTHER READING: Stchoukine, 1931; Wilkinson, 1929.

22   *A Feast in a Pavilion Setting*   20.1966

Mughal, ca. 1620, 23.4 × 14.6 cm. Very narrow red striped border. Later Hindi inscription on reverse: "Babur."

Gift of J. H. Wade

Comparative Material: (A) *Prince with Narcissus*, Mughal, ca. 1620; Stchoukine, 1929*b*, pl. XLIII. (B) *Portrait of Babur*, Mughal, ca. 1620; Stchoukine, 1929*b*, pl. XXXV*b*, or Pinder-Wilson, 1976, no. 102. (C) *Babur in a Pavilion*, leaf from the Moscow/Walters *Babur Nama*, Mughal, ca. 1593; Stchoukine, 1929*a*, pl. IV. (D) *Badiazammann Receives Babur*, leaf from the British Library *Babur Nama*, Mughal, ca. 1590; Suleimann, pl. 33. (E) *Birth of Rustam*, here attributed to Aqa Riza, leaf from a *Shah Nama* ms., Mughal, ca. 1610; Falk, 1976, no. 88(*i*). (F) *Lovers Picnicking in a Pavilion*, here attributed to Aqa Riza, Mughal, ca. 1610; Skelton, 1976, no. V49, color pl. 35.

In this illustration of a drinking party, an important noble kneels against a brocaded pillow opposite a lesser guest. An attendant behind waits with a *chauri*, while another in front kneels before a small table preparing to serve wine. A musician who has been playing a lute turns away from the group in displeasure. The figures wear Persian turbans and other accessories of dress that are blended with native details. They are gathered in a walled garden with a small *chenar* tree in front of a pavilion that is elegantly tiled along the roof but less tastefully ornamented inside. The two nobles sit on a carpeted dais with an array of fruits characteristic of Persia. Two books placed carelessly on the carpet complete the artist's picture of cultivated leisure.

As already mentioned, Jahangir's interest as a prince in the culture of his ancestors caused him to sponsor the immigrant painter Aqa Riza, whose various Persian styles were imitated by others for several decades. The spidery drawing and the ultra-refined detail of rugs, dishes, and clothing evident in this Cleveland miniature characterize one group of works showing his influence (see also A and B). In this group a slender figure type is used that along with the elegant detail implies an unworldly and idealized environment.

The pavilion setting, with its garden and ornate rugs, is much like several scenes from the *Babur Nama* manuscripts (C [illus.] and D). In addition, a Persian-influenced depiction of Babur (B, illus.) closely resembles that of the bearded figure in the Cleveland miniature. Despite the fact that this association may be intentional, the artist was not apparently creating an historical illustration. Other elements in the picture that imply a literary theme, such as the intimate drinking party and the emotional musician who turns away from his companions, are equally generalized. The unidentified subject was probably produced as a single composition that follows certain poetic conventions without illustrating a specific reference. In a manner common during the early seventeenth century, the artist merely alludes to historical as well as literary models in order to suggest cultivation and refinement by familiar means.

Figure 22.

Although the stiffness of the drawing indicates a slightly later date, the Cleveland painting resembles works that can be attributed to Aqa Riza himself about 1610 (E, F). Because of his Persian background, Aqa Riza was well acquainted with classic literary conventions and set the fashion for doing non-specific idealized scenes (F). In addition to the subject matter and the preciousness of the style, such specific features as the heavy square faces in many of Aqa Riza's works were adapted by the artist of the Cleveland miniature (cf. the head of the spurned musician in the Cleveland painting with that of the lute player in F).

Aqa Riza and his imitators, like this artist, favored a limited, decorative space in their miniatures. Backgrounds are composed of simple tilted planes that tend to block out

Figure 22(B). *Portrait of Babur*. The British Museum, London (titled: *Babur Seated in a Chair Reading*). Reproduced by permission of The Trustees of The British Museum.

Figure 22(C). *Babur in a Pavilion*, from the Moscow/Walters *Babur Nama*. Musée du Louvre, Paris. Photograph courtesy of Documentation photographique de la Réunion des musées nationaux.

Figure 22, detail.

distant details: no faraway Akbari town intrudes upon the upper corner of these compositions. This limitation turns scenes inward and accentuates the pleasure garden as separate from the world, a romanticization originally characteristic of Persian painting.

Aqa Riza was not a consistent artist, but certain of his attributed compositions show remarkable taste and decorative ability (E, F). The artist of the Cleveland miniature seems to have been intuitively skilled in arranging his color scheme of corals, lavender, and green, but his choice of details here is not as sensitive as that of the more experienced and better trained Aqa Riza. The back wall of the pavilion, for example, with its niches, panels of entwined trees, and cartouches framing deer, reveals the artist's comparative lack of skill in organizing elaborate patterns. However, this miniaturist still achieves a pleasantly complex surface design that expresses his sense of the refined paradise garden. The soft colors, elegant dishes of food, and decorative freshness of the young tree with its birds all contribute to the creation of an idyllic setting.

FURTHER READING: Godard, 1936; Wilber; Wilkinson, 1929.

83

23 *Fighting Cock* 44.501

Mughal, ca. 1620, 18.3 × 12.1 cm, 37.3 × 25.4 with border. Brown and coral inner border; eighteenth-century dark blue flecked outer border. Spurious inscription to an artist: "Dilaram Pandit Kashmiri."

Gift of Herbert F. Leisy

Ex collection: Kevorkian.

Published: *Islamic Art* (Cleveland: Cleveland Museum of Art, 1944), p. 26.

This picture of a fighting gamecock with huge spurred feet seems to date from the Jahangiri era when animal portraiture was at its height, although it is a rather rough picture. Later animal or bird pictures were almost invariably done with less detail and were often prettified by soft landscape backgrounds, whereas this cock stands austerely against a plain green ground. Although this bird has been boldly posed, the unknown artist has revealed his inexperience by the awkward drawing of the foot held in the air. In addition, he has applied his paint in a thick impasto that fails to convey the texture of the bird's feathers as do the best Mughal studies by favored imperial painters.

The study is inscribed "Dilaram Pandit Kashmiri," but the order of the name is incorrect and the inscription therefore seems to be a later addition without relevance to the picture.

Figure 23.

24 *Portrait of Raja Bikramajit*   45.170

By Lal Chand, Mughal, ca. 1620–30, 17.4 × 10 cm,
33.3 × 22.2 cm. with border. Background slightly rubbed
near feet, inner border torn. Coral inner border with floral
motifs; outer border of colored flowering plants with gold
details. Inscription: "jan-fishan namak ba-halal"
(life-shedding [or heedless of life] and faithful).

Purchase from the J. H. Wade Fund

Ex collection: Heeramaneck.

Comparative Material: (A) *Portrait of Raja Bikramajit*, by
Bichitr, Mughal, ca. 1616; Leach, 1981, fig. 154. (B)
Jahangir Embracing Shah Jahan, by Balchand, leaf from
the *Shah Jahan Nama* (fol. 43v), Mughal. ca. 1630; *Los
Angeles County Museum Bulletin*, 1973, p. 23. (C) *The
Submission of Rana Amar Singh to Khurram*, by Lal
Chand, leaf from the *Shah Jahan Nama* (fol. 46v), Mughal,
ca. 1630. (D) *Sketch of Jahangir with Khurram*, Mughal,
ca. 1650–60; Coomaraswamy, 1926, pt. 6, pl. 33. (E) *Sketch
of Jahangir Embracing Shah Jahan*, Mughal, ca. 1655; P.
Brown, 1924, p. LVIII; Wilkinson, 1949, pl. 7; Welch,
1976, no. 18. (F) Finished version of *Jahangir Embracing
Shah Jahan*, by Murad, leaf from the *Shah Jahan Nama*
(fol. 49r), Mughal, dated 1657; Archer, 1960, pl. 28.

This miniature by Lal Chand is a compelling depiction that
is noteworthy among the many examples of Mughal standing portraits because the artist has treated an intense man
with a stylistic forcefulness complimentary to the courtier's
personality. The ugliness of the face has not been softened;
instead, the artist has created an uncompromisingly angular
design that accentuates the sharp nose and the brooding
energy of the visage. The most emphatic note in an otherwise plain, almost stark, composition is the brilliant lemon
yellow shawl, which by its acidity throws the sallow face into
greater prominence. The two firm triangles of arms and
jama skirt add further strength to the composition. Lal
Chand retains the early Mughal custom of using a strong
outline, so that although Raja Bikramajit's face is well-
modeled, his body is presented with two-dimensional
directness.

Bikramajit was a title that originally belonged to a ruler of
Ujjain credited with building astronomical observatories.
This title, evoking the greatness of India's past, was be-
stowed upon Hindus by the Mughal emperors. The Raja
Bikramajit portrayed here, whose personal name was
Sundar Das, was a close friend of Prince Khurram and, from
his young manhood to his early death in 1623 (during the
prince's rebellion against his father), was one of Khurram's
most trusted military subordinates. He was raja of the prov-
ince of Bandhu where his family had been important *zamindars*,[1] but he became a significant *mansabdar* whose
actions altered events at court solely through his association
with the prince. His biography relates directly to Lal
Chand's forceful character study, and the circumstances of
his early death affect the dating of the Cleveland miniature.

Although Emperor Jahangir was clearly afraid of combat,
his son Khurram proved adept, and as a culmination to
decades of Mughal struggle brought the final, most im-

placable enemy in Rajasthan, the Mewar Rana, to submission. The scene of Khurram leaving for this campaign in
his own regnal history was done about two decades later but
is probably accurate in showing the important personages
(B, illus.). While the prince embraces his father, Bikramajit
stands in the center apart from most other nobles, apparently a leader of Khurram's troops. During the ceremony of
Amar Singh's submission to Khurram in 1614, Bikramajit—
this time wearing his sword as an army commander—is
singled out as one of Khurram's three favored generals in
the foreground of the composition (C, illus.), and when the
victorious party is welcomed back by Jahangir, Bikramajit
stands second among the officials who hold trays of jewels as
rewards for service (F).

A few years later (in October 1617) after a much-lauded
Deccani engagement by Khurram, the emperor gave a lavish ceremony for his then-favorite son, granting him unprecedented privileges as well as titling him Shah Jahan.[2]
Almost immediately after this Sundar Das was honored as
Bikramajit, "which among Hindus is the highest title."[3]
Thus the prince and his comrade seemed to have been a
highly successful team who won battles against enemies that
had stalemated Mughal armies for years.

For the next two years, Bikramajit conquered and recon-
quered Kangra Fort—another trouble spot—and his performance pleased Jahangir, who received him on a number of occasions.[4] Then from 1620 until 1622 Bikramajit
apparently went to the Deccan with Shah Jahan who was
again fighting there. In 1622 the scene changed as the
prince, knowing his father was ill and supposing that his
weaker brother Shahriyar was being manipulated toward
the throne, decided to march in rebellion toward Agra to
seize treasure that would finance a full-scale revolt.
Bikramajit, clearly the prince's most trusted and able officer, was chosen as leader of the raid.[5] The doting father,
Jahangir, who feared both the rebellion and the fighting
prowess of his son's party, became intensely bitter, calling
Shah Jahan "Bi-daulat," or "the wretched one."

Jahangir saw the phases of the rebellion in allegorical
dimensions, recounting it in his diary with wild metaphors.
He described his relations with his son in the tragic terms
of a betrayed parent, but his appraisal of Bikramajit, whom
he now called only Sundar, was totally black. Jahangir attributed the instigation of the rebellion to him, believing he
was Shah Jahan's "guide to the desert of error" or "the
ringleader of the people of error and the chief of the sedi-
tious."[6] The events of the first battle are known only from
Jahangir's account that describes an imminent rebel victory
when a bullet "from a mysterious hand" killed Sundar Das.
It was never discovered who fired what the emperor considered a most fortuitous shot, but with the loss of this general,
the rebel forces fell apart. Villagers later cut off Bikramajit's
ears for their pearl earrings and then conveyed the rest of
the head to Jahangir. When Shah Jahan heard the news, he
retreated to Mandu. His father felt that the prince's courage
had abandoned him at the death of Sundar Das.[7]

Figure 24.

Figure 24(A). *Portrait of Raja Bikramajit*. The Metropolitan Museum of Art, New York; Purchase, 1955, funds given by The Kevorkian Foundation supplementing the Rogers Fund (titled: *Portrait of Patr Das, Rai Rayan Bakramajit*).

Because of his valued service to Shah Jahan, Bikramajit was significant enough to be the subject of several single portraits as well as to have been included posthumously in a number of group scenes of the *Shah Jahan Nama*. These depictions give very different views of this Rajput, but since they were undoubtedly based on his short-lived prominence, all show him as a mature man probably about twenty-five to thirty-five years old (the same age or just slightly older than his companion Khurram).

A portrait now in the Metropolitan Museum (A, illus.), more elegant and subdued than the Cleveland one, shows Bikramajit wearing both a white shawl and a *jama*. The artist has experimented with the effects of white on white tones against a dark background in an extremely sophisticated and refined manner. Since this portrait is signed by both Jahangir and Shah Jahan,[8] it was done during Bikramajit's lifetime, prior to Shah Jahan's rebellion. Because it is close in setting, pose, and border ornamentation to a portrait of Shah Jahan by Abu'l Hasan, verified by Shah Jahan's later inscription as dating to his twenty-fifth year, or ca. 1616, the Metropolitan portrait of Bikramajit, his close associate, may date from the same period, when Bikramajit was esteemed by the emperor.[9] While the Metropolitan miniature portrays Bikramajit as the titled courtier and the more austere Cleveland miniature reveals him as the hardened soldier, a third portrait in the Chester Beatty Library shows him as a handsomer man in a purple *jama* with a red and white shawl over his shoulders and his hands extended in a conversational gesture.[10]

The posthumous portraits of the *Shah Jahan Nama* contain both frank and more flattering portrayals of the raja. Some show heavy features or smallpox scars, others do not. Since numerous Shah Jahan-period courtier portraits were made from common sketches kept in some imperial studio storage and reused, this variety indicates the momentary prominence of the man; on a subtler level it may hint at his complexity.

For purposes of comparison with the Cleveland miniature, the most significant *Shah Jahan Nama* page is one also painted by Lal Chand (C, illus.). Working at the beginning of Shah Jahan's reign to preserve the events of the new emperor's battle record in the great regnal history, Lal Chand undoubtedly re-created the surrender of Mewar in 1614 from accurate sketches in the file of the imperial studio (which must have been incredibly extensive). Mughal painters were accustomed to reconstructing the physiognomies of aged or dead courtiers with great veracity, and Lal Chand

Figure 24(B). *Jahangir Embracing Shah Jahan*, from the *Shah Jahan Nama*, fol. 43v. Royal Library, Windsor Castle. Reproduced by gracious permission of Her Majesty Queen Elizabeth II.

Figure 24(C). *The Submission of Rana Amar Singh to Khurram,* from the *Shah Jahan Nama,* fol. 46v. Royal Library, Windsor Castle. Reproduced by gracious permission of Her Majesty Queen Elizabeth II.

the group has been completely scattered and some of its pages altered by the mounting of new miniatures, less is known about its original construction than about most Shah Jahan volumes. However, the group clearly contained some of Shah Jahan's most distinguished smaller miniatures mounted in sumptuous flower or flower and animal borders. Besides Lal Chand, the artists represented include, among others, Payag, Muhammad Ali, and Mansur. Pages are in the Chester Beatty Library, The Freer Gallery of Art, and private collections.[11] Leaves of calligraphy have also been found from this album, indicating that it was apparently arranged like other Mughal examples with paintings and calligraphy on alternating double pages.

There has previously been some confusion between these leaves and calligraphy pages from the late Shah Jahan Album (see [28*iii*]). The folios of the late Shah Jahan Album, however, measure approximately 37 × 26 centimeters, while these leaves are only about 33 × 22 centimeters. The ornamental borders of the smaller album are either superbly imaginative—incorporating chimera with jungle animals—or freshly natural; this one, a typically composed Shah Jahani design of flowering plants, is nevertheless of a quality that raises it above similar examples.

The painter Lal Chand, although not a highly renowned artist, is known from inscriptions on several miniatures; he seems to have been painting from late in Jahangir's reign until roughly the middle of the seventeenth century. A notation on a painting in the Goenka collection, Bombay, indicates that Lal Chand was one of Shah Jahan's painting librarians, which leads to the supposition that he may have been recognized as a competent artist but was more talented at organizational work. He produced an illustration for a Shah Jahan-period *Gulistan* of Sa'di (formerly in the collection of the Marquess of Bute) and did several portraits in addition to the *Shah Jahan Nama* scene.[12] The Cleveland portrait of Bikramajit is one of his most powerful and skillfully rendered works.

1. Jahangir, 1: 325.
2. Ibid., p. 395.
3. Ibid., p. 402.
4. Jahangir, 2: 25–26, 114.
5. Ibid., p. 249.
6. Ibid.
7. Ibid., p. 256.
8. Conversation with R. Skelton, 1977.
9. Gascoigne, p. 186.
10. Arnold and Wilkinson, 1: 36, no. 32.
11. Chester Beatty Library, Ms. 50; Falk, 1976, no. 100; Beach, 1981, no. 28.
12. Other works by Lal Chand include Pinder-Wilson, 1976, no. 159; *Sotheby,* 26 March 1973, lots 10 and 11, possibly lot 31; *Sotheby,* 6 Dec. 1967, lot 140; *Sotheby,* 12 Dec. 1929, lots 122 and 136 (Kevorkian album, now Metropolitan Museum); *Sotheby,* 7 July 1980, lot 86; Martin, 2, pl. 218A; Arnold and Wilkinson, 1: 35, no. 29; Rampur Museum, album 3, portrait of Muhammad Ali Beg.

has here made Bikramajit look both younger and less stern than he does in the Cleveland miniature. This latter portrayal is difficult to date stylistically, but the strength and clarity of the design in addition to the large scale of the figure make it characteristic of the period from 1620 to 1630. While Lal Chand could have done two diverse reconstructions of the then-long-dead Bikramajit at the beginning of Shah Jahan's reign, it seems more likely—because the two portrayals are surprisingly distinct—that the Cleveland picture was done about 1620 when Bikramajit was still popular at court. In this case the inscription would have been added later as a nostalgic tribute to his courage. In 1620, after Bikramajit had pleased the emperor by his success in the Pahari area and before he went off to the Deccan, it is quite logical from Jahangir's eulogies that this courtier would have been the subject of distinguished portraits.

The now-dispersed album to which this miniature belonged was a small-sized, extremely refined one assembled in the early or middle years of Shah Jahan's reign. Because

25 *Oval Portrait of Shah Jahan* 20.1969

By Hashim, Mughal, ca. 1628–32, 5.4 × 3.7 cm
oval. Slightly damaged at bottom. Signed: "amal-i
Muhammad Hashin."

Gift of J. H. Wade

Published: Beach, 1978, no. 64.

Comparative Material: (A) *Bust Portrait of Jahangir,* by
Hashim, Mughal, ca. 1620; Arnold and Wilkinson, 1: ms.
7A, cat. no. 12 (repr. in Gascoigne, p. 114). (B) *Bust
Portrait of Shah Jahan,* by Abu'l Hasan, Mughal, dated
1628; *Sotheby,* 26 March 1973, lot 3. (C) *Portrait of Shah
Jahan in His Fortieth Year,* by Bichitr, Mughal, ca. 1632;
Welch, 1963, no. 43. (D) *Drawing of Suleiman Shikoh and
His Tutor,* by Hashim, Mughal, ca. 1645; Welch, 1976,
no. 20.

Figure 25.

The art of Hashim, the painter of this portrait, is as calculated and precise as that of a watchmaker. Bodies are sum-
marily sketched or are cut off, as here, by circumscribing a
frame around the face. In his concentration on faces, it is as
if the painter had held a magnifying glass over the human
visage, satisfied to let everything else in the environment
fade away. To a certain extent the artist must have been
capturing a subjective reflection of his own temperament
in this perusal. Mughal portraits of the same subjects by
other artists tend to show stolid, cynical, or cruel expressions, whereas Hashim's sitters are coolly but more be-
nignly viewed.

Hashim's career began with illustrations for the 1598
Razm Nama.[1] This manuscript, with its disparate styles and
lapses into a Rajasthani idiom, must have been in part a
training project for young artists like Hashim and Payag.
Other painters, like Paras or Kanha, had been responsible
for coloring pages in various Akbari manuscripts but had no
great talent.[2] The production of the 1598 *Razm Nama* in the
imperial studio has been questioned because its styles are
varied and without the control or finish of manuscripts such
as the *Chingiz Nama* of 1596. The issue is unresolved;
Paras, for example, had worked on the imperial *Chingiz
Nama* two years previously,[3] but his continued employment
in the studio is not an inevitability. Thus Hashim started his
career either in a noble's employ or by working on a manuscript without royal priority. He was fortunate to have
progressed and prospered later in life, unlike most of his
colleagues on the *Razm Nama* project who disappeared into
obscurity.

Despite working on such a project, Hashim somehow
came to the attention of Jahangir, although he must have
had fewer advantages than other aspiring painters whose
fathers are known to have been notable artists and who were
born in the palace. His rise was relatively unusual, and it is
a tribute to his ability that he came into favor with Jahangir
after the emperor had discharged numerous painters and
set demanding individual standards. Since the artist worked
into Aurangzeb's reign, he must have been very young
when he started his career.

Figure 25(D). *Drawing of Suleiman Shikoh and His Tutor*, by Hashim. The City of Bristol (England) Art Gallery, Oriental Section.

Hashim's talent is narrower and more limited by personal preference than that of certain contemporaries. In the Jahangir and Shah Jahan reigns he therefore stands apart from the most prestigious portraitists like Govardhan, Abu'l Hasan, and Bichitr. Around 1620 an interest in southern European Baroque art transformed the Mughal portrait style. Bichitr and Abu'l Hasan turned out a series of important full-length official portraits.[4] Hashim's tendency toward precision was not in accord with the broader planes, larger scale, and sweeping ornateness of this style of painting. Nevertheless, he was commissioned to produce some significant work in the latter half of Jahangir's reign.

Jahangir was interested in assessing his rivals and enemies through their portraits—as shown by his dispatch of Bishndas to Persia to paint Shah Abbas's likeness. Around 1618–20 Hashim depicted a group of Deccani rulers and ministers. Presumably the painter did not actually go to the Deccan because his picture of Ibrahim Adil Shah II inscribed by Jahangir is a rearranged version of a Deccani portrait (the face of the model portrait, which would have been in traditional Deccani three-quarter view, has been redone in profile by the Mughal artist).[5]

Hashim also did portraits of the emperor himself. Jahangir, who enjoyed distributing his likeness, invented the so-called "jewel portrait" set in gold to be given to his courtiers and worn on gold chains or in turbans.[6] A small portrait of Jahangir, similar to the jewel type but mounted on an album page, is signed by Hashim (A). It is stylistically close to the Cleveland miniature of Shah Jahan that is a true example of the jewel portrait. In this latter picture, the pale blue-green halo denoting imperial status has been ingeniously combined with the oval of the darker green background so that the two form the eye of the peacock's tail—a symbol of the utmost regal elegance.

Although this miniature was published once as a portrait of Prince Dara Shikoh,[7] it has been otherwise identified as a likeness of Shah Jahan. The boyish-looking Dara with a moustache evolved into a heavy, bearded man who resembled his father.[8] However, Shah Jahan's features, such as the narrow, slanted eyes, are distinctive, and although Dara was sometimes haloed in group pictures, it is doubtful that he would have been in a formal portrait miniature. In this miniature the emperor wears some exceedingly beautiful and elaborate turban ornaments that befit his status and that are interesting historically, as they are among the first painted records showing the influence of European jewelry on the court. The most spectacular decoration on the maroon turban is a branched ornament of European inspiration with a large emerald at the center and long stems of jewel-encrusted gold that end in pearls.[9] The black feather aigrette that droops over the back of the turban appears to be attached to the ornament. At the front of the turban, suspended over Shah Jahan's forehead, is a very large emerald with a pendant pearl of the type described in Jahangir's diary that were given as gifts to the sovereign by his chief *mansabdars* in order to increase their influence and power. Shah Jahan also wears pearl earrings, a short necklace of pearls with either a cameo or a portrait miniature in the center, a longer rope of pearls, and a rope of pearls interspersed with precious stones.

Since the Cleveland miniature includes a halo as an integral part of the design, it dates after 1627, when Shah Jahan came to the throne. Its date can be assessed by comparison with two other portraits that are better documented by their respective inscriptions (B and C). The earliest is a formal half-length portrait of the emperor by Abu'l Hasan done in the first year of Shah Jahan's rule. It is a grim picture in which the angularity of the emperor's facial features has either been portrayed frankly or has possibly been exaggerated. The new ruler at age thirty-six appears tight-lipped, rapacious, and somewhat sly. The second portrayal, by Bichitr (C), actually looks earlier because the face has been softened. Shah Jahan was pleased with this version of himself and inscribed the picture "a very good portrait of me in my fortieth year." The Hashim portrait is the picture of a fairly young man and is therefore not likely to follow the

Bichitr. Although Bichitr had flatteringly depicted the emperor, artists could not continue indefinitely to paint a youthful sovereign. Thus the Cleveland miniature can best be placed between the Abu'l Hasan and Bichitr pictures.

Hashim's miniature is much more like Bichitr's portrayal in spirit than like Abu'l Hasan's, but because it is a tiny, concentrated work the face is more revealing. The ruler appears benign and untroubled, with a luminous complexion. A drawing by Hashim done around 1645 (D, illus.) is very similar to the Cleveland miniature in its treatment of the subject. Both pictures are among the best examples of the artist's meticulous delineation of the human face.

In the latter part of his working years Hashim's style became somewhat of a formula. Continuing to accentuate the face by eliminating distractions, the artist finally weakened his designs.[10] The earlier Jahangir portrait (A), the Deccani portraits, the Cleveland miniature, and the Suleiman Shikoh drawing were produced at the height of the artist's powers when his keen perception and technical competence combined harmoniously in the creation of modest works of great strength.[11]

1. Gray, 1950, p. 147.

2. Ibid.; for Paras name connected with the *Razm Nama* see Pinder-Wilson, 1956, p. 65; for Kanha see Binney, 1973, no. 25.

3. Paras's work for the *Chingiz Nama* is illustrated in Knizkova, pl. 21.

4. Ettinghausen, 1961, pls. 12 and 14.

5. See R. Skelton, "Documents for the Study of Painting at Bijapur," *ArtsA* 5, no. 2 (1958): 104; he notes that the portrait is taken from a Deccani original. Skelton also notes that Jahangir sent Ibrahim a picture on himself in 1618, and that an exchange may have occurred around this date, which would accord with the appearance of Ibrahim, who was in his late forties. Since this miniature is inscribed in Jahangir's own handwriting, there is no doubt that the picture dates from his reign. Most probably the other Deccani portraits by Hashim were also commissioned about this time; see Falk, 1976, and further references. In addition, Victoria and Albert I.M. 21-1925 is inscribed "the portrait of (Malik) Amber, by Hashim."

6. P. Brown, 1924, p. 151; Welch, 1963, p. 227.

7. Beach, 1978, no. 64.

8. Gascoigne, p. 202.

9. This ornament is similar to the one held by Shah Jahan in the portrait made by Abu'l Hasan during his twenty-fifth year, but the two are probably not the same because Hashim's version does not include a large diamond mounted below the emerald as in Abu'l Hasan's well-known picture (Gascoigne, p. 186).

10. See, for example, Martin, 2, pls. 185 and 186.

11. For other Hashim work see Arnold and Wilkinson, pl. 72; Welch, 1963, fig. 18; Pinder-Wilson, 1976, no. 138; Gray, 1950, nos. 741 and 759; Godard, 1937, figs. 70 and 97; *Sotheby*, 26 March 1973, lot 2; Beach, 1981, cat. 18a.

FURTHER READING: Beach, 1978, pp. 126–30.

26 *Portrait of the Aged Akbar* 71.78

Here attributed to Govardhan, Mughal, ca. 1640–50, 25.2 × 16.8 cm; 27.5 × 18.8 cm with border. Brush drawing in *grisaille* and gold has pin pricks for tracing; additional strips of paper on each side widen the composition.

Purchase, Andrew R. and Martha Holden Jennings Fund
Ex collection: MacDonald.

Comparative Material: (A) *Portrait of Akbar*, inscribed Govardhan, Mughal, seventeenth century, *Sotheby*, 12–13 Dec. 1929, lot 107 (now Metropolitan Museum of Art, 55.121.10.22). (B) *Portrait of Akbar*, Mughal, ca. 1650; Welch, 1963, fig. 17.

This portrait of Akbar in old age is attributable to the artist Govardhan, who has modelled his brush drawing techniques on observations of European prints. The emperor stands in the center of a plain holding a necklace; behind his head is a huge golden sun emanating rays that symbolizes the glory of the empire conquered under his leadership and also serves as the imperial halo that had become traditional by Shah Jahan's reign. The details of Akbar's costume, such as the border of his *patka*; his long, straight sword; and his *katar*, are also decorated in gold, as if echoing the sun's brilliance. Two birds of paradise hover above the celestial orb as angels extend a crown. Below the monarch are a lion and heifer, which probably symbolize an age of peace under inspired rule.

The work was probably done about 1640–50 as a study for Govardhan's painting of the same composition mounted in Shah Jahan's royal albums. (A, illus.). The fact that the artist altered certain aspects of the design as he progressed can still be seen from the varying tonality of the paper; the right side of Akbar's *jama* has been narrowed, his feet have possibly been moved, and the lion's head shifted. It is also evident that the emperor once held a globe rather than a necklace, both of which were standard accessories for the depiction of the Mughal sovereigns.

At some time the drawing was used as a tracing, although it is surprising that Govardhan himself would have prepared such a detailed work for this purpose. The pin pricks of the tracing follow the outlines of the figure and such details of decoration as the border on Akbar's *jama* or the design on his slippers (the tracing holes can be seen only with magnification). It can also be noted from magnification that the heavy outline around the figure and the animals was added after the sketch was originally done, and that it does not altogether follow the earlier contours. This extremely dark and clumsy outline blunts the forms and obscures the impact of the complex cross-hatching done in lighter, more delicate lines. The quality of this fine linear work can be judged particularly in the complex shading employed for the form of the heifer. The bone structure of the animal, the shift of its backbone, and the volume of its stomach are all brought out by Govardhan's buildup of lines and a subtle highlighting of the animal. Such technical achievements as

Figure 26.

well as the gray tone of the drawing show that the artist was quite familiar with the Western engravings he was attempting to imitate.[1]

Although probably the most talented and versatile artist of his period, Govardhan was of uneven temperament, and he produced certain works that are quite weak. Some of the strengths of the Cleveland miniature are concealed by the harsh outline and can easily be underrated, but they stand out in comparison with Govardhan's painting of the subject. In particular, the face of Akbar in the drawing is very sensitively handled, giving a substantial, glowing picture of dignified age through skillful modeling and highlighting, whereas the face in the painted version is weak and structureless. Akbar's narrow, drooping shoulders also make the painted portrait a less convincing and vigorous study. The heifer in the drawing is much more rounded and lifelike than the animal in the painting. The angels of the drawing have been badly damaged by the addition of the heavy outlines, yet their figures in detail still show a fleshiness characteristic of Govardhan's work.

Few portraits of the aged Akbar date from the emperor's lifetime, since his continuing vitality was renowned and helped to ensure dynastic stability. However, by Shah Jahan's period, Akbar was characteristically portrayed as elderly, and numerous portraits share the same stereotypical conventions (B). Govardhan has employed this general conception of the emperor, but the work escapes superficiality because the artist's careful treatment of the face emphasizes the humanity of his long-dead subject. At the time Govardhan did this portrait, the royal symbols of lion, lamb or heifer, and angels were being repeatedly employed. Several portraits of Shah Jahan are arranged in this manner with the animals below his feet and angels hovering in the clouds holding either crowns or parasols.[2]

1. British Museum 1945.5-8.02 is a Western engraving of the French dauphin surrounded with a lion and lamb in flowers and three angels holding a crown. Similar works were apparently the source for Govardhan's symbols and imitation of engraving style.
2. See Arnold and Wilkinson, pls. 63, 86.

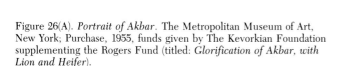

Figure 26(A). *Portrait of Akbar*. The Metropolitan Museum of Art, New York; Purchase, 1955, funds given by The Kevorkian Foundation supplementing the Rogers Fund (titled: *Glorification of Akbar, with Lion and Heifer*).

27 *Portrait of an Unidentified Noble*
from Shah Jahan's Court

47.4

Partially colored drawing, Mughal, ca. 1640–50,
14.4 × 10.2 cm., 39 × 27 cm. with border. Decorative
calligraphy on reverse on dark blue paper with gold fleckᵉ
Inner surround of dark blue floral decoration, alternating
with small bands of calligraphy; second inner border of
buff; eighteenth-century outer border of dark blue with
gold flowers.

Purchase, Edward L. Whittemore Fund

Ex collection: Heeramaneck.

Published: *Islamic Art* (Cleveland: Cleveland Museum of
Art, 1944), p. 27.

Comparative Material: (A) *Shah Jahan Receives His Three
Eldest Sons on Their Return from Lahore*, by Bichitr, a leaf
from the *Shah Jahan Nama*, Mughal, ca. 1640–50;
Gascoigne, p. 146. (B) *Shah Jahan Being Weighed during
Nauraz*, by Bola, a leaf from the *Shah Jahan Nama*,
Mughal, ca. 1640–50; Randhawa and Galbraith, pl. 6.
(C) *Drawing of a Courtier from Shah Jahan's Court*,
Mughal, ca. 1640–50; Coomaraswamy, 1926, pt. 6;
pl. XLIV.

This partially colored drawing is the portrait of an unnamed
notable of Shah Jahan's court who is depicted frequently in
episodes of the *Shah Jahan Nama*. Each of these folios
shows the same general version of this man whose mis-
shapen face bears a serious expression and whose eyes appear to be squinting unnaturally (A, detail illus.; B). A scene
depicting Jahangir honoring Khurram with the title of Shah
Jahan after his triumphant return from the Deccan in 1616
(fol. 194r) is historically the earliest in which this courtier is
found. Since this official does not appear in any other scenes
portraying Shah Jahan as an heroic prince, it can be assumed that he was present at Jahangir's court but had
no personal relation with the future emperor and took no
active part in events shaping Shah Jahan's life. His presence
continues in court scenes at least through Shah Jahan's
tenth regnal year (fol. 213v), after which he ceases to appear. Because he is portrayed as unalteringly middle-aged
during the events of twenty years, many renderings were
probably posthumous.

In most of the *Shah Jahan Nama* miniatures (including
A), the rotund courtier has an important position at the front
of the assembly, often slightly set off from the group. His
hunched shoulders and conspicuous stomach denote a court

Figure 27.

functionary rather than a soldier or man of action. In the double-page composition of folios 119v and 120r showing the wedding procession of Dara Shikoh, this man rides a horse at the front of a processional group. His repeated frontal placement suggests that he may have been one of the four masters of ceremony with charge over the arrangement of various court functions. These men are placed prominently in the *Shah Jahan Nama* illustrations, and this speculation would explain his significance at such gatherings as *durbars*, the reception of the Persian ambassador, and Shah Jahan's annual weighing.[1] The fact that this man does not appear in battle scenes though he is mounted on a horse for Dara's wedding also supports his identification as a ceremonial official.

Unfortunately, while folio 50v of the *Shah Jahan Nama* (A) includes the names of most-depicted personages, the identifying inscription for this courtier, which was written across a shield, has been damaged and is now unreadable. The Cleveland drawing may have served as a study of this man's face and was probably done about the same time as some of the *Shah Jahan Nama* folios, since its precise treatment is similar to the finished paintings from this work. It has been pointed out that the drawing was intended only as a preparatory work and not originally for preservation. It was applied to the decorated border with the addition of a paper strip along the top edge, and only in this way was it fitted to its elaborate mount.[2] Another drawing of this type, again of a courtier from Shah Jahan's reign (C), appears in a border similarly embellished with calligraphic cartouches.

1. The *Shah Jahan Nama* folios in which this man appears are 50v, 70r, 72v, 97v, 119v, and 120r, 194r, and 213v. A Lucknow copy of a portrait of this official in the India Office Library (J.23.3) identifies him wrongly as Riza Bahadur (Riza Bahadur was another of Shah Jahan's courtiers who was a master of ceremonies). There may have been some basis for the confusion if the two men held the same office (see Binyon and Arnold, pl. XX and p. 81).

2. S. C. Welch, conversation, 1976.

Figure 27(A), detail. *Shah Jahan Receives His Three Eldest Sons on Their Return from Lahore,* from the *Shah Jahan Nama,* fol. 50b. Royal Library, Windsor Castle. Reproduced by gracious permission of Her Majesty Queen Elizabeth II.

28   Three Leaves from the Late Shah Jahan Album

Assembled ca. 1650–55.

The following three folios are from the so-called *Late Shah Jahan Album* assembled at the end of that monarch's reign, probably from about 1650 to 1655, since one of the scattered pages is dated 1653.[1] The album included miscellaneous subjects, some of which were produced earlier in the reign, such as the Cleveland picture of a prince visiting *yogis*. The majority of miniatures, however, are standing courtier portraits of Shah Jahan's retainers done expressly for this book about 1650. The borders of this album are distinctive, as each of the miniatures is framed by a composition of figures that has some correlation with the main subject. Govardhan's composition of *yogis* and a prince is surrounded, for example, by a design of other holy men with a courtier meant to attend the prince placed in the center.

While some borders have been shown to be explicitly meaningful to the particular central courtier,[2] others have only a more general relevance. The Cleveland portrait of Asaf Khan is surrounded by various types of retainers who are echoed on another page picturing Shahnawaz Khan, also a Muslim and military commander (see below); since the leaves could not have faced each other, the folios were unrelated and show that artists may not have attempted to do more than approximate suitable border subjects.

It was Jahangir whose inquiring, restless mind led him to favor the album of miscellaneous subjects over a cohesive literary theme. His albums alternated double pages of calligraphy surrounded by figural borders with those of miniature paintings in plainer borders. This pattern of miniatures followed by calligraphic pages was then preserved as a standard of fashion throughout the Mughal period. In this album Shah Jahan has, however, reversed Jahangir's association of figural borders with decorative calligraphy. Although in some ways this reversal violates the exquisite taste of the Jahangiri era, the attendant figures also serve to diversify the many standing portraits in the album. When compared with Jahangiri border depictions, these figures have fuller proportions and are more completely colored. In terms of quality, they are less imaginatively conceived and not as fluidly drawn or positioned.

This *Shah Jahan Album,* reportedly taken from Delhi at the time of Nadir Shah's invasion, was brought to Paris, broken up, and sold about 1909.[3] Unfortunately, no record exists of the album's construction or arrangement except for a note that about one hundred pictorial leaves were dispersed.[4] Its facing portrait pages were certainly coordinated by subject matter, and there may have been a loose hierarchical order of imperial and courtier depictions interspersed with or followed by miscellaneous subjects. Many of the now-scattered miniatures have similar compositions, and it is to be assumed that borders surrounding calligraphic passages were also repetitive. The album is more conventionalized than the sumptuous, intimate record of the royal family mounted earlier in Shah Jahan's reign (Minto, Wantage, Kevorkian group).

Since its early twentieth-century sale, this album has been popular largely because the amplification of the main subject by the surrounding genre figures in the borders has a pleasing appearance. When complete, the album must have given the stirring impression of an active court filled with dignified officers and their alert servants. Its overstated imperial symbols have the rousing elements of a military march and were obviously intended to convey the brilliance and supremacy of the imperial court. However, its pages have also been described several times as lacking in originality.

The quality of the earlier Shah Jahani miniatures in the group tends to be good, but those pictures prepared specifically for the album are somewhat weak. The contrast can be noted, for example, in the difference between the Cleveland miniature of the prince with *yogis* and the later, somewhat bland portrait of Asaf Khan. Small details also betray the lack of sensitivity developing among court painters; the gold floral illumination of the Mughal manuscript borders had been breathtakingly refined, but here, despite elegant ornamentation framing the calligraphy, the gold plants appearing behind border figures on the other side are stenciled with surprising carelessness. A partial listing of known pages has already been published.[5]

1. *Sotheby*, 3 April 1978, lot 99.
2. Victoria and Albert Museum, 1982, nos. 69 and 70.
3. Martin, 1:85.
4. Ibid.
5. Beach, 1978, pp. 76–77.

28i *Prince and Ascetics* 71.79

Here attributed to Govardhan, Mughal, ca. 1630, mounted 1650–55, 20.3 × 14.3 cm, 37.5 × 25.2 cm with border. Upper left corner of outer border obliterated. Coral and gold inner border; figural outer border with portraits of ascetics.

Purchase, Andrew R. and Martha Holden Jennings Fund

Ex collection: MacDonald.

Published: Beach, 1978, no. 22 (repr.).

Comparative Material: (A) *Group of Servants*, by Govardhan, Mughal, ca. 1625; Arnold and Wilkinson, 3: frontispiece. (B) *Ascetics*, attributed to Govardhan, Mughal, ca. 1625; Welch, 1973, no. 63.

This miniature showing a young prince visiting two *yogis* who apparently live in a narrow cave on the outskirts of a village reinterprets a traditional subject with much originality. Both in literary descriptions and in Mughal history, courtly personages sought out holy men inhabiting caves in isolated areas. Although based on Persian miniatures depicting the ruler's search for wisdom, this theme was especially popular in the early Mughal period because of frequent visits to holy men by Akbar, Jahangir, and Dara Shikoh. Only the young prince in this miniature follows a stereotyped concept with prettified features that emphasize his refinement. His figure may be modeled loosely on the handsome Dara Shikoh, who was renowned for his association with sages throughout Shah Jahan's reign. His generalized face and body, however, contrast strongly with the portraitlike treatment of both *yogis;* one of these men wears the round bone earrings of a *kanphat* and plays a *vina,* while his bearded companion wrapped in a cloak sits beside the customary ascetic possessions of a shell and a long-necked water vessel. Behind these figures a few villagers stand in front of a thatched house talking amid a herd of goats.

Govardhan, like the Akbari painter Basawan (see [17]), seemed compelled to depict ascetics, apparently because he also was deeply interested in assessing how the face and body mirrored psychological states. The ascetic utilizing his body to discipline his mind brought it to a pitch of emotional expression that these two painters understood and captured. The ascetics in this picture exemplify two different types of wisdom acquired with age and self-restraint: the one on the left appears as if he had disciplined himself to a sensitive austerity, while the man on the right seems to have mellowed to a greater humanity with the years. Their faces look as if the rendering may have been based on observation of real ascetics.

An inscribed Govardhan miniature depicting a group of servants (A, illus.) has many parallels to the Cleveland painting. The most obvious is the physical resemblance of the ascetic in the foreground of the composition to the ascetic with the *vina* in the Cleveland picture. The figures in each miniature show Govardhan's creation of strong facial features by giving the illusion of skin tightly stretched over

Figure 28*i*.

Figure 28i(A). *Group of Servants,* by Govardhan. Chester Beatty Library, Dublin.

Figure 28i(B). *Ascetics,* attr. to Govardhan. Private Collection. Reproduced by permission of the Fogg Art Museum, Harvard University, Cambridge, Massachusetts.

Figure 28i, detail.

bone structure. In his depiction of ascetics, as well as in other works, the treatment owes much to European art despite the Indianness of the subject (that this is true of background elements also can be seen from the rural vignette in the Cleveland painting viewed from a quasi-Western perspective).

Few of the paintings central to defining Govardhan's career are inscribed; most are attributed to the artist. Because his manner was individual, however, elements can be traced from inscribed miniatures to attributions. One picture essential for comparison of drawing techniques is an unsigned work widely accepted as representative of Govardhan's oeuvre (B, illus.). This painting and the Cleveland miniature, which both treat ascetics, differ in mood but can be seen as two aspects of a single personality. Comparison enriches the understanding of Govardhan's great abilities and scope as an artist. Both works focus on figures that the artist has made an intense effort to describe, but the disparity springs from Govardhan's different manner of visualizing his subjects. The painting of the five ascetics is a mature, rather cold work, ultimately disturbing both spatially and emotionally. The figures appear to be separate studies that are uneasily united. The young boy seen from the back is positioned ambiguously in a dreamlike space, while the ascetic to his left—very aware of the world—surprises the viewer with a challenging, almost sardonic expression.

By contrast, the Cleveland painting concentrates on the idealization of beauty, and thus has a slight decorative element. The more bizarre undercurrents in Govardhan's work expressed in his study of the five ascetics remain hidden. The picture is less a three-dimensional work and more an essay in refined line drawing. The upward-thrusting tree trunk and its long root lines are shadowed and highlighted with a concentration much like that focused on the drawing of the ascetics' hands or faces. A nervous ecstasy animates such portions of the picture, but the total effect of the composition is quiet and subdued. The border figures are interesting genre studies, done later, when the picture was mounted, and in a slightly coarser style not related to Govardhan's work.

Govardhan's awareness of Western art and his sensuous perception of form are the factors that link the Cleveland miniature and the two comparative works (A and B). The cloak around the bearded ascetic in the Cleveland painting is given the significance of a passage of still life and demonstrates Govardhan's sensitive response to European renderings of texture and luminosity.

The dating of the Cleveland picture is based on Govardhan's emotionally complex depiction of the *yogis*, as well as on the conventionalized rendering of the prince, which is similar to that of figures in the album Dara Shikoh prepared during the 1630s and presented to his wife in 1641–42.[1]

1. Falk and Archer, pp. 383–93, fols. 17v, 18, 19v, 27v, 35v, 36, 38, 43v, 45v.

28ii *Portrait of Asaf Khan* 45.168

Mughal, ca. 1650, 19 × 11.9 cm, 38 × 24.8 cm with borders. Slight cracking of paint around central figure. Coral inner border; figural outer border bears the number "22" at bottom left.

Purchase from the J. H. Wade Fund

Ex collection: Demotte (?).

Published: H. C. Hollis, "Portrait of a Nobleman," *CMAB* 33 (Dec. 1946): 180–82.

Comparative Material: (A) *Portrait of Asaf Khan as Commander-in-Chief*, by Bichitr, Mughal, ca. 1630; W. G. Archer, 1960, pl. 27; Hambly, p. 91; or Pinder-Wilson, 1976, no. 152. (B) *Shah Jahan Receives His Sons on Their Return from Lahore*, by Bichitr, leaf from the *Shah Jahan Nama*, Mughal, ca. 1640–50; Gascoigne, p. 146. (C) *Delivery of Wedding Presents at the Time of Dara's Marriage*, by Murad, fols. 121v and 122r of the *Shah Jahan Nama*, Mughal, ca. 1640–50; unpublished. (D) *Durbar of Shah Jahan*, Mughal, ca. 1640–50; Binyon and Arnold, pl. XXXVI; or P. Brown, 1924, pl. XXIV. (E) *Portrait of Shahnawaz Khan*, by Ram Das, Mughal, ca. 1650; Binney, 1973, no. 62.

Asaf Khan was a central figure in the courts of both Jahangir and Shah Jahan and was, therefore, portrayed numerous times during these reigns. He was made Jahangir's vizier on the death of his father, who had held that office, as well as being related by marriage to both sovereigns.[1] Depictions of him cover young manhood, middle age, and older years when he is shown with a full beard. His position in group portraits during these years was an important one, and artists carefully observed his features rather than presenting a single, easily identifiable stereotype. Several individual portraits of him present different artists' views of his physiognomy. Because Asaf Khan was a man with even rather than exaggerated features, he is, however, more difficult to recognize than other officials. The changes occurring with age, although not great, increase the problems of identification.

Among the single inscribed portraits of Asaf Khan is one by the artist Bichitr (A) that extols him as commander of the imperial army. In a group portrait also by Bichitr (B), Asaf Khan at the upper left behind the young princes can be distinguished by his resemblance to Bichitr's single portrait (A). Asaf Khan's position behind the princes is also repeated in a number of additional *Shah Jahan Nama* leaves, such as a page identifying him by inscription as the man riding behind Shah Jahan's three younger sons delivering wedding gifts to their brother Dara Shikoh (C).[2] In four other unpublished miniatures of the *Shah Jahan Nama*, this same figure is behind the princes or beside the throne.[3] In these scenes Asaf Khan is generally bearded (when short, the beard juts from his chin; but when longer, it appears straight, as in the Cleveland portrait).

The Cleveland picture has been called "Alla al-Mulk Tuni" because it was equated with a mistakenly identified portrait of Asaf Khan in a *durbar* scene.[4] In this scene (D,

Figure 28*ii*.

Figure 28*ii*(D). *Durbar of Shah Jahan*. Bodleian Library, Oxford, MS. Ouseley, Add. 173, no. 13. Reproduced by permission of the Curators of the Bodleian Library.

illus.) the bearded figure in question stands on the balcony level with Shah Jahan and behind the princes, and from his position as well as his appearance is undoubtedly Asaf Khan.[5] Alla al-Mulk Tuni, a sharper-featured man, is depicted in quite a different manner in another miniature of the *Late Shah Jahan Album*.[6] The identity of the figure in the Cleveland portrait is established not only on the basis of the court scenes from the *Shah Jahan Nama* but also from the relationship with the individual portrait by Bichitr (A). Although Asaf Khan is unbearded in this latter work, the resemblance to the Cleveland painting is strong.

In the border surrounding the main portrait, the supporting figures include two Muslim *mullahs* expounding from religious books (showing the orthodox devotion of this royal family member) and an attendant with a vase of narcissi who represents the cultured aspect of the khan's character. His valued military service is symbolized by the officer holding his sword, the attendant with bow and arrow, and the two armed men kneeling with a shield and cover. These figures are repeated in different costumes and with a few minor changes of accessories around another miniature from this album depicting Shahnawaz Khan, who was also a respected military hero (E, illus.). The style of the rendering shows that the two pages were done by different artists, and since both are versos, they probably had no relationship in the arrangement of the album. Such repetition, however, demonstrates the way in which this volume was designed and composed as Shah Jahan's reign drew to a close.

1. Bhattacharya, p. 64; Godard, 1937, pp. 217–18.
2. Asaf Khan is identified as Yaman ud-Daula, one of his titles.
3. Asaf Khan appears in fol. 123v standing behind the three youngest princes in Dara's wedding procession; in fol. 146v he is behind Shuja, who bids the emperor goodbye; in fol. 216v during the celebration of Aurangzeb's appointment as Deccani viceroy, he is at the left of the throne; in fol. 217v he is at the left of the throne for Aurangzeb's marriage.
4. Hollis, *CMAB* 33 (Dec. 1946): 180.
5. Binyon and Arnold, p. 86, wrongly asserted that the emperor in the *durbar* was Aurangzeb and that the bearded courtier was Alla al-Mulk Tuni; the same figure was then mistakenly called the tutor of the princes by P. Brown, 1924, p. 88.
6. Victoria and Albert Museum, 1982, no. 69; see also Binyon and Arnold, pl. 26; *Sotheby*, 7 April 1975, lot 130.

Figure 28*ii*(E). *Portrait of Shahnawaz Khan*, by Ram Das. Edwin Binney 3rd Collection.

101

Figure 28*iii*.

Figure 28*iii*(A). *A Page of Persian Calligraphy.* The Los Angeles County Museum of Art, from the Nasli and Alice Heeramaneck Collection, Museum Associates Purchase, M.78.9.15, verso (titled: *Page from an Album Assembled for Shah Jahan,* ca. 1630-35).

28*iii*   *A Page of Persian Calligraphy*   77.207
       Framed by an Ornamental Border
       of Vines, Birds, and Deer

From the *Late Shah Jahan Album,* Mughal, ca. 1650, 36.8 × 25.2 cm overall. Very slight discoloration and paint removal; slightly trimmed. Verse penned by the calligrapher Mir Ali al-kalib.[1]

Gift of Herbert F. Leisy in memory of his wife, Helen Stamp Leisy

Ex collections: Demotte, Heeramaneck, Leisy.

Comparative Material: (A) *A Page of Persian Calligraphy* (framed by an ornamental border of vines, birds, and deer), from the *Late Shah Jahan Album,* Mughal, ca. 1650; Beach, 1978, no. 23 recto. (B) *A Page of Persian Calligraphy* (framed by an ornamental border of vines, birds, and deer), from the *Late Shah Jahan Album,* Mughal, ca. 1650; A. Welch and S. C. Welch, *Arts of the Islamic Book* (New York: Cornell University Press), 1982, no. 73.

Mughal artists followed the long Persian tradition of enhancing the purely abstract curves of calligraphy with delicate vine traceries in surrounding borders. On this page the flowering vines are stylized in a manner characteristic of Shah Jahan's preference for a fantasy that at first appears naturalistic. Different types of blossoms placed on the same tendril combine with various leaves and, although conventional, give an impression of growth and freshness. The birds and animals superimposed on the vine scrolls by contrast are recognizable Indian species treated in some detail: brightly colored kingfishers in the upper right, female and male sambar (*Cervus unicolor*) at the bottom, and nilgai in the middle and upper portions.

Shah Jahan was a traditionalist who loved order both in the political realm and in art. In contrast to the spontaneously energetic decoration of the Akbari and Jahangiri reigns, his artists returned to classical types of Islamic geometric arrangement. Despite the fact that this ornamental border has some pictorial elements, the vine scrolls are carefully treated as circles and ogival arches. Parallels are found in Mughal architecture, Shah Jahan's best-loved art form around which he coordinated all the other decorative arts of the mid-seventeenth century. Ornamental patterns in his two Red Forts are done with comparable control, again made to appear natural by their fragility as well as by added leaves and flowers. Although the cool, structural precision of such designs masked by their soft natural details

Figure 28*iii*, detail.

103

is very beautiful, one can sense its underlying rigidity and brittleness. The crowded vitality of the earlier decorative arts is much more Indian. By contrast, Shah Jahan seems to have rejected such energy for a dreamlike perfectionism that symbolizes his reaction against Akbar's desire for Hindu-Muslim coalescence. The always-pushing, multiplying, purely organic vegetal decoration of Hindu monuments intimates a different manner of perceiving the universe that eventually could not be reconciled with Islamic geometric and abstract concepts of order. Thus to a great extent Shah Jahan's decorative arts and white marble buildings signal the dynasty's retreat into an idealism unrelated to the predominant cultural environment or to real political conditions.

The great importance of purely decorative manuscript borders such as this one in the court art of Shah Jahan's time is proven by the examples in the Minto album that have been signed as independent creations.[2] Although few elements in the album under discussion are unique to one page, the standard of workmanship for the calligraphic borders remains extremely high. The vine scroll, for example, on the Cleveland page is painstakingly outlined in gold on each side of its narrow stem, and the leaves are likewise carefully outlined and veined.

Like other pages of calligraphy from this album, this one was separated from the miniature on the reverse by the French dealer Demotte before being sold. Most other examples were further altered by mounting paintings over the original calligraphy.[3] Among the few remaining leaves retaining a calligraphic verse is one that is a mirror image of the Cleveland verso page, with the same delicately colored birds and deer at regularly spaced intervals determined by the rhythmic looping of the vine tendrils (A). The two compositions could easily have formed a double page opening in the original album, although there were probably other pages that repeated the same design. Another leaf (B), similar but with slightly different bird and animal species as well as a vine scroll that does not touch the central calligraphy, shows that artists also did very subtle variations of designs. Since apparently more than one hundred ornamental pages were prepared, it is probable that, as in other albums, many were repetitive.

1. This calligrapher, much admired in Shah Jahan's era, also wrote other poetic verses included in this album; see Falk, 1976, no. 98(i).
2. James, p. 39; Skelton, 1972, pl. LXXXVIIIa.
3. Falk, 1976, no. 96(i).

29 Portrait of Prince Murad Baksh 17.1066

Mughal, ca. 1655, 20 × 12 cm. Outer paper torn and frayed, paint gone in many areas; inner square of paper stained, slightly torn across shield, paint on sword eaten away. Persian inscription identifying prince on reverse.

Gift of The John Huntington Art and Polytechnic Trust

Comparative Material: (A) *Portrait of Murad Baksh*, Mughal, ca. 1655; Gangoly, 1961, pl. 5b. (B) *Portrait of Murad Baksh*, Mughal, ca. 1670; *Sotheby*, 7 April 1975, lot. 129. (C) *Portrait of Murad Baksh*, Rajasthani, ca. 1670–90; *Sotheby*, 7 July 1975, lot 103.

Murad Baksh, the subject of this portrait, was Shah Jahan's fourth and youngest son, born in 1624 while his father was in revolt against Jahangir. The next generation's struggle for succession found Murad unwisely allied with his clever brother Aurangzeb, whose calculated betrayal led to Murad's execution in 1659.[1] In the years between, Murad had served as a general fighting rather purposeless battles that represented no territorial gain to the empire. In his occupation, Murad chose brawn over brains, and his sportive eagerness to fight was coupled with an indifference to the men under him.[2]

When the four princes began competing for the throne, Murad evolved shallow plans for his own elevation without fully evaluating Aurangzeb's ambitions. This heedlessness led to his imprisonment and execution, but since Murad had accompanied his own imperial claim with the murder of a minister and the plunder of a city to finance his army, his demise does not seem unfitting.[3] His own passions and crimes, brutal and uninteresting, apparently dulled his awareness of danger.

Murad's portraits substantiate this account in showing a stocky, able-bodied, emotionless prince. Details and coloration are handled well in the Cleveland miniature, but the artist has not been inspired by his sitter. He has simply combined the requisite jewels and rich fabrics with a noble stance, and in this way produced his picture. Little personal variety is expressed in any of Murad's portraits; a miniature from the Baroda Museum (A) is virtually identical to the Cleveland painting except for adjustments of color and pattern. A later version (B) is obviously based on these sources for both pose and costume. A half-length portrait of Murad (C) is a Rajasthani adaptation of another much-used compositional formula.[4]

The Cleveland and Baroda miniatures were probably done just before the struggle for succession when Murad would have been in his late twenties or early thirties. Prior to this date he would have looked younger, while it is almost certain that he would not have been portrayed following Aurangzeb's accession. Since many examples of nearly identical portraits are found in this era, the comparisons possible between the Cleveland and Baroda pictures are not unusual. However, Murad was not treated either like his brother Shuja or the much-portrayed Dara, who was both the favored son and an aesthete; Dara especially is shown in

Figure 29.

more situations and in a greater variety of poses. Murad, though selfish and vain, probably cared little about being the subject of miniature paintings; in addition, he was less popular than his two older brothers. Portraits of the young Aurangzeb are also somewhat rare, perhaps for similar reasons. The Mughal royal family was quick to discern that eventually all but one royal prince was expendable, and Murad seems to have been a superfluous son.

1. Gascoigne, p. 220.

2. Haig, p. 203; Gascoigne, p. 213.

3. Haig, p. 213; Gascoigne, pp. 206, 213.

4. A conventionalized depiction of a clean-shaven prince in a love scene has been conjectured to be Murad Baksh, but is more likely to be a generalized princely representation based on the appearance of the royal sons (W. G. Archer, 1960, pl. 46). Other examples of portraits identified as Murad Baksh include *Sotheby*, 1 July 1969, lot 114, and Schultz, pl. 189; if the latter is Murad Baksh, which seems doubtful, he must be much younger; *Sotheby*, 11 July 1972, lot 51, may also be a portrait of the prince.

FURTHER READING: M. Quamruddin, *The Life and Times of Prince Murad Baksh* (Calcutta, 1972).

III. Subimperial, Popular Mughal, and Bazaar Mughal Painting

Manuscript painting in various Sultanate styles that can mainly be considered provincial Persian was done for the nobility in India prior to the Mughal invasion. Even for several decades after Babur's conquest in the early sixteenth century, the same type of painting was carried on without much influence from the imperial court—largely because during Humayun's life and the early part of Akbar's reign the court was like any other of the previous, limited Sultanate governments. Eventually, Akbar's vigorous miniature style came to serve as a popular model because of his political dominance as well as his charisma. As the Akbari studio became increasingly productive, the emperor encouraged nobles to copy his *Ramayana* and *Razm Nama*[1]—an offer that was probably also made with other manuscripts.

In the best-documented instance, the *Ramayana* was used for reference by Akbar's statesman-general Abd ar-Rahim, the Khan Khanan, to produce his own copy of the epic (see [35]). This privileged noble, whose murdered father had been Akbar's guardian and aide, had been raised as a member of the imperial family and retained a special position in the realm because of Akbar's sentiments as well as his own abilities. His artistic patronage was independent and surprisingly unsophisticated, considering that he should have had more knowledge of developments within the royal studio than others. His atelier is very significant, however, because as a poet and manuscript-lover himself, he is associated with more illustrated works than any other noble; and his large staff of illuminators and artists is the only subimperial group to be described by a contemporary historian. While Abu'l Fazl mentions noble patrons of manuscripts unspecifically in his writings, Akbar's foster brother Aziz Khan Koka is the only other Akbari official linked with a specific work.[2] In the Jahangiri or Shah Jahani eras, in addition to Prince Dara Shikoh who apparently had his own artists, Asaf Khan is mentioned as among those commissioning paintings, and Shah Jahan's Kashmiri governor Zafar Khan was the patron of paintings executed about 1640.[3]

These officials are presumably a few of a restricted but fairly numerous group who commissioned miniatures as a secondary interest associated with literature. Almost no patron in India was exclusively interested in painting for its own sake, as was clearly demonstrated by such men as Abd ar-Rahim or Zafar Khan, who spent their funds and energy on large literary collections. Both had poet-protégés and commissioned as many copies of works in the author's own handwriting as was possible. Despite the charm of the Khan Khanan's illustrated manuscripts, they are simplistic and old fashioned in comparison with imperial prototypes and were certainly less significant to this bibliophile than his prized examples of calligraphy.

Two leaves in the Cleveland collection come from Abd ar-Rahim's *Razm Nama* that is dated on several folios to 1616/17 and is one of his later productions in a style continued from the earlier *Ramayana* [35*i*, 35*ii*]. This style was one of several unrelated ones that painters in the Khan Khanan's workshop employed, apparently whether their employer was residing in Gujerat or in the Deccan. These painters (who included a few Muslims, Rajputs, and a native of the Deccan) were each capable of working in more than one of the Khan Khanan's subimperial manners but generally created doll-like, slightly Persianized figures.

Among the best quality Mughal-influenced works are the ones that are less conservative than the Khan Khanan's illustrations and have a local flavor. Bikaner, the Rajasthani desert state that enriched its culture by imitating the arts of the imperial court, was a center for high-quality, as well as more folkish, illustrations. Among the most elegant of these Mughal-influenced productions that were probably done in Bikaner is a scene copied from an unknown imperial source but made more lush outside the formalized Muslim atmosphere of the court [36]. Since few works of any one type exist, the source of such subimperial styles is difficult to assess, but this painter and others clearly blended some knowledge of Mughal techniques with a Rajput sensibility.

As with other classifications of artistic work, distinctions are relative rather than absolute. The term "subimperial" is generally used to denote paintings related to those of the court atelier but less refined. In certain known instances paintings in court-related styles were also done for patrons besides the nobility, such as the illustrated letter produced by the artist Salivahana for the Jain sect in 1610.[4] Works like this letter merge with miniatures on the next social level of patronage—sometimes termed "Popular Mughal"—that are generally bright-colored, vital, and stiff. The Popular Mughal artists working for a variety of patrons struggled to master the Mughal techniques that only slightly mask their

Figure 32, detail.

late Akbari work.[2] The two pictures, closely related in composition, show the limited training of their artists, who used a standard setting with similar pavilions and courtyards. In both miniatures the ruler, surrounded by courtiers, is posed in the same manner on an almost identical throne. Unfortunately, the subject matter of the two leaves gives no clue to their literary source, although it can be inferred that they come from a modest illustrated volume probably done for an Akbari court noble and that the subject was neither poetic nor historical but dealt with unusual fables or stories.

The Cleveland scene represents rather rough or crude Hindu entertainers performing before a king. While the figures wear demonic masks, the three are actually a group of rustic dancers with primitive religious associations, rather than being either demented or supernatural. The rows of bells worn by the man on the right are common ornaments of shamans officiating at village shrines,[3] while the necklace is that of a Lingayat Shaivite. Like the bells, the animal bone held by the same dancer probably had a shamanistic use. The customs depicted in the context of a straightforward court scene reveal a strange juxtaposition of folk and courtly life, due to veneration of holy or quasi-holy men. Because the artist himself appears to have been a minor painter and seems familiar with the role of the performers, he may have been of Hindu origin.

1. See Pinder-Wilson, 1956, pp. 62–65, pls. XIX and XX.
2. *Sotheby*, 11 April 1961, lots 42 and 43; these two lots were equated at the time of the auction with two other Akbari leaves from the small Clive album, to which they have no actual connection, however (*Sotheby*, 17 Jan. 1956, log 332a).
3. *Gods of the Byways*, an exhibition of Rajasthani religious practices at the Museum of Modern Art, Oxford, 1982, included photographs of *bhopa*, or shamans, wearing bells (not reproduced in catalogue).

Figure 32(A). *A Vizier Pleading before a King.* Collection unknown. After *Maggs Bulletin* no. 5 (April 1963), no. 92.

111

33 *Kakubha Ragini*   60.50

Popular Mughal, ca. 1610, 21.5 × 16 cm. Staining on right
half; paint obliterated, especially in bottom portion; edges
torn.

Purchase, Mr. and Mrs. William H. Marlatt Fund

Ex collection: Heeramaneck.

Published: Lee, 1960, no. 54.

Comparative Material: (A) *Todi Ragini*, Popular Mughal,
ca. 1610; Stchoukine, 1929*b*, pl. LXXIV. (B) *Kamod Ragini*,
Popular Mughal, ca. 1610; Ebeling, no. 40.

This *Kakubha Ragini* leaf is similar to a *ragamala* series in
the India Office Library (A and B). The works are associated by their figure treatment and simple compositions,
although the Cleveland miniature was done by a slightly
better artist; for example, though it was quickly done, the
sketchy bushes, flowers, and tree leaves are gracefully
handled with a suggestion of differing species. Both sets,
however, represent a folkish style produced commercially
that mixes Mughal with Rajasthani elements.

While such leaves for popular consumption are superficially varied, the artists' basic approaches—determined
by the necessity of rapid, low-cost production—are much
the same. Like other paintings of its caliber, the Cleveland
Kakubha leaf has a limited palette. Many popular Mughal
paintings such as this leaf and the India Office set depend
heavily on dark green and blue paints, which presumably
were cheap and easily obtainable. The lavender and the
orange used for Kakubha's costume were employed spar-
ingly where they would have the most effect. The flaking of
pigment shows that the artist began by painting the entire
leaf yellow. Without a preliminary brush drawing, he then
combined the applications of local color with relatively
sketchy freehand outlining and detailing.

FURTHER READING: P. Chandra, 1960, pp. 25–57; Khandalavala, M. Chandra, and P. Chandra.

Figure 33.

34 *Radha and Krishna Caught*   47.503
in a Storm

Leaf from a *Rasikapriya*, Popular Mughal, ca. 1615–20,
13 × 13 cm. Rubbed. Narrow dark blue border trimmed,
but some remains on two sides.

Purchase, Edward L. Whittemore Fund

Ex collection: Heeramaneck.

Comparative Material: (A) *Meeting at a Festivity*, leaf from
a *Rasikapriya*, Popular Mughal, ca. 1615–20;
Coomaraswamy, 1926, pt. 6: pl. XIII. (B) *Heroine Whose
Lord Is Steadfast*, leaf from a *Rasikapriya*, Popular
Mughal, ca. 1615–20; Coomaraswamy, 1926, pt. 6: pl. XI.

This tiny miniature in Popular Mughal style is probably part
of the *Rasikapriya* manuscript that is now mainly in the
Museum of Fine Arts, Boston (A and B). Costume, ornament, and figure style match those in the Cleveland leaf,
but few of the variously sized illustrations remain mounted
with the text, which increases the difficulty of identification.[1] In general the compositions involve only two lovers, but when group scenes occur (as in A), the designs
are relatively simple, with only a few planes, as in this
miniature.

The manuscript, with figures characteristic of early
Jahangiri painting, is done in a delicate style lacking forceful
or spectacular movement. Colors such as the blues and
greens of the Cleveland miniature are generally subdued.
In this scene Radha and Krishna embrace, unworried by
lightning and rain clouds, while the village *gopas* and *gopis*
run for shelter.

1. Coomaraswamy, 1926, pt. 6: 19. At the time Coomaraswamy
wrote, he was aware of forty-four miniatures from this manuscript,
which he believed were nearly all that would have existed; the
Cleveland miniature conforms to the average size of illustrations.

Figure 34.

35 Two Leaves from the Khan Khanan's Razm Nama

Subimperial Mughal, ca. 1610(?)–17

The Cleveland Museum has two pages from the subimperial *Razm Nama*, done for Abd ar-Rahim, Akbar's khan of khans (Khan Khanan), which has pages dated 1616 and 1617.[1] The *Razm Nama*, the Persian translation of the Hindu *Mahabharata* epic, presumably interested the Khan Khanan because like many within Akbar's circle of influential courtiers he was sympathetic to the emperor's syncretistic religious policies. The chronicler Badauni says that the *Razm Nama* was repeatedly copied at Akbar's court, and that the grandees were commanded to make editions of it in order to learn about Hindu India.[2]

Abd ar-Rahim was raised at court under the supervision of the slightly older Akbar following the murder of his father, who had been Akbar's judicious tutor and guardian. Because Rahim was acccorded rank and the privileges of imperial intimacy he acquired considerable sophistication and had the freedom to try his abilities in several directions. This highest-ranking noble and army commander, in addition to being a bibliophile, was a writer of stature in Hindi as well as other languages. Renowned for religious tolerance, he undoubtedly would have been aware of the great works of Hindu literature, but as far as is known had only a *ragamala* and the two epics—the *Ramayana* and *Razm Nama* that were first produced for Akbar—illustrated in his own studio.[3] The khan's library was the largest of those belonging to Akbar's nobles, employing about ninety-five men in various phases of book production.[4] The attribution of this dispersed *Razm Nama* manuscript to Rahim's studio is based not only on inscribed paintings by artists in his atelier (like the prolific Fazl) but also on its similarity to the nearly complete *Ramayana* in the Freer Gallery, Washington, with a long colophon describing production under the khan.[5]

Considering the Khan Khanan's status and the size of his library, it may at first appear strange that the paintings in his *Ramayana*, *Razm Nama*, and other manuscripts do not correspond more closely with the great developments in the imperial studio. Not only is it odd that his rank did not automatically insure a certain level of sophistication for miniature painting, but the colophon of the *Ramayana* specifically states that Akbar's imperial volume was borrowed so that the Khan Khanan's artists might copy the design.[6] Other manuscripts apparently done for the Akbari nobility (the Barmecide text, for example) reveal greater technical virtuosity and show that there were more knowing connoisseurs of miniature painting than the Khan Khanan.[7] The khan did not lack funds to spend on book production, but he was primarily interested in texts rather than illustrations. He was apparently a literary rather than a visually educated connoisseur. He lavished money particularly on well-known calligraphers, but his artists for the most part were illuminators or even bookbinders in addition to being part-time illustrators.[8] They were also not exclusively from families of painters. For example, a Hindu artist was the son of a Rajput warrior whose father had been killed in battle by the khan. Abd ar-Rahim provided for this orphan by having him trained in the painting studio, and although his work was competent, the khan's action was unusual for his day.[9] In addition, it is clear from accounts of his artists that the Khan Khanan was relatively indifferent to searching out painters with established reputations.

These workers were both Muslims and Hindus from various parts of India, including a man specifically mentioned as coming from Ahmednagar in the Deccan.[10] There has been speculation about where the Khan Khanan had his library, since he was shifted to various parts of the empire during his career. For a time the studio was in Gujerat where he served as governor; it was then probably moved to the Deccan, since he spent much of the remainder of his life fighting in that area.[11] His known recruitment of an Ahmednagar artist supports this theory.

Because he was such an able soldier and administrator, the Khan Khanan was influential up to the time of his death in 1626, although he was often in temporary disgrace during Jahangir's rule.[12] Abd ar-Rahim was cultured but also a rough-and-ready type who was thoroughly Akbar's man and not at all related intellectually to the dilettantish and sensual Jahangir. It is thus not surprising that this *Razm Nama* done during Jahangir's reign basically continues the style of the *Ramayana* produced in the Akbari era from 1589–98. By the time of the *Razm Nama*, his artists' style—enhanced with only a few features introduced in Jahangir's time—could be considered extremely conservative and indicated that the crusty patron was continuing to live to some extent in the golden age of the past. Among other elements, the *Ramayana* and *Razm Nama* share landscape and vegetational forms derived from the same period of imperial painting. The coarsely modeled rocks, the stones with flowers sprouting out around them, the dark trees with yellow leaf outlines, and the bushes hanging from cliffs that occur in the two Cleveland *Razm Nama* pages are only some of the features employed throughout both manuscripts.

Akbar's imperial copy of the *Razm Nama* was completed by 1586, after which the emperor's translators and artists commenced working on the *Ramayana*.[13] The Khan Khanan became interested in this version of the *Ramayana* during its preparation; according to the colophon, he borrowed it directly upon completion. He had not shown such an early interest in the *Razm Nama*, however, and for this reason the *Ramayana* and *Razm Nama* preparations were rather different. Although the Khan Khanan's *Ramayana* does not duplicate the style of the imperial copy, many of the compositions are borrowed from this source.[14] Despite the fact that the evidence of scattered leaves is imperfect, the compositions of the Khan Khanan's later *Razm Nama*, presumably done in the Deccan, seem to be independent of an imperial prototype. This is not surprising, because the imperial copy had been done so much earlier and also because the Khan Khanan was not as close to Jahangir as to his father. That Abd ar-Rahim commissioned the *Razm Nama* long after the court had almost entirely stopped producing illustrated manuscripts and was no longer interested in Hindu subject matter shows both his independence and his genuine admiration for Hindu culture. Jahangir did not perceive the political necessity for interchange. In many ways he was anti-Hindu, so that although Akbar had requested his nobles to copy the epics, Abd ar-Rahim's project was an anomaly by the time it was completed.

According to the colophon on the Khan Khanan's *Ramayana*, this manuscript was done over an inordinately long period of eleven years.[15] However, the implication is that the artists made drawings from Akbar's imperial *Ramayana* in 1589, the very year it was finished, and then worked these sketches into paintings over the years in another locality. The *Razm Nama* also may have taken a long time to produce. It is highly probable that it was begun well before the dates recorded on a few individual folios; however, that the style of the Khan Khanan's painters remained relatively consistent for about twenty-five years from the conception of the *Ramayana* to the completion of the *Razm Nama* is amazing.

The Khan Khanan is known to have commissioned illustrations for at least six other manuscripts, including a fable book, Islamic poetry, and the traditional *Shah Nama*.[16] The styles of these works vary somewhat from the Hindu epic illustrations. The poetry scenes particularly are more likely to be in pastel colors and with stiffer, more symmetrically arranged compositions that are meant to imitate Persian painting. None of the other volumes that bear a colophon or single-dated miniature was completed as late as 1617. Abd ar-Rahim's biography was, however, prepared in 1616, and artists are described as being consistently at work in his studio at this time.[17]

1. Several leaves of the manuscript are dated 1616. See, for example, Gray, 1950, p. 158, cat. no. 711; one leaf in the Lewis Collection, Philadelphia, is dated 1617.

2. Badauni, 2: 302.

3. R. A. Dwivedi, p. 84, states that the Khan Khanan was a scholar of Sanskrit as well as Hindi, wrote in Braj and Avadhi, and had Hindu and Muslim friends without distinction. In summary, Dwivedi remarks that universality was the outstanding trait of this courtier.

4. Nadvi, p. 335. Akbari and Jahangiri nobles other than Abd ar-Rahim undoubtedly had book-producing establishments for which certain records exist. In addition to extant illustrated manuscripts of various types, there is some literary information of sub-Imperial libraries. It is difficult, however, to discover which nobles were interested in works of literature or history: many seem to have been absorbed only in theology, medicine, or the sciences. Secondly, it is difficult to find explicitly stated references to illustration of miniatures in this class of atelier and to distinguish which nobles merely supported gilders or border illuminators on their staffs (see Nadvi, pp. 329–45). Historians do, however, unequivocally state that painters existed in big libraries as distinct from gilders ("Big libraries had their own bookbinders and gilders.... A number of painters were attached to almost every big library whose duty it was to illustrate the manuscripts." Bhanu, p. 300). The Khan Khanan's *Ramayana* contains 130 miniatures, and the number of scattered leaves from the *Razm Nama* indicates that it was also an extensively illustrated manuscript. Whether studios other than the Khan Khanan's had the capacity for such projects is an unexamined issue.

5. For Fazl, see Welch, 1963*b*, p. 229 and fig. 16; see also *Sotheby*, 15 July 1970, lot 12; *Sotheby*, 1 Dec. 1969, lot 135; *Sotheby*, 9 July 1974, lot 309; *Christie*, 25 May 1978, lot 92; colophon of *Ramayana* is given in Beach, 1981, p. 135.

6. Beach, 1981, p. 135.

7. Welch, 1963*b*, p. 230.

8. Nadvi, pp. 333–34.

9. Nadim is the orphan (Haq, p. 625; Nadvi, p. 333); Nadim's work occurs in the Khan Khanan's *Khamsa* of Dihlavi in Berlin, in the Freer Gallery's *Ramayana*, and the Khan Khanan's *Khamsa* of Nizami in the British Library.

10. Haq, p. 627.

11. Naik, p. 269.

12. Abu'l Fazl, *Ain*, I: 364.

13. Skelton, 1970, p. 48.

14. The fact that compositions have been borrowed by the Khan Khanan's painters can be checked from comparisons of plates in a forthcoming book by Asok Das on Akbar's *Ramayana* with leaves of the Freer manuscript; see also statement by Ettinghausen, 1961, text for pl. 3.

15. Beach, 1982, p. 135.

16. In addition to the Khan Khanan's *Ramayana* and *Razm Nama*, his atelier also produced the following: Jami's *Panj Ganj*, Chester Beatty Library Ms. 20; *Khamsa* of Nizami, British Library (Titley, nos. 307, 330, and 404(79); *Khamsa* of Dihlavi, Berlin; Laud *Ragamala*, Bodleian Library, Oxford; *Shah Nama*, British Library, Add. 5600; *Zafar Nama*, Sotheby, 1 Dec. 1969, lot 196; possibly *Iyar-i Danish*, Sotheby, 9 July 1976, lot 309.

17. See Haq, 1931*b*, pp. 625–26. Haq quotes the *Maathir-i-Rahimi* on the artist Bahbud: "'He is still alive and passes his time in the library'"; and on the artist Mushfiq: "'He has passed his life from an early age down to the present day in the library.'"

FURTHER READING: Beach, 1981, pp. 128–55; Bhanu; Haq, 1931*b*; Nadvi; Naik; Singh; Zafar.

بسر یا خلاص کرد و خود بر سر اسرالنسال آمد و هر کس که همراه او آمده بود هر یکی سله زیر بر بسته کرد روی
آنلاخنند ارجن چون شنبد که نیل الدجم آمده است و در غضب شده و اینه خود را نیل
بانله بوسر نیل الدجم آمد و پیچ نیر و انداختن نیل الدجم هر جه نیر و داده هم بشکست
و خنده کرده گفت که شما مرا بزنید و بید ارجن آن خنده آن زیر آن نهان شد در غضب
و کمان کما نند و خود را بدست گرفته بنوعِ بر نیل الدجم و مردمش نیر باران کرد که آن
الدجم با رایه و اسپان و فرزندان فیح که نزدیک او بود دند زیر تمام نهان شد س لبا
واصلا هیج ازرایش نماید آن نی شد نیل الدجم از هوش برفت بعد مدتی مدید ارجن روی
آمد با آتش که دامه او بود او داد و بو کفت که نوحالا بیش برو و جنگ لیکن که دیکره طاقت جنگ بیار
نماند آتش بیش رفت و ناگاه آتش در سیاه ارجن افتاد اسب مردمان بسیا د سوختن کرد
و در بوشتهای فیلان جون آتش درگرفت فیلان رو بکبن نهادند و اسیان و سنگران
میکریختن کرفتند و در لباس سپاهیان آتش درگرفت ارجن جون این حال مشاهده کرد بر نری
دلله جون بنداخت باران از آسمان فرو بیشود برکمان نهاده بیند لخت ناگاه بارانی عظیم
باریدن کرفت اما آن باران نتوانست که آتش را بکشد بلک شعله آن زیاده کشت ارجن
جون دید که باران فایده نکرد هر دو دست خود را بر بیشانی نهاده دو جانب آن آتش کرد رو

ربی آتش نبو د بزرگی هیئت من ترا تعظیم میکنم بعد لزان کفت ای آتش ما این چمله
میکنیم فایله آن بیشتر بتو میرسد و این کمان کانداختم تو بر آن این داده و میان ما و تو به
که دوستی است در هر وقت که دشتنان اسب سراجه جدا شتند کرفته اند و مردم ما را
میخواهند که بکشند تو در هر وقت ما دمی سونی این قصه آتش را جمین که شاکر بر باس
بود با جمیمی کرد نبیره ابه من بسر ارجن بود و میکفت جمین ازجمین بیرسید کجی
بود که آتش دامه او دا جدا شله بود و کلام دخنر بود که او را با آتش داده بود دند و من حنی
مانم ام که می شنوم که آتش لینک که ارجن را می سوخنا این قصه را ای سوخنا من بکوجمین کفت

35i *The First Adventure of the White Horse* 64.52

Page size 38 × 22.4 cm (painting covers entire surface).
Some scraping of paint along bottom and top edges; some
faces damaged.

Purchase, James Parmelee Fund

Comparative Material: (A) *First Adventure of the White
Horse*, by Tulsi, leaf from the imperial *Razm Nama*,
Mughal, ca. 1586; Hendley, 1883, pl. XC.

This Cleveland miniature illustrates the first in the series of
the white horse adventures recorded in the *Razm Nama*.
This episodic section of the text deals with an early Hindu
ceremony performed over the course of a year during which
a freely roaming white horse is believed to have accessioned
the territory he crosses in the name of the ruler who owns
him. The horse in the *Razm Nama* adventures belongs to
the Pandava king Yudhishthira, and his movements are observed by Yudhishthira's brother Arjuna. In this tale
Arjuna, who is responsible for defending the horse's symbolic acquisition of territory by combat against various local
forces, confronts King Niladhwaja. Niladhwaja is at first
beaten by Arjuna but calls upon his son-in-law, the fire god
Agni, to help him. Arjuna, retaliating against the fire created by Agni, shoots arrows that miraculously produce water, but nothing avails against the power of the fire god.
However, the Pandava hero recalls that he has been of
service to Agni in a battle against Indra. When reminded of
his debt, Agni voluntarily retires, and the forces of the
white horse prevail.[1]

The composition of this miniature is bisected by the
golden river of fire sent by Agni that crosses the landscape
diagonally. Arjuna stands prominently near the center of
the composition with his hands raised in supplication, apparently begging Agni's favor. The men in armor are dispersed in a vividly colored landscape of blues, pinks, and
browns. Although the artist seems to have been aware that
the distant men shown on the far side of the river should
appear small, he has generally followed the older formula of
making the most significant personages, such as Arjuna,
inordinately large. The subimperial *Razm Nama* leaf, like
pages of the Khan Khanan's *Ramayana*, is more brightly
colored and has more two-dimensional patterns than
Akbar's own versions of the epics. Here there is, however,
some concept of spatial breadth, which derives from imperial art and is skillfully manipulated to give the sense of
Agni's vast powers of destruction. Compositionally, the
Razm Nama is somewhat more complex than the *Ramayana*, which commonly has more limited backgrounds and
fewer figures.

Both this *Razm Nama* page and the following Cleveland
leaf are among the examples that show that the Khan Khanan's artists were not depending on imperial compositions
for models.[2] The imperial version of the first white horse
adventure (A) depicts a crowded battleground with the opposing groups locked in close combat and fire roaring up
among warriors on the right in a sheet that engulfs and
unites their bodies. In the later *Razm Nama* scene, since

Figure 35i, detail.

the artist has perceived the tale differently and has chosen
to interpret Agni's fire as a miraculous river, he has not had
to depict the antagonistic forces in motion but has shown
them stalemated on either side of the flames. Such a composition with forms arranged in a tentative, static manner is
typical not only of the Khan Khanan's artists but also of the
entire subimperial idiom. By contrast, the imperial composition has the swirling crowd configurations, strong
unified rhythm, and other hallmarks of the sophisticated
Mughal style developed in the 1580s. If numerous figures
are depicted in the *Razm Nama* of ca. 1616, they tend to be
treated in isolated groups—as, for example, in this Cleveland picture with its several separate figure-islands. The
color scheme of bright blues and pinks, the huge rubberlike
rocks, and the hesitant figures in this Cleveland leaf reveal
the mixture of diffidence and spiritedness typical of the
Khan Khanan's painters. In spite of a certain stiffness, the
Razm Nama and *Ramayana* are both animated, since the
artists were too inexperienced to solve all the problems of
illustration by using stereotypes. Their approach is therefore ingenious, both when conveying details of the natural
world and when solving unusual narrative problems.

1. Hendley, 1883, 4: 31.
2. In addition to the Cleveland examples of the Khan Khanan's
Razm Nama, there are other episodes that can be contrasted with
their imperial counterparts. *Sotheby,* 1 Dec. 1969, lot 135,
though picturing the same episode as Hendley, 1883, 4: pl. CIV,
is not based on its design. *Sotheby,* 15 July 1970, lot 12, is also
distinct from the corresponding imperial miniature shown in
Hendley, 1883, 4: pl. CXIII.

117

مزهبين از مردم درخشنبید نا آن جواهر جود ستارکی آسمان می‌نمود و حایلهای مروارید و لعلوبا
را با آت کلهای بی‌خوش بو برکردن ارجن و دیگر راجهاو بزرگان انداختند و برسر هرکلام ازان
براجهاو بزرگان خوان خوان جواهر و زر و کل تثار و میکردند و بجر باهن یافتند زنه بیکه در بکر
در هر بیش ارجن دادند و بیت دوانت کرد و گفتند که شما محذوم و صاحب و ولی نعمت و منم اگر چه
ازشما متولد شده ام و شما بیدا میداد اما من غلام شما یم و ما دومن چیزیکار است که برتربکن
انک قدم مبارک شما باو رسید و بود او از صورت بنهنی برآمده آدم شده و نام من
بیوباهن است و من ناداننه ابن اسب و کروفته بودم حالا ابن ولایت و ملک نشور
و مال و خزینه ابنخ در تقرقی منست هم بیشکشتی شما است و من غلام شما یم و آمده م
که غلامی شما بیکنم و بد ملازمت شما شمشیر میزده باشم آمده ام و آدم که بنظر رحمت و عنایت
در من نگاه کنند و جنابخ و جنابخ فرزندان شما در ملازمت شما هستند مراهم نظور در
خلاصت نگاه داد ید بجر باهن ابن سخن گفتنه باز سوخود را برهنه کرد و دندوت کرد
بعد از ان بیش آمده سرود پای ارجن نهاد و گفت امید وادم که بدست خودسر
از خاک بردار بد یداز من درمیان عالمیان سراز اران بروم بروم بروم وجوبنا سی و انسا
و هنس اللدجو و سانک و دیگر بزرگان بیش ارجن آمده کفتند که ابن فرزند شما سجرا
بدست مرحمت سوی او بار از خاک برداد بدا ینخبین بسری بیچ باد شاه کردن داشت
است شما جوا بار و بنظر شفقت و مرحمت نظر بکنید و مهر بدید و با رو مند اوید
جون خداو تد نعالی بلا یبی بار جن نقد برکرده بود و مقادر شده بود که او کشنه شود
در خاطر ارجن انداخت که از سخنی آن بزرگان در غضب آمده و پای خود را برسر باهن
جنان محکم زد که دوی آن جوان بر زمین خورد بر زمین سراز ان زمین برداشتبنو و کفت
ای بدرکنا من جبت من کرنو جبسبر من نسی

35ii *Vabhruvahana Approaches Arjuna*   60.44

Page size 35 × 24 cm (painting irregular). Dark staining, tears along bottom edge, some paint removed on left edge. Text on reverse.

Purchase, Mr. and Mrs. William H. Marlatt Fund

Ex collections: Beckett, Heeramaneck.

Published: M. Marcus, "A Page from a Dated Razmnama," *CMAB* 48 (January 1961): 13–15.

Comparative Material: (A) *Arjuna Spurns Vabhruvahana*, by Daswanth and Miskin, a leaf from the imperial *Razm Nama*, Mughal, ca. 1586; Hendley, 1833, 4: pl. C. (B) *Arjuna Spurns Vabhruvahana*, leaf from a *Razm Nama*, subimperial Mughal, dated 1598; British Library, Or. 12076, f. 44a, unpublished.

The second Cleveland leaf of the Khan Khanan's *Razm Nama* illustrates another portion of Arjuna's defense of the white horse. In this seventh adventure, which takes place in the country of Manipura, Arjuna is submissively approached by the king, Vabhruvahana, who offers his allegiance. Arjuna, however, scorns the offer and turns away from Vabhruvahana, who is in truth his son. Vabhruvahana then kills his father, but, after learning the truth of the relationship, goes on a quest that restores Arjuna to life.[1]

In this miniature, Arjuna kneels on a rug facing Vabhruvahana, who is shown as a very young man and weaponless, in contrast to the mature Arjuna armed with his miraculous bow, a sword, and *katar*. Two brahmins(?) with books and writing boxes have come to speak on Vabhruvahana's behalf and kneel with hands outstretched to Arjuna. The difference between the Khan Khanan's earlier *Ramayana* and this *Razm Nama* of ca. 1616 lies mainly in the style of figures. Here, the man in the lower right behind the horses, the man on the left by the tree, and Arjuna himself all have recognizable Jahangiri traits. Like these men, the horses are treated somewhat more naturalistically than they might have been in the Khan Khanan's *Ramayana*.

In the imperial version of the episode drawn by Daswanth (A)—a painter renowned for the power of his compositions—the dramatic potential of the encounter is fully exploited. Arjuna, naked to the waist, is shown stepping on the back of the kneeling Vabhruvahana, who has lost his crown and is falling forward with his hair streaming behind him. This is a much more intricate composition than that of the Khan Khanan's *Razm Nama* example, where much of the pictorial space is occupied by text. In Daswanth's miniature numerous attendants are depicted who convey the idea of Vabhruvahana's influence and nobility as well as heighten the suspense of the quarrel between the two. Vabhruvahana's disarranged hair and swirling shawl along with Arjuna's draperies and the stamp of his foot effectively suggest the impending chaos and tragedy. The landscape is extensive, complex, and rhythmically organized in comparison with that of the Cleveland miniature.

Though the stiffly posed figures in the Cleveland scene are appealing, the illustration has not been conceptualized with any intensity. Whereas Daswanth visualized the incident in the most artistically challenging manner, the later, more limited artist has avoided any development of the father-son confrontation despite its being specifically described in the text. (The meeting between Arjuna and Vabhruvahana is so generalized that it could be any encounter between dominant and submissive figures.)

Still another *Razm Nama* illustration of the Vabhruvahana story (B, illus.) is significant because the manuscript was produced between the two previously discussed versions and is based on the imperial illustration by Daswanth. This illustration from the dispersed *Razm Nama* completed in 1598 is, however, much more stilted than Daswanth's scene. Arjuna is poised to step on the back of his kneeling son, but the activity is frozen rather than tumultuous. This *Razm Nama* manuscript was prepared by imperial artists of mediocre ability in conjunction with artists possibly in the employ of a noble who was the patron.[2] When this illustration is compared with the Cleveland scene, it demonstrates that the Khan Khanan's seventeenth-century *Razm Nama* was indeed an independent production and that his artists were not aware of the imperial designs used as models for the 1598 volume.

Figure 35*ii*(B), *Arjuna Spurns Vabhruvahana*, from a *Razm Nama*, Or. 12076, fol. 44a. The British Library, London. Reproduced by permission of The British Library Board.

The 1598 volume was probably done sometime following the command given by Akbar for nobles to copy imperial volumes in order to familiarize themselves with the Hindu classics. Badauni implies that many such volumes were done (though not necessarily illustrated). The instability of the nobles, who forfeited their possessions at death or on losing *mansabdar* status, indicates that numerous illustrated texts, which have long since disappeared, were probably done for these officials.

1. Hendley, 1883, 4: 32.

2. For information on the 1598 *Razm Nama* see Gray, 1950, p. 147; also R. Pinder-Wilson, "A Persian Translation of the *Mahabharata*," *BMQ* 20, no. 3 (1956): 62–65, esp. p. 65, fn. 7. It has been conjectured by Skelton (1976, pp. 250–51) that the unknown artists working on this project were young recruits belonging to painter families who were starting in the imperial atelier. This hypothesis is based on inscriptions listing these painters as "sons of...”; however, in only a few cases are the fathers' names identical to those of Akbari artists. Since these names generally do not reappear on later Akbari manuscripts, it seems likely that most painters worked temporarily in the imperial studio for this project but were regularly in the hire of the influential *mansabdar* who had requested the *Razm Nama*. Some of the names are identical to artists working for the Khan Khanan. (The artists Kamal and Qasim worked on the Khan Khanan's *Ramayana* and British Library Add. 5600 attributable to this noble's studio as well as the 1598 *Razm Nama*. Painters named Bhagwati, Shamal, and Dhannu worked on the 1598 *Razm Nama* and Add. 5600.) If this official indeed commissioned the manuscript, which would have been consistent with his Hindu sympathies, the style was unrelated to that of his later *Razm Nama* volume of ca. 1616/17.

36 *Lovers Embracing*   71.91

Popular Mughal, probably done at Bikaner, ca. 1630–50, 14.9 × 10.1 cm, 24 × 16.8 cm with border. Painting cut out and remounted in smooth beige paper of the type used in Bikaner.

Purchase, Andrew R. and Martha Holden Jennings Fund

Ex collection: MacDonald.

Comparative Material: (A) *Lovers and Attendants*, Mughal, ca. 1620–30; Arnold and Wilkinson, pl. 54. (B) *A Girl Playing the Tambur*, Rajasthan, Bikaner, ca. 1650; *Sotheby*, 11 Dec. 1968, lot 19. (C) *Jahangir Celebrating Holi*, Mughal, ca. 1620–30; Arnold and Wilkinson, pl. 56. (D) *Women in a Garden*, Popular Mughal, Bikaner, ca. 1660; *Metropolitan Museum of Art Bulletin* (Autumn 1978), p. 45.

In this miniature a prince in a wide Jahangiri turban embraces and kisses his mistress who holds a wine bottle and cup. A gold *pan* box and shallow dish are beside her. The two are seated out of doors on a carpeted dais against a sumptuous brocaded pillow. The blue carpet has a very beautiful though irregular pattern not characteristic of rug design. Richly dressed in contrasting pastels tied with gold sashes, the couple is waited on in this idyllic setting by an unattentive maid holding a fan.

Scenes of lovers embracing were productions of the Mughal court with such appeal for artists of other centers that they were borrowed and imitated at all levels from the smaller courts to the bazaars.[1] Despite variations of style,

Figure 35*ii*, detail.

Figure 36, detail.

their compositional origins are recognizable because Rajasthani paintings illustrating love poetry treat themes symbolically, while the embracing lovers of Mughal scenes mirror an essentially realistic situation. The poses of lovers in Rajput *ragamala* scenes are governed by classifications and rules not followed in the Mughal scenes.

The Cleveland painting is a sensitive combination of several styles in a single picture of romantic love. The composition and the delicacy of feeling captured by the artist originate in Mughal miniatures such as those by Balchand or Govardhan (A).[2] There probably was a Mughal prototype whose design was almost exactly copied by the miniaturist of the Cleveland work, as is demonstrated by such details as the prince's face. It is rendered in a complex fashion, but the artist's misalignment of the eyes and the misunderstood foreshortening of facial features prove that he was adhering closely to a model rather than relying on his own invention.

The precision, the shading of drapery, and the round fleshy forms evident in this miniature must have been inspired by the Mughal tradition (A, C). The lush shades of heliotrope, violet, and orange as well as the blooming flowers across the foreground come, however, from Deccani sources. Such a combination is characteristic of Bikaner, although few comparisons exist for this particular refined style. One related example with the same rich treatment of details but with figures of a more recognizably Bikaner type was originally part of the same album as the Cleveland painting (B, illus.). Several other paintings in eclectic styles (including [37]) were also part of this group of works mainly attributed to Bikaner when it was sold at auction.[3] Many mid-seventeenth-century miniatures closely related to imperial Mughal compositions have mixed influences and are

121

Figure 36(B). *A Girl Playing the Tambur.* Photograph courtesy of Sotheby Parke Bernet & Co., London.

difficult to attribute, but they were probably produced in Bikaner, since its artists acquired sophistication through the state's unusual connections with the imperial court.

In the Cleveland picture the grapevine entwined around the tree trunk is a symbol of love and union that also appears in other miniatures.[4] The petallike segments of cloth on the women's bodices, common in paintings from the Akbari period on, originated as fastenings, but quickly became decorative in nature. Finally, the women's pointed skirt reflects a fashion that was unusual by the time this miniature was painted.

1. Khandalavala and M. Chandra, 1960, no. 18, fig. 27; E. Kuhnel, *Moghul Malerei* (Berlin: G. Mann, 1955), pl. 4.

2. Another miniature that has obvious parallels to the Cleveland romantic scene is one that has been called *Jahangir Embracing Nur Jahan* and attributed (perhaps incorrectly) to Govardhan, originally by Stchoukine (see "Portraits Moghuls," *RAA* 7 [1931/32]: 171).

3. *Sotheby,* 13 Dec. 1965, lots 29–36.

4. Pinder-Wilson, 1976, no. 129; Arnold and Grohmann, pl. 86.

Figure 37(A). *Jahangir in the Harem During Holi.* Chester Beatty Library, Dublin (titled: *Jahangir Playing Holi with the Ladies of His Palace*).

37 *Girls Spraying Each Other at Holi* 71.83

Rajasthan, Bikaner, ca. 1640–50, 19 × 12.5 cm. Very slightly rubbed; pasted to several sheets of paper; probably trimmed.

Purchase, Andrew R. and Martha Holden Jennings Fund

Ex collection: MacDonald.

Comparative Material: (A) *Jahangir in the Harem during Holi,* Mughal, ca. 1620–30; Arnold and Wilkinson, pl. 56. (B) *Megha Raga,* Rajasthan, Bikaner, ca. 1640; *Sotheby,* 2 May 1971, lot 143.

The harem women in this miniature are in a garden with water channels celebrating the spring festival of *holi* in typical fashion. Several play tambourines, while in the foreground a girl shoots a squirt gun of colored water as her companion fills another. On the right three women fight playfully to smear each other with red powder, as do some of the others in this large circle of figures. This scene—painted quite freely—borrows its foreground from a more complex Mughal picture (A, illus.). The provincial artist seems to have been interested solely in capturing the spirit of the harem girls, which he does with more animation and naturalness than is expressed in the original. Though unable to follow the most complicated postures of the Mughal miniature exactly, he has given some of the girls more graceful hand poses. Most of the figures are copied in small groups, with the less significant personages of the Mughal prototype omitted. The compositions of the groups are so specific as to be unmistakably borrowed.

Unfortunately, the artist failed to plot any overall design for his work. His interest or imagination gave way after doing the figures, and he concluded the miniature weakly, with no hint of the carpets or the rich pavilion wall of the original. The two girls at the top of the picture who are presumably his own inventions are less easily handled than those of the foreground circle. The disparity of scale between the large women of the foreground and the cramped garden shows the miniature—a small work—to be a kind of experiment only roughly completed.

This work is linked to the previously discussed painting [36] by similar dependence on Mughal composition and by the fact that both came from the same album of assorted miniatures.[1] The style employed here is, however, a more purely Rajasthani one. Though familiar with Mughal painting, the artist of this miniature was less skilled in adaptation and has struggled to grasp the essentials of his prototype. His usual style is seen in the garden trees and the two figures at the top of the composition that do not appear in the Mughal model. Both figures and vegetation are close to the rendering in a *ragamala* combining Bikaner with Mughal elements (B).

The group of miniatures (including this one) that were sold together at auction mainly classified as coming from Bikaner are in rather diverse styles and depict varied subjects such as a bird, or the love scene of catalogue number 36.[2] Several, like this Cleveland painting, are abstracted from known Mughal works. They demonstrate the eclecticism of Bikaner art and its various compositional or stylistic links with Mughal painting.

1. *Sotheby*, 13 Dec. 1965, lots 31, 36.
2. Ibid., lots 29–36.

Figure 37.

IV. Late Imperial, Provincial Mughal, Deccani, Kashmiri, and Company Style Painting

Late Imperial Painting

By the end of Jahangir's reign Mughal court protocol had become stifling. Since the two succeeding emperors, Shah Jahan (r. 1627–58) and Aurangzeb (r. 1658–1707), were both rather cold men who apparently welcomed formality as a means of holding themselves aloof, the constricted atmosphere at the court grew increasingly oppressive. In addition, ceremony was used to mask the escalating economic problems of the dynasty, which reached catastrophic proportions by the end of the seventeenth century. And because the political system had been organized so that the nobility was kept insecure, anxiety-ridden individuals willingly conformed to any social conventions required by the emperor.

Miniature painters tended to follow the trend toward artificiality in the court, so that by about 1650 it is unusual to find a courtier portrait that shows any genuine spirit reflected in the sitter. It is surprising, therefore, that certain pictures done between 1660 and 1680 are fresh, original, and relatively informal. The portrait of an unknown young woman [38] that was presumably commissioned by a noble is an example of the tasteful, personally meaningful commissions being made by aristocrats. In fact, Aurangzeb himself seems to have been a relatively interested, intelligent patron during the early years of his reign.

While his father, Shah Jahan, was imprisoned, Aurangzeb merely attempted to maintain stability and consolidate his hold on the throne he had usurped. The miniatures that have survived from this period are slightly better than those commissioned by his father. However, after Shah Jahan's death in 1666, the emperor took steps that revealed how deeply he was influenced by Islamic fundamentalist reformers. In 1668 he dismissed musicians from the court and attempted to banish them from the homes of nobles living in the capital, ordering instruments broken if music was heard. He attempted to impose other moral restrictions but without much success, and he reinstated old prejudices against Hindus, such as requiring them to pay a large poll tax. In 1680 painters were ousted from the court, but whether they received the same harsh treatment as musicians is not recorded.

Judging from the fact that Aurangzeb's successor, Bahadur Shah, during his short reign from 1707–12 had some creditable paintings done in a style that continued the imperial tradition of Shah Jahan and Aurangzeb, court painting was probably never completely terminated. (Music for court ceremonies is known to have been maintained.[1]) However, for more than twenty-five years, the number of paintings produced in Delhi must have been severely curtailed (especially when Aurangzeb moved to the Deccan in 1680 in order to superintend his wars there). Painters went to Rajput courts both in Rajasthan and in the Pahari area, where their influence on local styles was profound.

In the first decade of the eighteenth century the imperial painting style was still based on that of Shah Jahan's magnificent regnal history, the *Shah Jahan Nama*, but was no longer very naturalistic. An equestrian portrait of Aurangzeb done either in his late reign or in Bahadur Shah's short reign is a good example of the clean, precise, but very limited type of painting that can be associated with the court [41]. A slightly later picture of drugged *yogis* [42] may indicate that the nobility had some imagination and freedom to commission informal or caricatured subjects in the early part of the century.

By the time the prohibition on miniature painting was lifted in the reign of Aurangzeb's son Bahadur Shah, the position of the Mughal emperors had shifted dramatically. Bahadur Shah himself had little power, and his successors were tools of unscrupulous ministers who did not flinch at murder within the imperial family to forward their objectives. In this period, patronage of painting was confused and many styles were prevalent. Individual works such as the composition of drugged *yogis* are often very interesting, but in general miniature painting was tied to political conditions. Painters were undoubtedly working blindly and hoping for strong patrons who would provide adequate direction.

The emperor Muhammad Shah, while not intelligent enough to govern decisively, at least had the shrewdness to survive a long reign (1719–48), during which he reestablished an imperial style that was then carried by painters to the provincial areas of Oudh and Bengal. The Muhammad Shah style preserved the clean, decorative contours that had evolved in Bahadur Shah's period but also frequently looked back to Shah Jahan's golden age. Subjects such as intimate terrace scenes were more superficial, less noble or stately than before, however. There was a new emphasis on the use of white in miniatures to provide striking contrasts with a few vivid colors.

Provincial Mughal Painting

As imperial power disintegrated after Muhammad Shah's death, painters migrated from the court to the provincial Mughal areas. In the later eighteenth century Lucknow in Oudh assumed the role of chief imperial city; its painters refined the Muhammad Shah style for the nawabs there. These toughened men were ambitious de facto rulers, originally subordinate to the emperor, who attempted independently to keep their territories under more orderly control than Delhi. Even Oudh and Bengal succumbed to the pressure of events, however, and opposed by the British either forfeited power or held it, subject to foreign approval.

Paintings for the *nawabs* were produced in the Bengali capital of Murshidabad only from about 1750 to 1765, after which political and economic disaster forced painters to work for wealthy Bengali families or for the British. The high point of miniature production under the *wazirs* (or rulers) of Oudh, chiefly Shuja ud-Daula (r. 1754–75), extended from about 1750 to 1775, many of the most significant works being done shortly after real political power in the area had been seized by the British following the 1764 battle of Baksar.

The Cleveland Museum has a selection of different types of painting done in either Lucknow or the short-term Oudhi capital (from 1765 to 1775) of Faizabad. Lucknow was one of North India's most urbane centers almost wholly devoted to pleasures of gaming, sport, and the arts. The fact that the miniatures not only echo the taste of the nawabs but also of the city's foppish bourgeoisie is an unusual circumstance, since culture in the Mughal period did not generally center around city life.

The inhabitants of Lucknow pursued enjoyment as zealously as if it were a vocation and developed standards of connoisseurship for even the most obscure pursuits. Their artistic interests lay primarily in dance, drama, poetry recital, and other performing arts that could be savored, criticized, and gossiped about collectively by an urban audience. Since the city seems to have been as devoted to assembly and to conversation about its pleasures as it was to the activities themselves, the condensed, intensely private world of the true miniature painter became slightly outdated.

In such an extroverted, fashion-conscious environment, it was inevitable that the decorative aspects of miniatures would become accentuated, both for status and for enjoyment. Among the best Lucknow pictures are those that are refined and extremely detailed, such as the Divali night scene with golden splashes of fireworks lighting up the background [46]. Such compositions involving women were probably the most popular eighteenth-century type, and perhaps because female activities were severely restricted in this period, the miniature sometimes gave fulfillment to dreams of bathing in hidden streams or wandering in forest glades [48]. The Muslim tradition did not usually associate feminine seclusion with tension, however, and in contrast to Rajput painters who depicted solitary heroines pining in the wilderness, the late Mughal artists generally showed groups of pretty women relaxing in leisure activities.

There are few dated Oudhi works that would permit the development of a chronology, but in general the looser, flatter compositions seem to postdate those with tight, precise, Muhammad Shahi details. Among the painters, Mihr Chand, who incorporated both Western modeling and seventeeth-century Mughal motifs in his eclectic work, was most significant. There were few Lucknow painters who did not imitate some of the features that he developed by studying old Mughal paintings or Western engravings. Second in influence was Mir Kalan Khan, who had worked for Muhammad Shah and had brought his nervously twisting, manneristic style sprinkled with bizarre Western touches to the Oudh capital. A lesser-known artist, Aquil Khan [47], typifies the Oudh characteristic of maintaining several styles simultaneously and shifting from one to another without infusing personality into any composition.

At the end of the century, when the country had been pacified under British control, a weakened imperial following crept back to the traditional capital of Delhi, which had been isolated by so many different clashes during the eighteenth century. Here during the first decade of the nineteenth century, under Akbar Shah II (r. 1806–37), artists evolved a manner of painting that was to remain unvaried in hundreds of examples. The Akbar Shah miniatures almost always copied other compositions, such as those from Shah Jahan's royal albums, although copies of Hindu themes such as *ragamalas* were also produced. All have heavy, stippled shading and regularized Western facial features obviously borrowed from cheap English or French prints prevalent in India at that time (see [51]).

Despite some life flowing back to the court, imperial Delhi was not destined to recover its artistic eminence. The crises of the previous century had been too demoralizing. Nineteenth-century visitors noted that although imperial ceremonies were still carried out, they seemed tawdry, and that Shah Jahan's buildings were dirty and severely vandalized.

The vale of Kashmir, visited by the emperors Akbar, Jahangir, and Shah Jahan in the seventeenth century for recreation, also attracted Muslim immigrants whose talents enriched the court. Persian poets especially, but also a few artists, came to the area drawn by the patronage, the surroundings, and the valley's reputation as a center of Islamic scholarship. The paintings done here by immigrant artists were often composed of Persian motifs with common conventionalizations: figures with long, squinting eyes, and curling locks of hair over the ears [55] were popular. Because Kashmir did not sponsor a unified type of miniature production (except on a folkish level), its paintings cannot properly be termed those of a school.

The British filled an artistic vacuum on the subcontinent, since political conditions had seriously eroded traditional patronage. Their curiosity and supervisory discipline—the same qualities that had fostered good work under Akbar and Jahangir—produced a resurgence of originality in the eighteenth and nineteenth centuries by artists eager for challenging assignments. Natural-history subjects especially, but also genre scenes of various types, are the most vital works. The British prompted artists to observe their own environment with scientific accuracy, which painters had not done since the days of the early Mughal rulers.

The term "Company style" painting can be generally interpreted as that done during the period of British dominance that bears traces of the British watercolor style. The Indian artist learned these new watercolor techniques in a variety of ways: (1) he might be trained by British matrons who wished him to paint scenes of native customs, occupational groups, or flora and fauna in a way they found acceptable; (2) he might be employed by the East India Company to do drafting or some other art-related occupation and find that he could produce watercolor scenes after hours; or (3) he might be a traditional artist who tried to learn new styles because only such innovation allowed him to continue making money. Although the British were the wealthy group in the nineteenth century, paintings that could be considered Company style works were also done in the watercolor manner for Indian patrons. Such works contrast with the late Delhi copies of imperial miniatures or *ragamalas* that were affected by European prints but basically continued the Indian miniature tradition.

The Company paintings done in transparent pigments with broad brushstrokes had traits exactly opposite to those of previous miniatures with their carefully prepared surfaces and minute brushstrokes. The skills of the traditional miniaturist had, however, been undermined in the eighteenth century by carelessness and tasteless commerical production, so that technically many of the Company paintings are far superior to the works they superceded.

1. R. C. Majumdar, p. 234.

38 *Jewel Portrait of a Young Girl* 68.71

Drawing, Mughal, ca. 1660, 3.3 × 2.4 cm, 4.6 × 3.8 cm
with borders. Torn, cracked, rubbed.

Gift of the Arthur L. Parker Foundation

Comparative Material: (A) *Portrait of a European Woman*,
Mughal, 1650–60; Stchoukine, 1929*b*, pl. XXIVa. (B)
Lovers in a Garden, by Balchand, Mughal, ca. 1645;
Welch, 1973, no. 65.

In this tiny oval drawing an appealingly innocent young
woman with long, flowing hair is posed in her jewels and a
tall *chaghtai* cap. In contrast to the generalized depictions
of beauties with impressively dramatic profiles, this woman
is more carefully rendered in a three-quarter view that
reveals her wide cheeks and rounded nose. The fact that she
is graceful and dignified but not strikingly handsome is, like
the three-quarter rendering, evidence of the artist's intention to create a portrait.

The simple jewel miniature has been drawn in an unusually delicate style with a slightly geometric but very sensitive line. This balance between illustration and abstraction
is one reached shortly after the middle of the seventeenth
century. The same drawing style and feminine facial type
also occur in another miniature of the early Aurangzeb period (A, illus.); since relatively few examples of paintings
exist from Aurangzeb's early reign, each instance revealing
freshness and artistic originality is significant. The un-
studied quality of the Cleveland representation is particularly intriguing because female depictions done during Shah
Jahan's reign are often rather cold and formal. In general,
only works by the emperor's major artists give such a charming, personalized view of female subjects (B).

The accuracy of female portraiture is an unresolved issue
in Mughal art (see [44]); however, an unaffected sketch like
this Cleveland miniature, despite abstraction, is more likely
to represent a particular woman than one of the much-
copied feminine idealizations. Though it would not be worn
in public, the jewel portrait may well have been a gift for a
betrothed man or young husband.

Figure 38.

Figure 38(A). *Portrait of a European Woman*. Bibliothèque Nationale,
Paris, fol. V. 6200, pl. XXIVa (titled: *European Lady in Red*).

39 *Portrait of Mirza Muizz*   17.1067

Mughal, ca. 1680–1700, 22 × 13.4 cm. Background paint
somewhat scraped. Inscription: "Mirza Muizz."
Gift of The John Huntington Art and Polytechnic Trust

The inscription identifies the subject as Mirza Muizz, a
courtier of Persian descent who held various offices in the
Aurangzeb era. From the length of the *jama* and the long-
waisted proportion of the body, the depiction can be judged
to date from about 1680–1700. The mirza is wearing a fur-
trimmed coat, originally a Persian type but adapted to Indian dress; both the coat and the pose, common in courtier
miniatures of the period, are comparable to a slightly earlier
portrait of Prince Murad Baksh [29].

Figure 39.

40 *Drawing of an Elephant*   69.65

Mughal, ca. 1700, 12.8 × 18.1 cm, 20 × 25.3 cm with border. Eighteenth-century dark blue border with gold flecks.

Purchase, Edward L. Whittemore Fund

Comparative Material: (A) *Drawing of an Elephant and Mahout*, Mughal, ca. 1670; *Sotheby*, 12 Dec. 1972, lot 37.

This drawing is somewhat like that of a miniature done a few years earlier (A). The artist of the Cleveland sketch has attempted to depict the elephant's mass and weight mainly by means of an outline. Apparently he has not intended to capture any particular mood of energy or wildness, as in earlier versions of the subject, but has worked from a purely descriptive standpoint. No motion is implied: the elasticity understood by Jahangir's animal portraitists has been neglected. Emphasis is on the firm outline and the refined but dry contour lines.

Figure 40.

41 *The Emperor Aurangzeb* 71.81
    on Horseback

Mughal, ca. 1690–1710, 30.5 × 22.3 cm.
Purchase, Andrew R. and Martha Holden Jennings Fund
Ex collection: MacDonald.
Comparative Material: (A) *Equestrian Portrait of Dara Shikoh*, ca. 1633; Skelton, 1976, no. V71, pl. 128.
(B) *Bahadur Shah Enthroned, Surrounded by His Sons*, Mughal, ca. 1710; Binney, 1973, no. 71.

In this miniature the elderly Aurangzeb sits resolutely astride his horse holding a spear. His disciplined pose shows that the emperor attempted to maintain the military stoicism for which he was famed (and cursed) into the last part of his life, although in his final years he is commonly shown bent with age and carried in a litter. Here his haloed face is fixed in the vacant, strained expression typical of his later portraits. His horse is ornamented with a rich saddle blanket, an aigrette, a necklace, and a long switch caught in a jeweled martingale. His attendant—who because of his proximity to Aurangzeb and his resemblance is probably one of the emperor's family—holds a jeweled parasol as a sign of regal power. The portrait is a strange mixture of the austere and the lush, which is typical of this transitional era at the turn of the century; some of the colors, for example, are soft and sensuous in contrast to the rather bleak composition. The background is pale aqua, with a few lines of cloud traced in orange or lavender at the top of the scene. The absence of any other setting seems an unconscious reference by the artist to the severe, isolating effect of autocracy that was finally becoming apparent in the court.

Though Aurangzeb had disrupted the imperial portrait tradition by his rejection of artists in 1680, this equestrian picture is very much in the mainstream of Mughal painting. Its clean, luminous formality can be viewed not only in relation to past works but also as an important stage in the continuing development of painting under Muhammad Shah. It is especially interesting because it celebrates the grand and glorious aspects of Mughal sovereignty near the end of Aurangzeb's life or directly after his death, when other depictions of the emperor—small, plain, and almost completely repetitious—show him as a stooped, broken man. Despite the fact that Aurangzeb's Deccani wars had torn the empire asunder, artists were thus still capable of creating miniatures that maintained the illusion of imperial prestige.

If there is not a marked contrast in its elegance when compared to an earlier equestrian depiction of Dara Shikoh (A), however, there are some discernible stylistic alterations. Although all the stylizations of the later period are present in a basic way in the portrait of Dara, the process of abstraction and of modeling arbitrarily to create luminosity has been carried much further in the Cleveland miniature. For example, while the tightly arched neck of Dara's mount is almost a pure curve, the resolution of form into geometry has become more absolute in the portrait of Aurangzeb.

There is little evidence available to distinguish whether paintings were done at the end of Aurangzeb's reign or during the short reign of his son Bahadur Shah (r. 1707–12); this emperor apparently revived official painting on a modest scale, but Aurangzeb himself may not have maintained as absolute a prohibition on the arts as was once assumed from contemporary statements. A portrait of Bahadur Shah surrounded by his sons (B) is more detailed than the Cleveland picture, but the two miniatures, which may have been done at the same time, have a similar atmosphere of formalism, suspended animation, and remoteness.

Figure 41.

42 *Opium Smokers Served Melons*   71.90
     and Bread

Mughal, ca. 1700–1720, 18.5 × 29 cm. Paint rubbed and
scraped, lower left section torn and replaced, probably
cropped along left side, face of figure in white seated in
right foreground restored.

Purchase, Andrew R. and Martha Holden Jennings Fund
Ex collection: MacDonald.

Published: Repr. in Leach, 1981, fig. 163.

Comparative Material: (A) *Musician and Servants,* by
Bichitr, Mughal, ca. 1635–40; Stchoukine, 1929*b*,
pl. XLIV. (B) *Intoxication,* Deccan, Hyderabad, ca. 1700;
Wiener Gallery, *Indian Miniature Painting* (New York,
1974), no. 9. (C) *Opium Smokers Served Melons and
Bread,* Provincial Mughal, Lucknow, ca. 1770; Freer
Gallery of Art 07.276R, unpublished.

This composition weaves more than thirty figures of differing types together in an ingenious manner with a great deal
of lively characterization and movement. Most of the subjects are *yogis* who are probably being entertained at the

behest of a ruler or official, since such a gesture was a
common way of appearing magnanimous and gaining spiritual merit. Servants bearing loaves of flat bread climb the
steps to a porchlike structure covered with straw matting as
two of the official's musicians look on. A man who seems to
be one of the host's representatives is seated in the right
foreground with his shield before him smoking a hookah. A
young man of some social importance wearing a gold-
flowered *patka* is passing out melons to the guests, while a
servant carries a tray of them on the right.

The *yogis* themselves are of various types—some, like
the two women seated near the center of the picture, retain
their worldly status and are obviously intended to appear
refined; others, like the old man in a feathered headdress
seated in the lower left, are similar to figures caricatured by
other artists as cranks or religious hypocrites. They are the
most emaciated and dissolute of the *yogis*, clearly wasted by
their years of addiction. The artist has depicted his subjects
in different drugged states induced either by the *bhang*
prepared in basins or smoked through hookahs. Several
figures on the right, for example, are bent in stupefaction.

Figure 42.

This subject matter originates in both the Mughal and Persian traditions. The Mughal interest in genre is revealed by the background vignettes in Akbari history manuscripts or the treatment of painters, papermakers, and others around the borders of Jahangiri albums. Only a few miniatures, however, are devoted entirely to what could be termed genre (A). Large compositions with numerous figures of an earthy type such as those in the Cleveland miniature are unusual. The Persian tradition from which this painting derives is one of portraying drinking or drug scenes that include different stages of intoxication. These illustrations, however, are rarely naturalistic; instead, they reflect the sensations of intoxication rather than the observations of an onlooker (B). In the Cleveland painting a clear sense of environment is conveyed by the hills and buildings in the background. The figures are not shown whirling metaphysically in space but are surveyed from a human point of view, with emphasis on the serving of food and the physical state of the smokers.[1] The two servants who bend over trays piled with flat bread are the most obvious examples of the artist's interest in genre, but other figures are similarly depicted.

A comparison of this picture with another version from the Freer Gallery (C, illus.) shows that both human and abstract qualities are masterfully realized in the Cleveland leaf. The artist of the Cleveland miniature avoided stereotypes of bony ascetics and created much more developed characters: the man carrying a tray of melons in the upper right and the bearded man in the upper left are two examples.

Figure 42, detail.

Figure 42, detail.

Figure 42(C). *Opium Smokers Served Melons and Bread*. Courtesy of the Freer Gallery of Art, Smithsonian Institution, Washington, DC.

133

Figure 42, detail.

The Freer painting is in an album of Mughal and Provincial Mughal miniatures, the majority of which are recognizably copied from other sources. The confused logic and carelessness of the Freer drawing indicate that this version could not be the original of a fairly complex composition. The artist of the Cleveland page, while far from being a mere copyist, may also have followed a previous composition, since the practice of repeating designs was quite common in the eighteenth century. The quality of the Cleveland miniature, therefore, arises from the painter's characterization of types more than from uniqueness of concept.

Like many of the best early eighteenth-century painters, the artist of the Cleveland scene had a great talent for measured, dignified line drawing. He was exceptionally skillful in enhancing the ordered and rhythmic qualities of his work by abstraction without destroying the naturalism of his figures. The soft coral, yellow, and green tones of the work are thin, allowing the line to dominate the finished painting.

Because the Cleveland miniature does not include two figures that appear on the left side of the Freer painting, it has probably been trimmed (only part of a figure remains at the top left). The lower left corner has been torn off and replaced with a clumsy restoration of the man in the feathered headdress, who should actually be posed with his hands in the basin, as in the Freer copy.

1. For a scene of opium preparation and smoking, see *Maggs Bulletin*, no. 3 (June 1962), no. 35; details of the open bowls and the jars seen on the left in the Cleveland miniature are similar.

43 Oval Portrait of a Woman in a Chaghtai Hat 20.1967

Mughal, ca. 1740–50, 9.5 × 7.4 cm. Some rubbing. Mounted on plain paper.

Gift of J. H. Wade

Comparative Material: (A) *Woman in a Chaghtai Hat*, Mughal, ca. 1740–50; Godard, 1937, fig. 65. (B) *Woman in a Chaghtai Hat*, Mughal, ca. 1750; Arnold and Wilkinson, I, ms. 11A, no. XIV, not illus. (C) *Courtesan in a Chaghtai Hat*, by Sahabuddin, Rajasthani, Bikaner, dated 1748; Sharma, no. 62, pl. 56. (D) *Courtesan at a Palace Window*, Rajasthani, ca. 1750; Skelton, 1961, pl. 81.

The many late Mughal versions of this scene exemplify the impersonality of feminine depiction (A-C). The hat is the beauty's sole distinguishing feature; a towerlike confection festooned with jewels, it is anchored by a rope of pearls under her chin. The embellishments of the hat generally include bands of pearls falling behind the ear and an artificial bird in flight.

The *chaghtai* hat was customarily worn as a mark of distinction during the reigns of Akbar and Humayun (see [18i]); it was a badge of female rank and honor that also happened to be decorative. At the time of its usage in this group of pictures, however, the hat was only a costume detail with vaguely remembered associations. Although intended to be merely ornamental, many compositions of this type were sold to the British in India as representing historical subjects such as Babur's sister and others.

The Mughal versions of this composition are so similar in style that they were likely produced within a short time. Their prettified, meticulous but bland style classifies them as mid-eighteenth-century examples. By contrast, the Rajasthani illustrations of the same subject deriving from Mughal prototypes are bold and energetic drawings that reflect a more vital spirit and the complete detachment of their courtesan types from historical associations (D).

47 *Princess and Attendant in*   55.297
Trompe l'Oeil Window

By Aquil Khan, Provincial Mughal, possibly Lucknow,
ca. 1760, 12.5 × 7.8 cm, 44 × 31.6 cm with borders.
Conventionalized study of a flowering tree on reverse.
Small paint smears on white border area. Border imitates
textile, with bright yellow floral inner surround and
gold-flowered outer areas. Signed at lower right next to
hookah (can be seen with magnification).

Gift of George P. Bickford

Published: W. Ward, "Two Rajput Paintings and a Rajput
Textile," *CMAB* 43 (1956): 62–65.

Comparative Material: (A) *Zainat Afza Begam in a Window*,
by Aquil Khan, Provincial Mughal, Lucknow, ca. 1760;
Falk and Archer, 1981, no. 203.

This miniature is signed by Aquil Khan, an artist of the
mid-eighteenth century who produced numerous works in
vastly different fashionable styles. Like other painters of his
era, he was capable of jumping eclectically from one idiom
to another; only the minute, surreptitiously placed signatures reveal his oeuvre. One of three signed miniatures by
Aquil Khan in the India Office Library is among the several
portraits of women by the artist that could be compared to
the Cleveland example (A, illus.). The India Office painting,
conventionalized in quite a different manner, is, however,
less delicate than the Cleveland miniature.

Here the heroine, with her attendant behind her, sits in
a window with a gold awning above and a rug of the same
pattern below. Obviously meant to be a princess, she is
haloed and heavily bejewelled. In one hand she holds the
stem of a hookah between hennaed fingers and with the

Figure 47, detail.

Figure 47(A). *Zainat Afza Begam in a Window*, by Aquil Khan. The
British Library, India Office Library and Records, London.

other hand grasps a short flower garland. The window surrounding both this picture and the India Office miniature was a frequently used motif from the mid-seventeenth century but was particularly characteristic of the eighteenth century. The composition seems to have originated in the appearance of the Mughal emperor at his palace window in *darshan* each morning, but the conceit was also often utilized for silhouetting beauties, as here. In this example the window, created with artificial devices, opens rather illogically onto a tree-filled garden rather than an interior vista. Above the trees the artist has put in a favorite type of eighteenth-century sky composed of rolling clouds shot with orange and gold sunset rays to enhance the color and drama of his very carefully planned decorative design.

The vivid floral border of the Cleveland painting is so large that the small picture at the center is engulfed by its brilliance. Although in typical provincial style designed to resemble a textile hanging, the work was done with unusual care, probably at least in part by Aquil Khan himself. Each of the stylized carnations in the middle section is depicted with far more dots of paint than are necessary and the thousand or more flowers have been completed in incredibly precise fashion. The artist knew how to coordinate colors very attractively, so that the rich saffron yellow of the inner surround is repeated in the attendant's dress and the flowered gold is repeated in the elegant rug and pillows surrounding the princess.

Aquil Khan's eclecticism has created difficulties in identifying the city or cities in which the painter worked. It has been conjectured that he may have lived in Delhi,[1] but Lucknow was a flourishing center, whereas Delhi was under many harsh pressures after Muhammad Shah's reign. This type of picture with its ornate border looks like a Lucknow work, although this may be attributable to Aquil Khan's imitative abilities. Other miniatures by the artist include compositions of both Murshidabad and Lucknow/Delhi types.[2] Aquil Khan's completely unrelated works help to illustrate that the eighteenth-century artist was not hired to originate either styles or compositions but to handle popular themes in an appropriate manner. He may, however, have specialized in subjects such as idealized females, since there are other compositions of women in windows signed by him.

1. Falk and Archer, 1981, p. 121.
2. Ibid., nos. 204 and 205.

48 Princely Ascetic in the Forest Visited by Ladies   71.95

Provincial Mughal, Lucknow, ca. 1760, 19.6 × 13.8 cm, 32.7 × 26.5 cm with borders. Floral inner surround, elaborate floral outer border in diaper pattern with gold ground.

Purchase, Andrew R. and Martha Holden Jennings Fund
Ex collection: MacDonald.

Comparative Material: (A) *Princely Ascetic Visited by Ladies*, Mughal, ca. 1730; *Sotheby*, 26 March 1973, lot 34.

The heroine of this picture is a bold woman who is conscious of her allure and stares directly into the eyes of her lover. She is surrounded by more demure companions and by attendants who wait on her or prepare to play music. The women's gold costumes, the hookah, the elaborate dishes that include a *pan* box and long-necked wine bottles, and the carpet laid down under the trees all suggest refinement. The company is in a clearing next to dark, flowery woods and between two ponds filled with blooming lotuses. Illustrations of women coming to the forest were a common theme of romanticized eighteenth-century Mughal painting that seems to symbolize a feminine desire to escape restricted boundaries. In this instance, as in many others, the romantic scene purports to be one of religious withdrawal following a long literary tradition of isolated ascetics discovered by pretty women in the forest. Here, the women have

Figure 48(A). *Princely Ascetic Visited by Ladies.* Reproduced by permission of Sotheby & Co., London.

found a handsome prince (undoubtedly by mutual connivance) who wears a band around his knees like those generally worn by ascetics practicing meditation. He seems, however, to have lapsed into dreamy reverie. Most of the women wear transparent gold bodices, but the heroine and prince are attired completely in gold. The prince, in a feathered turban, has a garland of flowers around his neck and jeweled anklets and armlets.

This genteel gathering in the forest is copied from an earlier picture (A, illus.) with few apparent changes. Even the foliage of the trees that seems to divide the male and female positions is patterned in the same manner. The romantic aura of the Cleveland version has been enhanced, however, by its increased tightness and stylization. The polarity between the prince and his mistress has been increased so that more tension is generated by the meeting of their eyes, which are both widened and uptilted in the Cleveland version. Not only are the facial features completely modified but the bodies are more geometric.

Such conventions as the widened eyes and tensed bodies are not characteristic of Lucknow (they of course resemble the type adapted at Kishangarh); however, the miniature is mounted on a lavish, textile-like, gilt-flowered border often used in the provincial Mughal center, and the subject is very typical of paintings done in this city in various imitative styles.

Figure 48.

49 *Yusuf and Zulaykha Meeting*   39.164

Provincial Mughal, Lucknow, ca. 1764, 21.5 × 15 cm,
40.5 × 28 cm with borders. Text on reverse in gold-flecked
border; seal in upper right with date equivalent to AD 1764.
Dark blue inner border with gold scrolling; outer border of
rust with gold flecks (gold cartouche in top center bears title
of scene).

Gift of Leonard C. Hanna, Jr., Coralie Walker Hanna
Memorial Collection

Comparative Material: (A) *Ladies Being Entertained by
Actors*, in the style of Mir Kalan Khan, Mughal,
dated 1742; Binney, 1973, no. 79.

That this miniature picturing Yusuf and Zulaykha was produced in 1764 or slightly earlier is established by the dated
owner's seal appearing on its reverse side. Scenes from the
Persian account of Joseph and Potiphar's wife were frequently illustrated in provincial Mughal painting because
easily understood romantic subjects became increasingly
common when paintings began to be commissioned by
wealthy city-dwellers. In this version, as in others, Yusuf is
dressed in clothing associated with Persia. The sharp, thin
faces of the lovers imitate those in works by the popular
mid-eighteenth-century painter Mir Kalan Khan (A), who
had begun his career under Muhammad Shah and then
migrated to Lucknow. The border of the miniature with an
inscribed cartouche at the top is also imitative of works done
for the highest social class in Lucknow. It resembles folios
in a large album or group of albums probably done for Shuja
ud-Daula, the powerful *nawab* of Oudh (r. 1754–75). The
miniaturized landscape of this Yusuf and Zulaykha scene
with its *gavial*, or crocodile, rising in front of a ship is
characteristic of both late Mughal and provincial Mughal
painting, while the silver-flecked sky and silver moon appear in other Provincial Mughal examples done about this
time.[1]

1. Binney, 1973, no. 103.

Figure 49.

Color Plate XV. Kedara Ragini [83].

Color Plate XVI. The Attractions of Music [87].

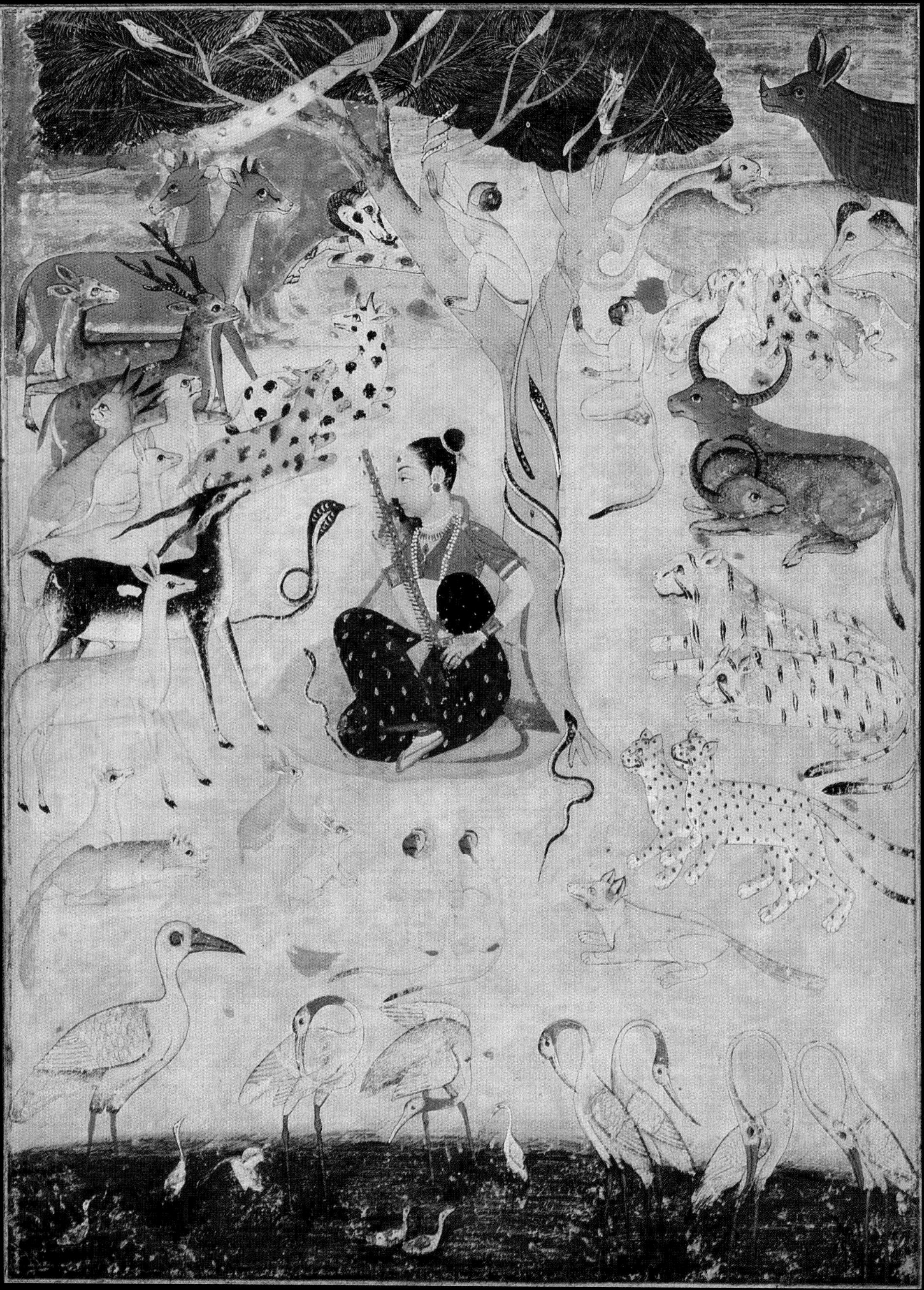

50 *Portrait of Aurangzeb* 20.1968

Provincial Mughal, probably Faizabad, ca. 1770,
23.5 × 14.9 cm. Upper portion spotted.

Gift of J. H. Wade

Comparative Material: (A) *Portrait of Aurangzeb*, Mughal,
ca. 1680–90; *Arts of Asia* 2 (July/Aug. 1972): 38.
(B) *Portrait of Aurangzeb* (?), probably Mughal,
ca. 1670–80; Binney, 1973, no. 135.

Although this portrait of Aurangzeb follows the painting
conventions used during his youth, it is an eighteenth-
century copy—probably produced in Faizabad, Shuja ud-

Daula's capital from 1765 to 1775, where painters (generally
men with previous attachments to the *nawab*) unin-
terruptedly carried on the Oudh *nawabi* styles. The handling of the figure is tighter and more rigid than would be
characteristic of ca. 1680 (when this portrait should rightly
have been done). The face is harshly outlined and the hands
have little substance. The stiff pose with a sword and flywhisk was often used for Aurangzeb (A and B).

Figure 50.

51 *Bhairava Raga* 24.972

Provincial Mughal, Delhi, early nineteenth century, 18.7 × 12.5 cm, 35.6 × 22 cm with borders. Slightly rubbed at top. Border with gold floral scrolls on buff ground.

Gift of Mrs. Francis F. Prentiss for the Dudley P. Allen Collection

Comparative Material: (A) *Bhairava Raga,* Provincial Mughal, Lucknow, ca. 1760; Gangoly, 1935, pl. IIIC. (B) *Bhairava Raga,* Provincial Mughal, Lucknow, ca. 1770–80; Coomaraswamy, 1926, pt. 5, pl. XXXI. (C) *Dhanasri Ragini,* Provincial Mughal, Lucknow, ca. 1760; Gascoigne, p. 207.

This miniature is an example of a style commonly used in early nineteenth-century Delhi, generally by artists copying older compositions. The Hindu *ragamala* design of Shiva as Bhairava being rubbed with sandal paste as he is adored by female attendants is a standard one (A and B). By the nineteenth century it was also widely employed by artists working for Muslim rather than exclusively Hindu patrons.

Figure 51.

52 *Tiered Court Scene* 73.237

Late Imperial, Delhi or possibly Rajasthan, ca. 1800, 39.7 × 28.8 cm.

Gift of Mr. and Mrs. Michael de Havennon

Comparative Material: (A) *Terrace Scene,* Late Imperial, possibly Ajmer, ca. 1800; McNear, no. 92. (B) *Nawab on a Terrace,* Provincial Mughal, Lucknow, ca. 1770; *Sotheby,* 9 Dec. 1975, lot 238.

This fantasy represents one popular direction for miniature painting as the imperial Mughal era drew to a close. Intricate, operetta-like scenes were produced with huge casts of tiny figures suspended in luxurious palace and garden settings. Some centers like Delhi were so impoverished that patrons relied on such spectacular (but relatively inexpensive) possessions to camouflage their situation, while other centers like Alwar were newly influential and enjoyed the prestige of gaudy trappings.

In the Cleveland design there are more than one hundred figures hidden within the tiered architectural structures. The figures show no emotion and lack individuality but are coordinated into a dense surface pattern of colored and gilded detail that mimics elegance. The most crowded and dramatic area is at the top of the composition where Rama is shown attacking Ravana before the golden city of Lanka. Sita is imprisoned at the center of the fortress with demons crouching in the niches of the outer walls. Depicted as white rather than blue, Rama leads an army of men without any monkeys or bears. The lower terrace scenes do not relate to this illustration, nor is their iconography clear. Two golden boats with animal heads carry a god and his attendants, while women fly kites from the roofs. Two blue gods, probably both Vishnu and his incarnation Krishna, are shown at the center of the picture with Brahma and Ganesha. In the lower portion Krishna appears in a Holi celebration.

The imprecise iconography shows that the effect of the work was mainly intended to be decorative. In the late eighteenth and nineteenth centuries as the Hindu-Muslim power structure collapsed, specific incidents of Hindu mythology were confused and amalgamated.

Although this composition is done in a Delhi style, the same types of painters were working in other nearby centers like Alwar, which is known to have produced hundreds of both Hindu and Muslim miniature subjects in the early nineteenth century. Since a miniature (A) very similar to the Cleveland work was obtained from the raja of Ajmer, it seems probable that this city, which had always been closely associated with the imperial court, was also doing miniatures in a Delhi style. The Cleveland painting with its Hindu subject matter may thus have been from an outlying center, such as Alwar or Ajmer, where there were Hindu patrons.

Figure 52.

53 *Sleeping Youth*   44.494

Deccan, possibly Golconda, ca. 1630, 20.4 × 11.4 cm (painting only). Somewhat rubbed. Light blue border.
Purchase from the J. H. Wade Fund
Published: *Islamic Art* (Cleveland: Cleveland Museum of Art, 1944), frontispiece.
Comparative Material: (A) *Young Man Beneath a Plane Tree,* Deccan, possibly Golconda, ca. 1630; Welch, 1959, fig. 20. (B) *Youths in a Garden,* Persian, early 17th century; Marteau and Vever, pl. 169.

This miniature, once thought to be Persian, is made up of Persian-derived elements, but these have been altered by the inexperienced artist who was used to working in a looser Deccani style. The miniature shows that the artist seems to have been interested in pigment texture and warm color harmonies that would have been typical of the evolving Deccani aesthetic. In the scene a youth dozes with a fan in his hand apparently after drinking wine from the decorative long-necked bottle before him. Seated alone in a hilly landscape, he rests on his arm in the crotch of a spindly willow tree that has a nest and two birds very obviously placed in it—one of the artist's unconsciously humorous touches. The gold sky has a few small clouds that like the plants and rocks of the landscape are intended to enhance the scene decoratively in a traditional manner.

In comparing the miniature with a Persian composition that it paraphrases (B, illus.), it is evident that the artist of the Cleveland scene has made the young man's body too large and ungainly to be acceptable by Persian standards.

Figure 53.

Opposite top
Figure 53(A). *Young Man Beneath a Plane Tree.* Anonymous Loan to the Fogg Art Museum, Harvard University, Cambridge, Massachusetts; reproduced with permission.

Opposite
Figure 53(B). *Youths in a Garden.* After Marteau and Vever, *Miniatures Persanes . . . exposées au Musée des Arts Décoratifs 1912* (Paris: Bibliothèque d'art et d'archéologie, 1913), pl. 169.

The comparison also shows that the Deccani artist has centered the hero, moved various accessories, and thus lessened the sophistication of the original design. The turban that lies before the young man in the Persian miniature has been rearranged as a pillow in the Cleveland scene, an ingenuous touch typical of the more naive artist's approach.

Although every motif of the scene derives from Safavid ideas, the miniature style is proven to be non-Persian mainly by the artist's unfamiliarity with calligraphic line drawing. Whereas a native Persian artist would have used the curving form of the willow tree to exhibit brilliant calligraphic skills, this painter's outline is unimaginative. He has failed to outline most of the plants on the hillside at all but has blended the hues of the large iris in a way that demonstrates his more sensuous appreciation of pigment. The soft or vague calligraphic strokes used for the young man's curling hair, his features, and his costume also help to distinguish this leaf from Persian productions of the same era. Since the sharp, rhythmic strokes of Safavid master artists had become a widely imitated cliche, the softness of this artist's work stands out all the more emphatically by contrast.

The rulers of the Deccani kingdoms looked to various Islamic cultures, but especially to that of Persia in the sixteenth century for artistic inspiration and leadership. By the beginning of the seventeenth century the area had achieved much creative independence, however, and painters were capable of assimilating Persian characteristics into their new native idiom fairly fluently. This miniature is datable to the seventeenth century because of its particular kind of Persian model. The Cleveland scene and one of a young man beneath a *chenar*, or plane tree (A, illus.), that seem to be by the same artist are therefore unusual because the painter has had such difficulty with Persian prototypes at a relatively late date. He seems to have been a man with some natural sensitivity who had not had thorough training in a court and was thus out of the mainstream of artistic development. Other near-contemporary artists were more skilled in adopting Safavid Persian motifs to native Deccani ideas about color or design.[1]

This work and comparison A are attributable to the same painter because of their styles as well as the similar compositions of young men beneath trees.[2] Both works are charming but slightly awkward in the same way (in comparison A, the artist has had trouble mastering the pose, which was undoubtedly borrowed from a Persian source like that of the Cleveland miniature). The small flowers and the iris in each scene are not only comparable motifs but are done in the same manner, and the landscape settings are similar.

1. Welch, 1973, no. 77.
2. Cary Welch has previously discussed this Cleveland picture, analyzing the reasons for a Deccani attribution as well as relating it to comparison A (1959, p. 144).

54 *Radha and Krishna Embracing* 62.241

Leaf from a *Gita Govinda*, Deccan, Aurangabad (?), ca. 1650, 13.5 × 14.5 cm. On plain paper. Some paint flaking, as in blue background and overskirt of woman on the left in pavilion; green pigment in strip at lower right eaten away.

Purchase, Norman O. Stone and Ella A. Stone Memorial Fund

Comparative Material: (A) *Radha and Krishna in a Bower*, leaf from a *Gita Govinda*, Deccan, Aurangabad (?), ca. 1650; Binney, 1973, no. 130. (B) *Radha with Attendants*, leaf from a *Gita Govinda*, Deccan, Aurangabad (?), ca. 1650; Czuma, no. 55. (C) *Krishna Fluting*, leaf from a *Gita Govinda*, Deccan, Aurangabad (?), ca. 1650; Krannert Art Museum, *Art of India and Southeast Asia* (Champaign, IL, 1964), no. 85. (D) *Radha and Sakhi in the Forest*, leaf from a *Gita Govinda*, Deccan, Aurangabad (?), ca. 1650; Sotheby, 12 Dec. 1972, lot 47. (E) *Woman and Lover*, leaf from a *Gita Govinda*, Deccan, Aurangabad (?), ca. 1650; Sotheby, 7 July 1975, lot 86. (F) *Two Women*, leaf from a *Gita Govinda*, Deccan, Aurangabad (?), ca. 1650; Sotheby, 7 July 1975, lot 87.

The style of this *Gita Govinda* series has been previously analyzed in a study that traces three manuscripts of the type (a *ragamala*, this *Gita Govinda*, and a *Rasamanjari*) and describes their common characteristics.[1] The paintings of the group amalgamate features from Rajasthani, Mughal, and Deccani miniatures, and it is clear that they were produced by artists under the influence of all three areas. The figures, for example, as in this leaf, are tall like those of Deccani miniatures but have the typical jewelry and faces with wide open eyes characteristic of Rajasthani painting. Some naturalism in the drawing as well as certain costume details such as turbans are attributable to Mughal influence. Research on this mixed style was begun after the discovery of a *Rasamanjari*, which has become the key manuscript of the group because it contains a colophon dated 1650 specifying that the portion of the text in which the paintings appear was produced at Aurangabad in the Deccan.[2]

Aurangabad and the huge fort of Daulatabad outside the city were strategically located bases used by the Mughals from 1633 on for the launching of their southern campaigns.[3] Mughals and Rajasthanis thronged the city during fifty years of war and for purposes of administration afterwards, settling there with large retinues during prolonged periods of fighting. The wealth circulating in the area, the enforced waiting in military camps, and the cultural interchange indicate that Aurangabad may have been an ideal environment for the development of several mixed schools of painting. Consequently, diverse types of miniatures—linked only by the fact that they combine Mughal, Deccani, and Rajput characteristics—have been attributed to the city itself without further documentation. This practice has made general attributions appear specific when a more logical approach is to see Aurangabad as an important center in a fairly large area affected by the cross-cultural currents of the Deccani wars. In various ways the wars seem to have introduced new painting motifs or styles to countless states and *thikanas* of Rajasthan or the Northern Deccan. Even when an attribution of this complex historical period can be made directly to Aurangabad (as in the case of the *Rasamanjari* dated 1650), the social and political factors that affected the city raise difficult questions, since artists from many backgrounds were coming into the area with their patrons, mixing in different circumstances and then leaving again. Painters who had been trained in the dissimilar styles of Bikaner, Bundi, and Mewar were those whose work altered most through contact with Mughal and Deccani art. In this case the patron of the *Rasamanjari* manuscript was the prince of a Mewar *thikana* and the group's most prominent features—such as the use of intense, plain-colored backgrounds; simple compositions; and particular figural details—all derive from Mewar art.

Prior to the discovery of the *Rasamanjari* colophon, the stylistic group was assumed by several authors to come from some *thikana* of Mewar. The most solid attribution was to Ghanerao, a *thikana* controlled for a time by Mewar, where the *ragamala* miniatures belonging to the group had been discovered on palace walls.[4] Because the predominant element of these miniatures is Mewari, it seems most logical that the artists who developed the style were Rajasthanis who worked temporarily at Aurangabad and were accommodating themselves to a new cosmopolitan atmosphere.[5] Striking carpet patterns, some of the textile prints, and the more unusual colors (such as lavender) are attributable to polished Deccani or Mughal styles.

The Ghanerao *ragamala* is a more refined manuscript than either the *Gita Govinda* or the *Rasamanjari*. The three works do not seem to have been produced by the same artist, nor were they all necessarily painted at Aurangabad rather than in some Mewar *thikana*. The essential point is that they share the same features created by the exchanges of the wars over the Deccan plateau. Other miniatures that are related though not actually in the group show the popularity of this style.[6]

The *Gita Govinda* set, known from various published leaves (see comparatives A-F) as well as additional unpublished examples, has somewhat rudimentary backgrounds in contrast to the more sumptuous paintings from the *ragamala* found at Ghanerao. The Cleveland leaf, like other miniatures of the *Gita Govinda* set, has a simple composition made up of a few horizontals and verticals with tall figures filling most of the frame. There is little detail or suggestion of open space in these leaves. In the Cleveland painting and several other *Gita Govinda* leaves, compositional divisions are relatively symmetrical; the distribution of two personages in the Cleveland miniature on either side of the painting's center line is typically planned. Textile patterns, especially on rugs and furnishings, are less rich or carefully drawn than in the *ragamala* miniatures, though certain patterns are common to the three manuscripts of the group. Whether seated or standing in an embrace, the fig-

Figure 54.

ures are poised and their long-waisted bodies controlled and upright. Women, who are shown with exaggeratedly arched backs, are restrained in a manner characteristic of much Rajasthani art that points up the essentially Rajput character of the style.

1. Doshi, pp. 19–28.

2. Ibid., pp. 20–21.

3. The town of Khirki was not named Aurangabad by Prince Aurangzeb until 1651, a year actually covered by the V.S. date of the colophon. Khirki and the important neighboring fortress of Daulatabad were primary positions of the Deccani strategist Malik Amber. Though Khirki was attacked and ruined by Shah Jahan in 1622, it was not until 1633 that it was permanently retained under Mughal control. The 1620's base of Mughal operations was Burhanpur, but from the 1630s on, Khirki and Daulatabad quartered mixed Mughal/Rajasthani troops; therefore, the *Rasamanjari* colophon refers to a new name but not a new location for the Mughal army (Haig, 4: 262, 269).

4. Doshi, p. 25. For published paintings not listed by Doshi from either one or more *ragamala* series belonging to this stylistic group, see: Doris Wiener Gallery, *Indian Miniature Painting* (New York, 1974), no. 59; Ebeling, no. 270; *Sotheby*, 11 Dec. 1973, lot 56. An additional *Rasamanjari* picture is published in Pal, 1976, no. 34.

5. Though the *ragamala* paintings of this stylistic group are not associated with a Rajasthani scheme or organization, many follow accepted Rajasthani compositions. Their classification is discussed by Ebeling, p. 21.

6. The long-faced, rather stiff-backed woman; the architecture; and the sense of patterning in Khandalavala and P. and M. Chandra, nos. 159A and C, are similar to the group defined by Doshi. Goetz, 1950, color pl. 7, is the result of a different mixture of Mughal, Rajasthani, and Deccani elements, but the figures of Radha and Krishna are like those in the Aurangabad *Gita Govinda*.

FURTHER READING: Ebeling.

Figure 55.

55 Encampment in the Mountains 71.282

Kashmir, ca. 1650, 34 × 21.1 cm, 40.2 × 27.7 cm
with border. Some paint scraped. Gold inner border,
eighteenth-century dark blue and gold floral outer
border. Later poetic inscription at top in sky.

Gift of Doris and Ed Wiener

Comparative Material: (A) *Encampment in the Mountains*,
Persia, Qazwin, dated 1582; Grube, 1968, no. 79.1.

This decorative miniature contains small details of all kinds.
Such features as the bizarre multi-colored rocks and the
elaborately patterned tents reveal the artist's ornamental
treatment. Because the painter has stressed so many elements with rather harsh colors, the miniature is not attractive; but it is intricate and ingeniously planned as well as
interesting to art historians, since it is one of only a few
works attributable to seventeenth-century Kashmir.

The nomadic encampment depicted is in a steep mountain valley by a winding stream. Various common activities
are going on, some of which are humorously portrayed, as
in the foreground where an old man and a boy are attempting to load two recalcitrant camels. Also in the foreground a mare suckles a colt, a boy dozes with a flock of
sheep, and a woman milks a goat. The artist has focused on
a woman and her attendants grouped around the largest
tent conversing with an elderly bearded man. (The formality of the meeting seems to indicate that the man is a
visitor.) Above, the mountains are full of antelopes, birds,
and various kinds of cats as well as a few people, such as the
two woodcutters who are wending their way down toward
the camp with loads of sticks on their backs.

This scene is an elaborate adaptation of a Persian landscape setting. Many stock characters of the mountainous
nomadic camp scenes that were a popular Persian compositional type (A) have been amalgamated by this artist into
his single composition. The woman milking, the boy with
his flute, the leopard snarling on a crag, and the returning
woodcutters are all familiar motifs. The arrangement of the
central group of figures implies that a narrative subject,
possibly Laila receiving Majnun's messenger, has been
worked into the genre scene. The Persian tale of Laila, who
was forced into an arranged marriage but continued to be
the object of her school companion's love, was so familiar
that it was often illustrated by single incidents.

Kashmir was an area frequented by the Mughal emperors
and their nobles during the first half of the seventeenth
century; consequently, it supported a small group of painters. From the little that is known, these men seemed to
have arrived from centers such as Bukhara where they had
been trained in painting. The only painter documented by
name as working in the area during the mid-seventeenth
century was Muhammad Nadir of Samarkand, who signed
illustrations of a *Yusuf and Zulaykha* manuscript dated
1650.[1] Although Muhammad Nadir had enough familiarity
with Mughal painting to do naturalistic works, his usual
style was more conventionalized. His figures have the long
curling locks and the delicate features also seen in this
miniature. Somewhat similar figures are also employed in a
few Deccani works,[2] but the cold grayish colors and thick
paint used here are found in Kashmiri miniatures. While
this picture has been previously classified as Deccani, its
style is more formal and stilted than in Deccani works.[3]

1. Chester Beatty Library, Dublin, Ms. 31, with leaves inscribed
as done in Kashmir by Muhammad Nadir of Samarkand in 1650
(unpublished); for a published leaf of this manuscript see Binney,
1973, no. 63, or Falk and Archer, no. 90.
2. See Fogg Art Museum, *Annual Report* (Cambridge, Mass.,
1972–74), back cover; Welch, 1973, no. 77.
3. Archer, 1960, pl. 31, shows a nomadic camp scene done in
Golconda that is in a rather different style.

56 A Green Parrot 72.285

Company School, ca. 1820, 35.5 × 28.5 cm. Edges slightly frayed. Inscription in Persian: "Cagilah" (parrot).

Gift of Edgar A. Hahn

Comparative Material: (A) *Green Parrot*, Company School, ca. 1795; *Maggs Bulletin*, no. 16 (March 1970), no. 38.

Different kinds of the abundant Indian parakeet were among the birds most frequently depicted by Company School artists. In this case the work shows a common green bird with a pink breast that compares stylistically with a painting of a similar green parrot done somewhat earlier (A).

The artists commissioned by the British in India recorded occupational groups, religious customs, and outstanding scenic spots. In general, however, the natural-history subjects often painted were more specialized commissions. The British patrons of such works tended to have a genuine scientific interest in the Indian environment rather than simply a passing curiosity about the exotic. Among the stylistic modifications they required were shading and transparent watercolor washes in the European manner.

For the Indian population, such exacting studies were a novelty that may have attracted artists selling paintings in bazaars or working for Hindu and Muslim patrons. Certainly the influence of European painting on traditional production was evident in many ways during the nineteenth century. Both the Cleveland miniature and the comparison are inexpensive, simple paintings that may have been marketed in large numbers for either English or native buyers. Each is quite flat and lacks any indication of bone structure in the parrot. Since the artist's concern for scientific accuracy is slight, the two works were apparently intended for decorative purposes. The painter of the Cleveland picture handles watercolor in a way he would have learned from seeing works done for the British, but awkwardly, with only a general idea of his model; for example, he applies surface details of feathers and leaves over transparent color washes but without elaboration or painstaking delicacy.

FURTHER READING: M. Archer, 1972; M. Archer and W. G. Archer, 1955.

Figure 56.

57 *Juggler*   82.119

Company School, Lucknow or Patna, ca. 1840,
17.2 × 12.7 cm. Pale yellow border. Urdu inscription at
bottom corner on reverse.

Gift of Mr. and Mrs. William E. Ward

This small painting must have been taken from a book of
trades and castes of the type popularized by British patrons.
English curiosity was aroused by the many Indian occupations that were strange to Europeans, and picture
books of trades became the most common request of Company School patrons. The modeling and the pale wash tints
of this miniature show the extent to which European taste
had affected the market. Lucknow and Patna, both centers
within a reasonable distance from Calcutta, attracted fairly
large numbers of Europeans to whom commercial painters
catered.

Complete books of trades and castes at the India Office
Library and the Victoria and Albert Museum that are contemporary with this illustration and in the same style do not
include this subject. Although the word "Juggler" has been
written in English about an inch below the painting, the
more usual pictures of such performers show them balancing or tossing series of objects. If this man is correctly
described, he must earn the cowrie shells in front of him by
causing the balls on his bow to move and vibrate.

Figure 57.

V. Rajasthani and Central, Eastern, and South Indian Painting

The Traditional Inheritance of the Rajput Painter

Two major changes took place in Hindu art during the Muslim period. The first, in the Sultanate era, was the shift of emphasis from temple building to miniature painting in North and Central India. Although the construction of temples never stopped, it was arrested by the Muslim destruction or defilement of existing temple sites and by Muslim control of tax revenue. Muslim governments, however, never made any sustained attempts to obliterate the social focus of Hinduism and Jainism on temple worship. The temple thus continued as a center, and the miniature painter never developed a communal importance equal to that of earlier decorators and sculptors; however, it is clear that an alteration of direction that fitted new social conditions took place as miniature painting evolved and became the more progressive art form. The painter became both the new transmitter of traditional ideas and the major artistic voice of his own time.

The great Hindu caves or temples that had been decorated with sculpture and wall paintings by guilds of workers for more than a millennium were the classic expressions of the Indian artist. The productions of the Hindu miniaturist show that he was a more ruralized and limited artist than the great wall-painters, but although he differed in numerous respects from these craftsmen, he was influenced by the idealism that had brought about their vast communal projects. The surrender of ambition to a collective religious purpose, as expressed in the cooperation between temple sculptors and painters, had always been deeply attractive to the Indian artist. Religious dedication, sublimation of ego, and a desire to create universally meaningful images were all part of the enduring motivations that earlier artists passed on to the Rajput painter. The centuries of large-scale projects that must have reflected communal piety drew to a close with the completion of medieval temples at sites such as Konarak in the thirteenth century. But if communal Hinduism faltered because of the confrontation with Islam, the Rajput miniaturist could develop a more private type of *bhakti*, amalgamating India's past into the new art form of manuscript illustration that had been independently evolved by both Muslims and native Jains.

In the Rajput society of the Sultanate period, the process of artistic creation was a universalized and impersonalized one—that is, the artist was motivated by hereditary obligation rather than by personal passion, and, like his predecessors, he created works of broad symbolic import (the particularized recording of individual features in portraiture, for example, was introduced only through Mughal contact). That the Rajput's art was centered around abstraction rather than naturalism seems related to the Hindu perception of order as transcending temporal existence. Because the symbolic components of objects were more real than objective appearances, commonly accepted symbols formed the actual subjects of pre-Mughal miniatures; thus the idealized man whose bodily parts could be compared to a lion, an elephant, and so on was much more substantial than a man whose temporary appearance could be portrayed naturalistically because the former embodied an age-old, universalized rather than transitory concept of order.

The relative unconsciousness of personalities that was revealed by the lack of personal credit given to painters can also be attributed to Indian religious views. The concept of an artist as a genius probably did not exist because the continuity of collective thought was more real to the Jain or Hindu than any single talent. The artist sublimated himself to the ideals and symbols that had always had significance within Hinduism; this position was altered only when miniature painting in Rajasthan was suddenly redefined by the Mughal invasion.

The Effect of the Mughal Conquest on Rajasthan

Because of their potential strength, the Rajasthani maharajas inherited a perpetually tense relation with the Mughal court. At most times actual conflict was repressed, but every emperor was wary of dealings with these volatile rajas. Although the Rajput warrior caste as a whole was always quick to inflate controversy into strife, the Rajasthani rulers were geographically and politically much more significant than their Rajput cousins in the Himalayas. The great Mewar fortresses of Chitor and Ranthambhor were bastions essential for dominating the entire Rajasthani area of dusty plains, dry grass-covered hills, and large deserts. This territory was not only vast but was also the key to holding the south and far west. Both temperamentally and because of their situation, therefore, the Rajasthani rulers from the beginning were assessed as being dangerous and were thrust into uneasy associations with the advancing conquerors.

The nature of the struggle, and even of Rajasthani painting, during the Mughal period was decided by the character of the young emperor Akbar. Concluding that only Hindu and Muslim cooperation would ensure the success of his dynasty, Akbar attempted to win allies rather than to create a repressive government. Because of his physical prowess and his incredible successes in battle, the Rajput rulers were stirred, although their feelings were torn between animosity, envy, and admiration. The canny emperor knew that he appealed to their own caste sense of valor and honor, but at the same time he upset the traditional separatist position of Hinduism. He was the hero who exactly fitted Rajput warrior stereotypes, the dynamic leader whom their own clans had failed to produce in several centuries of struggle against the Muslims, and yet he was an enemy. Although Akbar won over the conquered Rajasthani states by his charisma and diplomacy, the states never completely capitulated but simply acknowledged his personal fascination and the superiority of Mughal organization. Neither group fully trusted the other, nor did a real Hindu-Muslim amalgamation occur. Such dichotomy created enormous confusion in the Rajput's position, which manifested itself culturally—for example, in the variant principles adapted for miniature painting by different rulers. However, the hold that Akbar established over the Rajput imagination was considerable, and it provided the impetus for Rajput imitations of the imperial court and its miniature painting.

Although miniature painting styles could be said to have altered rapidly in the few years before Akbar's death, the entire upheaval of artistic ideals was more complex and prolonged. The secularization of painting that Akbar precipitated was the second major artistic change during the Muslim period. Its implications were profound and affected the two different strata of Hindu society—raja patrons and artist retainers—in diverse ways.

Everything that Akbar struggled to achieve contradicted the tenor of customary Hindu life—in particular, his view of reality as measurable in physical, finite terms conflicted with attitudes that had long been expressed in Rajput painting. To Akbar time was not a metaphysical continuum, it was a finite limitation against which he worked. Everything he achieved, from forced marches to administrative changes, impressed his Rajput allies by speed. His sense of space or geography was also objective in comparison to their own traditional views: it had certainly fostered territorial ambitions that were much greater than theirs. At the core of the turmoil he introduced was a belief in individual dynamism and free will, which made him a creation of modern, as opposed to traditional, society. His greatest distinction was that he envisioned the possibility of complete political

or social change by challenging stable collective thought through the assertion of individual will.

Despite the fact that Akbar's personal philosophy was not understood or accepted in a comprehensive manner, it had an impact on Rajput painting styles. The new concept of time was translated into freer figural movement, and space was depicted as more nearly three-dimensional. In general, perceptions of nature became more closely related to physical observation, and the development of portraiture and the identification of artists by inscriptions were confirmations that the individual was acknowledged in various new ways.

While the sculptor had always been directed by the Brahmin class even if royalty had paid for his work, the painter in the Mughal period found that he was working directly for rajas who often gave him secular commissions. The changes that occurred in Rajasthani painting were prompted by many of these rajas who not only wished to emulate imperial magnificence but also desired to see themselves flatteringly depicted in their own surroundings. The rulers who held themselves aloof from the materialism of the Mughal court, such as those in Mewar, were more likely to continue exclusively religious commissions in pre-Mughal styles. But for the ruling class, art increasingly came to be a matter of pleasure—an indulgence of the ruler's desire to see himself portrayed in various sports, pastimes, and state duties.

The painters were probably more conservative than the nobility they served. The countless illustrations of texts such as the *Bhagavata Purana* or *Ramayana* that were still produced in most courts apparently continued to inspire sincere devotional creativity. For some artists the possibilities of expressing themselves in more naturalistic styles seem to have been liberating; yet even these men if born in Rajasthan almost certainly preserved traditional ideals of loyalty to their patrons. The desire for self-surrender remained an essential motivational impulse. The artist merely transferred the religious awe that made him creative to his Rajput overlords, who were credited with supernatural descent and with religiously sanctioned authority over their subjects. His sublimation was therefore approved by both mythology and the caste system. Since the ruler was a manifestation of godpower, he was worthy of receiving the painter's deepest adulation; and the artist's bond with his overlord was thus far removed from being a simple contract for employment. The quality of this association, including its ceremonial sanctity, is one of the chief reasons that the Rajput patron was significant. The artist's humility conditioned him to work only as an act of dedication, so that it was accordingly difficult for him to develop ideas outside such a relationship.

Although illustrations had been done for rulers prior to the Mughal conquest, the development of courtly painting was greatly accelerated by the new recognition that such miniatures enhanced royal status. Thus sponsorship of painting quickly became a common Rajput pastime. The amount and quality of output depended largely on individual rulers since some states that were not wealthy or influential supported disproportionately large studios and produced very interesting paintings. Painters might migrate from their home states, but in general they held secure positions that could be passed to succeeding family members, as is shown, for example, by many inscriptions noting familial ties on miniatures from the state of Bikaner. A single style to which each painter conformed might predominate rather consistently over long periods of time in Rajasthani centers like Bundi, but, on the other hand, in courts like Kota several different but equally strong styles could coexist simultaneously.

Single miniatures in states like Mewar were sometimes produced by more than one person—probably a master artist with assistants, who were likely to be relatives—and manuscripts commonly were cooperative studio projects. The artists lived near the court, taking their work in for approval; the way commissions were given probably varied from state to state, but evidence is that in certain states painters were required to produce presentation pictures at set times, such as festival days. Artists were at the command of the rajas, giving attendance for long periods when required (as on the hunting trips of Mewar or Kota rulers).

Of the five Rajasthani and central Indian areas well represented in the Cleveland collection, Malwa and Mewar had established pre-Mughal patterns of culture and had remained least affected by either imperial styles or subject matter. In Mewar, for example, miniatures illustrating religious texts were highly significant, while portraits and other secular subjects became common only during the first half of the eighteenth century. By contrast, the rajas of Bikaner were open to Mughal styles from the period of earliest contact. During the early seventeenth century, many artists who worked in Bikaner owed more to Mughal than to Rajasthani painting techniques and could be classified as Popular Mughal painters [36, 37]. On the other hand, artists from Kota used Mughal techniques only to enhance their native imagination and drawing abilities. Finally, of the five areas, mid-eighteenth-century Jaipur was perhaps most derivative. Its social atmosphere was much like that of Mughal cities like Lucknow, which flourished contemporarily. Some works from Jaipur show that Provincial Mughal artists apparently came to this city of rising fortune and plied their talents commercially. The Jaipur miniatures owned by the Cleveland Museum are Rajasthani in character, but they are from *ragamala* sets comparable to ones produced in Lucknow because they were made in great quantities for city dwellers enjoying a new, wealthy status.

Painting in Malwa and Mewar

The paintings usually attributed to the state of Malwa have proven difficult to place specifically. There are several stylistic groups, some of which probably originally came from the neighboring central Indian area of Bundelkhand, since many miniatures were discovered in the collection of the Bundelkhand state of Datia.[1] In 1652 a Malwa-style poetic manuscript called the *Amaru Sataku* was illustrated at Nusratgarh, but this city cannot be positively identified.[2] A 1680 *ragamala* set is from Narsingh, probably the seventeenth-century Malwa capital of Narsingarh (see [84]). The several styles found prior to these dates have no specific provenance recorded, however, nor are their relationships to one another clear. As discussed in the entry for [81], the style represented by a *Rasikapriya* set dated 1634 probably existed at the same time but has no relation to the many stark early *ragamala* sets such as [82, 83]. Since these are the two major stylistic divisions during the first half of the seventeenth century and their artists were prolific, it is surprising that neither group can be more specifically identified. The most definite statement that can be made from the scanty data associated with the state is that the Malwa school is not monolithic, as it has often mistakenly been considered, but has pronounced substyles that must have been characteristic of various, perhaps widely separated, centers.

More than those of any other area, the Malwa miniatures preserved the pre-Mughal types of painting associated with both Hinduism and Jainism. The repressed passion in early Rajput painting, reflected in contorted poses and dramatic color blocks, reappears in many seventeenth-century Malwa works. The extensively illustrated Malwa *Rasikapriya* dated 1634 [81] has the small angular figures and stylized vegetation reminiscent of Jain painting, while the other common Malwa painting types preserve the red and dark blue traditional color scheme typical of both Rajput and Jain miniatures. Despite the fact that Muslim Sultanate paintings were produced in Malwa's capital, Mandu, they had little effect on seventeenth-century painting with this overwhelming Rajput character.

The other arts and the lush landscape of this central region are also equally crucial to understanding seventeenth-century illustration, although such influences must be understood on a more intuituve level. Malwa's romantic literature, from the nature imagery of the Gupta poet Kalidasa through the lyrics of the heroic sultan Baz Bahadur, affected the paintings done in the Mughal era by its passionate intensity. Artists anticipated the viewer's familiarity with various ancient poetic images and also paralleled the terse expressionism common in love poems that had many hidden levels of meaning.

Akbar's forces conquered Malwa in 1561, but the court had little influence on this remote state. A century and a half before, after Delhi had been razed by Timur, this heartland area had developed as an important Sultanate center; but since Akbari or Jahangiri culture was almost solely confined to the north, Malwa was eclipsed. Its art was like its rugged, still-wild terrain, with little direct connection to the transformations caused elsewhere by the Mughals.

Thus the conservative Malwa painting styles altered slowly without much outside influence; they continued to reflect the values of the Rajput warrior caste throughout the seventeenth century. The reckless Rajput courage demonstrated in customs such as *jauhar* (clan suicide in the face of defeat) is paralleled in the abstract boldness of both Mewar and Malwa paintings. In addition, the simple but intense color combinations of brilliant red and cold blue employed in Malwa seem appropriate to the fervency and unyielding pride of the Rajput's temperament.

Many works of Hindu literature were illustrated in Malwa during the Mughal period; these include the *Ramayana*, *Bhagavata Purana*, *Amaru Sataku*, and *Rasikapriya*. Written in neighboring Orcha in 1591 by Keshav Das, the *Rasikapriya* was still a comparatively new work when illustrated in Malwa in 1634. Keshav Das (ca. 1555–1617) came from a family of eminent Sanskrit scholars and poets and was well acquainted with some of Akbar's court poets as well as being a friend of his patron, Raja Bir Singh Deo. He composed the *Rasikapriya* in Hindi, which distinguishes it from the *Rasamanjari*, an earlier text of the same type written in Sanskrit. Both works classify heroes and heroines in different stages of maturity or experience who react in varying ways to the same amorous situations. Most of the attention is given to the reactions of women—from the adolescent sweetheart to the attractive wife—who are cleverly analyzed in circumstances caused by very aggressive lovers, philandering males, and so on. The *Rasikapriya*, unlike the *Rasamanjari*, uses Krishna as the hero who fills all roles. In an exceedingly involved work, Keshav Das multiplied the circumstances of love into 360 categories. Though he is considered one of the Braj Bhasha group of devotional poets who wrote on the Krishna theme, his work is actually secular, intended for the entertainment of the Orcha court. His metaphoric and convoluted *Rasikapriya* text includes both poems and critical commentary on poetics.[3]

A gradual Mughal influence on Malwa painting is seen in alterations of costume, architectural motifs, and figure types; but the abstract elements of Malwa miniatures remained little changed for many decades. By 1690, however, the difficulties artists were encountering in merging novel details with their ancient two-dimensional formats had become apparent. The tight, geometric arrangement of shapes that was the basis of traditional composition was weakened by the painters' confused admiration for Mughal styles or was submerged in meaningless lacey elaboration meant to prettify the harsh older painting manner. Adverse political conditions that resulted in the Maratha takeover in 1738 also contributed to the deterioration of traditional Malwa painting, and in the eighteenth century styles attributable to central India are quite different. Few examples of the tensely arranged blue and red type of illustrations were done.

Both the Mewar ruling clan's position as the foremost of the Rajasthani clan-families, and the state's tumultuous political history affected artistic developments during the Mughal era. From Delhi, successive Muslim invaders noted the strategic location of Mewar's forts, and, in 1300, Chitor on a rocky plateau was conquered after bitter fighting that ended in *jauhar*. When the fortress was rebuilt in the fifteenth century it evolved into an extremely splendid center with many impressively large public buildings. Rana Kumbha (r. 1433–68), one of the most celebrated Rajput leaders, was not only a great builder who strengthened the state but was also a patron of the arts. Although primarily interested in the colorful bardic romances so typical of his period, he probably also developed paintings that corresponded with this literary tradition.

Because of its prominence and the intense pride of its nobles, Mewar was considered by other Rajputs as the psychological center of resistance against the Muslims. Its defeats were therefore extremely significant, not only for strategic reasons but also because of their effect on Rajput morale. The second conquest and *jauhar* at Chitor occurred in 1535; a child, the future Rana Udai Singh, was the sole survivor. During the third siege by Akbar's forces in 1568 with little hope of Rajput escape, Udai Singh understandably relinquished the tactilely futile struggle to his generals, retreating to found a new capital of Udaipur, which later became an important painting center. His successors were pursued across Mewar territories, but mainly through knowledge of the terrain and sheer determination, they were able to fight a guerrilla war that was unique in Rajasthan until they were at last forced to a decisive capitulation in 1614.

Despite this resistance, the painting style in Mewar changed in response to Mughal influence more rapidly than in the Malwa area. The *Rasamanjari* leaf of ca. 1615 from the Cleveland collection [90] is, like Malwa paintings, dependent on the pre-Mughal Rajput tradition for its primary color scheme and furnishings, such as the bed with its tasselled pillow. Nevertheless, the architecture in the Cleveland scene is clearly Akbari in its combination of bracketing, kiosks, and dome. Both the costume and the profile of the hero, who is being rebuked by the young heroine for his unfaithfulness, reveal Mughal influence. The masculine qualities of early Mughal painting could clearly be advantageously blended with this bold, rather brusque Rajput style.

The Muslim painter Sahibdin, who developed into Mewar's most eminent artist under the religiously devoted patron Jagat Singh I (r. 1628–52), began his career working in a popular Mughal manner that lacked stylistic definition. Because of the commercial appearance of his miniatures, it can be ascertained that the painter was probably without a steady patron during his initial development. Sometime after being welcomed at the Mewar court, Sahibdin began to explore aspects of traditional Rajput painting, and his experimentation opened up new, creative possibilities for others in the Mewar atelier. Without Sahibdin's imaginative reorganization of Mewar painting, the long-lived school would have lacked real avenues of development. His personal evolution thus led to a greater redirection of the entire atelier.

Since he was aware of Mughal compositions, Sahibdin enlarged the customary Rajput horizontal format but filled it with burgeoning landscape and figural forms that had a traditional basis. His Mughal training clearly afforded him the technical freedom to express his perceptions of Rajput life and the Rajasthani landscape.

Following Sahibdin's inspiration, the mid-seventeenth-century painters—probably the most expressive in Mewar history—created miniatures that are harshly contrastive and yet compellingly vivid. These compositions, which lack superficial prettiness, are imbued with an air of challenge or conflict that gives many clues to the Mewari temperament. The shapes and colors appear not only to be derived from the surrounding landscape but also to reflect the Rajput's response to his environment; for example, the Mewar artists almost invariably used pungent yellow-green combined with hot colors that seem to express visually how the landscape feels in heat. The sour color combinations of pinks, yellows, and yellow-greens appear to show that the Mewaris had come to terms with a landscape of oppressive extremes and in fact had identified with their environment in a profoundly joyous manner.

Although the Mewar atelier lapsed into dry illustration of religious texts during the second half of the seventeenth century, it was revitalized around 1700 by Amar Singh II (r. 1698–1710). As prince and rana, he introduced new secular subjects, Mughal stylistic elements, and new complexity in composition [91]. Although the change occurred shortly after his reign, it was because of him that the Mewar painters altered their depictions from expressionism to renderings based on actual observation. The popular mid- and late eighteenth-century pictures were relatively naturalistic scenes of estates, hunts, and festivals that demonstrate a new kind of receptivity to Mughal prototypes. The traditional Mewar style was not, however, completely rejected: many of these very large, maplike panoramas have familiar pungent colors and squat, large-headed figures. These late works, when considered with ones from the religious center of Nathadwara (see [93]) and also from the Mewar *thikana* of Devgarh, give an indication of the breadth and influence of the eighteenth- and nineteenth-century Mewar school.

Krishna Paintings in Rajasthan, Especially in the Mewar Area

Much art in Mewar and elsewhere in Rajasthan derives from the Krishna worship that became immensely popular just prior to the Mughal conquest, in part as a reaction to Muslim incursions in the North. The most intense Krishna worship had a mystical aspect that was quite different from Muslim Sufi ecstasy and thus emphasized Hindu separatism. Krishna's mythical deeds were in many ways incomprehensible to outsiders, and the passionate, idolatrous type of love given to this figure also helped to create a cult exclusive to Hinduism that followed the religion's own historical trend of development. Finally, mysticism not only helped to define the identity of an invaded people but also provided escapism from the prevailing politico-economic conditions of the Sultanate and Mughal periods.

The worship of this blue incarnation of Vishnu in Rajasthan was both general—as is exemplified by the varied single miniatures portraying Krishna as a hero—and associated with specific scriptural texts. The beliefs concerning the god/hero evolved over several centuries as this deity was made progressively more accessible and immediate to his devotees by poets and philosophers. He first appears in literature as a somewhat stern, remote warrior chieftain whose spiritual authority is given little explanation but who manifests himself in the early *Bhagavad Gita* as a transcendent god. A sixth-century text described Krishna's birth, childhood, and *avatara* mission to destroy the demon Kansa; and an important elaboration of his role was presented in the *Bhagavata Purana*, composed around the ninth century in South India. This text was associated with the beliefs of the Vaishnavite sect of Alvars, who enlarged the concept of the word *bhakti* from mere concentration on a deity to a whole-hearted, devotional surrender or worshipful trust, from which the succeeding literature of the Krishna movement arises.[4]

Seen, however, in the context of later times, the *Bhagavata Purana* itself is a somewhat abstract, moralizing treatise that discusses Krishna as an object of love but also concentrates on the social responsibilities of his princely role. It is the twelfth-century *Gita Govinda* that passionately describes Krishna as the god with whom each individual soul craves unity. Both of these latter texts were illustrated in numerous instances during the pre-Mughal and Mughal eras, the Mewar artists being among the most prolific creators of such scenes.

The poets who gathered near Mathura in the late fourteenth and fifteenth centuries to write about Krishna while living in the place associated with his early life as a village herdboy had a profound influence on Rajasthani culture. Poetry, painting, and musical composition for several centuries reflected their intense desires for union with the divine. One of the most single-minded of these devotees, Mirabai, was originally from Rajasthan: the daughter of a Mewar rana who abandoned secular life after being widowed, she endured social opprobrium to wander in the area of Brindaban, celebrating Krishna.

Many of the poets in Brindaban were disciples of the philosopher and proselytizer Vallabhacharya, who conceived the idea of salvation through *pushti marg* (the way of joyful well-being) as opposed to asceticism. The subject of their poetry was Krishna as a youthful cowherd or lover who in his playful activities (*lilas*) gave symbolic indications of his full, transcendent power to devotees. Vallabha based his cult of Shri (Lord) Nathji around his discovery of a supposedly ancient and thus awe-inspiring Krishna image to which he gave that title. The Shri Nathji icon supposedly found protruding from the ground, represented the god Krishna with his hand upraised, a gesture that symbolized Krishna's balancing Mt. Govardhan to shelter his friends the cowherds from the torrential rain sent by Indra. Indra's storm unsuccessfully challenged Krishna's attempts to establish a more direct, meaningful, and earthy form of worship for the cowherds, and the Govardhana image therefore represents the beneficent triumph of a new order with a village, or folk, basis.

In accordance with the belief of salvation through *pushti marg*, Vallabha's sect celebrates Krishna's *lilas* with huge feasts and opulent rituals. Such festivals require not only large, elaborate, painted scenes for the phases of temple worship but also miniatures for commemorations by devotees [79, 93]. In the course of daily worship, the cult accentuates practices already inherent in Hinduism: feeding, bathing, dressing, and otherwise caring for the Shri Nathji icon and others as if they were living humans.

Because of Aurangzeb's late seventeenth-century persecutions of many noteworthy Hindu shrines, the Shri Nathji icon was moved from the prominent religious city of Mathura, where various temples had often been damaged by Muslims in the past and which was dangerously near the Mughal capital. The sculpture was shifted to Nathadwara, which was barely a settlement but was near the Mewar city of Udaipur, where it could be protected by the Mewar rana. The town that subsequently grew up at this location was devoted to the Shri Nathji cult and the sale of religious objects to its pilgrims. The ceremonials that have developed at Nathadwara combine local folkish aspects of the original unsophisticated Krishna legend with luxurious, ritual practices of *pushti marg*.

Painting in Bikaner, Kota, and Jaipur

Unlike the two areas thus far surveyed, Bikaner did not have an ancient history as a territory. It was created in 1459 by a scion of the Rathor clan of Marwar in a desert area with a few oases and irrigated valleys. After wresting the land from local tribes, the new ruler founded a capital city.[5] Since cattle herding and trade provided the only sources of revenue, Raja Rai Singh propitiously allied himself to the Akbari court by offering his daughter in marriage to Prince Salim. An able general, Rai Singh played a significant role in expanding the Mughal empire, and he also served as governor of several areas. In return he was awarded fiefs whose revenues enabled him to have stone transported about two hundred miles for building the large fort of Bikaner.[6]

The raja also molded his rough, frontier state into an area that attracted poets, scholars, and possibly Mughal artists. The refinement typical of Bikaner painting perhaps stemmed from a desire to transform the barren desert environment. The soft painting styles, however, seem little related to the lives of the interminably fighting warrior-patrons. The Bikaner Rajputs coming from such rugged terrain were undoubtedly as formidable and proud as men from any part of Rajasthan, but in contrast to other Rajasthani miniatures the colors of Bikaner paintings almost always suggest pastoral serenity, and the figures are slight in comparison with the usually robust types.

Bikaner's close political dependence on the court and its lack of a rich traditional heritage must both have been factors that encouraged patrons to emulate the more highly developed Mughal school. The Bikaner artists borrowed careful, precise line-drawing techniques but employed these decoratively rather than naturalistically, in contrast to the Mughals. Since they lacked the intellectual curiosity of Mughal artists, many of their works are insubstantial; but the best Bikaneri miniatures have subtle, evocative landscapes and coloration [66]. The Mughal influence on the Bikaner school was not only stylistic but was also evident in the number of Muslim artists working for the court and in their habit of carefully inscribing miniatures with personal information.

Perhaps fortunately for the desert state, several of its leaders had great ability and performed well in Mughal service, although the authority of these able Rajputs was systematically compromised by their overlords. From Akbar's era on, the emperors considered it expedient to promote rivalry among chieftains in order to prevent them from fomenting rebellion—a policy that culminated in designs of Aurangzeb that estranged many Rajputs. The state of Bikaner reacted docilely, however, because the ruling family was absorbed in clan feuding. No estrangement altered the predominantly Mughal style of Bikaner painting, which had been further enriched by Rajput contacts with the Deccan during the decades of Mughal wars there.

In the 1640s Karan Singh (r. 1631–74), who was a fairly astute art patron, while serving with Mughal forces in the South, introduced Deccani elements to miniatures being done for him. The exotically colored, elegant Deccani styles enlivened the somewhat subdued or pallid Bikaner manner of painting. In addition, such attractive decorative painting created a bridge between the sometimes disparate Mughal and Rajput elements of the Bikaneri style.

Karan Singh spent much of his life in Mughal service in the Deccan despite Aurangzeb's attempts to dominate Bikaner. The wily emperor tried to allot Bikaner territory to other Rajputs, to slight or even to punish Karan, and, finally, to support an illegitimate heir. Karan's legitimate son Anup (r. 1675–98) outmaneuvered Aurangzeb, gained the title of raja, and reestablished order in his state. Apparently choosing the only viable outlet for his talents as a general, this ruler then fought side by side with the Mughals for twenty years in the Deccan. Such an action revealed the traditional Rajput's desire to spend his life in warfare, as well as his inability to cooperate politically with others of his caste. This complex attitude was reflected in the continuing dependence of Bikaner artists on Mughal or Deccani painting coupled with their independence from other Rajasthani schools. Anup Singh's military position gave him an opportunity to acquire Deccani miniatures as well as Persian and Turkish paintings and South Indian bronzes[7]—an appreciation of other traditions that was unusual among Rajputs and that parallels the assimilation encouraged in the Bikaner atelier.

The proximity of the state of Amber to Delhi and Agra naturally made it incline to Mughal influence, and its raja's early voluntary alliance with Akbar was pivotal in securing the cooperation of further Rajasthani leaders with the emperor. Akbar's first Rajput marriage was to an Amber princess, which of course promoted the influence of the state at court. Like Bikaner, Amber's fortune was also significantly improved by the Mughal service of its capable rajas. The successive Amber rajas Bhagwan Das and Man Singh were Akbar's leading generals and among his close associates.[8]

A *ragamala* leaf painted in Amber [60] parallels the imperial miniature style in its delicate restraint and precise detail. From the remaining evidence, the entire life style within the great Amber fortress was affected by imperial fashion and protocol. Courtly artisans had a surprisingly accurate view of imperial decoration but rendered this model in a refreshingly soft, original manner. In decorating the reception chambers of the Amber fort, the architects imitated specific Mughal features like the white architecture with its *pietra dura* panels and bottle niches, and artists then apparently borrowed from their colleagues to create refined miniature settings.

A larger body of *ragamala* leaves without specific documentation are attributed to Jaipur, the planned city that succeeded the fortress of Amber as the capital of the state. Its founder, Sawai Jai Singh II (r. 1699–1743), became the most powerful Rajasthani ruler, and, as a strong personality during a period of weak leadership in Delhi, he was able to enjoy wide influence and to complete numerous projects such as the construction of large astronomical instruments in several Indian cities. Both during and after his prosperous rule, many studios in Jaipur or the small surrounding principalities apparently produced *ragamala* sets having similar compositions but styles varying between those with tall, slender women [63] and those with heavier

Rajasthani types [62]. Such *ragamalas*, probably commissioned by families whose affluence was assured by the long rule of Jai Singh, are somewhat unusual in the Rajasthani tradition of court patronage. Urban culture was not characteristic of Rajput society, but Jai Singh was an expansive thinker who imitated successful Mughal urbanization.

The *ragamala* typically used in Rajasthan consisted of thirty-six painted compositions paralleling musical arrangements that describe different amorous moods. Both music and paintings were organized so that six melodies classified as males each presided over five associatable wifely melodies. Sung at particular seasons or times of day, the *ragamala* compositions had always been a popular subject for illustrations but became increasingly so with the broadening patronage of the eighteenth century. For painters, the *ragamala* was conveniently prescribed, could be repeated often, and formed an attractive set; for patrons, the themes were familiar, not too complex or literary, and concerned the favorite topic of romantic love.

The state of Kota was formed in 1625 by partition from Bundi in a typical Mughal gesture that rewarded the younger Kota branch of the family and simultaneously slighted the Bundi house, thus creating rivalry. Continually fanned by the Mughals, this rivalry was further exacerbated by Rajput hauteur and avidity for petty warfare. In spite of tensions, however, for several decades, up to about 1680, Kota painters borrowed from the Bundi repertoire of *ragamala* designs and romantic scenes using compositions taken verbatim from Bundi pictures.[9] Nevertheless, the early Kota miniatures have an individual freedom, and even wildness, apparent in figural or architectural exaggerations and fiercely swirled skies.[10]

In slightly later paintings the entire style becomes more strikingly individual because of the Kota flair for drawing. By the reign of Ram Singh I (1686–1708), artists had begun to draw a large variety of subjects with a tremendous passion to comprehend animation in particular. Their appetite to learn about life through observation was unusual in India and could be better paralleled by the Japanese artist Hokusai's characterization of himself as "mad about drawing." Like him, the extraordinary Kota artists learned to transcribe landscape elements and animals with very confident, fluid calligraphic lines. All the qualities of thought such as intuition, spontaneity, and whimsicality that develop from working improvisationally by sketching are emphasized in Kota miniatures. Although the artists' perceptions of reality were never analytical, Kota paintings often have an effect of startling accuracy that derives from sympathetic observations.

Although the Kota artists were followed by those of Mewar in the mid-eighteenth century, they seem to have been the first to render landscape as the real subject of compositions. Because they were interested in drawing, they sought to depict underlying structural contours of landscape. Their more conservative Bundi cousins often arranged flat trees in overlapping rows that artificially simulated spatial recession, whereas they captured the rhythm of jungle growth and its density in a much bolder way. The Rajasthani landscape is generally dry, if not barren, as, for example, the states of Jodhpur or Bikaner. In states like Mewar and Kota, however, the jungle—open and sunlit rather than dense—has long grasses interspersed with small, twisted trees and rock outcroppings. Trees in Kota miniatures are rounded and have branches reaching outward so that they appear to encompass air and, if colored, are rendered in subtle greens.

As a part of the environment they so skillfully built up, the Kota artists stressed the relationship of animals to ground cover as well as to other species. These painters sensitively placed men and animals deep in foliage or landscape pockets so that vegetation envelops them, whereas even in Mughal art, forms tend to perch on terrain in a more artificial manner. The deer and the lion are the two usual personalities of this world—the one light-bodied and delicately wary, the other muscular and bold. The all-important subject of the Kota hunt miniatures is the jungle itself, which is always portrayed as a dominant but vital, not hostile, presence.

Umed Singh (r. 1771–1819), a Kota ruler portrayed in a Cleveland drawing [76], succeeded at the age of ten, but his regent, Zalim Singh, arranged for the young raja to be amused with hunting while Zalim governed the affairs of state. Thus the hunt scene, already a popular subject, was made to serve a political end. As Zalim Singh was enjoying a long career that involved the expansion of the state's power, land reform, and dealings with the Marathas, Raja Umed Singh continued hunting, and paintings served as flattering records of his exploits. Because such hunting scenes became so important during his reign, styles multiplied. One highly conventionalized type showing short figures and barriers of nail-headed rocks stretching across the horizon became usual from around 1770 and remained in common usage well into the nineteenth century. Other styles, however, evolved and blended with one another, indicating the Kota artists' delight in independent observation and drawing—qualities that kept the spirit of the school alive well into the nineteenth century, when its paintings constituted one of the most important chapters in the final episode of Rajasthani art.

1. Krishna, pp. 12–13.
2. M. Chandra, 1951/52, 1: 63.
3. R. A. Dwivedi, 1966, p. 84; W. G. Archer, 1957b, p. 90.
4. Hopkins, p. 6.
5. Tod, 2: 137–39.
6. Goetz, 1950, p. 42.
7. Ibid., p. 47.
8. Gascoigne, pp. 81–82.
9. In Beach, 1974, compare fig. 26 with fig. 68, or fig. 17 with fig. 62.
10. See two leaves of the earliest-known Kota *ragamala* in Spink, no. 78; and in Beach, 1974, fig. 62.

58   *A Raja on an Elephant*   69.36

Drawing with slight color, Rajasthan, Ajmer area, possibly Sawar, ca. 1680–1700, 39.5 × 61 cm. Disintegrated along fold lines and has been rejoined; extraneous script added on right; section of another drawing used to fill lower left corner; small tears, wrinkles, and holes; some discoloration and staining. Torn inscription at top left: "Maharaja L [?]. . . ."

Purchase, Edward L. Whittemore Fund

Comparative Material: (A) *Elephant Attacking a Horse and Rider*, Popular Mughal, probably Ajmer area, ca. 1640; *Sotheby*, 26 Nov. 1968, lot 379. (B) *Rampaging Elephant*, Popular Mughal, probably Ajmer area, ca. 1650–60; Beach, 1966, no. 168. (C) *Elephants Given Water*, Rajasthan, Ajmer area, possibly Sawar, ca. 1760–80; Beach, 1974, fig. 81. (D) *An Elephant Being Subdued*, Rajasthan, Ajmer area, possibly Sawar, ca. 1670–80; Beach, 1974, fig. 80. (E) *Maharaja Pratap Singh of Sawar on an Elephant*, Rajasthan, Sawar, early eighteenth century; *Sotheby*, 4 May 1977, lot 426.

This drawing of a raja astride a prancing elephant is a large work whose scale contributes to its majestic appearance. Color has been applied mainly in the center of the composition on the elephant's saddle cloth and the accessories of the raja himself. Unfortunately, the inscription at the upper edge of the picture identifying the ruler and his principality has been almost entirely obliterated, and the royal portrait is too generalized to permit identification. With his elephant goad in his hand, this raja sits confidently astride his beast, who is obviously in a frisky, playful mood. Retainers march alongside armed with spears or prongs holding fireworks to head off and distract the pachyderm should he prove intractible. The damaged state of the paper does not obscure the vigorous quality of the drawing, which is fairly simple and like other Rajasthani miniatures depends on a strong silhouette.

Many miniatures of elephants (an exceedingly important subject in Rajasthani painting) are related, although not attributable to the same school. Associations between Mughal art, the art of the Ajmer area, and that of Kota have not been fully explored, but it appears that elephants were the primary subjects of a particular group of Rajasthani painters who may have acquired Mughal characteristics in Ajmer and then shared them with Kota artists or even migrated to Kota.

In the energetic Akbari period, the elephant—whether dashing warriors to the ground in battle or trampling criminals—was a dynamic creature well understood by artists. Many painters working for the imperial studio who showed an uncanny aptitude for capturing its spirit were certainly Hindus. Their mastery of naturalistic techniques complemented their strong instinctive sympathy, and it is these Akbari works that seem to be the antecedents of the Rajasthani elephant sketches despite a lapse of time before the appearance of known Rajput drawings.

The exuberant vitality and expressionism of Akbari

Figure 58, detail.

Figure 58.

animal-painters disappeared in Jahangir's more formal era. The elephant who had been portrayed with sweeping, leaf-like ears; bulbous legs; and a head with an exaggerated cranium was depicted with cooler, more scientific accuracy by the artists of Jahangir and Shah Jahan. The extremely individual Akbari beast reappears, however, in the drawings of Ajmer, Bundi, and Kota.

Because Ajmer was a state closely linked to the Mughal court, it was an area of much Muslim-Hindu interaction. As a center of Sufism, Ajmer had welcomed Akbar and Jahangir during several pilgrimages, and Jahangir had held court here from 1614 to late 1616. The first paintings of elephants that may have come from this state are Popular Mughal works that show the early transfer of Mughal art to the common culture (A and B). These works do not, however, demonstrate the existence of a cohesive style. A lively Rajasthani style evolved slightly later in the seventeenth century that appears to depend on Akbari conventions (C and D).

The artist of the Cleveland miniature has acquired Mughal mannerisms secondhand, perhaps from an artist like the one who drew a powerful sketch of elephants being watered before a citadel (C). In studying the heads of the animals, it is evident that the repeated sketching lines meticulously depicting structure in the earlier miniature are treated more as pattern in the Cleveland drawing. In this latter miniature the artist has exaggerated the curving mouth in an abstract manner, while in the earlier work, closer to a Mughal source, the rolls of the elephant's jowls give an illusion of weight as they hang over his tusks. The figures in the earlier sketch are more casually drawn than those in the Cleveland miniature, but despite a difference in approach, both are related as Ajmer types.

The Cleveland artist has given a spirited but symbolic rendering of form that is midway between Mughal inspiration and the stylized elephant pictures done in Ajmer in the early eighteenth century (E). These latter miniatures, which are numerous, show the continuing popularity of this genre, but the elephants themselves now are rarely drawn in action, and in this respect differ greatly from the earlier Clevelant scene. Many of the eighteenth-century pictures are documentable by inscription to the Ajmer *thikana*, or fiefdom, of Sawar, whose painters produced ruler-portraits, garden scenes, and epic illustrations as well as animal miniatures. Little specific information is known about painting in the rest of Ajmer; it is therefore difficult to attribute the unidentified raja in the Cleveland drawing to a particular area within the state.

The Cleveland drawing has been damaged in much the same way as the two other Ajmer works (C and D). The paper has disintegrated along fold lines, and clumsy restoration has been undertaken in places. The inept restorer used any available pieces of paper, even including parts of other old drawings: a nearly complete figure, probably by the same artist, with long curly locks and robed in a fully colored Persian or Deccani costume has been inserted horizontally at the lower left corner.

59 *Bitch with Her Litter* 69.77

Rajasthan, Ajmer, probably Sawar, ca. 1780, 22 × 16.5 cm, 25 × 18.7 cm with border. Narrow black inner border; orange outer border.

Gift of Mr. and Mrs. William E. Ward in memory of her father, Charles Svec

Comparative Material: (A) *Dog Portrait*, by Bagta, Rajasthan, Devgarh, dated 1806; Andhare, fig. 44. (B) *Raja Amar Singh II of Mewar with Four Salukis*, Rajasthan, Mewar, ca. 1700; H. Waters and D. Waters, *The Saluki in History, Art, and Sport* (London: Newton Abbot, 1969), p. 89.

Isolated in a large, deep gray background, a female dog presides like a schoolmistress over her neatly dispersed litter of puppies. A mongrel herself, she seems to have an unstinting regard for her foolishly smiling offspring whose origins are even more questionable than her own. The puppies with eyes still closed reflect an air of simple contentment.

Other miniatures show how far this family ranks below standards of canine snobbery. The dog valued in India during the Mughal era was the saluki, originally brought to the subcontinent from the Near East and bred for hunting.[1] Because dogs were not highly regarded, a sovereign like Jahangir had far fewer dogs than horses, elephants, or hawks. But those he did own and gave as presents were mainly salukis.[2]

Rajasthani portraits of dogs show that the saluki was prized by the Rajputs and that standards of appearance were controlled. In other miniatures the salukis stand in exhibition postures (A). Their noses are long, straight, and pointed, and they wear not only elaborate collars but often bejeweled anklets. The dog in the Cleveland miniature wears no collar and has a blunt nose and a head of less than ideal shape.

Though humor or satire is unusual in Indian painting, it does appear at times, and, in fact, seems to be consciously intended here. The bitch, gazing off over the heads of her puppies, seems totally unaware that nothing will make them proper dogs. Certainly the motley circle of puppies, with masklike eye patches and contrasting paws, seems whimsical. Although some valued salukis had spotted coats (B), here the spots are clearly accentuated for effect. The ugliness of the puppies is skillfully contrasted with their engaging smiles and helpless clumsiness. Possibly the artist intended a further irony, for although he gently lampoons the family group, the liveliness of these outcasts simultaneously makes a comment on the usual portraits of bejeweled court dogs.

On a technical level the Cleveland miniature is more complex than the standard dog portrait. Indeed, if it were not competently done, it would lose its understated meanings. The artist has conceived his animals three-dimensionally—a departure from the drawing formulae used for other dog portraits whose silhouettes are conventionalized (A).

Figure 59.

Horse and elephant portraiture was an important category of miniature production in both the Mughal and Rajasthani courts. Dog portraiture was, however, characteristic of Rajasthan in the eighteenth and nineteenth centuries and was mainly confined to the states of Ajmer, with its *thikana* of Sawar, and Mewar, with its *thikanas* such as Devgarh. Although no apt parallel is known for this theme, the concise style of the Cleveland miniature is typical of Ajmer. Furthermore, the sober colors are comparable to those in other eighteenth-century animal portraits done in Sawar.

1. Waters, p. 17.

2. Foster, pp. 103–4. While Jahangir's other animals numbered in the thousands, he had only four hundred dogs. Salukis are shown in early Mughal miniatures, such as the British Museum *Akbar Nama* folios (Martin, 2: pl. 182). Jahangir hunted with "Arabian dogs" (Jahangir, 1: 126, 288), which the translator of the *Tuzuk* amplifies to "greyhounds." The word "saluki" is derived from an Arabian city, and these dogs are classified as a type of greyhound (Waters, pp. 96–99).

60 *Kanhra Ragini* 60.46

Rajasthan, Amber, ca. 1700, 29.6 × 18.4 cm. Right edge torn irregularly, removing from one-half to two inches of the horizontal dimension; fold across center resulting in damage to two men's faces; stain in trees at top; tear at top running through trees and pavilion roof. Fragmentary border, but was once dark blue and red.

Purchase, Mr. and Mrs. William H. Marlatt Fund

Ex collection: Heeramaneck.

Published: Lee, 1960, no. 42.

Comparative Material: (A) *Kanhra Ragini*, Rajasthan, Amber, from a set dated 1709; Ebeling, no. 168.
(B) *Vasanta Ragini*, Rajasthan, Amber, ca. 1700; Ebeling, C27, or Spink and Son, 1976, no. 42.

Figure 60, detail.

In this miniature from a *ragamala* set, the key figure is represented as Krishna, with his peacock crown and blue complexion. He stands in a pavilion with two attendants behind him as two retainers salute him with raised arms and two others in the lower left attend an elephant on which a *mahout* is seated with his head bent in tribute. The theme of *kanada, kanaro,* or *kanhra*—the *ragini* portrayed here— is bravery in elephant hunting. The mood of love represented is one of heroic triumph; peerless physical beauty is celebrated as well. The attendants praise the valor of their king, who is usually identified with Krishna because of this hero's legendary slaying of the elephant demon. Often a slaughtered elephant with its tusks removed is shown in compositions of Kanhra. The components of the Cleveland miniature, however, are among the common alternatives; the prescribed elements are the elephant near the base of the miniature, the two saluting men, and the lord with a sword over his near shoulder and an elephant tusk in his opposite hand.[1]

Almost no study of the early Amber school has been done, although the court was one that must have sponsored painting. Both its close political association and its location near the imperial capitals indicate that there would probably have been Mughal-influenced miniatures at an early date. Various architectural elements such as the audience hall of the now-deserted Amber palace show that Mughal influence was strong in other artistic areas. The first large group of paintings known to have been done in Amber are *ragamala* pages, like this Cleveland miniature, which were produced about 1700. These numerous partial sets have quite consistent stylistic features, although their *ragamala* iconographies are of two disparate types. Details of the Cleveland miniature—trees, figures, fretwork fences, and delicately patterned architectural panels—are done in a common style that is somewhat related to that of earlier Popular Mughal paintings.[2]

In his book cataloging *ragamala* painting Klaus Ebeling noted that Amber artists used two different *ragamala* iconographies and labeled one as Amber tradition, distinguishing it from the more widespread Rajasthani type.[3] The Cleveland Kanhra leaf belongs to the Rajasthani tradition with iconographic features common to several states, while comparison A exemplifies the composition that evolved only in Amber, wherein the lord is shown at the base of the picture symmetrically positioned between four attendants who do not salute him with raised arms as in the Cleveland miniature. The lord holds a sword and elephant tusk, but no elephant is present. Since the arrangement of five standing figures is duplicated in other Amber-tradition illustrations, Kanhra is made almost indistinguishable from various other *ragas* or *raginis*.

Only one of the four sets discussed by Ebeling as being from Amber is of the Rajasthani type. *Kanhra Ragini* is one of a large group of leaves from a single collection forming the core of this set;[4] thus, without doubt the leaf belongs to this particular series. The Cleveland miniature must then

167

Figure 60.

belong to a further Amber *ragamala* of the Rajasthani type. Its damaged condition implies that possibly other leaves from the set may have been destroyed.

In spite of serious damage to the outer areas of the Cleveland miniature, the quality and simple restraint of the Amber style can be easily seen. The Krishna figure with a soft face in repose and fleshy cheeks is echoed in a further Amber page (B). In the Cleveland painting the artist has lavished attention on this central personage by means of certain details: the dark jewels are appliqued, the tiny white beads of his necklaces are raised, and the gilt *patka* is daintily flowered. The painting thus combines a dignity or refinement characteristic of Mughal art with a warmth and gentleness probably attributable to Hinduism.

1. For various examples of this iconographic type see Pal, 1967, no. 40, pl. XVIII; Ebeling, C29, no. 155; Gangoly, 1935, pl. L, figs. A, B.
2. For stylistic similarities with Popular Mughal painting, see Coomaraswamy, 1926, pt. 6: pls. XI, XII; and Khandalavala, Chandra, and Chandra, 1960, no. 15B, fig. 25.
3. Ebeling, *ragamalas* 44–48, pp. 186–88.
4. Ebeling, p. 186.

61 Gaudi Ragini 68.109

Rajasthan, probably Jaipur, ca. 1700–1725, 25.5 × 19 cm, 30.7 × 23.8 cm with borders. Narrow dark blue inner surround, orange outer border.

Gift of The American Foundation for the Maud E. and Warren H. Corning Botanical Collection

Comparative Material: (A) *Malavi Ragini*, Rajasthan, probably Jaipur area, ca. 1660; Archer, 1958, pl. 10. (B) *Kakubha Ragini*, Rajasthan, probably Jaipur area, ca. 1660; W. G. Archer, *Indian Painting* (London: Iris Books, 1956), pl. 8. (C) *Malkaus Raga*, by Ram Kishen, Rajasthan, Malpura, from a set dated 1756; Archer and Binney, no. 36.

The stylistic group to which certain seventeenth-century *ragamala* pages (A and B) belong has proven difficult to relate to other contemporary pictures or to attribute to a location. This group, however, has features that are continued in eighteenth-century miniatures such as the Cleveland leaf of *Gaudi Ragini*. The known seventeenth-century pictures belong to an almost complete *ragamala* series that was in the Kanoria collection, Patna, and is now mainly in the Victoria and Albert Museum; in addition, scattered leaves of the type exist from at least one other *ragamala*.[1] The kind of stylized execution employed and the standard compositions for this group imply that a large number of sets was originally created from one master series of *ragamala* drawings. The group is distinguished by repetitive compositions for most indoor or outdoor scenes; by warm yellow, pink, and orange color schemes; and by various motifs such as those used for architecture (for example, a particular type of white palace building with balconies and tiny decorative bands occurs in any scene with a pavilion setting). Figures are narrow-waisted and fragile looking, unlike many Rajasthani types.

The female figure in the Cleveland *Gaudi Ragini* leaf is much like the heroines of the seventeenth-century miniatures (A and B). In addition, the Cleveland scene has unusual horizontal bands that are frequently employed in the earlier *ragamala* series as building units (see A). The arc-shaped hill, the central position of the heroine, and the foreground pond with water lilies are all typical features of the seventeenth-century *ragamala* type (B), which can be compared with the Cleveland scene.[2]

The colors of the Cleveland miniature—chartreuse, dark blue, and brown—are not common, however, and this leaf has not proven associable with any known *ragamala* series. The inscribed title of *Gaudi* or *Gauri Ragini* is a variant one, since the heroine of Gaudi is usually surrounded by peacocks rather than deer. The composition of the Cleveland Gaudi miniature is almost identical to that of a miniature labeled *Kakubha Ragini* (B). (Differences in *ragamala* labeling often occur in conventionalized *ragamala* groups.)[3] In each composition the heroine stands alone before a lily pond with flower garlands in her hands and deer beside her.

The provenance of both the early and late groups of miniatures remains uncertain. The early miniatures have been

Figure 61.

attributed to Malwa or Jaipur, while the later types have been termed Jaipur, Central India, or, in some cases, Bikaner.[4] Little documentation exists for either group. The environs of Jaipur appear a probable location because a set dated 1767 of the later *ragamala* type is known to have been done in Ranthambhor—at this time under the influence of Jaipur.[5] Furthermore, there is a *ragamala* set inscribed as being from Malpura and dated 1756 that has the same small figures as the seventeenth-century *ragamala* type (cf. C with A and B).[6] Rows of flowers across the page and certain architectural features and compositions are also similar. Malpura was a city near Jaipur, which was under Jaipur's protection and served as the Jaipur market area. Thus it seems probable that the *ragamala* style centers around Jaipur though it may have been quite widely employed throughout this area of Rajasthan. The eighteenth century was a time of stylistic diffusion and of styles being freely passed about and imitated. Jaipur and its environs were commercially successful, with a new wealthy class encouraged by the powerful Maharaja Sawai Jai Singh II (r. 1699–1744) who foresaw the necessity for an expanded type of urban life in Rajasthan. Amber, the old capital of his clan, had been situated for strategic reasons on a rocky outcrop, but, because of this placement, had a limited size and population. The scientifically minded raja created Jaipur with a planned grid of streets and squares. Its inhabitants, by utilizing the setting to commercial advantage, created a thriving community but one with only a superficial culture. The maharaja himself was interested in the pragmatic applications of art to architecture rather than in concerning himself with purely aesthetic expression in painting. Jaipur's citizens were leading altered lives, had more money to spend, and maintained somewhat tenuous links with the Rajasthani culture of the past. All these factors enhance the probability that the eighteenth-century group of *ragamala* miniatures under discussion was created in the Jaipur area where the newly affluent could have commissioned such attractive but repetitive compositions with only loose traditional associations.

1. In addition to comparative miniatures A and B, the Victoria and Albert/Kanoria *ragamala* has been published in Ebeling, color pl. 12, and M. M. Deneck, *Indian Art* (London: Hamlyn, 1967), pl. 39. Pages of a fragmentary *ragamala* of the same type are in the Bickford collection (Bhairavi, Desvarari).

2. For a discussion of the relationship between the seventeenth- and eighteenth-century miniature groups see Ebeling, pp. 94–98.

3. *Kakubha* and *Gaudi Raginis* in this style can apparently be shown with either deer or peacocks around the heroine (see [62]). The two themes have identical settings.

4. W. G. Archer, 1958, p. 22; Archer and Binney, p. 66; Ebeling, pp. 94–98.

5. Ebeling, p. 94.

6. Ibid., p. 212; the date of this set is misprinted in several other sources.

62 *Kakubha Ragini* 71.92

Rajasthan, probably Jaipur, ca. 1750, 22.9 × 15.5 cm, 27 × 20.5 cm with border. Gold inner border; red outer border.

Purchase, Andrew R. and Martha Holden Jennings Fund
Ex collection: MacDonald.

Comparative Material: (A) *Kakubha Ragini*, Rajasthan, probably Jaipur, ca. 1750; Philadelphia Museum of Art, 17-1964-10, unpublished. (B) *Kakubha Ragini*, Rajasthan, probably Jaipur, ca. 1750; *Times of India Annual* (1965), p. 64. (C) *Todi Ragini*, Rajasthan, probably Jaipur, ca. 1750; Gangoly, 1935, pl. XVb. (D) *Todi Ragini*, Rajasthan, probably Jaipur, ca. 1750; *Sotheby*, 27 March 1973, lot 80. (E) *Todi Ragini*, Rajasthan, probably Jaipur, ca. 1750; Archer and Binney, no. 51.

This composition is much like that of the previous catalogue entry. Here, however, the female figure in the center is surrounded by peacocks. (In some miniatures it is deer who are attracted to her.) Many near-duplicates of this arrangement are found in the large group of *ragamalas* that can be loosely associated with the Jaipur area during the mid-eighteenth century; for example, the basic composition of a woman between a lily pond and a key-shaped hill with deer or peacocks beside her was an obviously popular one. Certain more specific correlations are also evident, such as the presence of two men on the left looking over the brow of a hill in many miniatures (A-E). A low, fluid strip of land runs directly in front of the heroine, and, finally, a white pavilion appears at the top of each design. In addition, certain compositions of *Kakubha Ragini* have the same text as the Cleveland scene, thereby demonstrating the closeness of the type (cf. A and B).

Figure 62.

Such proliferation and uniformity hint at the conditions under which these *ragamala* sets must have been illustrated. They were probably produced in fairly large commercial workshops located in several neighboring areas since the figures differ in the paintings.

The Cleveland Kakubha scene, like others from a subgroup of these *ragamalas*, is brightly colored in fuschia, red orange, and pink; and its figures are quite stocky. The explosion of heated colors and crowded forms (such as the closely packed, junglelike trees in the background) gives the Cleveland scene an intensity it might otherwise lack as one of many similar compositions. The colors, the giant buds of the banana trees, and the peacocks—standard imagery of Rajasthani painting for several centuries—symbolize the frustrated longings and desires of the waiting heroine.

63 *Gunakali Ragini*   54.261

Rajasthan, probably Jaipur, ca. 1750, 23.6 × 15.6 cm, 30.5 × 22.9 cm with border. Orange-red border.

Purchase, Edward L. Whittemore Fund

Published: Lee, 1960, no. 46b.

Comparative Material: (A) *Malavi Ragini*, Rajasthan, probably Jaipur area, ca. 1660; W. G. Archer, 1958, pl. 10. (B) *Gunakali Ragini*, Rajasthan, probably Jaipur area, ca. 1750; Gangoly, 1935, pl. XXIVb.

Like the two previous catalogue entries, this scene is part of a large mid-eighteenth-century group of *ragamala* miniatures that have similar dimensions, texts, compositions, and iconographies.[1] Although the sets are standardized in many ways, the figure types are widely variable. This seems incongruous since other prominent features—architecture and compositional patterns, in particular—remain much

Figure 63.

the same. This miniature with its slender, elongated women and the previous miniature [62] with short, stocky figures illustrate the two most common varieties within the group. Clearly the two *ragamalas* are products of different studios and may be from different localities—possibly two towns in the Jaipur area, although there is no specific evidence of provenance for either type.

As already mentioned (in [61]), the entire mid-eighteenth-century group is linked with an earlier *ragamala* type by numerous stylistic details. Many of the earlier *ragamala* leaves have bands of flowers across the upper portion of the composition (A), while in the Cleveland Gunakali scene the floral band has been moved to the top of a wall. Rows of thin horizontal steps are shown in many of the earlier *ragamala* group (A) as they are in the Gunakali leaf. The white architecture with its balconies and bottle niches is also much the same in each period.

The mid-eighteenth-century *ragamala* group has numerous repetitive compositions seemingly for each *raga* or *ragini*. The Cleveland Gunakali scene is nearly identical in all respects with a further contemporary depiction of the same subject (B). The major change in the comparative scene is the addition of two figures, but this is of slight importance because the other figures are arranged and posed in the same fashion as in the Cleveland Gunakali leaf.

1. Ebeling, p. 96.

64 *Jai Singh III of Jaipur*   25.1337
(*r. 1818–1835*) *Riding*

Drawing, Rajasthan, Jaipur, ca. 1820, 10 × 14.3 cm. Fold marks.

Purchase from the J. H. Wade Fund

Comparative Material: (A) *Raja Jagat Singh of Jaipur (r. 1803–1818) on an Elephant*, Rajasthan, Jaipur, ca. 1810; Gray, 1950, pl. 96. (B) *Raja Pratap Singh of Jaipur* (r. 1779–1803), ca. 1800, Rajasthan, Jaipur; Coomaraswamy, 1926, pt. 5, pl. CXVI. (C) *Raja Pratap Singh of Jaipur*, Rajasthan, Jaipur, ca. 1800; *Maggs Bulletin*, no. 14 (Dec. 1968), no. 107.

This small drawing is typical of nineteenth-century Jaipur portraits (cf. A-C). The raja in the Cleveland sketch wears a wide sash and a huge helmetlike turban with a chin strap—both characteristic of Jaipur costume. His profile is expressionless, and the drawing style is controlled and slightly blueprint-like, as is usual within the nineteenth-century Jaipur tradition.

Figure 64.

65 *Krishna and the Gopis*   46.359

Rajasthan, Jaipur, mid-19th century, 14.4 × 12 cm.
Damaged; paint removed on upper right.
Gift of Mr. and Mrs. Arthur D. Brooks

This painting of Krishna and the *gopis* is painted in a folkish
style that is vastly different from the elaborate and detailed
nineteenth-century miniatures done for the Jaipur court.
The short, flat figures, like those of catalogue entry 60,
suggest that the miniature was produced somewhere in the
Jaipur area.

Figure 65.

Figure 66.

66 *Worship of Shiva* 67.240

Rajasthan, Bikaner, early 18th century, 26.7 × 20.3 cm,
31.2 × 24.5 cm with border. Some paint removal in various
places. Narrow gold inner border; mottled green outer
border.

Gift of Dr. and Mrs. Sherman E. Lee

Comparative Material: (A) *Krishna and Gopis*, Rajasthan,
Bikaner, ca. 1690; Welch and Beach, no. 23.

Figure 66, detail.

This unusual miniature is divided into two scenes that are
treated somewhat independently. Despite an enigmatic arrangement, three of the figures seem to be the same female
personality shown at different moments. In the upper part
of the design this heroine sits despondently on a carpet in
a white pavilion. She is then shown reverently greeting a
young ascetic from the steps of the building. Not only are
her facial features the same, but her jewelry and costume
are identical (to distinguish her from the other women in
the miniature, she is shown in each sequential episode
wearing a blue-gray *choli*, a red and gold-flecked skirt, and
a transparent veil). The brahmin ascetic with his tuft of hair
is bare-chested except for a narrow scarf and a rosary; he
is posed with arms extended in what appears to be a gesture
of explanation as well as beneficence. Below this scene,
Shiva and Devi are seated in a small shrine on the god's
tiger skin. Shiva's trident, horn, and other symbols of
asceticism are beside them. Shiva and Devi gaze at the
suppliant heroine, who approaches them on the left with
her hands raised in an *anjali* position. Around her, five
other women offer dishes of rice and ewers of water to the
holy pair.

Since the miniature's theme has not been selected from
a commonly illustrated literary work, its meaning remains
obscure. However, it appears that Shiva and Devi may be
a vision meant to resolve the problems of the languishing
woman. The sorrow of heroines in Indian painting is associated with desertion or unfulfilled love, and it is probable
that the ascetic is making some pronouncement on the
woman's state, or may himself be her desired lover.

The miniature is predominantly done in shades of deep
emerald green with the hillock on which the shrine is situated in yellow greens and the tree foliage in dark green.
These various green tones must have provided relief from
the dust and heat of the desert state; Bikaner painters produced a number of similarly serene pastoral compositions.
The treatment of foliage in the Cleveland miniature parallels that of other works: the same unusual protruding
branches and groupings of light leaves against dark tree
masses are found in comparison A, among others. The grace
and fragility of the figures are also typical; for example, the
ascetic who appears in the upper right is modeled with the
gentle, pretty face and thin limbs characteristic of many
male figures in Bikaner paintings (A).

Figure 66, detail.

67 *Lovers Embracing* 68.107

Rajasthan, Bundi, ca. 1760, 26 × 15 cm, 28.7 × 17.9 cm with border. Slightly rubbed; border damaged at upper right. Narrow yellow inner border. Red outer border.

Purchase, James Parmelee and Cornelia Blakemore Warner Funds

Comparative Material: (A) *Umed Singh of Bundi (r. 1749–ca. 1773) with His Sons*, Rajasthan, Bundi, ca. 1765; Beach, 1974, fig. 39, or W. G. Archer, 1959, no. 32. (B) *Umed Singh of Bundi Kills a Wild Boar*, Rajasthan, Bundi, ca. 1760; W. G. Archer. 1959, no. 22. (C) *Lovers Embracing*, Rajasthan, Bundi, ca. 1760; Randhawa and Galbraith, pl. 16. (D) *Lovers Embracing*, Rajasthan, Bundi, ca. 1760; W. G. Archer, 1959, no. 27. (E) *Lovers on a Terrace*, Rajasthan, Bundi, ca. 1760; W. G. Archer, 1959, no. 28.

This decorative scene showing a seated lord embracing his mistress is found in several versions with nearly identical compositions (C and D) as well as in variations with only slight differences (E). Each of the paintings is in the same period style with the heavy faces and short stocky figures employed for depictions during the rule of Umed Singh of Bundi (r. 1749–73) (A and B). The artists of the Bundi tradition had always depended upon compositional prototypes that endured over many decades, and this conventionalization was especially typical of *ragamala* scenes, which these romantic compositions imitate. The lack of inscriptions indicates that these scenes of embracing lovers are not from *ragamala* sets, but they depend on designs used for such subjects as *Malkaus* or *Pancham Ragini*.

While the Bundi habit of reworking designs was typical of the state's most creative periods through the seventeenth

Figure 67.

century, the era in which these miniatures of lovers were produced was one of excessive repetition of similar subjects. The traditionally delicate Bundi painting had also become rather artificial and fussy. The state itself, a contested pawn of Jaipur, was being devastated by the Marathas originally called in to help restore the authority of its rulers. Umed Singh thus had little independence or power. Any patronage was probably divided between his impoverished court and Bundi nobles—one of several reasons for the many versions of this love scene.

The three nearly identical compositions of lovers are adjusted so that each appears unique at first glance. In comparison C, for example, the pavilion differs, and in D the embracing couple is reversed. More significant are the many intricate and selective changes in color or pattern: the artist of the Cleveland miniature utilized a floral pattern similar to one used in another scene (C) that covers the terrace, continues into the pavilion, and is transformed in the rug design. The colors in these miniatures are rich and contrasting—as, for example, in the Cleveland leaf where orange, reds, yellows, and yellow greens appear against a cool blue. Innumerable variations of color or details are possible, but the slightly cloistered, mannerist style remains unaltered.

The demand for semi-erotic themes in the politically indolent but jaded court seems to have generated numerous related depictions, which have, however, been stripped of the ardor and tension present in romantic miniatures by Kota or earlier Bundi painters.

68 *Desakh Ragini*   65.32

Rajasthan, possibly Raghugarh, ca. 1770–90, 22 × 13 cm, 24.3 × 15.9 cm with border. Border slightly rubbed; slight paint flaking. Dark blue border. Inscription at top: "Meghmallar's Ragini Desakhar."

Sundry Purchase Fund

Comparative Material: (A) *Gujari Ragini,* Rajasthan, possibly Raghugarh, ca. 1770–90; Skelton, 1961, pl. 17. (B) *Kakubha Ragini,* Rajasthan, possibly Raghugarh, ca. 1770–90; Skelton, 1961, pl. 18.

This version of *Desakh Ragini* belongs to a large group of almost identical *ragamalas* done in the latter part of the eighteenth century in a derivative Bundi style (A and B). The *ragamala* themes are treated according to Bundi tradition, and stylistic conventions also conform to those used in the state. The details are, however, more florid and charming than those of contemporary Bundi pictures. Pools are crowded with birds, trees are bursting with leaves, and figures are abundantly decorated with jewelry or garlands (the two Cleveland miniatures from the group are plainer than most in this style).

Because one *ragamala* set of this group was found in a collection that also contained large numbers of ruler portraits from the state of Raghugarh in Central India, the *ragamala* group has been tentatively ascribed to this area also.[1] But such a connection is tenuous, since many Rajasthani collections contain material from several places. The attribution is supported, however, by a Raghugarh seal found on the back of the following miniature [69]. Most of the Raghugarh portraits are in a much bolder, simpler style with little relation to the Bundi idiom.[2] Certain of the later eighteenth-century depictions contemporary with the *ragamala* miniatures are more ornamental, but stylistic association is still not provable.[3] It was, however, common for the same artists to be able to paint concurrently in more than one manner. Some states reserved certain conventions for portraiture and a more decorative manner for other depictions; the problem thus lies in determining the range of diversity possible in any *thikana*. Bundi and Kota were artistically influential states, and many small *thikanas* would have had painters at least partially working in substyles based on Bundi-Kota models.

Not enough is known about the smaller painting ateliers in Rajasthan and Central India to understand how each was affected by the larger states. Raghugarh was close to the southern border of Kota but rather far from Bundi, which these *ragamala* paintings resemble more closely.[4] Whatever the locale of this group, there are some additional miniatures of a decorative character, generally with female subjects, that should be classified with the *ragamala* scenes.[5]

Desakh is an athletic *ragini* with the figures depicted as either women or men. Since *raginis* are considered to be feminine melodies but Desakh is heroic in mood, there is often a dichotomy in the way the subject is treated. The idea behind the athletic theme is that the woman Desakha is competitive; the central post is a phallic symbol, indicating the sexual prowess Desakha hopes will result from her gymnastics. She wishes to dominate her lord's other wives by force of will and muscular strength as well as by the alluring suppleness that results from her exercises. Desakh often differs from other *ragamala* compositions in having a plain or austere setting in keeping with the vigorous theme. In this case, the hill upon which the gymnasts perform is bright red, indicating fertility. The acrobats seem to be men with the type of turbans often seen in Bundi painting.

1. Beach, 1974, pp. 45–47.
2. Leach, 1982, nos. 136 (not illus.) and 289.
3. Beach, 1974, figs. 120 and 121.
4. *Gazetteer of India and Pakistan,* U.S. Military Survey, 1953, map 54H.
5. *Tooth* 1974, no. 25, and 1977, no. 48 are comparable to the very simple Raghugarh ruler portraits; 1974, no. 38 is more akin to the *ragamala* leaves. For other styles that have been attributed to Raghugarh, see *Sotheby,* 11 Dec. 1973, lot 202; *Sotheby,* 12 April 1976, lot 165; Sharma, cat. no. 52, pl 54; Pal, 1967, no. 28; Beach, 1974, fig. 124 (series also represented in Sharma, cat. no. 48, pl. 46).

Figure 68.

69 *Gaudi Ragini*   75.40

Rajasthan, possibly Raghugarh, ca. 1780–1800,
20.3 × 11 cm. Plain paper surround. On reverse, seal of
Raghugarh state reads: "Raja of Raghugarh."

Purchase, Edward L. Whittemore Fund

Ex collection: Raja of Raghugarh.

Comparative Material: (A) *Kakubha Ragini*, Rajasthan,
possibly Raghugarh, ca. 1770–90; Skelton, 1961, pl. 18.
(B) *Gaudi Ragini*, Rajasthan, possibly Raghugarh,
ca. 1770–90; Waldschmidt, 1975, 2: fig. 2.

Like the previous miniature, this illustration is part of a
stylistic group that follows the Bundi tradition of compositional arrangement and uses conventional Bundi figure
and tree types. The fact that the group may have come from
Raghugarh, somewhat distant from Bundi, has been discussed in the previous catalog entry. The juxtaposition of
some of the *ragamala* pictures with about five hundred
portraits of Raghugarh rulers in an Indian family collection
may be circumstantial,[1] but the attribution of provenance is
strengthened by the Cleveland page bearing a Raghugarh
seal on the reverse.

Figure 69.

The special elements that characterize the group are all exaggerations of details that were originally taken from Bundi painting; the most prominent is a way of painting elongated eyes for both male and female figures and, humorously, even for the birds in the scenes. Even such small details as the painting of leaf clusters, whorls in the water, and swaying feminine skirts characterize the group and tend to indicate its derivation from the Bundi idiom.

Scenes are repeated in this group as they were in Bundi itself, and occasionally *raginis* related in theme will share the same composition; for example, Gaudi and Kakubha—typical of the several *ragamala* and *nayika* subjects that show the solitary heroine waiting for a lover—were similar enough to sometimes look alike. Thus a miniature picturing the heroine Kakubha (A) is much the same as the Cleveland leaf showing Gaudi walking through the forest, although the heroines are reversed. Both leaves compare closely with designs of earlier Bundi pages.

A further miniature of *Gaudi Ragini* (B) from a group of twenty-two leaves in the National Museum, New Delhi, not only shows a woman in the same position as the Cleveland miniature but also has similarly placed peacocks and monkeys. Because the Cleveland page is in a tighter style and accentuates conventionalized details, it may have been done about ten years after its comparison. The Cleveland artist's "mistake" in putting the heroine's foot on the back of a peacock shows his desire to maintain a previously evolved format.

Such a standardized process of composition indicates that many sets would have been made in this style: at least three are now known[2] that were almost certainly produced by tracing from a group of master designs, as was done in Bundi. An artist who owned a series of such designs may in fact have migrated from Bundi to a *thikana* where he could find patronage. This *ragamala* group appears to have been done within about two decades and was probably the output of one artist or one artist-family perhaps working in the central Indian area of Raghugarh.

1. Beach, 1974, p. 45.
2. Three versions of *Vasanta Ragini* from different sets of this group have been published: Skelton, 1961, pl. 16; Beach, 1974, fig. 123; Waldschmidt, 1975, 2: fig. 2. Other published pages include Skelton, 1961, pl. 17, and Ebeling, no. 179.

FURTHER READING: Beach, 1974, pp. 45–50.

70 Page with Two Scenes of Sita's Abduction

68.108

Here attributed to Rikhaji; from a *Ramayana*, Rajasthan, Kishangarh, ca. 1745, approx. 28.5 × 20 cm (page and painting sizes variable). Coarse floral borders frayed and somewhat rubbed in places.

Purchase, James Parmelee and Cornelia Blakemore Warner Funds

Comparative Material: (A) *Reconciliation of Chandana and His Family*, leaf from a *Chandana Malayagiri Varta*, Rajasthan, probably Marwar, dated 1684; Khandalavala and P. Chandra, 1960, cat. no. 143d, fig. 100. (B) *Page from "Chandana Malayagiri Varta,"* by Rikhaji, Rajasthan, Kishangarh, from a set dated 1745; Czuma, no. 93. (C) *Page from "Chandana Malayagiri Varta,"* by Rikhaji, Rajasthan, Kishangarh, from a set dated 1745; Brooklyn Museum 69.125.5, unpublished.

Both sides of this Cleveland Museum leaf illustrate scenes, from a *Ramayana*, of Sita's abduction. The first side depicts the brave bird Jatayu attacking Ravana, who is treated as an ordinary human being rather than a demon with multiple heads and arms. (It is unusual for a painter to ignore the dramatic possibilities presented by the demon king Ravana, but this artist seems content to portray his story in a plain fashion, as a very human narrative.) Ravana throws rocks into the mouth of the defeated bird just before flying off with Sita thrust into a knapsack. On the reverse, Laksmana informs a mourning Rama of the abduction, while Jatayu looks on amid a landscape of cramped mountains and rivers that form a herringbone pattern.

The style represented by this miniature and its comparisons probably originates in Marwar in the later seventeenth century and is carried into Kishangarh by the otherwise-unknown artist Rikhaji in the mid-eighteenth century. A painting (A) from a Popular Mughal manuscript probably from Marwar[1] illustrates the story of *Chandana Malayagiri*, rarely treated in Rajasthani painting. Another miniature (B) from Kishangarh, dated 1745, is from a manuscript of the same work that utilizes some of the stylistic elements of the 1684 manuscript in a cruder fashion. This second *Chandana Malayagiri* appears to be a rustic relation of the earlier copy, and despite a manuscript colophon mentioning Kishangarh, its artist may originally have come from Marwar. The two manuscripts share the same type of prominently flowered border. The format of the later manuscript (B) has been changed, but like the 1684 version, the page incorporates a large block of text. Another leaf from the 1745 *Chandana Malayagiri* text (C, illus.) includes the high turbans, the sharp sideburns, and the great moustachios characteristic of eighteenth-century Marwar painting. Since the style shows no relation to that associated with Kishangarh, Rikhaji apparently migrated to the state. The usual paintings produced for the small Rajasthani court of Kishangarh are, however, so elegant that Rikhaji must have been employed by some patron unconnected with the major noble families.

Figure 70, obverse.

ल्समेदलेऋगेस्राकोम्ही ज्ञाबुडावतमुफगमा साजिकरुचक
चुरही रावणमाहरोनाम ८४ ज्ञबेरावणसीतांमलेरलका
ढमेगळोबे ज्ञवैश्रीरामजीकसीतरेखु लरुस्माबैस्रोराव
न्सागरामयकारखु सीतानदेषेनैन लुनीमढियादेषके
लघमणसुकहैवे १९ पाकुंबनफलमीले उठयकु
नरुपत एतमेखी ताहरगए बीयतमासीबीयत १०नत
बमणबायकरामजीसुकहै ताइमादिसलाल मे
कमज्ञमा रोकदीव चीया बीएएकहीबारा रावेकालु
रामचंद् १ एतमेगीरधवीपेषी ज्ञाच्यारामहठुर

ज्ञवैश्रीरामजीडुसताबिगमीसीताबीज्ञागउपफ्त्रोलबमणहीमलामहे
ताव ३६

Figure 70(C). *Page from "Chandana Malayagiri Varta."* The Brooklyn Museum, Brooklyn, New York, 69.125.5.

The Cleveland page from a *Ramayana* manuscript is stylistically identical with leaves from the 1745 *Chandana Malayagiri* manuscript by Rikhaji (B). The heavy pigments and choice of colors—dark red and green—are the same, as are the floral borders. Both stories are illustrated by depictions on the front and back pages combined with large sections of text on thin, brittle paper.

1. Compare with M. R. Anand, *Album of Indian Paintings* (New Delhi: National Book Trust, 1973), p. 127.

71 *Krishna Receives a Flower Garland* 82.65

By Sitaram, Rajasthan, Kishangarh, ca. 1770, 42 × 32 cm. Most of both red towers in foreground repainted—particularly discernible in bottom of the right tower and top of the left one; some trees in left foreground have also been repainted. Inscription: "amal-i Sitaram."

Purchase, John L. Severance Fund

Comparative Material: (A) *The Boat of Love*, by Nihal Chand, Rajasthan, Kishangarh, ca. 1750–60; Dickinson and Khandalavala, pl. IX, or Leach, 1982, no. 125. (B) *Raja Approaching the Zenana*, Rajasthan, Kishangarh, ca. 1760; Leach, 1982, no. 150.

This miniature shows Krishna riding boldly into a lake to receive a garland from one of Radha's attendants who leans over the railing of a terrace directly overlooking the water. Since Kishangarh buildings were by Lake Gundaloo, the idea of riding to the women's quarters through water seems to have been usual; depictions of this occur in other paintings as well (B). In this case, Radha is seated on a gold throne with two of her attendants, while two other women row a boat at the left. The elegant architecture of Radha's palace is conceived in three sections that run across the miniature in parallel lines without joining. The artist has drawn the walls mainly as airy façades with no depth, thereby giving the scene a stagelike appearance. The first wall pierced by *jalis* with a small pavilion in the center and towers at each end is a bright red, imitating the Mughal palaces of Agra or Delhi that are ringed with red sandstone. (The two towers have been mainly repainted.) Behind this façade is a large park filled with both palms and dark green deciduous trees. It is interrupted by a second wall of white marble that includes three fairly large verandas topped with kiosks. A white marble terrace, apparently designed for leisurely promenades, is located in the background near the horizon.

The inscription, like others written on Kishangarh miniatures, simply gives the artist's name in Persian and was probably written by a librarian. Without this notation to Sitaram the miniature probably would have been ascribed to the artist's father, Nihal Chand, because it is close to the older artist's documented work, and because his reputation as the originator of the mid-eighteenth-century Kishangarh style has inspired many hypothetical attributions.

Sitaram is mentioned by Eric Dickinson in his book that helped to introduce the Kishangarh school to outsiders through examples long hidden within the state's palace. The author notes that miniatures ascribed to Sitaram were in the collection when it was shown to him and says that the artist was a descendant of Nihal Chand, apparently on the basis of inscriptional evidence.[1] Few, however, have seen the Kishangarh palace miniatures, and the Cleveland painting can thus be viewed as an important illustration of the artist's style.

Sitaram has here carried on Nihal Chand's work in an extremely sensitive fashion but without much innovation. He has used the same horizontal spatial divisions running

Figure 71.

Figure 71, detail.

across the painting and the same vista extending vertically up the picture that his father habitually employed (A, illus.). In addition, specific conventions such as those for the sky, trees, and figures are much the same. Certain passages, like the subtle streaking of the grayish sky with red, are handled in an even more refined manner that demonstrates Sitaram's personal skill.

Savant Singh (r. 1748–57, died 1764), the verse-writing raja of the small state of Kishangarh who spent his time meditating on Krishna and Radha's ideal world in Brindaban, had Nihal Chand externalize his poetic vision by combining Mughal and Rajasthani painting elements. This mixed type of miniature painting had begun under his immediate predecessors but was most expressively employed during his patronage.[2] Although obviously unsuitable for Krishna the prankish cowherd, the settings created by Nihal Chand fitted Krishna, the god of love who was eulogized by Savant Singh as ruling in princely splendor over a kingdom of the romantic imagination.

Kishangarh had been unusually dependent on the imperial court since its formation by Mughal fiat in the early seventeenth century. Its rajas, because they were not politically competitive, were sometimes close associates of the emperors, and apparently Mughal culture had become customary in the state. The early Kishangarh paintings now known (generally portraits) are difficult to distinguish from conventional Mughal works. If they reveal a Rajasthani personality at all, it is mainly the formality or pride of the

Figure 71(A). *The Boat of Love*, by Nihal Chand. National Museum, New Delhi.

187

Rajputs that is distinctively apparent in the disciplined poses. Savant, who was an intimate friend of Muhammad Shah and was well-acquainted with the luxuries of his court, was thus accustomed to paintings that had a Mughal flavor.

If specific motifs as well as the elegance of the Nihal Chand style seem mainly derived from imperial painting, the cohesiveness of the works is due to the Vallabha worship long prevailing in Kishangarh. The state's founder was a Vallabha devotee, and his successor, who was a disciple of Vallabhacharya's great-grandson Gopinath, took the step of establishing a family idol in the state.[3] Nihal Chand's genius lay in blending the lyrical sweetness of devotional subject matter with Mughal opulence and Rajput hauteur.

Savant Singh's devotion found expression first in poetry written under the pseudonym Nagari Das and secondly in paintings commissioned from Nihal Chand. Despite the fact that Savant went into self-imposed exile with his consort, Bani Thani, in Brindaban in 1757 several years before this miniature was apparently produced, his personality dominates the work.[4] As in other Kishangarh paintings, Krishna seems to be acting out a role with an understood narrative significance. The comparative painting by Sitaram's father, Nihal Chand (A), very precisely illustrates one of Savant's verses describing Krishna and Radha boating on the Jumna and as night falls, entering a grove "where love alone can find its way." Further works are known that are actually inscribed with the raja's Krishna poetry.[5] The aura of per-

sonal feeling and memory mingled with devotion exemplified by Nihal Chand's boating scene (A) is typical of the Kishangarh paintings of this period. The Cleveland painting by Sitaram has the same dramatic quality of lovers in a vast romantic landscape focusing only on each other, and it quite probably also illustrates one of Savant's verses.

Certainly the painting is like much of Savant's poetry, which is a reverie on a mythical Brindaban actually inspired by the Rajasthani scenery of Kishangarh with its prominent Gundaloo Lake. Savant's poetry was written to appeal to the imagination, and in this miniature Sitaram has created an architectural fantasy with pavilions apparently stretching to infinity, indicating the allegorical nature of the setting. In such a poetic painting, the vast forests and limitless landscape vistas that contrast with the compulsively crowded works from other states seem to symbolize the sources of the imagination.

Whatever the romantic situation depicted in the Cleveland miniature, Krishna conforms to a conventional image of heroic bravado, while the female figures are elegantly passive. Although later Kishangarh artists tended to caricature the figure type that evolved in Nihal Chand's painting by exaggerating its obvious conventions, Sitaram has here achieved a delicacy and refinement equal to his father's. The arched backs, flowing gestures, and curved eyes convey sensitivity and restraint as well as the grace of Radha and Krishna's relationship.

As is demonstrated by this painting, the artistic association between Nihal Chand and his son was close, but Sitaram's age in comparison with his father's and his importance in the Kishangarh court are uncertain. Nihal Chand is pictured in middle age with other personages of Sardar Singh's retinue (son of Savant Singh, r. 1757–66) at an evening music party, but Sitaram is omitted.[6] In 1773 a *durbar* record stating that Nihal Chand should be provided with gold leaf proves that the artist was still working. Thus it must be assumed that Sitaram probably painted with his father for the Kishangarh house over several decades and that the two helped perpetuate the memory of Savant Singh, who had achieved a reputation of near-sainthood in his native state by the time of his death in the Brindaban area in 1764.

1. Dickinson and Khandalavala, p. 16.

2. Ibid., pl. VIII.

3. Ibid., p. 6.

4. Randhawa and Galbraith, p. 103.

5. Dickinson and Khandalavala, p. 36; a poem by Nagari Das appearing on a painting is recorded on p. 40, pl. XI; pls. I, III, VII, and XIII by Nihal Chand and his followers also look as if they may illustrate poems.

6. Ibid., pl. X; see controversy over Nihal Chand's depiction in W. G. Archer, "Review of *Kishangarh Painting* by Eric Dickinson and Karl Khandalavala," *LK*, no. 6 (1959), pp. 85–86, 88.

7. Dickinson and Khandalavala, p. 16.

FURTHER READING: W. G. Archer (see fn. 6, above), pp. 82–88; Dickinson and Khandalavala.

Figure 71, detail.

72 *Lovers and Old Crone* 80.29

Rajasthan, Kishangarh, ca. 1780–90, 19.7 × 13.5 cm.
Purchase, Edward L. Whittemore Fund

This Kishangarh painting shows Krishna the lover appearing on a terrace before his mistress, who is chaperoned by a crone. Krishna, wearing a gold turban and a *jama* decorated with elaborate jewelry, is emphasized as the ideal figure, while the old woman remains partially hidden in the pavilion.

In contrast to major pictures of the Kishangarh atelier, this work is small and focuses on a confined area. The dramatically lit sunset-sky and the full tree behind Krishna (both typical Kishangarh features derived from Muhammad Shah imperial works) are treated confidently, but the artist has had difficulty in rendering the pavilion, the space around it, and the young woman.

Figure 72.

73 *Krishna and Radha under* 64.389
Mt. Govardhan

Drawing, Rajasthan, Kota, ca. 1720, 30.3 × 20.2 cm.
Paper damaged and replaced with portion of another
drawing at left edge, script is bleeding through at top from
reverse side. Obscured poetic inscription on reverse.
Sundry Purchase Fund

Comparative Material: (A) *Shuddhamallara Ragini*,
Rajasthan, Kota, ca. 1660–80; Spink, fig. 78. (B) *A
Banqueting Scene*, Rajasthan, Kota, ca. 1705; Welch, 1976,
no. 46, or Beach, 1974, fig. 77. (C) *Arjun Singh of Kota
Worshipping Krishna and Radha,* Rajasthan, Kota,
ca. 1720; Sotheby, 12 Dec. 1972, lot 112.

This unfinished Kota scene shows Krishna, Radha, and the
cowherds coming together under Mt. Govardhan when, in
order to protect the people of his village from the storm

Figure 73.

created by Indra, Krishna lifted Mt. Govardhan and, balancing it on one finger, sheltered his companions. The Cleveland drawing is an unusual illustration of this particular legendary incident, since other compositions are arranged formally and symmetrically with Krishna balancing the mountain in an iconographically prescribed pose.[1]

In the Cleveland drawing Indra appears as in other depictions of this storm riding amidst the lightning on his elephant. Peacocks, the harbingers of rain, are clustered on Mt. Govardhan, which has levitated on its own while Krishna stands surrounded by playful cowherds.[2] Across a stream filled with wading and splashing birds, Radha looks on in the midst of the *gopis*. No one appears to be endangered by the storm. The joyous animation and casual posing of the figure groups make this scene appear less like an awesome miracle than like a celebration for the approach of the rainy season.

An earlier Kota scene (A) that depicts Krishna dancing with *gopis* conveys this idea of male and female celebrating the revivifying monsoon. Kota paintings often extol a lighthearted or informal aspect of Krishna's presence. The artist has here created a lively illustration suiting the character of the god Krishna though setting aside the usual iconography of the religious legend. Such a rejection of conventionality is a trait of Kota painting manifesting itself in various ways thematically as well as stylistically.

Spontaneous, sketchy, and energetic, this work forms part of one stylistic branch of Kota art. The scrawled drawing technique appears toward the end of the seventeenth and the beginning of the eighteenth century (B). The artist of the Krishna and Radha scene has followed figural stereotypes, yet has also drawn freely and repeats strokes or changes details at will in a manner that conveys his vitality. The spirals of lightning and the streaks of rain in the religious scene appear in finished form in the painting of *Shuddhamallara Ragini* (A). Tumultuous skies distinguish Kota paintings and are an element that reveals the dynamism and exuberance of Kota artists.

The repeated drawing of certain lines and the sketchy alteration of forms in the Cleveland work suggest that it was at first meant to be painted but was left unfinished, possibly because the artist made another drawing after his conception was clearer. The conventionalized faces with heavily lidded eyes; beaklike noses; and short, wide skull shapes in the Cleveland drawing are generally characteristic of Kota pictures done in the first half of the eighteenth century. Such stylizations help to date the execution of this unfinished work that is most closely related to scenes done about 1720, such as a portrait of Raja Arjun Singh worshipping Radha and Krishna (C).

1. See Barrett and Gray, p. 156, *Krishna Supporting Mt. Govardhan*, by Shahadin.
2. Sherman E. Lee suggests that the mountain may rise as the result of Krishna's music.

74 Krishna and the Gopis Gather for the Rasamandala   60.45

Rajasthan, Kota, ca. 1720–30, 41.5 × 28.5 cm, 50 × 32.5 cm with border. Paint flaking badly, especially green tone. Red border; corner severed. Inscription at top in Sanskrit (damaged): "Moved by the coming of the Lord, the *gopis* went up to him and were overcome by the sight of Krishna, who was shining with moonlike splendor; then the Lord, who was a (love) thief, wearing yellow garments, smiled slightly with his lotuslike mouth. Radha said to her *sakhi*, 'He is certainly the God of Love.'" At the bottom in Hindi: "On the banks of the Jumna, the *gopis* are expressing their grief and sorrow as Krishna tells them he is leaving them."[1]

Purchase, Mr. and Mrs. William H. Marlatt Fund

Ex collection: Heeramaneck.

Published: Lee, 1960, no. 28.

Comparative Material: (A) *The Gopis Adore Krishna*, Rajasthan, Kota, ca. 1720–30; *Arts in Virginia* 11 (Fall, 1970): no. 14. (B) *Krishna and the Gopis Showered with Flowers*, Rajasthan, Kota, ca. 1720–30; Boston Museum of Fine Arts, 59.706, unpublished. (C) *Picnic of Krishna and the Gopis*, Rajasthan, Kota, ca. 1720–30; Beach, 1966, no. 170. (D) *Arjun Singh of Kota Worshipping Krishna and Radha*, Rajasthan, Kota, ca. 1720, *Sotheby*, 12 Dec. 1972, lot 112.

The paintings cited as comparative material (A, B, C) and others in this style, though not all from the same series, show Krishna with a crowd of *gopis*. This subject was a popular one in Kota during the early eighteenth century, and the theme is treated fairly uniformly. In the Cleveland painting and others from Virginia (A) and Boston (B, illus.), the setting is an idyllic place beside the river where Krishna traditionally meets the *gopis* to bathe and dance with them. This area, which represents freedom from the restraints and the strictures of usual daily life, is here treated as a disk of land—a self-contained world in which the *gopis* exist with perfect relation to the god. The tiny male figure standing in the upper left of the Cleveland miniature, reverentially bowing outside this "other world," represents a devotee. The prominent circle of the full moon in each of the paintings, echoing the earthly circle, not only indicates the particular evening when the *gopis* have their assignation with Krishna but also probably symbolizes perfect time.

The Cleveland and Virginia paintings depict the *gopis* reaching out toward, and adoring, Krishna, while the Boston miniature shows boats of celestials showering the group with flowers. All three are from similar large-sized sets; the sizes themselves differ, however. For example, the Virginia painting (40.6 × 30.5 cm) is shorter than the Cleveland miniature; and since its text passages are complete, it seems to be from another series rather than being cropped. Though these miniatures belong to sets, they do not seem to illustrate sequential happenings of a narrative, but rather the various aspects of an epiphany. The exaltation of union with the divine is celebrated with different manifestations of rejoicing and worship.

Figure 74.

Each of the miniatures is painted mainly in orange combined with shades of green (*verdigris*, which is quite damaged from chemical alteration). Stylistically, each miniature follows conventions of the Arjun Singh era (1720–24). Both Krishna and the female figures in the Cleveland painting have the heavy half-shut eyes and beaky noses used to portray Arjun Singh himself. In addition, the figure of Krishna, with a thick chest, broad head, and plumbed turban, is almost identical with a depiction that shows Krishna being worshipped by Arjun Singh (D). The painting manner utilized for this miniature group is graceful but fairly loose and rough. Quickly drawn, thick outlines around the eyes are typical of its easy, spontaneous rhythm.

1. Translation by J. Losty; although the Sanskrit verse is clearly from a Krishna text like the *Gita Govinda*, the source has not been identified.

Figure 74(B). *Krishna and the Gopis Showered with Flowers*. Courtesy, Museum of Fine Arts, Boston, John Ware Willard Fund.

Figure 74, detail.

75 *Krishna and Balarama*   38.302
Approaching Mathura

Rajasthan, Kota, ca. 1740–50, 14 × 30.7 cm. Damaged and
somewhat retouched.

Gift of N. M. Heeramaneck

This scene from a Kota *Bhagavata Purana* set shows Krishna and Balarama surrounded by *gopas* and cows arriving at
the walled town of Mathura. A folkish painting that retains
the old horizontal format of palm-leaf pages, this small scene
has garish colors and simple details. It is spirited, nevertheless, as can be noted from the treatment of the cows and
playful calves.

Figure 75.

76 *Umed Singh of Kota Hunting Lions*   64.51

Brush drawing with slight color. Rajasthan, Kota, ca. 1785–90, 39 × 52 cm. Fold lines, some white ground paint flaking at left, slight tear in left foreground, and paper very worn in some areas.

Mrs. J. Livingston Taylor Collection by Exchange

Comparative Material: (A) *Durjan Sal of Kota Hunting*, Rajasthan, Kota, dated 1788; Beach, 1974, fig. 91, or W. G. Archer, 1959, no. 41. (B) *Raja Umed Singh of Kota Shooting Tigers*, Rajasthan, Kota, ca. 1790; W. G. Archer, 1959, no. 40.

This large hunt drawing is quite different from a previous Kota work [73], which is more sketchy and free. Here the basic composition has been laid out in red ochre with bold, more exact drawing over this in black. The strokes are broad and decisive with none of the wavering delicacy of the draw-

ing of Krishna in catalog entry 73. Only in doing the faces of the lion, lioness, and cubs has the artist used a finer brush and taken pains to render detail. In the remainder of the work he is concerned with the strong general rhythms of the entangled trees and spreading grass clumps.

The drawing is close to different types of finished work (A and B) and could have been painted in either style. The gold and silver elaboration of the vegetation in the hunt scene of *Durjan Sal* (A, illus.) is more a matter of finish than of structure and probably covers a similarly firm line drawing.

The Cleveland drawing was apparently being prepared for painting and therefore reveals one manner in which the Kota artist worked. The red underdrawing often does not make correct allowances for overlap because another object was drawn later. The black lines clarify the drawing by establishing how overlap occurs, which branches are to be

Figure 76.

Figure 76(A). *Durjan Sal of Kota Hunting.* Victoria & Albert Museum, London.

re-angled, and so forth. Changes, however, continued to be made at the second stage of designing. In the upper center the tree and the monkeys have been altered, and some of the contradictory lines of the tree have been covered with white pigment. The positions of the attendants in the upper right corner have been modified by more emphatic black drawing. Transparent color has been used in certain areas to suggest later hues, and some opaque white has been applied as a ground. Though there are confused areas remaining in the composition, none presents insoluble problems, and it is difficult to determine why this work was abandoned.

The miniature of Durjan Sal hunting dated 1788 (A) parallels the Cleveland drawing in many ways, most significantly because both pictures include rhythmic waves of vegetation in their design. Few other miniatures reveal the animation of the jungle itself through such powerful and concentrated sweeps of growth. Though the lions in the two pictures are very similar, they follow common conventions; their grimaces, masklike faces, and flexing claws have been emphasized in a nearly identical manner. In both the Cleveland drawing and the Durjan Sal miniature, the men on foot are obscured by trees but are equal in size to the lions. By contrast, in some earlier miniatures enormous, muscular lions dwarf the hunters,[1] and in certain later works the human heroes are made to tower over the beasts—indicating that the artist had creative license to symbolize the psychological aspects of the hunt differently in various eras.

Figure 76, detail.

The lion cubs whose positions are rendered in a very lifelike fashion (possibly from observation) are a distinctive element in the Cleveland drawing. (In most other hunt scenes, lion and lioness are shown together but without cubs.) Interestingly, the artist seems to have rendered the family with warmth but without any reaction to the idea of death.

The haloed raja shown drawing his bow in the Cleveland miniature is probably Umed Singh, titular head of Kota from 1771–1819. The raja succeeded his father at age ten, but his energies were channeled into hunting by his regent Zalim Singh in order to leave the latter free to govern the state. Several extant pictures of Umed are identified by inscription or by encircling haloes. In the Cleveland drawing Umed is in his prime, and this is consistent with a dating based on stylistic considerations of ca. 1785–90, when he would have been in his middle and late twenties. The raja's facial features can be compared with those in a painting of a tiger shoot (B).

As was customary, only the raja aims at the lions in the Cleveland drawing; the attendants are present to aid in discovering the animals and to kill them in an emergency should the raja fail to do so. Thus, Umed, unable to assert his power in the political world, could satisfy himself by facing the king of beasts.

1. Beach, 1974, fig. 86; Welch, 1976, no. 53.

FURTHER READING: W. G. Archer, 1959; Beach, 1974.

Rajasthan, Kota, ca. 1810, 34.3 × 27.3 cm, 38.1 × 31.1 cm with border. Rubbed on left side across form of one monkey, slight tear, and slight rubbing on right side. Narrow gold inner border, dark blue outer border.

Purchase from the J. H. Wade Fund

Ex collection: Heeramaneck.

Published: W. G. Archer, 1959, no. 43, and 1960, pl. 62; Beach, 1974, fig. 102; Lee, 1957, 180–83, and 1960, no. 40; and R. Reiff, *Indian Miniatures* (Rutland, Vt: Charles E. Tuttle, 1959), pl. 10.

Comparative Material: (A) *Ram Singh I of Kota Hunting at Mukundgarh*, Rajasthan, Kota, ca. 1720–30; Beach, 1974, fig. 60. (B) *Bhoj Singh of Bundi Slays a Lion*, Rajasthan, Kota, ca. 1740; Beach, 1974, fig. 86. (C) *Durjan Sal of Kota Hunting*, Rajasthan, Kota, dated 1778; Beach, 1974, fig. 91, or W. G. Archer, 1959, no. 41. (D) *Krishna (or Rama) Hunting by Night*, by Bhimsen, Rajasthan, Kota, dated 1788; Beach, 1974, fig. 92. (E) *Ladies Shooting Tigers from a Tower*, Rajasthan, Kota, late eighteenth century; Gray, 1950, no. 463, color pl. 8, or W. G. Archer, 1959, no. 44. (F) *Ram Singh II of Kota Hunting*, Rajasthan, Kota, ca. 1840; Beach, 1974, fig. 103; W. G. Archer, 1959, no. 45; Barrett and Gray, p. 158.

This painting, both charming and significant, has been published frequently and has figured as a key work in most evaluations of Kota art. An essay on its style written before many comparable Kota paintings appeared is still notable as a penetrating characterization of a group of miniatures aptly termed "super-real" by the author.[1] However, the miniature's frequent exposure and its prettiness have caused it to be taken for granted and have tended to prevent its thorough analysis. The various simple elements that contribute to the artist's rendering of nature have never been studied, nor has the miniature's subject matter been compared with the themes in other Kota paintings.

By taking careful note of various areas of the painting, it is apparent that the artist was representing the animals, reptiles, and plants of a specific ecosystem. As super-realistic, the miniature thus not only has an ultra-clear or "magic" aspect but a foundation in realism, and some consideration of these factual elements gives added dimensions to a painting that superficially appears fanciful. It is also illuminating to evaluate the human presence in this miniature in nineteenth-century terms, since the scene provides in part a primary social document that records the quality of Rajasthani life, much as does the account of Colonel Tod who traveled in Kota a few years later. Such an evaluation emphasizes the individuality of the feminine hunting theme in a Rajput social context.

Much of the spirit conveyed here arises from the painter's observations of natural complexity; because it is rendered in some detail, the artist has obviously considered the varied terrain significant in itself. His description of plants and of land formations is unusually accurate in spite of conventionalization. He has delineated clearly the lush growth

Figure 77.

Figure 77, detail.

around the pond from the scrubby bushes and trees of the rocky hillside. Watchtowers on top of rocky outcroppings were part of the Kota landscape and can still be found in the area. In general, hunt scenes from the states of both Kota and Mewar depict such courtly preserves very accurately.

More than other Kota pictures, this one is teeming with different species of wildlife that are portrayed accurately, although stylized. With a sense of whimsy, the artist has made some species more difficult to find than others. As soon as the viewer recognizes that the artist has set up a kind of game for him, he begins the search for other smaller, better-hidden images. Moving from the foreground, the larger creatures include wild boar; a black buck and its paler mate; an Oriental civet; two lions; several species of birds; langur, or Asiatic monkeys; two rabbits; and fifteen axis, or chital, deer.

In three areas the artist's ingenuity and humor further challenge the viewer. The steep rocks capped by a watchtower are inhabited by two Indian sloth bears, a peacock, a mongoose and snake (?), birds, and a pair of cheetahs. A beehive hangs above the two cheetahs, and the head of a wolflike animal is visible through a cleft in the rocks. The artist completes his ecological lesson with insects and reptiles in the foreground rocks. In the crevices behind the pair of boars are a turtle, a scorpion, two mice or rats, a spider in a web, a cobra, a bee, and two weaver (?) birds.

The microscopic elements in the distant background area derive from eighteenth-century Mughal or provincial Mughal painting, which often featured elaborate panoramas along the horizon. Here the artist has shown a man in a boat, a man on an elephant hunting a bounding deer with a dog, various kinds of birds, a man herding cows, two

199

Figure 77(E). *Ladies Shooting Tigers from a Tower*. Museum and Picture Gallery, Baroda. Photograph after L. Ashton, *The Art of India and Pakistan* (London: Faber & Faber, 1950), color pl. B.

temple groups, more deer, and some people drawing water from the river.

Such creatures as the bears, the cheetahs, and the civet are very unusual in any Kota scene, and the combination of so many types of large animals seems unparalleled. It is the inclusion of the insects in the rocks and the complex depiction of the total natural system that is most surprising, however.

It was once supposed that the freedom and accuracy of Kota painters, reflected in works such as this one, might result from imitation of British amateur artists who carried their sketchbooks throughout India.[3] It has now, however, been well established that, many decades prior to the proposed British contact, Kota artists were doing drawings and sketches of tremendous energy and spontaneity.[4] Mughal art was undoubtedly very influential, yet Kota artists recorded observations in an original way.[5] Several styles involving different combinations of the observed and the conventionalized existed concurrently in Kota, and the theory of a development into naturalism (perhaps through Western influence) is unsupported by evidence from the corpus of miniatures. Because any Kota painting combines observed with conceptual aspects, naturalism has to be evaluated by relative standards; it seems artificial, therefore, to judge that artists were either moving toward or away from it in an absolute fashion.

The individual animals of the Cleveland miniature are conventionalized in varying degrees. The artist, following earlier hunt pictures (A), has almost personified the axis deer, as is apparent in comparison with the radically different portrayal of the species in an early seventeenth-century Mughal picture [19]. The observed element in this rendering is the rhythmic neck-thrusting movement of the herd in concert, so that curving and bending "like a particularly appealing corps-de-ballet"[6] it sees in all directions. The lesser Oriental civet (*Viverricula Indica*),[7] walking coolly out of the picture with a bird in his mouth, is completely unexaggerated or undramatic and looks as if he comes from a sketch. Since he is rarely depicted in the hunts, there is no stereotype for his species. The great accuracy with which he has been portrayed here can be gauged from one of the few other representations of his kind (D).

Hunting, described by Tod as a major event in otherwise tedious lives,[8] was taken very seriously in Kota. The miniatures themselves record the numerous types of hunts and

Figure 77(F). *Ram Singh II of Kota Hunting*. G. K. Kanoria Collection, Calcutta. Photograph after W. G. Archer, *Indian Painting in Bundi and Kotah* (London: Her Majesty's Stationery Office, 1959), pl. 45.

the elaborate preparations made for them. Interestingly, the Cleveland picture contrasts with many of these scenes in its simplicity and apparent casualness. In the case of large Kota hunts, beaters surrounded and drove the quarry, as described by Tod and also documented in many paintings.[9] In his discussion Tod notes the important presence of women in hunts undertaken by the Kota raja Durjan Sal:

> In these expeditions, which resembled preparations for war, he invariably carried the queens. The Amazonian ladies were taught the use of the matchlock, and being placed upon the terraced roofs of the hunting-seats, sent their shots at the forest-lord, when driven past their stand by the hunters.[10]

This statement is corroborated by the inclusion of women with men in certain miniatures (A and D). Both Mughal and Rajput heroines had been known for hunting and riding with men; however, the unaccompanied women in the Cleveland miniature and another similar composition (E) have more suprising freedom.

While Tod states that Durjan Sal's ladies sat on the roofs of decorated hunt pavilions as the animals were driven by, the women in the Cleveland miniature are participating in another type of hunt: the towers shown in the Cleveland miniature and its comparison (E, illus.), often situated near ponds, were used mainly for awaiting the spontaneous appearance of animals coming to drink at dawn and sunset.[11] If these pictures represent real rather than idealized happenings, however, it is suprising that the women do not have more attendants to wait on them during their long vigils.

The closest compositional parallel to the Cleveland miniature shows the stocky Ram Singh II in the act of shooting lions (F, illus.) that have been attracted by the presence of a tethered bull—a common practice for smaller hunts. The contrast between the two miniatures, which are otherwise quite similar, arises from the difference in their male and female subjects. Since the hunt had much to do with the ruler's status and pride, it is logical that the miniature of Ram Singh stresses his dominance and his skill in shooting. Thus he appears as an unusually large figure sitting stiffly on the roof of the pavilion supported according to correct protocol by two nobles; he has already killed one lion. The Cleveland huntresses, who in contrast to Ram Singh have not fired a disturbing shot, peer out demurely from within the hunt tower. It is significant that this miniature, without a decoy animal, accentuates the animals' freedom of movement, the wildness of the landscape, and the intricate balance of natural elements in it.

In many Kota pictures in order to dramatize the contest of strength between man and beast, the lions are presented as fully aware of the hunters, their great, muscular forequarters straining and their teeth bared in fury. In the Cleveland miniature, although there are small indications that certain animals are wary, most are pictured as undisturbed. The lions, for example, remain unconscious of

their specific danger—one lion raises its head, but the other drinks calmly. Both are delicately treated; the arched paws and carefully stretched bodies reveal their catlike balance rather than their ferocity. Animals near the pavilion (like the monkeys picking mangoes or the civet carrying off his bird) behave naturally, and the emphasis is on the animal's lives and on their relationships in the natural world.

In many ways this picture is thus oriented toward women and, in fact, may have been painted for that audience. The exclusive presence of the huntresses and the witty game of locating small creatures suggest this intent, as does the focus on natural freedom rather than prowess. The *linga-yoni*, the combined male/female reproductive symbol behind the pavilion, is another indication. This symbol is not repeated in the similarly composed painting of Ram Singh II (F) or in other miniatures. In place of traps, lures, or mechanical shooting devices (see D), it seems to impart a sense of blessing rather than to accentuate depletion. Sherman Lee says of its presence: "As the primeval Hindu symbol of generation, it dominates the page, not in itself, but as a symbol multiplied and made manifest in a teeming but lyrical vision of nature."[12]

The Rajput clans throughout India were noted for their love of hunting, but the Kota and Mewar painters were Rajasthan's accomplished hunt landscapists. Miniature painters in Mewar accompanied hunting parties and must have done so in Kota also, since it seems clear that the Kota artist's experience parallels that of the waiting hunters. Like them, the artist acquired a knowledge of animal habits and small but characteristic gestures of animal movement. He carefully observed details of vegetation and foliage in much the same way that the hunter would have absorbed minute environmental details from long periods of waiting in the bush. The Cleveland miniature also illustrates specific ways in which the painter adapted the hunter's perceptions of animal migration.

The animals portrayed in this picture are both diurnal and nocturnal; sunset was a time when numbers of them would be seen together going to the pond. Smothered in foilage, the pond was apparently a meeting point between two habitats, which the artist has carefully represented. Animals who prefer treetops (like the monkeys) have been brought together with those (like the deer and antelope) who live in more open country.[13]

Equestrian hunting seems to have been less significant in Kota than in other Rajasthani states where it was extremely popular. This contrast in turn led to different practices in miniature-painting; the typical equestrian-hunt scene, which was not done often in Kota,[14] is usually only superficially observed and is highly conventionalized. The artist was not a participant in the same way that he would be in shoots where hunters waited for quarry. The stationary hunter anticipating the arrival of game studied the whole environment, and the composition of the Cleveland miniature mirrors the waiting hunter's sense of the totality of nature as well as its momentary changes. Animals in equestrian

Figure 77, detail.

scenes rarely show any potential for spontaneity, whereas the Cleveland miniature subtly captures nervous animal movements that are only momentarily observable. Unlike painters in other Rajasthani states, the artist of the Cleveland miniature also employs his picture as a window on a continuous scene. The lion lifting its head is sensitive to an unseen presence and the civet moves toward a destination beyond the border of the painting. This view parallels the hunter's watchful desire to interpret what occurs outside his immediate range. The technical facility to produce such effects is probably rooted in Mughal art, but the interest in hunt pictures of this type must have been conditioned by Kota society.

Two different assessments of this miniature's date and stylistic position in Kota art have been made.[15] The first estimation, a pioneering effort, was based upon then-known Kota paintings and evaluated this miniature and others on the basis of naturalism.[16] In this case the subjective term has proved to be an unstable measurement of dating. Mid-eighteenth-century works that have since come to light have dynamited any single application of the word "naturalism" in reference to Kota art and underscored its complete relativity. A painting of the Bundi ruler Bhoj Singh (B) considered alongside the Cleveland hunt scene illustrates this point effectively. The expanse of forest, the

Figure 77, detail.

Figure 77, detail.

individual trees, and the positions of the men in the foliage (B) are very realistic. In the Cleveland miniature the concern for landscape detail predominates over general truth. Many animals are accurately portrayed, yet it could not be said that "the understanding of animals is altogether keener" here or that this type of painting marks a break in demonstrating reliance on sketching rather than memory.[17] The two works, both in keeping with Kota traditions, are different manifestations, making different claims upon the word "naturalistic."

The second assessment of date is based on narrower, more specific criteria. Milo Beach believes that the technical finesse revealed by the Cleveland miniaturist is related to Mughal artistic training and was unlikely to have been acquired after around 1810.[18] He also notes that the huntresses lack the elongated eyes or other exaggerations of Ram Singh's era.[19] In considerations of dating, both Archer and Beach link the Cleveland miniature with the picture of Ram Singh II (F), more easily classifiable because it depicts this Kota ruler. The miniature of Ram Singh shares obvious passages as well as its general design with the Cleveland miniature. Since it should postdate the Cleveland scene, the Cleveland figure type and other elements can be assessed by moving back in time from the probable date of the Ram Singh miniature.[20] The final conclusion based upon historical and stylistic considerations is that the miniature must have been done early in the nineteenth century.

Beach believes that the Cleveland miniature represents the culmination of the super-real style first appearing in a late eighteenth-century scene of Durjan Sal (C) and in related works.[21] Yet the Cleveland painting is not a direct development from this work, since it includes a number of essentials occurring in other Kota paintings. The miniature of Durjan Sal hunting (C) is much more intensely outlined and rigid than the later Cleveland painting. The lyrical mood of the Cleveland scene, the number of animals, and their easy movements can be associated with a softer style of Kota painting (D). The "super-real" classification of Kota art is an important one,[22] but most Kota works have a strong individual quality that finally evades the charting of style. The Cleveland miniaturist has combined aspects of many past styles freely. The painting is a witty adaptation utilizing previous developments but also exuding the artist's own sense of playfulness.

1. Lee, 1957, pp. 182–83.

2. *The Emperor Shah Jahan Hunting Deer,* from the *Shah Jahan Nama,* Barrett and Gray, p. 113.

3. W. G. Archer, 1959, p. 51.

4. Welch, 1976, nos. 45–47, 53.

5. The Mughal painting of Shah Jahan hunting (Barrett and Gray, 113), contains ideas used later in Kota such as the recording of an extent of space, extremely defined clumps of vegetation, and abrupt changes of scale.

6. Lee, 1957, p. 182.

7. E. P. Walker, *Mammals of the World,* 2 vols. (Baltimore: Johns Hopkins Univ. Press, 1964), 2: 1227.

8. Tod, 2: 474.

9. Ibid., 562, also 2: 415 mentions three types of artificial barrier constructed for these hunts—ditches, palisadoes (fences), and circumvallations (presumably earthworks). The miniatures also show the use of large nets to entrap the animals.

10. Tod, 2: 415.

11. Paintings E, F, and others show hunting seats with ponds in front. In hunts with beaters, the miniatures show men facing the quarry on foot or shooting from trees or treehouses rather than from the hunting seats.

12. Lee, 1957, p. 183.

13. Walker, 2: 1457.

14. W. G. Archer, 1959, no. 36.

15. Ibid., p. 51—Cleveland miniature, ca. 1840 (*Ram Singh Hunting,* ca. 1830).

16. Ibid.

17. Ibid.

18. Beach, 1974, pp. 39–41.

19. Ibid., p. 41; Welch, 1973, p. 51, has observed a correlation of the Kota and Devgarh figure styles. There seems to have been a pool of artistic resources in Rajasthan during the later eighteenth and early nineteenth centuries. Contacts between the two states of Devgarh and Kota included royal marriages and gifts of hunting dogs (see Andhare, p. 45, and Beach, 1970/71, p. 23); they also must have extended to artistic stylizations. However, the heavy shading on the faces of the Cleveland huntresses and the shape of their facial features is a logical outgrowth of Kota conventionalizations seen in such paintings as those of the Kota *ragamala* series, ca. 1775 (Beach, 1974, fig. 100; and Pal, 1967, cat. nos. 11, 13, 34, 47, 51, etc.). The relationship of Chokha's work to that of the Cleveland miniature is indirect, and since the Kota style is more consistent then that of Devgarh, influences are likely to have extended outward from Kota.

20. W. G. Archer, 1959, p. 51) reverses the positions of the two paintings. F, a somewhat weaker picture, depends on the Cleveland miniature rather than vice versa. The animal outlines, for example, are spiritless by comparison (note the running gazelles in the two foregrounds). In addition, the pavilion, pond, and vegetation in F have been adjusted from the Cleveland miniature to accord with the ponderous weight of Ram Singh II.

21. Beach, 1974, p. 40.

22. The super-real group of Kota paintings generally includes works that are technically precise, have massed vegetation, and details in gold or silver paint; for other characteristics see Lee, 1957, pp. 182–83.

FURTHER READING: E. P. Gee, *The Wild Life of India* (London: E. P. Dutton, 1964); J. MacKinnon and K. MacKinnon, *Animals of Asia, the Ecology of the Oriental Region* (New York: Time-Life Books, 1974); P. Pfeffer, *Asia, a Natural History* (New York: Random House, 1968).

78 *Three Ladies Shooting from*
a Hunt Tower

78.50

Sketch, Rajasthan, Kota, ca. 1830, 28.5 × 26 cm. On reverse: sketch of Krishna on Kaliya; Devi.
Anonymous Gift

This casual sketch of women shooting from a hunt tower was certainly not the model for the finished painting in the Cleveland collection [77], but it is interesting because it shows that the composition was sufficiently known and appreciated to be copied. The color patches on the sketch seem to indicate that the artist was planning to do another version to be painted. He presumably abandoned this drawing because he had not rendered the hunt pavilion in correct perspective. Only a few of the animals present in catalog entry 77 are included in this cruder sketch. In typical Kota fashion, the artist has drawn freely on both sides of the sheet; the reverse has an incomplete scene of Krishna dancing on the serpent Kaliya as well as an illustration of Devi surrounded by gods.

Figure 78.

79 *Vallabha Priest Worshipping*   78.71
   a Krishna Image

Rajasthan, Kota, mid-19th century, 24.5 × 18.8 cm.

Purchase, James Albert and Mary Gardiner Ford Memorial Fund

Published: Beach, 1974, fig. 118.

Comparative Material: (A) *Ram Singh II Worshipping Shri Mathuranathji*, Rajasthan, Kota, ca. 1865; Leach, 1982, no. 285.

This Kota painting showing a Vallabha priest holding a lamp with four burning wicks depicts the performance of *arati,* a reverential act of worship involving circular motions with a lamp before an image—in this case a small, bejeweled Krishna flanked by his consorts Radha and Rukmini. While there is little similarity between the diminutive Krishna and the sect's main image of Shri Nathji housed in the nearby town of Nathadwara, the elaborate practices of Vallabha worship are very much the same. As in other states with

Figure 79.

Vallabha observances, the small Krishna image in the Cleveland painting is viewed as an exalted human being and placed on a tiered dais to be entertained by priests with toys or miniature objects, such as the cows or elephants associated with the Krishna legend.[1]

The sect was known for the wealth required from its devotees and for the sumptuous trappings of its devotional places. Here the small dais has a roof of gold with silver pillars and either silver or mirrorwork tiers. The bibelots arranged for Krishna's amusement are also gold and silver. The shrine itself frames the god with a niche composed of strips of red and green glass between mirrored panels that in some cases are painted with flowers. On its roof is perched a tiny kiosk with a couch and above that a further arrangement of pillows topped with some artifact dedicated to the god (possibly a hat or crown). In back of the shrine hangs a rich red and green silk interwoven with gold threads of the type made in another area of India (Benares?) and donated by wealthy adherents. In front of this is an elaborate arrangement of blue, green, and clear glass hanging lamps. The scene appears to be set partially out of doors since palms appear in the foreground before a fence. The colored glass and mirror panels are characteristic of eighteenth- and nineteenth-century Rajasthan and simulate palace decoration, since the Vallabhas believed Krishna should enjoy princely rather than his childhood rural surroundings. (The Shri Nathji image owns an imposing palace in the center of Nathadwara.) The priest, though simply dressed, wears elaborate jewelry, including pearl and emerald necklaces and heavy emerald-studded gold bracelets. He exemplifies Vallabha's creed of accepting the pleasure of aesthetic richness and the fact that the founder himself had forsworn the asceticism commonly associated with religious worship. The miniature is apparently one of a series commonly done by artists residing in Nathadwara to commemorate the variety of sectarian ceremonies throughout the sacred year.

During the nineteenth century the main Vallabha image kept in the state of Kota was that of Shri Mathuranathji, a somewhat larger icon with no attending females that was worshipped by the Kota rajas (A). The Vallabha sect was, however, very powerful in the state, and the figure in the Cleveland miniature was one of the several minor images involved in Kota's complex and expensive Vallabha devotions. In his description of Rajasthan, the early nineteenth-century British political agent Colonel James Tod comments at length on the wealth that flowed into the great Vallabha center at Nathadwara from all over India and even from abroad. Many Vaishnavites tithed, and some sent goods as well as monetary tributes. Tod mentions that Shri Nathji was refreshed with foreign perfumes and tempted by Persian raisins, pistachios, or other various exotic sweetmeats as well as by receiving a rich supply of Kashmiri shawls, Bengali silks, and Gujerati brocades. The opulent setting in the Cleveland miniature is thus characteristic of the widely accepted material extravagance in the sect.

In Kota as well as Mewar much valuable property, including a well-stocked lake for the god's pleasure, was held in Krishna's name. These resources were protected by state troops. As in Nathadwara, valuable textiles and other luxuries were given by the raja or his officials.[2] While the Vallabha cult had wealthy adherents in many areas, Kota was one of the main centers where the sect also enjoyed major political importance, especially during the tenure of the autocratic prime minister Zalim Singh in the late eighteenth century.

Ram Singh II of Kota (r. 1827–65) was one of the most enthusiastic Rajput patrons of the nineteenth century. While the style followed by his artists is regimented compared with that of the eighteenth century, these painters were well-disciplined craftsmen who created polished works in exciting, often original, tones of vivid color. Because of the elegance of Kota devotional illustrations, and the appearance of Ram Singh himself in many scenes (A), it appears that the state artists also produced scenes for the Vallabha order. Their miniatures, mainly distinguishable by a rhythmic, wiry line and by Kota figural conventions such as the heavy-lidded clamshell eye, are more refined than those produced for pilgrims at the purely religious center of Nathadwara. In this particular miniature the rich reds and greens combined with the sparkling decorative details of jewelry are an excellent example of the Kota adaptation to the requirements of the Vallabha sect.

1. Leach, 1982, no. 284.
2. Tod, 1: 420–24.

FURTHER READING: Jindel.

80 *Page of Sketches* 79.22

Rajasthan, Kota, ca. 1866, 28 × 18.6 cm. Inscription on
reverse: "Shri Maharaji Chatter Singhji."

Gift of Mrs. A. Dean Perry

Comparative Material: (A) *Raja Chattar Singh Riding to the
Gangaur Festival*, Rajasthan, Kota, ca. 1870; W. G. Archer,
1959, fig. 54.

From at least the late seventeenth century, Kota artists used
drawing to far better advantage than most of their Rajasthani colleagues: they were freer, more playful, and more experimental in putting forms down on paper. Many times they
simply doodled rather than executing a planned sketch, but
these random scrawlings show how they delighted in abstract shape and movement. Even late into the nineteenth
century when forms were mainly prescribed, an element of
exuberant creativity survives, as in this page of sketches.

Figure 80, obverse.

Here the artist has repeatedly formed the stock face considered a basic male or female ideal so that its geometrical relationships are stressed—the curves of the forehead and the fleshy chin, the wide eye, and the hooked nose supposed to be like a parakeet's beak. The uniformity of the type is emphasized by the profiles of a man and a woman facing each other who have identical features and beneath them, humorously, by a figure with female breasts whose face has been turned into that of a bearded man. The artist has done somewhat looser, more individualistic doodles of the two hennaed feet, an excited mastiff, and an older man.

On the reverse an unfinished drawing (illustrated here in a turned-upright position) labeled Maharaja Chattar Singh (r. 1866–89) that seems to be contemporary with the other sketches shows the raja as a youngish man riding. A few retainers are roughed out below him. In view of Chattar Singh's apparent age, the drawing was probably done around the time of his accession, in 1866.

Figure 80, reverse

81 *Krishna's Insomnia* 38.303

Leaf from a *Rasikapriya*, Central India, Malwa, set dated 1634, 17.8 × 13.8 cm, 20.5 × 16.5 cm with border. Rubbed in several places. Red border, uneven. Inscription: "She comes to embrace me only after I appease her in millions of ways. [Even while embracing me] she keeps her mind wide awake and often looks around in the midst of sleep [i.e., Krishna cannot sleep soundly]. Although my beloved is away, she [Sleep] does not trust me for a moment. I can never know her. Behaving like a newly wedded shy wife, she runs away from me in the middle of the night."[1]

Gift of N. M. Heeramaneck

Ex collection: Heeramaneck.

Published: V. Dwivedi, 1968, fig. 3.

Comparative Material: (A) *Krishna Kills the Horse Demon*, leaf from a *Bhagavata Purana*, Central India, Malwa, ca. 1634; A. K. Coomaraswamy and N. M. Heeramaneck, *Loan Exhibition of Early Indian Sculptures, Paintings, and Bronzes* (New York: College Art Association, 1935). (B) *Krishna Fluting*, leaf from a *Rasikapriya*, Central India, Malwa, 1634: Spink, fig. 72. (C) *Krishna Tied to the Mortar*, leaf from a *Bhagavata Purana*, Central India, Malwa, ca. 1634; Brooklyn Museum, 42.407, unpublished. (D) *Erotic Scene*, Central India, Malwa, ca. 1634; George Bickford collection, unpublished. (E) *Desvarari Ragini*, Central India, Malwa, ca. 1634–40; Krishna, pl. B.

The Indian dealer Heeramaneck at one time owned most of the leaves of this *Rasikapriya* now in Western museums (e.g., B is in The Nelson-Atkins Museum of Art, Kansas City, Missouri, acc. no. 34-106) and private collections. A colophon on what is presumed to be part of the same set in the National Museum, New Delhi, is dated 1634. Leaves of other literary works exist in much the same style, indicating a prolific and stable studio production probably lasting over a period of years without much change. One of the dis-

Figure 81.

tinctive features of seventeenth-century Malwa painting is that it altered slowly. In addition to the *Rasikapriya*, similar manuscripts probably done from about 1630–40 include a *ragamala* (E), an erotic manuscript (D), and two *Bhagavata Purana* sets (also formerly in Heeramaneck's possession)— one of which is rectangular and the other squarish (cf. C and A; the latter is now in the Albright-Knox Art Gallery, Buffalo, New York). Up to about 1660, works were done with the slight figures and simple compositions characteristic of this group, but the type gradually became coarser.

The markedly conservative ca.-1634 style was dependent on developments that had originally occurred in Jain or pre-Mughal painting. The early Hindu *Aranyaka Parvan* dated 1516 is an example of an illustrated manuscript that already includes many of the idioms employed by the Malwa painters more than a century later.[2]

Whether the ca.-1634 group provided inspiration for the main developments in Malwa painting seems questionable. It appears that two important Malwa styles ran concurrently, but that this one was linked closely to the past, while the other was more influential in the generation of further works. The more revolutionary style, best exemplified by such series as the so-called Boston *ragamala* [82], has large figures and emphatic blue/red color schemes that contrast with the elfin figures and predominantly yellow and red hues of this *Rasikapriya*. The Boston *ragamala* set is flamboyant and confident, while the dainty *Rasikapriya* miniatures are drawn in a tentative, less expressionistic manner. Possibly these two contemporary strains each represent the production of a different center. From about 1640 to 1650, when the ca.-1634 style that had been so consistently and prolifically employed seems to have declined, the more explosive type of Malwa painting developed into its most expressive phase.

Krishna is the hero of the poetic verse illustrated by the Cleveland miniature, but in the situation depicted, this eminently successful lover surprisingly finds himself neglected by the woman he wishes to attract. The subtly described subject of the poetic verse is Sleep personified as a woman who only comes to Krishna after he has "appease(d) her in millions of ways" and even then is elusive and undependable.

This scene and others like it by the miniaturist are handled with a gentle blandness quite removed from the romantic ardor of the *Rasikapriya* poetry. In addition, the literary art had already achieved a sophistication far beyond that of this delightful but simple or naive painting style.[2] The poet's adroit description of insomnia is typical of Indian literary imagery from the Gupta era on, but unfortunately the painter was at a loss in imagining how to portray the situation. Krishna sits alone, with a fawn on either side of him, but the significance of his cleverly described flirtation remains hidden.

1. V. Dwivedi, 1968, Appendix B, p. 27.
2. Khandalavala and M. Chandra, 1974.

82 *Madhu Madhavi Ragini* 25.1336

Central India, Malwa, ca. 1630–40, 19.1 × 14.6 cm. Damaged lower left edge, some paint flaking in other areas. Fragmentary red border. Inscription in Hindi on reverse: "Madhu Madhavi, the ragini of Hindol: a heroine who has come to her lord. The eye sees less than all and is at variance with thought" (paraphrased from Coomaraswamy, 1916); title repeated in Persian.

Purchase from the J. H. Wade Fund

Ex collection: Coomaraswamy.

Published: W. G. Archer, 1960, pl. 33; Coomaraswamy, 1916, 2: pl. I; Gangoly, 1935, pl. LXXXII; Lee, 1960, no. 4A, and 1973, color pl. 16.

Comparative Material: (A) *Lalita Ragini*, Central India, Malwa, ca. 1630–40; Coomaraswamy, 1926, pt. 5: pl. III.

Madhu Madhavi Ragini, illustrated here by a pair of lovers, portrays the break in tension and the arousal of passion brought about by the coming of the monsoon. According to a poem on another Malwa leaf of the same subject, a woman in the garden, seeing the lightning flash and hearing birds welcome the storm, is stirred to think of her lover.[1] Correlation between human behavior and the natural world is such an integral part of the history of Indian literature and painting that the fructifying effect of rain on the landscape is almost automatically associated with images of human love. An early example of rivers, clouds, and storms personified that experience human love is found in Kalidasa's fifth-century lyric poem *The Cloud Messenger* written in Malwa. Similar expressions are characteristic of the Mughal period *ragamala* verses, though the associations of man and nature are by now so well understood that they are treated implicitly:

> When the lightning flashes she twists her body,
> Her passion is excited by the sight of the closely grouped (leaves) of the *tamala* tree.[2]

The same immediacy that appears in the poetry of Madhu Madhavi is also characteristic of the passion expressed by the artists of this *ragamala* set. The strong, basic color contrasts and exaggerated gestures throughout this series convey the romantic fervor of the poetry in which everything superfluous is abandoned to the prevailing mood. In the Cleveland miniature the details that convey the moment of the storm's advent are simple, yet dramatic, as the woman lifts her hand in a portentous gesture to feel the rain. The peacock, symbolically the mate of the rain, has risen almost into the storm and flings back its head, shrieking.

Fifteen of the twenty-three miniatures from this series that the pioneering scholar Coomaraswamy purchased in Delhi are now in the Museum of Fine Arts, Boston (where he was curator), while other leaves are dispersed in various collections.[3] Because the group represents one of the key phases of Malwa painting, it has been widely published; however, very little factual information concerning its history has emerged. As has been noted by others, this *ragamala* retains much of the intensity of the pre-Mughal

Chaurapanchasika style.[4] In the Cleveland scene, as in the *Chaurapanchasika*, abstract color and shape are utilized to bring out the passion of the amorous attachments. The Malwa style, however, is slightly more folklike and simple than the elegant *Chaurapanchasika*. The *ragamala* is notable for its limited compositional settings contrasted with figures in complex positions that reveal their deep romantic feelings. Though the heavy and hulking figures move awkwardly, the artist very skillfully establishes the emotional timbre of the scenes through the tensions of their poses, as, for example, in portraying the lover stretched on the bed in this miniature. The combined deep blue and red coloring of the backgrounds and the figures' exaggerated, dancelike movements create an impression of the repressed emotion inherent in Rajput culture.

This *ragamala* set has been variously dated since Coomaraswamy first published his discovery of the series in 1916.[5] The scholar was deeply affronted by the equation of Indian painting with the Mughal court and used this series in his attempts to explain the aesthetic qualities of Rajput painting. In his publications these miniatures played a significant role in establishing a standard of excellence and defining

Figure 82.

Figure 82, detail.

what Coomaraswamy believed to be the essence of native Indian painting. Without comparative material, he instinctively considered the *ragamala* leaves early productions and at first dated them to the mid-sixteenth century.[6] In 1916 he stated:

> Many valuable treasures have . . . been lost or destroyed in the course of the constant internal warfare which marks the history of Rajasthan. . . . Yet, since illustrated Jaina books of the early fifteenth century are known, it may well be that fresh discoveries of older Rajasthani paintings may also be made. Of examples available to the present writer, none can be claimed as older than the series of twenty-three *raginis* from which four examples are reproduced. . . . These are the nearest that we have to the unknown primitives of Rajput painting. There is not as yet the least tendency to treat the *raginis* as pictorial material; the painter is occupied entirely with expression.[7]

The art-historical evaluation of dates for Rajput painting by Coomaraswamy's contemporaries rested upon costume styles and their appearance in Mughal miniatures. The German Indologist Goetz believed that the *ragamala* fell within the latter part of the Jahangiri period because the male figures did not wear *chakdar jamas;* he therefore convinced Coomaraswamy by 1926 to modify his opinions somewhat.[8] The later discovery of the pre-Mughal "kuladhar group" of Rajput paintings supported Goetz's point, since many male figures wear *kuladhar* turbans and *chakdar jamas* in these

earlier works. The significance behind this chain of events is that because Coomaraswamy believed the *ragamala* miniatures epitomized the culture of Hindu India, he dated them prior to the Mughal invasion. He was then prevailed upon to dissociate his aesthetic judgment from his concept of dating, yet he was eventually proved correct in assuming the existence of spirited expressionistic painting of this type during the pre-Mughal era.

While the period during which this *ragamala* could have been produced is now better understood, little conclusive documentation of the Malwa school has evolved. The 1634 *Rasikapriya* [81] and the Mughal-influenced *Amaru Sataku* of 1652 are the dated Malwa works closest to the presumed era of this *ragamala's* manufacture, but they differ from it stylistically. *Ragamala* sets discussed under [81] and [83] can be considered to form a stylistic group with this series, but like this set, they are undated or otherwise inscribed.

1. A. K. Coomaraswamy, letter to the Cleveland Museum.
2. Gangoly, 1935, text for pl. LXXXII.
3. See Ebeling, pp. 171–72 for a current list of miniatures and discussion of the set.
4. W. G. Archer, 1960, text to pl. 33.
5. Coomaraswamy, 1916, 2: text, pl. I.
6. Ibid., 1: 67, and 2: pls. I–III.
7. Ibid., 1: 12.
8. Coomaraswamy, 1926, pt.5: 71.

FURTHER READING: Ebeling, pp. 171–72; A. Krishna.

83 *Kedara Ragini* 64.452

Central India, Malwa, ca. 1650, 18.7 × 14.8 cm, 20.8 × 16.4 cm with border. Narrow red border, somewhat damaged. On reverse is seal of Datia state and seven-line inscription: "The heroine Kedara, longing for her lover, has assumed the character of a *yogi* and waits intently for his return. She has smeared ash all over her body, which is reduced to a skeleton. Absorbed in love, she sings her lord's praise. In this yogic garb, her body is terrifying and looks like a male body. She sees that night seems to be prolonged and anticipates dawn eagerly. Lovesickness is killing Kedara."[1]

Purchase from the J. H. Wade Fund
Ex collection: Maharaja of Datia, Heeramaneck.
Published: V. Dwivedi, 1968, pp. 19–27.
Comparative Material: (A) *Gaunda Ragini*, Central India, Malwa, ca. 1650; Czuma, no. 69. (B) *Asavari Ragini*, Central India, Malwa, ca. 1650; Archer and Binney, no. 45A. (C) *Varari Ragini*, Central India, Malwa, ca. 1650; Archer and Binney, no. 45B. (D) *Ragini*, Central India, Malwa, ca. 1650; J. McGregor, *Indian Miniature Paintings from West Coast Private Collections* (San Francisco: M. H. de Young Museum, 1964), pl. V. (E) *Kedara Ragini*, Central India, Malwa, ca. 1650; Ebeling, no. 278. (F) *Kedara Ragini*, Central India, Malwa, ca. 1630–40; Coomaraswamy, 1926, pt. 5: pl. IX.

Figure 83, obverse.

This miniature very movingly depicts the female ascetic theme common in medieval Indian literature and painting. The subject arises from the belief that meditation on an object (in this case the beloved) coupled with severe austerities is a means of acquiring power. In amorous circumstances, the heroine thus sought to bring her lover back to her, or to gain the exclusive attentions of her loved one, often in a polygamous relationship. The radical nature of the penance and of the heroine's outcast state is indicated by contrast with the protected lives socially prescribed for women.

Everything in this miniature suggests austerity or spareness; Kedara's attenuated frame is paralleled by the spidery legs of the antelope skin on which ascetics habitually meditated. Even her long, thin fingers poised over the *vina* emphasize her starved, lovesick condition. Every unnecessary line has been purged to convey the desolation of the environment. The blank pavilion door or the abstract background areas also express loneliness, and the two peacocks eagerly stretching their necks toward the sky mirror the yearning of Kedara. The heroine's intensity and tension are echoed by such details as the long, straight lines running horizontally across the composition that are as taut as the strings of her *vina*. The opposing red and blue background areas resonate visually much as Indian *ragamala* music vibrates between rich, contrasting sounds.

The unhappy Kedara, playing and singing praises of her absent lover, is suffering from a tragic hopelessness often described in the medieval period. The Indian literary tradition dwells in many texts upon the despair of a woman thwarted in love and the progressive symptoms she undergoes that may eventually lead to death. The poetic verse on the Cleveland miniature indicates the seriousness of Kedara's condition: "She . . . is reduced to a skeleton. . . . Lovesickness is killing Kedara." Another text questions whether Kedara will live to see the dawn of her interminably prolonged night of solitude.[2]

Although privation has severely reduced Kedara's form, her sex can be discerned from the difference between her loincloth and that of the ascetic in a second *Kedara Ragini* miniature owned by the Cleveland Museum in which the subject is clearly a man [84].[3] These two Malwa paintings illustrating the same ascetic subject have been compared from an iconographic point of view, but at the time it was thought that both dated from the same era.[4] It is apparent, however, that the simplicity, boldness, and lack of Mughal influence in this particular Kedara scene are characteristic of earlier productions. The increased detail in catalog entry 84 is closer to the dated Malwa Narsingarh set of 1680, while this miniature relates to the mid-seventeenth-century style of catalog entry 82, which has large, simple, and boldly arranged shapes.

Since the heroine of the Cleveland Kedara is emaciated, it is at first difficult to associate her figure with those of other dispersed miniatures coming from the same *ragamala* set, even though architecture and other elements are similar

Figure 83, obverse, detail.

(A–D). However, the inclusion of the Cleveland miniature in this series becomes clear when the ascetic subject is compared with still another Kedara illustration (E). This painting is from a complete *ragamala* series in the Bharat Kala Bhavan, Benares,[5] and it is virtually the twin of the scattered, partial set under discussion. This complete Bharat Kala Bhavan group is an aid to reconstructing the dispersed series that includes the Cleveland miniature and several other, unpublished as well as published, leaves. Like other paintings now classified as belonging to the Malwa school, the Cleveland miniature has a seal showing it was in the hereditary collection of neighboring Datia. This seal may help to establish the specific provenance of such *ragamalas* if some evidence comes to light concerning the existence of painting studios in seventeenth-century Datia.

Both the complete and partial sets use the same texts with the inscriptions written on the reverse of the miniatures.[6] The two series both have plainly colored bands above and below the illustrations, which in other sets would contain writing or floral scrolls (the Cleveland miniature has been called unfinished, but its austerity seems to represent a deliberate choice).[7]

214

The Cleveland and Bharat Kala Bhavan Kedara miniatures are stylistically identical, especially in their simplicity and spareness. Like other paintings of the two sets, their compositions are also closely related;[8] although the ascetic in the Cleveland miniature gazes at a flower rather than a burning fire (both symbolic of passion or sexuality) and the pavilion behind her is pointed rather than bulbous, most other features are alike. Interestingly, the composition of both these *raginis* differs from the nearly contemporary Kedara illustration of the so-called Boston *ragamala* [82]; though stylistically related, this miniature (F) shows the heroine acompanied by an attendant who plays the *vina* for her. This not only minimizes the impact of her intense solitude but also lessens her own expressiveness. Comparing the two compositional types fully brings out the pathos of the heroine's vigil as depicted in the Cleveland miniature, and the sensitivity of this second artist in conveying Kedara's disturbed emotional state with minimal elaboration.

1. This translation is paraphrased from V. Dwivedi, 1968, p. 27; in his article, Dwivedi gives a longer translation in addition to contextual information.

2. Ibid.; Ebeling, p. 134.

3. V. Dwivedi, 1968, p. 23.

4. Ibid., picture caption p. 19; p. 20.

5. Ebeling, *ragamala* no. 22, p. 172.

6. Compare the translation of Kedara given by V. Dwivedi, 1968, p. 27, and that for the Bharat Kala Bhavan Kedara leaf in Ebeling, p. 134. The slightly earlier Malwa set represented by [82] uses a shortened form of these texts, thus further establishing the relation between the sets.

7. V. Dwivedi, 1968, p. 23.

8. For further parallels between the two sets, compare miniature B, and Krishna, color pl. D.

84 Kedara Ragini 60.116

Central India, Malwa, ca. 1660–70, 19.5 × 13.6 cm, 20.4 × 14.8 cm with border. Floral scroll at base rubbed, portions of red border damaged. Labeled "Kedara" on reverse; numbered 35 on obverse. Inscription is translated in Lee, 1960, p. 19 (though wrongly identified as Malara).

Purchase, James Parmelee Fund

Published: V. Dwivedi, 1968, pp. 19–27; Lee, 1960, no. 8.

Comparative Material: (A) *Setmaller Ragini*, Central India, Malwa, ca. 1680; Ebeling, no. 281. (B) *Vilaval Ragini*, leaf from the Narsingarh *Ragamala*, Central India, dated 1680; Khandalavala, 1950, fig. 24. (C) *The Lovers*, leaf from an *Amaru Sataku*, Central India, Malwa, dated 1652; Khandalavala, 1950, fig. 20. (D) *Malasri Ragini*, Central India, Malwa, ca. 1660–70; Archer and Binney, no. 47. (E) *Dipsadhika Ragini*, Central India, Malwa, ca. 1660–70; Pal, 1976, no. 23.

This second Malwa illustration of *Kedara Ragini* includes some naturalistic elements, while the earlier version [83] is a starker, more expressionistic work. Though the move toward naturalism here can be considered quite relative, it can be seen in the carefully detailed drawing of the brick wall and the bottle niches. In addition, the face of the ascetic in this *Kedara Ragini* is closer to Mughal portrait painting. Mughal influence crept into Malwa very slowly through such avenues.

The resistance of Malwa artists toward change meant that compositional embellishment in many instances created pictorial tensions. More naturalistic detail as well as the proliferating decoration begin to break up the purely conceptual approach to form that is characteristic of the earlier Cleveland Kedara painting. A dichotomy exists in various pictures between areas of elaboration and the strong, plain blue/red areas that had always been typical of Malwa art. The second Cleveland Kedara is itself a balanced painting: the amount of detail is controlled, and illusionism is subordinate to the older abstract-design structure. When compared with [83], however, it exemplifies the problems of development within the traditional anti-spatial composition.

The Cleveland painting is related in its treatment to the 1680 set from Narsingarh, one of the few dated landmarks in Malwa painting (B).[1] Lack of other documentation has caused most miniatures with similar figures and architecture to be ascribed to the 1680 era, but the different centers of production as well as more precise dates for this large stylistic group remain to be determined. In comparing the Cleveland miniature with the Narsingarh *Vilaval Ragini* (B), it can be seen that the architecture of the latter, which covers the entire page, is far more complex and indicates recession. Thus the Cleveland leaf, though similar, is not totally comparable, and must have been produced between the dated Narsingarh *Ragamala* and the dated 1652 *Amaru Sataku* manuscript whose figures also show Mughal influence (C). Because of its nearly identical architecture and floral scrolling, another leaf (D) can be identified as coming from the same set as the Cleveland miniature.[2] Miniature E may be yet another page from this series.

A miniature in the Bharat Kala Bhavan (A) is a reversal of the composition of the Cleveland painting. Labeled as "Set-mallar," another *ragini* with an ascetic subject, it shows that there were often no clear-cut distinctions between ascetic themes but that these subjects in general portrayed the excruciating pains of desertion, longing, or unfulfilled love.

1. The meaning of the inscription for the 1680 set is in question, because the partition of Malwa between two factions and the creation of the city of Narsingarh occurred only in 1681, but this *ragamala* is generally accepted as being painted at the new city (see Archer and Binney, p. 53; Ebeling, p. 178; Krishna, pp. 11–12, 36).

2. This identification was first made in Archer and Binney, p. 62.

Figure 84.

85 *Pancham Raga*   61.43

Central India, Malwa, ca. 1660–80, 19 × 13.3 cm,
20.7 × 14.8 cm with border. Poetic verse damaged, some
paint rubbed or flaked in other areas; worm tunnel near
center. Narrow red border, somewhat damaged.
Inscription: "Panchama Raga—A lord with intense looks
and a disturbed mind who has the *chauri* moving (behind
him) gazes at the pleasure-seeking woman."

Purchase, James Parmelee Fund

This miniature shows a man approached by one of his mistresses while fanned by another with a *chauri*. The title
Pancham (meaning the fifth note) indicates that the *raga*
melody was organized around this sound, which was
thought to create a strong sensation. Probably for this reason the pictorial composition of Pancham often involves
musicians playing. However, the melody was also considered to excite passion,[1] and it is this aspect of the theme that
the miniature and its accompanying poetic verse illustrate

Figure 85.

Figure 85, detail.

here. Aroused and disturbed by the entrance of an alluring woman, the lord finds his self-possession deserting him.

This miniature is one of many stylistically similar *ragamala* illustrations, which therefore cannot always be distinguished by set. The type seems to have been produced in a single central Indian location from about 1650 to 1680, perhaps by the same studio group responsible for the illustrations of the Sanskrit romance *Amaru Sataku*, done in 1652.[2]

The *ragamala* illustrations, *Amaru Sataku* scenes, and some related erotic leaves are distinguished by floral scroll bands running across the bottom of the miniatures.[3] Like this scene, many of the compositions are static—they generally include a couple, or a few people, in a pavilion—and are often ornamented with lush, over-sized flowers or plants, probably symbolizing unity and fecundity in such romantic contexts. The figures, which can be simple (as in the previous illustration [84]) or more complex and naturalistic (as here), give the best indication of dating.

The floral scrolls originate in Persian art, as is demonstrated by the *Bustan* produced by a Herat-trained painter in Mandu, Malwa's capital, in 1503.[4] The *Chaurapanchasika* has floral bands running across portions of its illustrations,[5] and a late sixteenth-century manuscript in a recognizable Malwa style that retains traits of the *Chaurapanchasika* group has simple decorative bands across the bottom.[6]

In Malwa paintings of 1650–80, these floral bands range from geometric to more naturalistic types.[7] From the evidence of the 1652 *Amaru Sataku* pages, the same kind of scroll is repeated within a manuscript, though each leaf may show slight variations.[8]

Although the numerous *ragamala* leaves of the group cannot all be distinguished by set, floral scrolls might give some idea of series when examined along with page measurements and stylistic factors. The three *ragamala* pages equated in [84] all have scrolls of a creeper unfurling in a tight circular pattern against a background of blue and red. The present *ragamala* illustration is similar to these miniatures but has somewhat heavier figures above as well as a more ornate band of flowers arranged in scalloped triangles across the bottom.

1. Gangoly, 1966, 2: pl. XXVIII, notes.

2. The damaged colophon of this set is tentatively translated (N. C. Mehta, "Two Paintings from an Amaru Sataku," *JISOA* 3 [1935], 146–47) as stating that the paintings were done in a city called Nasratgarh, which has not been correlated with a known location.

3. See *Tooth* 1974, no. 3, for a leaf of another *ragamala*; the erotic series is pictured in Doris Wiener Gallery, *Indian Miniature Paintings* (New York, 1974), no. 40; various *Amaru Sataku* leaves are listed in note 8.

4. W. G. Archer, 1958, p. 3.

5. Miller, pp. 221, 229, 232.

6. *Sotheby*, 13 Dec. 1972, lots 76–78.

7. For a range of different types of scrolls, see Khandalavala and M. Chandra, 1960, cat. no. 55a, pl. 49; P. Chandra, 1971, no. 131; Doris Wiener Gallery, *Indian Miniature Paintings* (New York, 1971), no. 51.

8. See Khandalavala, 1950, fig. 20; Mehta, pp. 146–47; Gray, 1950, pl. 84–85 (wrongly dated to 1680); the *Amaru Sataku* scrolls are comprised of vine loops and narrow, curving leaves, some with flowers.

86 *Bangala Ragini* 56.9

Central India, Malwa, ca. 1680, 24 × 19.7 cm, 29.6 × 23.8 cm with border. Some flaking of paint, staining; red border, damaged. Inscription in Persian with title above panel of Hindi verse at top: "His body is decorated with a beautiful string of *munja* [grass]. He wears the skin of a young doe. He is a bell [vigorous] youth. His body shines with the brilliance of gold. He sings the sacred *samau* [hymn]—Vangalaragini." The text before the teacher reads: "Rama Rama Sita Sita Rama [invoking the deities Rama, Sita]/The Ragini equals the thousandfold expression of the delight in Rama,/the delight of the mind."[1]

Purchase, Edward L. Whittemore Fund

Ex collection: Heeramaneck.

Published: Lee, 1960, no. 10; 1957, pp. 180–83; and 1973, color pl. 18.

Comparative Material: (A) *Bangala Ragini*, Central India, Malwa, ca. 1670; Ebeling, no. 282. (B) *Bangala Ragini*, Central India, Malwa, ca. 1630–40; Gangoly, 1935, pl. IX. (C) *Bangala Ragini*, Central India, Malwa, ca. 1630–40; Gangoly, 1935, pl. X, or Coomaraswamy, 1926, pt. 5: pl. VIII.

Bangala Ragini, like the previous catalogue entries picturing Kedara [83, 84], is one of the ascetic *ragamala* subjects. Many verses describe Bangala as a beautiful woman attempting to win favor over her lord's other mistresses by practicing various austerities and reciting a magical mantra.

Figure 86.

The mantra used in the Cleveland miniature invokes Sita, symbol of the perfect wife, and her lord, Rama, as ideals of union. While in some instances the poetic verse may still refer to the subject as a woman, the illustration clearly depicts a man, thereby showing the abstract or symbolic nature of the *ragamala* concept. A *ragini* is considered to be feminine, representing a womanly drive for approval and satisfaction, although the artist and poet may employ either males or females to exemplify the subject; in this example both verse and painting depict a male *yogi*. Although Malwa had a distinctive tradition, the frequently used verse in the panel above the scene appears on numerous Bangala paintings from Rajasthan as well as Central India and is part of the basic Rajasthani textual tradition.[2]

The composition of Bangala has several variants, two of which are usual in Malwa painting. The first pictures a single ascetic holding the mantra that is being used as an incantation to influence the course of love (A–C). The Cleveland miniature, however, portrays the ascetic with two disciples who obscure the basic poetic meaning with needless elaboration.

Despite the additional figures in the Cleveland miniature, the position of the main ascetic is like that in a leaf of *Bangala Ragini* from a set in the Bharat Kala Bhavan, Benares (A), demonstrating how Indian artists employed standard poses. Both seated *yogis* are depicted with a small stand supporting the portion of scripture in front of them. In each case the illustrations are independent of the poetic verse describing a youth wearing an antelope skin with a string of grass around him. Such works make it clear that the artist had some license in interpreting scenes and also imply that he was probably illiterate and therefore more dependent on previous visual models than on the text.

Stylistically the Cleveland leaf is more complex than the Bharat Kala Bhavan Bangala scene, but there is a general relation to the entire Benares set, which consists of twenty known leaves.[3] The ornamental architectural details including a panel of scroll work are the same in the two Bangala scenes, although the pavilion towers in the Cleveland composition have been decoratively multiplied. This elaboration follows the late seventeenth-century tendency of Malwa artists to soften their stark compositions with additional detail or color. Here the ascetic is seated on a patterned carpet against a yellow flowered pillow. In addition, the artist has introduced features such as the tilted lotus pond, the pillared porch, and the ascetic in the doorway that imply space in a manner that was novel to Malwa painters. Like other miniatures dating from the end of the century,[4] this page is much larger than earlier examples that had carefully limited compositions and dimensions.

1. Translations by Dr. Stella Kramrisch; see Lee, 1957, p. 181.
2. See Ebeling, pp. 118, 124.
3. Ebeling, p. 179.
4. For an example of the late seventeenth-century style, see Ebeling, *ragamala* no. 34, p. 180.

Central India, ca. 1680, 21.6 × 16 cm, 32 × 24 cm with borders. Slightly rubbed; some staining around heroine's face. Brown and pink inner borders; late 18th-century outer border, dark blue with gold floral pattern.

Purchase, Andrew R. and Martha Holden Jennings Fund

Ex collection: MacDonald.

This miniature is filled with delightful, whimsical details of animals gathered around a heroine who is playing her *vina* in the wilderness. The dog suckling her puppies and the eagerly listening creatures at the feet of the heroine are among the most playfully treated. On the left, the artist has included several deer sitting contentedly in the presence of wild cats, while monkeys, who are notoriously afraid of snakes, are shown close to serpents wrapped around

Figure 87, detail.

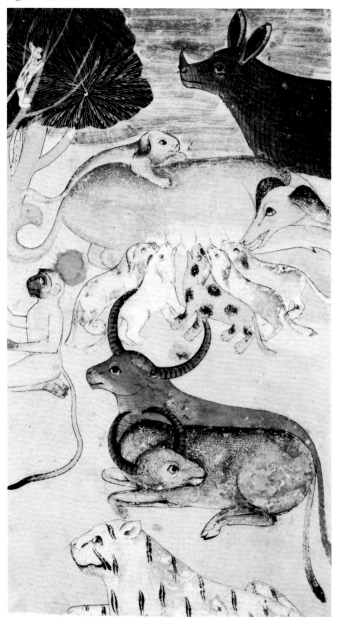

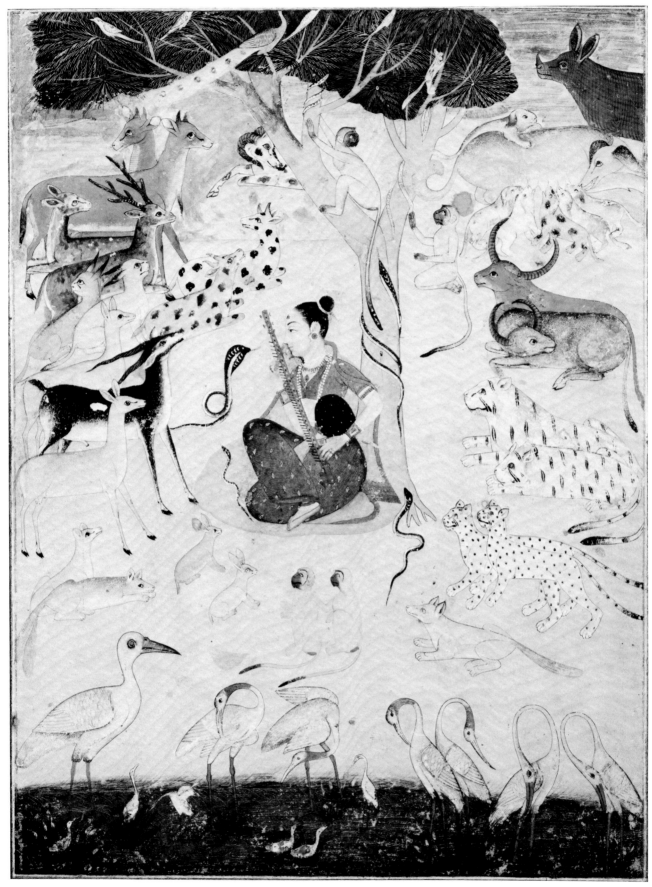

Figure 87.

the tree trunk. The unusual theme thus appears to be one of peace created by the charms of music. Although there are a few miniatures of Krishna as Lord of the Animals,[1] there is no precedent in painting for showing a woman surrounded by such a variety of wild creatures. While the woman playing the *vina* is comparable to *Todi Ragini*, who attracts deer, her seated pose among many animals is distinctive.

The miniature is also unusual stylistically because the soft pink, blue, and gray coloring is outside the ordinary range of Rajasthani or central Indian paintings, and the border is an eighteenth-century Mughal type. The heroine's face and figure resemble those in certain Malwa paintings done about 1680 under the influence of Mughal taste, like *Bangala Ragini* [86]. Her costume, however, is quite unlike those of Malwa *ragamala* heroines who wear boldly striped skirts.

This spirited, sensitive composition therefore differs from the conservative blue and red Malwa miniature types: it seems to represent the break that occurred with tradition in Central Indian painting toward the end of the seventeenth century. Since it is so distinctive, and since so little specific information is known about Central India, the miniature may even come from a school in this region that is not presently documented.

1. Czuma, no. 104.

88 *Jaswant Singh of Jodhpur* 81.5

Partially colored drawing, Rajasthan, Jodhpur, ca. 1660–65, 23.3 × 12.8 cm, 28.7 × 16.3 cm with border. Mounted on border of beige gold-flecked paper, damaged. Inscription above the drawing and on reverse: "Maharaja Shri Jasot Singh-ji Jodhpur-ka Raja."

Purchase, Andrew R. and Martha Holden Jennings Fund

Comparative Material: (A) *Raja Jaswant Singh in Durbar*, Rajasthan, Jodhpur, ca. 1660; Welch, 1976, no. 64. (B) *Jaswant Singh and His Courtiers*, Rajasthan, Jodhpur, ca. 1660; Leach, 1982, nos. 195 and 198. (C) *Jaswant Singh Listening to Music in a Garden*, Rajasthan, Jodhpur, ca. 1660; Topsfield, 1981, no. 12.

This portrait of the portly Jaswant Singh of Jodhpur (b. 1627, r. 1638–71) holding a straight sword seems to have been done around 1660–65, when the raja was between thirty-five and forty years old. Jaswant was the second son of Gaj Singh of Marwar, who was influential at the Mughal court and appears in various scenes by imperial painters.[1]

Whether Gaj Singh commissioned Mughal-trained artists to work in his native state has not yet been adequately established,[2] but he was certainly well aware of the imperial painting tradition, as his portraits by major artists such as Bichitr prove. The several paintings of his second son, Jaswant, in a mixed Mughal and Rajasthani style demonstrate that this raja wished to develop his own atelier based on imperial prototypes.

Because of the political situation, Jaswant and his father both had reason to fear and dislike their overlords, and it is surprising to discover Jaswant's adulation of Mughal culture as exemplified by his portraits. Clearly, despite his need to be wary in his dealings with the Mughals, Jaswant absorbed much from observation of court customs. Since neither he nor his father were allowed by the emperor to spend much time in their home state, they understandably acquired alien habits (for example, in miniature paintings both Jaswant and his father wear typical Mughal rather than more elaborate Marwari turbans).

Ironically, Jaswant owed his inheritance to the tensions created by the Rajput-Mughal alliance. Like all powerful Rajputs, Gaj Singh had been watched carefully by the emperor for signs of ambition or independence. Because of family apprehension, his hot-headed and reckless older son was passed over for the succession and exiled, so that any trouble he caused would not rebound on the clan or state.[3] When Jaswant Singh assumed power, he was not given the prominence at court that his father had been accorded. At the end of his life, since the large territory of Marwar was such a potential danger, the emperor Aurangzeb used old antagonisms in an unsuccessful attempt to deprive Jaswant's posthumously born heir of the succession rights.

The painters that Jaswant Singh employed during his reign have naturalistic styles similar to those in vogue in Shah Jahan's court. In the Cleveland miniature the artist has posed the raja in conventional Mughal fashion and has also attempted to give precise details of the *jama, patka,*

Figure 88.

and so on, as an imperial artist would. He may have been either a native Rajasthani painter who had undergone thorough schooling in Mughal draftsmanship, or conversely, he may have trained in the Mughal capitals and adapted the Rajasthani way of doing large almond-shaped eyes and decoratively treated sideburns in deference to his patron. The cultured and powerful Jaswant certainly had several painters, but this man seems to have been one of his favorite and most competent, who also did other, more fluid studies of the raja and his courtiers, all dating from about the same time (A and B). Another artist worked in a more decorative but still Mughal-influenced style (C).

While there is a dichotomy between the fiercely colored, somewhat crudely drawn works of outlying centers in Marwar like Pali and more sophisticated pictures, Jaswant's commissions as raja no doubt helped develop one important aspect of Marwari tradition. The fact that all the known works by the artist of the Cleveland miniature are restrained, with stiffly erect figures and more emphasis on drawing than on decorative color, helps to characterize the Jodhpur style as a masculine one. Jaswant seems neither to have used his artists for doing romantic pictures nor the typically Rajasthani legendary scenes in vivid colors. He instead was renowned for his interest in science, for commissioning numerous books, and for being something of an intellectual, which may also have contributed to his desire for understated, naturalistic miniatures.[4] The pride of the desert Rajputs, their stern way of life, and their associations with the court seem to have formed their taste for straightforward portrait studies, imitated in neighboring centers like Nagaur or Ghanerao, which are notable for dignified court depictions inspired by Jodhpur examples.[5]

1. Beach, 1978, nos. 24, 34.
2. *Sotheby, Parke-Bernet*, 27 Feb. 1974, lot 52, is possibly a slightly later copy of a seventeenth-century picture done under Gaj Singh's patronage.
3. Tod, 2: 34-35; he eventually assassinated several nobles in the emperor's *durbar* hall before being killed.
4. Ibid., p. 36.
5. Leach, 1982, nos. 42, 138, 197.

FURTHER READING: Tod, 2: 31-45.

89 Malkaus Raga 81.32

Rajasthan, Mewar, ca. 1610, 18.4 × 15.3 cm. Paint flaking; border, damaged, has been painted yellow in recent years although remainder of miniature is unretouched. The number *14* and a damaged inscription are at top.

Purchase, Normal O. Stone and Ella A. Stone Memorial Fund

Comparative Material: (A) *Malkaus Raga*, leaf from the Chawand set, Rajasthan, Mewar, 1605; Ebeling, color pl. 10.

This leaf is of particular interest because of its resemblance to the well-known *ragamala* series painted according to the colophon by an artist named Nasiruddin in Chawand in 1605.[1] Unusual because of its inscription, the Chawand series has long been the only one that could be positively identified as coming from Mewar at such an early date. Stylistically related to the *Chaurapanchasika* group, it was previously without comparison. This Cleveland leaf, however, is closely related although slightly more refined: Nasiruddin drew coarse, thick outlines around his figures, while this artist uses finer lines despite the similarity of the short, square-headed figure type. The two artists must have employed a common design source since the composition of the Cleveland miniature, like that of *Malkaus Raga* by Nasiruddin (A), has three men with a buck in the lower area and a ruler with a *vina* similarly posed above.

When first purchased, the Cleveland *Malkaus Raga* was thought to be part of the Chawand series.[2] The Chawand pages, however, are nearly square, with numbers in the lower right. They also almost always have titles followed by numbers in the upper right, and they have different border lines. Confusion over the identification arose because many conventions followed by the Cleveland artist (for example, the depiction of sky with a white wavy line and broad dashes) are the same as those employed by Nasiruddin. Such conventions—ultimately derived from early Rajput painting—are not products of personal invention but imply that there was a common artistic vocabulary used by a number of early seventeenth-century artists.

Pages from another contemporary *ragamala* almost certainly from a location in Mewar that have come to light demonstrate the popularity of the style.[3] It is impossible to predict the geographical extent of the particular idiom; the similarities between the Chawand set and the Cleveland painting indicate either that the rough guerrilla stronghold of Chawand to which the Mewar *rana* had been temporarily driven by Mughal troops supported more artists than might be expected or that the Cleveland leaf was produced at some other nearby location in Mewar.

Although the origins of *ragamala* painting are obscure, by the time the Chawand set was produced iconographies were quite well defined and already follow patterns that would be used for several centuries. (The irregular feature of the Chawand *ragamala* is that each *raga* has six rather than only five *raginis*.) The fact that the artist of the Cleveland page used a composition for *Malkaus Raga* much like the one from the Chawand set indicates the consistency of *ragamala* illustration by the early seventeenth century in Mewar.

1. Kanoria, p. 1.

2. Other leaves of this previously unknown set have been extensively repaired; this particular miniature, however, is without breaks and has been tested in the laboratory for indications of reworking and for correct fluorescence of pigments.

3. Three leaves of another *ragamala* set with taller figures seem to be from Mewar, ca. 1605–10; they are to be published in a forthcoming book by P. Pal on the Kumar collection.

FURTHER READING: Ebeling; Kanoria, pp. 1–5.

Figure 89.

Leaf from a *Rasamanjari*, Rajasthan, Mewar, ca. 1615–20, 21.8 × 15.4 cm, 25.5 × 18.8 cm with border. Red border, damaged. Inscription at top: "You are expert in flirtation; you are charming; you are my lord and wonderful in your youthful handsomeness." Inscription above heroine's head: "Madya Dhira Adhira." Numbered 28 at bottom.

Purchase, Mr. and Mrs. William H. Marlatt Fund

Ex collection: Heeramaneck.

Published: Lee, 1960, no. 14, and 1973, no. 277.

Comparative Material: (A) *The Young and Patient Heroine*, leaf from a *Rasamanjari*, Rajasthan, Mewar, ca. 1615–20; M. Chandra, 1957, pl. I. (B) *The Errant Husband*, leaf from a *Rasamanjari*, Rajasthan, Mewar, ca. 1615–20; W. G. Archer, 1957a, no. 24, pl. VIII. (C) *The Husband Attempts to Please Both His Wives*, leaf from a *Rasamanjari*, Rajasthan, Mewar, ca. 1615–20; Doris Wiener Gallery, *Indian Miniature Paintings*, (New York, 1974), no. 47. (D) *The Return of the Husband*, leaf from a *Rasamanjari*, Rajasthan, Mewar, ca. 1615–20; Archer and Binney, no. 3. (E) *The Heroine Awaits Her Lover*, leaf from a *Rasamanjari*, Rajasthan, Mewar, ca. 1615–20; Czuma, no. 60. (F) *An Offended Heroine*, leaf from a *Rasamanjari*, Rajasthan, Mewar, ca. 1615–20; Pal, 1976, no. 31. (G) *Kama Watching Young Girls*, leaf from a *Rasamanjari*, Rajasthan, Mewar, ca. 1615–20; P. Rawson, *Indian Painting* (New York: Universe Books, 1961), p. 135 (see W. G. Archer, 1957a, no. 22 for confirmation of series). (H) *Heroine Seated on a Chair*, leaf from a *Rasamanjari*, Rajasthan, Mewar, ca. 1615–20; Leach, 1982, no. 169. (I) *Heroine and Sakhi*, leaf from a *Rasamanjari*, Rajasthan, Mewar, ca. 1615; H. Mukerjee, "Problems of Mewar Painting," *RL* 27, no. 1/2, p. 19. (J) *The Meeting with the Wife of Another*, leaf from a *Rasamanjari*, Rajasthan, Mewar, ca. 1615; Mukerjee, p. 20. (K) *Kansa Instructing His Demons*, leaf from a *Bhagavata Purana*, Rajasthan, Mewar, ca. 1550; *Sotheby*, 11 Dec. 1973, lot 253.

This *Rasamanjari* series is known from approximately forty leaves in the National Museum, New Delhi; several that are owned by G. K. Kanoria of Patna; and others now scattered in various collections.[1] Although the compositions might seem to be repetitive, the charming inventiveness of the series emerges when looking at the group preserved in New Delhi, which includes a range of compositional types. The group is one of the significant manuscripts attributed to Mewar between the time of the 1605 Chawand *ragamala* and the 1648 *Bhagavata Purana* by Sahibdin,[2] a set generally considered to represent an apogee in Mewar art. A 1628 *ragamala* painted by Sahibdin and another *Rasamanjari* in his style are the other major productions that can be attributed to Mewar between 1605 and 1648.[3] From the evidence, it is clear that Sahibdin, a strong artist with sub-imperial training, redirected Mewar painting so that this spritely *Rasamanjari* from which the Cleveland leaf was extracted appears more conservative and less typical of the state than it probably did before Sahibdin came to Mewar.

Rana Jagat Singh I (r. 1628–52), who was the most influential Mewar patron of the seventeenth century, can be credited with establishing a cohesive style in his atelier based upon the talents of the painters Sahibdin and Manohar, whose styles differed but who utilized similar conventions. In comparison with their mature work, the *Rasamanjari* is done in a somewhat childlike manner and combines a number of Rajput and popular Mughal features. The pre-Mughal Rajput features resemble those in manuscripts such as the Prince of Wales *Gita Govinda*,[4] including the huge flowering branches; simple, segmented compositions; and primary colors. (The latter, of course, are also associated with Jain painting.) The short, plump figures with their overly wide eyes demonstrate the combination of Rajput and popular Mughal elements; the women's ornaments and tassels, for example, are distinctively Rajput, while the moustachioed faces of the men follow popular Mughal stylizations. Although the artist has thus altered old-fashioned elements with contemporary touches, he has not been sufficiently innovative to transform a pleasant miniature group into the reference point for a new style.

The date of the *Rasamanjari* was first placed within Jagat Singh's reign, and the miniatures were assigned ca.-1640 or ca.-1630 dating, but as critics studied this manuscript's relation with earlier art and the sophistication of the 1648 or 1649 scenes, the miniatures were reevaluated as being earlier.

The subject of the text has also been confused at various times; the work was first published generally as a *Nayakanayika Bheda* text (i.e., some unspecified work dealing with the characters of lovers in various situations), and apparently because Bhanudatta's *Rasamanjari* was rarely illustrated in Rajasthan, the manuscript was wrongly assumed to be a *Rasikapriya*.[5]

As identified by the inscription, the Cleveland leaf pictures Madhya Dhiradhira, a youthful heroine who is angry at her lover's philandering. On the verge of tears, she ridicules him in verse, complimenting her hero ironically on his charms; her statement simultaneously demonstrates her awareness of helplessness in confronting the rights accorded to men and acknowledges her resignation and bitterness. The simplicity and symbolic nature of the pictorial composition, however, fail to capture the innuendoes of the scene or to distinguish this youthful lady from the others of different ages that the author describes in similar circumstances. As can be seen from the other published examples, the artist has treated situations symbolically throughout the series rather than by showing specific action or emotion.

The paintings of this *Rasamanjari* range from the abruptly plain to the decorative, including many whose backgrounds are filled with blossoming plants. The Cleveland painting has a luxuriant floral scroll in it, a feature similarly used in manuscripts of the pre-Mughal *Chaurapanchasika* group (e.g., scrolls are found on pre-Mughal *Bhagavata Purana* miniatures [K]). The band is rare in Mewar art of this era though employed regularly in Malwa painting at a slightly later date.[6] In this instance the flowers of the scroll are ornate and full, closer to sources of Persian textiles or metalwork than are Malwa examples.[7]

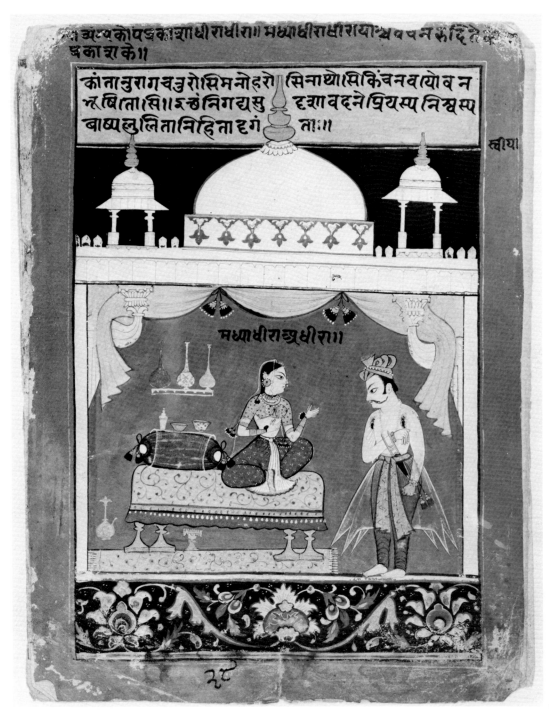

Figure 90.

1. National Museum 55.50/1 to 55.50/41; W. G. Archer, 1957*a*, nos. 22–25.

2. Khandalavala, 1950, pls. A and B; W. G. Archer, 1957*b*, p. 100.

3. Ebeling, p. 166; Leach, 1982, nos. 408, 412, 414, 416.

4. Barrett and Gray, p. 71.

5. A summary table of the published dates ascribed to the manuscript and also a listing of its text classification is given below:

    W. G. Archer, 1957*a*, pl. VIII, nos. 22–25, no title, ca. 1630.
Archer and Binney, no. 3, *Rasikapriya*, ca. 1615.
    M. Chandra, 1957, pl. I, *Nayaka-nayika Bheda*, ca. 1640.
Czuma, no. 60, *Rasamanjari*, ca. 1630.

    Pal, 1976, no. 31, *Rasikapriya*, ca. 1630.
Doris Wiener Gallery, *Indian Miniature Paintings* (New York, 1974), no. 47, *Rasamanjari*, ca. 1615 (same page in *Sotheby*, 13 Dec. 1972, lot 91, *Rasamanjari*, ca. 1615).

When this leaf was first published in Lee, 1960, no. 14, it was identified as *Khandita Nayika*, not labeled as to manuscript, ca. 1630.

6. Khandalavala, 1950, fig. 20.

7. A. U. Pope, *Masterpieces of Persian Art* (New York: Dryden Press, 1945), color pl. H.

227

91 *Shri Raga*   31.451

Rajasthan, Mewar, ca. 1680, 34.4 × 22.5 cm, 38 × 25 cm
with border. Somewhat rubbed. Yellow border on two sides
only. Inscription on reverse: "Shri."
Purchase, Edward L. Whittemore Fund
Ex collection: Coomaraswamy.

Comparative Material: (A) *Desakhar Ragini*, Rajasthan,
Mewar, ca. 1680; Coomaraswamy and Heeramaneck, 1935,
no. 55. (B) *Krishna Arriving at Radha's House*, leaf from a
Rasikapriya, Rajasthan, Mewar, ca. 1660; W. G. Archer,
1957a, no. 30. (C) *Portrait of the Heir Apparent Amar
Singh of Mewar*, Rajasthan, Mewar, ca. 1690; Gray, 1950,
pl. 90.

The miniatures of this *ragamala* set were produced at the
beginning of a transitional period in Mewar art when painting altered for the most part from religious to secular illustration. Artists became involved for the first time in doing
portrait subjects that had been common elsewhere in Rajasthan for nearly a hundred years. In the early decades of
the eighteenth century, both human and animal portraiture
became important, and artists also grew skilled at recording
local palaces or landscapes. After some practice, they developed such a remarkable aptitude for painting observed subjects that their works are among the best of this type done
in Rajasthan. In addition to discarding stereotyped themes,
painters also radically changed the formats of their paintings: compositions were enlarged and were gradually freed
somewhat from stiff, gridlike constructions.

The patron who was responsible for much of this development (inspired by Mughal prototypes) was Amar Singh II,
who ruled from 1698–1710. Amar Singh's father preferred a
second wife over the mother of his heir, a serious slight that
ultimately led to the prince's staging a revolt and attempting
to capture the state. Failing in this, he set up an independent court and probably had an influence on painting for
several years prior to his accession. Apparently it was he who
initiated portraiture in Mewar. A portrait of him as heir-
apparent (C) shows that he was requesting such Mughal-
derived subjects early in his life.[1] A circumstance that fur-
thered this aesthetic change was the Emperor Aurangzeb's
dispersal of painters from Delhi in 1680, which caused them
to seek work with Rajputs.

Whether this *ragamala* can be attributed to the influence
of Amar Singh, who would have been eighteen at the approximate time of its production in 1690, is uncertain but
probable. The speculation that the series may include portraits of the prince is also conjectural.[2] The different faces of
the heroes seem to be generalized types. Thus the noticeable resemblance between the portrait of Amar Singh
(C) and the hero of Cleveland's *Shri Raga* may be coin-
cidental. However, Amar Singh was one of the eighteenth-
century patrons most interested in portraiture, and it was
sometimes a habit for artists in such a state to make certain
other male depictions similar to those of true ruler portraits.

While this miniature series represents a highly significant
step in the development of eighteenth-century Mewar

painting, it has awkward features probably because painters
were not yet fully committed to a particular new approach.
They had now discarded the passionate symbolic style typical of mid-seventeenth century miniatures, but did not yet
comprehend the artistic possibilities open to them. These
ragamala miniatures therefore have traits of previous
Mewar sets combined with some new characteristics, such
as relatively large dimensions and a slightly freer drawing
style. The stage of artistic transition is perhaps best illustrated by the more complex compositions built of boxlike
compartments like those of earlier Mewar paintings that
have merely been expanded to fill bigger areas.

The fact that these *ragamala* scenes are more crowded
and complicated can be observed when they are compared
with a Mewar miniature of ca. 1660 (B), despite the fact that
basic elements like awnings and pillared porches are almost
unchanged. Figures and activities have been multiplied so
that an average of eight or ten personages are generally
grouped in each of these *ragamala* scenes. The paintings
have been described as "extraordinary, not only in their size
but also in their rich compositions and their almost epic
content."[3] This elaboration as well as the delicate details of
these miniatures can be attributed to Mughal inspiration.
Many of the textiles in the *ragamala* have small floral or
fleur-de-lis patterns and more refined architectural details
than had been usual. As can be seen from this composition,
such small patterns blend somewhat strangely with the bold
yellow and red areas of the usual, straightforward Mewar
style. Certain other Mewar paintings of the era are com-
parably refined,[4] though the more robust Mewar style continues also.

Shri Raga is one of eighteen leaves from the ca.-1680
ragamala recorded by Klaus Ebeling in his comprehensive
text on *ragamala* painting; a few additional pages are also
extant.[5] In the Cleveland composition, a lord holding a
flower sits with his consort on a divan listening to music in
his palace. A woman and a horse-headed musician before
the royal couple play a *vina* and cymbals; outside the com-
pound more women dance to the beat of a drum and cymbals. The decorative palace is typical of the Mewar type
with towers, ornamental cornices, many-flowered canopies,
and a garden. Although the Cleveland painting is inscribed
"Shri Raga" on the reverse, it has previously been termed
"Pancham," which Ebeling lists with quotation marks. The
kinnara (the horse-headed celestial musician on the right in
the Cleveland scene) is a popular symbolic figure found in
early Hindu sculpture as well as in classical Indian literature. As Ebeling notes, the *kinnara* was used only for *Shri
Raga* and was a kind of identifying element; without it the
scene could easily be mistaken for one of several *ragamala*
subjects that were often illustrated with musicians in palace
settings.[6]

228

Figure 91.

1. Among the numerous portraits commissioned by Amar Singh, the most distinctive type is that with pronounced outlines and schematic shading; for example, see Welch and Beach, no. 28; Skelton, 1961, pls. 10 and 11; Khandalavala and Chandra, 1960, no. 29, fig. 35; Archer and Binney, no. 6. The earliest, most graceful portrait drawing from Amar Singh's reign is pictured in Welch, 1976, no. 39.

2. Archer and Binney, p. 3.

3. Ebeling, p. 181; he discusses the unusual drama of the compositions and emphasizes that this is an expanded *ragamala* set originally of forty-two compositions; miniature A is one of the rare iconographies.

4. Czuma, no. 61.

5. *Arts in Virginia* 11, no. 1 (1970): no. 13; *Indian and Persian Miniatures from the Collection of Everett and Ann McNear* (Indiana: University of Notre Dame, 1967), no. 66.

6. Ebeling, p. 108; he corrects the title of the miniature to *Shri Raga* on p. 182.

92 *Shiva as Mahakala Dancing*   55.296

Rajasthan, Mewar, ca. 1700–10, 28 × 20.3 cm,
32.8 × 22.8 cm with border. Excessive paint flaking. Plain
unfinished cardboard border. Inscriptions, colloquially
written, are damaged, but loosely describe the iconography
of the scene.

Gift of George P. Bickford

Ex collections: Getty, Bickford.

Published: A. Getty, *Ganesha, a Monograph on the
Elephant-faced God* (Oxford: Oxford University Press,
1936), pl. 6b; Kramrisch, p. 182; W. Ward, "Two Rajput
Paintings and a Rajput Textile," *CMAB* 43 (April 1956):
62–65.

Comparative Material: (A) *Shiva Dancing after Killing the
Elephant Demon*, Rajasthan, Mewar, ca. 1760; Kramrisch,
p. 183. (B) *Chandi Dancing*, Rajasthan, probably Ajmer
area, ca. 1670; A. Mookerjee, *Tantra Asana* (Basel: Ravi
Kumar, 1971), pl. 91.

This subject is rare in miniature painting and is therefore of
significant iconographic interest. Shiva clad in his lion skin
is shown dancing with flying hair and a necklace of heads
almost to his feet; he is surrounded by admiring gods and
devotees. Another miniature of Shiva dancing (A, illus.) was
also done in Mewar but at a somewhat later date. Shiva
Mahakala (Transcendent Time) as the male principle of
cosmic dissolution is usually understood as more abstract
than his consort, or alter-ego, Kali, who is the active force
of Time's destructive energy. Mahakala, one of the several
aspects of Shiva's terrible form, Bhairava, thus contrasts with
the female Mahakali who is often portrayed in miniature
painting. When Shiva Mahakala takes form in Hindu sculpture, as at Elephanta, the god has eight arms and a complex
group of hand-held symbolic attributes such as a sword, a
basin of blood, and a veil that extinguishes the sun.[1] Here
the manifestation is comparatively simple, however.

The subject borders on Tantrism but is less emotional and
bloody than true Tantric paintings, such as one picturing the
female principle Chandi (B), who also wears a necklace of
skulls. Chandi, one of the aspects of Kali, is in a dancing
position much the same as that of Mahakala, which denotes
the ongoing rhythmic power of universal destruction; however, she is surrounded by severed limbs and holds an axe
and a bowl with a head. The Cleveland miniature, with its
grouping of worshipful gods, is more doctrinal than violent.
The subsidiary figures are Brahma with four heads, Shiva's
son Ganesha with his elephant head, and Vishnu in his
avatara form as Varaha, the bull. The chain of heads about
Shiva's neck is interesting because the heads appear to
have a macabre life; they turn in different positions and
have varying expressions, some of which are deliberate
caricatures.

The miniature, done with short, squat figures in the
Mewar style of ca. 1700–1710, is now very badly flaked,
thereby revealing much of the underdrawing. Certain details, such as the dog and swan at the bottom of the work,
also indicate that this was never a completely finished
composition.

1. Dowson, p. 193.

Figure 92(A). *Shiva Dancing after Killing the Elephant Demon*. Navin
Kumar, Inc., New York. Photograph after S. Kramrisch, *Manifestations
of Shiva* (Philadelphia: Philadelphia Museum of Art, 1981), p. 183
[titled *Bhairava Dancing*]).

Figure 92.

Figure 93.

93 *Pechwai Possibly Picturing*　　　37.454
Sarat Purnama
(the Festival of the Autumn Full Moon)

Rajasthan, Nathadwara, 1825–50, 257 × 169.5 cm. Paint
rubbed, cloth rather worn.

Purchase from the J. H. Wade Fund

Comparative Material: (A) *Panel of Gopis from Sarat
Purnama Scene*, Rajasthan, Nathadwara, 1825–50; Skelton,
1973, no. 10.

This *pechwai* is a good example of the older nineteenth-
century type of cloth temple hanging used as a backdrop for
the elaborate ceremonies of Shri Nathji worship in Nathadwara. Although the style of the *pechwais* verges on folk
art, with heavy figures arranged in simple poses, the money
expended on these religious accessories can be gauged from
their complex iconographic elements, their size, and the
frequent use of gold and silver paint. The most essential
aspect of the *pechwai* is its depiction of the life of an icon,
not of the god Krishna as a human being. Standing rigidly
with arm upraised, the painted image goes through various
phases of activity in the hangings that enhance the illusion
of artificial life created by the priests who bathe and dress
the Shri Nathji sculpture.

The elaborate costumes regularly changed by the priests
are among the most significant factors in the attempt to
make Shri Nathji's image seem animate. In the Cleveland
pechwai the icon is shown in the wide, round skirt worn
during any festival of dancing with *gopis*.[1] The orange-
colored skirt, the flaring peacock crest, and the particular
arrangement of jewelry are worn in combination on a few
occasions, the most important of which is the *Sarat Purnama*, or Festival of the Autumn Full Moon, occurring at
the end of the monsoon season when the *gopis* go to meet
Krishna in the forest and dance with him there.[2]

The iconographic formulas of the Shri Nathji cult are
involved and highly detailed. In the present example the
symmetrical arrangement of *gopis* in dancing postures, Shri
Nathji's costume, the full moon, and the starry sky with its
boats of celestial beings are all features of the *Sarat Purnama* iconography. There are, however, deviations that
may be significant enough to mark this as another, more
unusual festival. Shri Nathji generally stands against a white
backdrop but does not balance on a lotus, as here. In addition, the inner border scenes commonly give a summary of
Shri Nathji images at different festivals throughout the
year.[3] In this case, these border scenes picture *bans*, or
pilgrimage places, around the Mathura area[4]—a much more
unusual motif.

In this *pechwai*, as in other representations of Krishna's
lilas, the *gopis* stand on either side of Shri Nathji with
entwined arms upraised in dance poses. Below the feet of
the group is a landscape area depicting Mt. Govardhan and
its shrines. Both the large temple and the two small shrines
appear in identical position in other *pechwais*.[5] In the large
temple an enormous covered food dish represents the wor-

ship of the sect. An image of Krishna before this temple is
also being offered *puja* and is being worshipped by a herd
of cattle. *Gopas* and *gopis* stand facing each other beneath
the two smaller shrines. In the panels at the bottom of the
pechwai are several scenes of cows at sacred water tanks
and before shrines. The various shrines of the Mathura area
occupy the panels around the sides of the *pechwai;* not all
are devoted to Shri Nathji, but show Radha and other figures as well. Directly above the full moon at the top of the
pechwai is a scene of Krishna as a child.

The style of the *pechwai* shows it to be a comparatively
early example among those now extant. As in other examples (A), the very full *gopi* figures are done in a softer style
than that of later artists. Furthermore, the depiction of
female facial features corresponds to early nineteenth-
century miniature painting. Another indication of dating is
that the feet of Shri Nathji images are turned out in a
balletlike position in *pechwais* done prior to the mid-1870s,
whereas they tend to be treated in a foreshortened manner
after that date.[6]

1. Skelton, 1973, p. 91.
2. Ibid., p. 93.
3. Ibid., nos. 6–9.
4. Skelton, in conversation, 1977.
5. Skelton, 1973, nos. 3, 6–8, 14, etc.
6. Ibid., p. 28.

FURTHER READING: Jindel; Skelton, 1973; Spink.

Figure 94, obverse.

Figure 94, reverse.

94 *Devi Attacking a Demon*   68.72

Rajasthan, possibly Sirohi, ca. 1630, 12.5 × 10.2 cm
(painting), 12.5 × 27.2 cm entire page. Somewhat rubbed.
Partial text on front, full text on reverse (illus.).

Gift of George P. Bickford

Ex collection: Bickford.

Comparative Material: (A) *Folio from the Upadesamala
Prakarana*, Rajasthan, possibly Sirohi, dated 1634;
Khandalavala and M. Chandra, 1960, cat. no. 65b, fig. 58.
(B) *Illustration from a Sangrahani Sutra*, Gujerat,
ca. 1630; P. Chandra, 1960, fig. 42.

Sirohi, the tiny state in Rajasthan that included the Jain
temples of Mount Abu, was strategically located between
Mewar, Marwar, and Gujerat. The state was buffeted by
Mewar, from which it won independence in the late fifteenth century, and by Marwar. It absorbed influences from
both these states, but because of Jainism it was also closely
linked with neighboring Gujerat. This page (showing the
four-armed goddess on her lion boldly approaching a demon) has the same horizontal format and textual arrangement of contemporary Jain pages (A and B), though the
subject of Durga is a Hindu one. The provenance of many
folkish paintings suspected to be from Sirohi requires better
documentation, but this miniature has features—such as
the dark red, orange, and yellow coloring—that are characteristic of the state.

Figure 95.

95 *Gunakali Ragini* 60.283

Rajasthan, Sirohi, late 17th or early 18th century,
19 × 12.9 cm, 23.4 × 16.2 cm with border. Paint scraped
on orange border, especially left side. Inscription: "Number
27, Gaunakali Rag."
Gift of the Folio Club
Published: Ebeling, no. 221.
Comparative Material: (A) *Madhu Madhava Ragini*,
Rajasthan, Sirohi, late 17th century; Krannert Art Museum,
Art of India and Southeast Asia (Champaign, IL, 1964),
no. 83. (B) *Madhumadhavi Ragini*, Rajasthan, Sirohi, late
17th century; Ebeling, no. 220.

This miniature picturing women leaning against pillows and
delicately sampling *pan* is from one of many Sirohi *ragamala* sets and illustrates *Gunakali Ragini*, which should
have poetic connotations of a heroine desiring a lover. Sirohi
ragamala painting of this type was fairly short-lived, apparently lasting from the late seventeenth through the first
quarter of the eighteenth century. The idiom is a practiced
one, and the sharp-featured women as well as the detailed
pavilions appear to have been repeated fluently. The extremely consistent manuscript style has features relating
to both Mewar and Marwar, states situated on either side
of the small principality. Despite this association, such
things as hot Sirohi colors—especially a pervasive brick
red—easily distinguish the state from its neighbors.

In his study on *ragamala* painting, Klaus Ebeling has
noted that the iconographies of certain Sirohi leaves are
puzzlingly irregular. The Cleveland Gunakali miniature is
among the variant compositions that Ebeling noted and
published; he commented that it was uncertain whether the
design of ladies eating *pan* was a true Sirohi convention or
simply an error of labeling. The possibility of misclassifica-
tion was entertained because the Cleveland miniature was
the only painting of its type that Ebeling had encountered.
The other Sirohi Gunakali painting he knew was a composition, also deviant, of ladies making a garland.[1] Two compositions (A, illus.; B) that are almost identical to the Cleveland
miniature yet labeled *Madhumadhavi Ragini* indicate the
confusion and overlapping in the short Sirohi tradition.

As Ebeling points out, Sirohi artists originating their designs at a late date do not seem to have been wholly familiar
with the usual Rajasthani illustrations and thus devised certain original, somewhat enigmatic iconographies.[2] Various
elements of the Sirohi *raginis* are superfluous or inap-
propriate, having no correlation with the inscribed verses.

Neither the poetry of Gunakali or of Madhumadhavi has
any link with the social gatherings shown in the *ragini*
scenes under discussion. Gunakali's most usual Rajasthani
form is a lovesick woman arranging flowers in a vase. The
particular musical mode has definite, relatively fixed connotations of longing and sorrow for an absent lover that do
not fit with these illustrations. It can be assumed that the
failure to produce a correctly evocative atmosphere was
caused by the Sirohi artists' lack of knowledge and by a desire to produce simple and pleasing decorative compositions.

Figure 95(A). *Madhu Madhava Ragini.* Courtesy of The Art Institute of
Chicago, 61.122.

1. Ebeling, pp. 94, 250.
2. Ibid., p. 94.

96 *Hanuman Brings the Mountain of Healing Plants; Rama Extracts the Arrow from Laksmana as Hanuman and a Bear Prepare to Treat Him* (obverse); and *The Monkeys and Bears Fight Ravana and His Demons* (reverse)

79.21

Incised drawing: black ink and yellow pigment. Palm-leaf page from a *Ramayana* manuscript, Orissa, late eighteenth century, each approximately 4.8 × 40.2 cm. Inscriptions (obverse and reverse) in Oriya with names next to the main figures.

Purchase, Edward L. Whittemore Fund

Drawing with a stylus on palm leaf, though it gives a different effect from sketching with a brush, is amazingly fluid as practiced by eighteenth-century Orissan artists in a manner apparently developed much earlier. They clearly enjoyed showing their proficiency by rendering both fast action and florid detail simultaneously, as in the tumultuous battle scene on the reverse of this leaf. Incised and rubbed with ink before the excess is cleaned off with sand, the narrow palm leaves were generally divided into small sections by architecture or by partitions and decorated, as in this case, on both sides.

Orissa is a state with an impressive artistic heritage ranging from temple sculpture with a complex philosophical background to vibrant folk crafts. The palm-leaf manu-

Figure 96, obverse.

Figure 96, reverse.

scripts fall somewhere in between: they illustrate the Hindu classics in a style whose monumentality is fascinating when dimensions are considered (the rhythmic drawing is similar to that known from a few preserved Orissan murals);[1] at the same time, the scenes have touches of folkish wit, immediacy, and informality. There is a large corpus of eighteenth- and nineteenth-century palm-leaf material indicating the presence of many artists well trained in what must have been a very popular and fairly accessible art form.

The Orissans, who clearly enjoyed the Vaishnavite literature connected with Rama and Krishna, stressed the feeling for nature inherent within the literary descriptions of Krishna's pastoralism and Rama's self-discovery in his forest exile. Few illustrations lack trees filled with birds or small

flowering bushes. The same gentle, rippling curves move almost without interruption between human, animal, and plant forms; this unifies them in a buoyant mood that emphasizes the optimistic and delightful over the horrific aspects of Rama's struggle.

On the obverse of this leaf, Hanuman, who has flown to the Himalayas, arrives back in Lanka carrying the mountain sprouting with healing plants to cure Laksmana, who is in a comalike state, having been hit by a rain of magic arrows shot by the demon king, Ravana. (The only color the artist used for this leaf was yellow, for the body of the fallen Laksmana.) Rama extracts an arrow while Hanuman holds a branch of herbs, and a bear waits to give aid. On the reverse, the monkeys and bears, now holding fragments of the

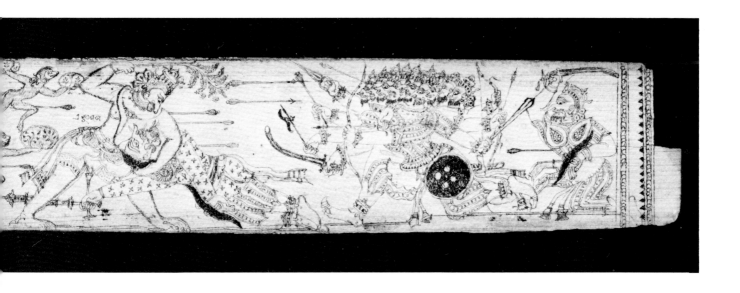

healing mountain, attack Ravana's forces with renewed energy. Ravana anxiously brandishes his weapons as a bear general vanquishes a large Lankan.

Many illustrations like this one have become separated since the books (joined together simply by a cord passing through a central hole) were easily dispersed; leaves are thus not only difficult to associate with others but also to date because they lack inscriptional documentation. This leaf, for example, is datable only on loose stylistic grounds by comparison with other complete manuscripts that retain their colophons and have been done with equal fluidity and precision.

Figure 96, reverse, detail

Figure 96, obverse, detail

1. Barrett and Gray, p. 73.

FURTHER READING: J. Losty, *Krishna: A Hindu Vision of God* (London: British Library Reference Room, 1980).

Figure 96, reverse, detail

Figure 96, reverse, detail

97 *Krishna with Radha and*   73.102
Two Attendants

Orissa, nineteenth century, on cloth, 19.5 × 15 cm
(image), 25.5 × 17 cm overall. Painting on reverse:
Jagannath, Subhadra, and Balarama in an arch.

Purchase from the J. H. Wade Fund

The three stylized deities—Jagannath, Subhadra, and
Balarama—on the reverse of this miniature are common
Orissan folk deities who appear consistently on all types of
materials, such as leather, paper, or cloth, used by popular
artists. The round, stonelike figures are barely recognizable
as anthropomorphic idols but are instead close to the purely
symbolic, village worship of actual stones or other natural
objects. The god-presence recognized as phenomenon
can take on various human personalities: thus, the dark
Jagannath and his light-skinned brother can substitute for
Krishna and his brother in the local area.

On the front, a thoroughly human Krishna and Radha
with two attendants appear in the usual Orissan folk style.

Figure 97, reverse.

Figure 97, obverse.

their development. While the Basohli artists received ideas about portraiture—the specialization of the Mankot school—the Mankot painters gained greater freedom in using color and ornamental details.

Although the idea of creating portraits came after Mughal contact (probably indirectly absorbed from Mankot as well as the result of direct contacts), the Basohli artists were almost impervious to other outside influences. Single-mindedly they worked on, seemingly driven by indigenous psychological motivations during a time when painters in other states were much more open to mixing various artistic approaches. The Basohli style was perhaps best suited to the creation of powerful, iconlike religious imagery. Despite some remarkably designed portraits, the style was too mannered for conveying the humanistic nuances of this genre. Although Basohli and Mankot painting were very similar, the latter was simpler and more rationally ordered, thus permitting greater honesty and flexibility in the rendering of portraits. Despite the long confusion over Pahari schools, the fervor of Basohli painters clearly distinguishes them from the cooler, Mughal-influenced artists of hill states like Bilaspur.

Early Portraiture in the Hill States and the Development of Painting in Guler

The fact that portrait painting in the hills was a major imperial influence as in Rajasthan is demonstrated, for example, by the many Mankot courtier depictions. These portrayals—which must have been quite accurate, although stylized—are closely related to types developed during the Shah Jahan and Aurangzeb eras because the same poses are attempted by the artist. At times when painters were not so self-consciously following a Mughal prototype, depictions were in a more pronounced folkish style, like that used for rendering a raja and his heir in the Cleveland collection [133].

Like others, Mankot rulers paid tribute to the emperor and went to Delhi periodically in the seventeenth century. In Bilaspur and Nurpur, states that also developed portrait styles, there were likewise some contacts (not always friendly) with the court. Nurpur rulers oscillated between service in the Mughal army and revolt.[3] Early Nurpur depictions of Raja Man Dhata (r. 1667?–1700) and his son, the enthusiastic patron Raja Daya Dhata (r. ca. 1700–ca. 1735), are similar to conventionally posed Mughal works done about the same time.[4] Daya Dhata, who commissioned an elegant *Rasamanjari* manuscript, permitted it to be illustrated with many heroic depictions of himself (see [136]). Since Bilaspur was one of the states bordering the plains, it was in a natural position to absorb influences from Delhi. Raja Dip Chand (r. 1650–67) fought in Aurangzeb's campaigns, apparently went to Delhi, and may have brought Mughal painters home from the capital.[5] Despite distortions, the one known portrait of Dip Chand's court is distinctly Mughal in its treatment, especially of the raja's facial features.[6]

Guler was a state that specialized in portraiture and the one producing the most naturalistic illustrations—at least from the late seventeenth century onward. A painter-colony is recorded there during the reign of Dalip Singh (r. 1700–41) (see [107]), who apparently commissioned many works.[7] About 1730 to 1740 the Guler painters were the source of a new wave of Mughal inspiration that soon affected other states, like Jammu. The artists responsible appear to have had some Mughal training: their compositions are spacious and open, and their drawing is evenly rhythmic, like that of Muhammad Shah's imperial painters. These artists excelled not only in portraiture but also in depicting idealized women who have even features with long, curving brows and cleanly traced profiles. Their bodies are drawn in a simplified manner, and their concisely rendered, fluid poses became characteristic of most sophisticated Pahari painting at the end of the eighteenth century.

Among the few artist-families who must have been instrumental in the development of the Guler style is that of Pandit Seu, who has himself left no paintings. Over several generations, members of the Seu family migrated to several states, spreading the style of painting that contemporaries clearly viewed as an advanced one. Thus while miniatures can be distinguished geographically and were affected in part by the wishes of raja patrons, the artist-family played an equally significant role in creating, or altering, painting styles. The most innovative member of the Seu family was Nainsukh, one of Pandit Seu's sons, who may have been trained at Muhhamad Shah's court, since his skill in creating naturalistic illusions could not have derived from Pahari models. Nainsukh spent most of his life in Jammu working for the introspective noble Balwant Singh (1724–1763), whose political stature was minimal but who was one of India's most sensitive and original patrons. Because of his own naturalness and lack of pretension, Balwant seems to have promoted Nainsukh's talent for capturing human poses and expressions throughout a long career. The artist passed his skills in drawing to other relatives, perhaps by means of sketches if not by actual training.

Painting in Kangra

The naturalistic style that had evolved in Guler was taken to Kangra, where the avid patron Sansar Chand (r. 1775–1823) found its gentle charm the perfect vehicle for illustrating Krishna literature. Sansar Chand consolidated his power in the first years of his reign; he recovered the strategic Kangra fort in 1786 and increased his territory for twenty years before being attacked by Gurkha tribesmen. After ignominious defeats, caused largely by the alienation of neighboring states, he lived in a servile, powerless condition in what remained of his territory. At the height of his influence he had a large atelier, and he was able to retain some of the painters during his impoverishment from 1806 to the early 1820s. Though several of his artists' names are known, they have not been successfully connected with specific Kangra paintings.[8] The cycle of literary works commissioned by Sansar Chand was much more extensive than at Guler. Known to have married for love and to have been celebrated as a romantic hero,[9] the raja largely selected Krishna and Radha themes that must have appealed to his sentimental temperament.

Krishna worship had become popular in the hills as miniature painting was first developing, so that the evolution of the art itself and religion became interconnected. Nevertheless, despite the frequency of Krishna illustration in Mankot, Basohli, and so on, a style had not yet been created that was capable of conveying all the moods of *bhakti* as expressed in literature. The Basohli style did not suggest the tender, playful qualities of the myth, for example, as conveyed by the Rajasthani painters of Bundi or Kota. Raja Sansar Chand's Kangra artists succeeded in bringing a new range of expression to the Krishna story as illustrated in the hills; they emphasized the romantic appeal of the god by soft colors, subtle landscapes, and evenly rhythmic contours.

Although the Pahari landscape in certain states (such as the westerly Chamba) is dry and barren, it is generally fertile with terraced fields, tree-covered slopes, and refreshing air that contrast greatly with the environment of Rajasthan. In the paintings of both Guler and Kangra such settings are the real subjects of many miniatures and imbue the classic myths or love scenes with unusual emotional qualities related to pastoral ideals. Scenes along the Beas River, which flows through part of Kangra, are common and show the Kangra artists' enjoyment of relatively naturalistic landscape settings. One of the most fascinating aspects of the Kangra style of lyric naturalism is that the Krishna story, supposed to have been enacted near Mathura, acquires a realistic air that it lacks in Rajput paintings done much nearer to Krishna's homeland. In the Kangra miniatures the god has been invested with the genuine characteristics of a Pahari herdboy growing up among the pasturelands of the Beas valley.

Before about 1770 the Kangra style was clearly dependent on Guler models but quickly became more florid. Landscapes in Guler miniatures are often austere, while Kangra paintings are filled with flowering as well as dense, leafy trees. A painting fragment picturing Shiva shows both the relationship in early Kangra painting to the Guler style and the distinctive Kangra treatment of landscape elements, in this case two entwined leafy trees [120].

Common Literary Subjects in Kangra and Other Pahari States

The subject matter of Pahari painting differs little from that of Rajasthan; the great traditions of religious and romantic literature provided an almost inexhaustible source for Pahari patrons, especially in the states of Basohli, Mankot, and Kangra. The *Bhagavata Purana*, *Gita Govinda*, and *Ramayana* were all popular subjects. The area was, however, steeped in the worship of Devi, the primal goddess of many personalities, and illustrations connected with her mythology—such as those of the *Devi Mahatmya*—were frequently done in both the early Basohli and the later Guler and Kangra styles, in contrast to their rare production in Rajasthan.

The worship of different aspects of the female personality probably added depth to the exploration of feminine moods in art. Although the heroines of literature and miniature painting rarely shared the Devi's cool power, they give fascinating glimpses of a similar complexity of temperament. Pictures of women were by no means confined to the Hindu tradition, but they received quite different emphasis because of Hindu philosophical and artistic ideals. In contrast to late Mughal miniatures that merely depict pretty women at leisure, Pahari and Rajasthani miniatures almost always have underlying emotional connotations. The tension of unrequited love or of lovers separated is perhaps the most powerful theme.

The theory of Hindu drama, dance, and poetry that had evolved prior to the golden age of the classical Gupta period was that of alternating, or contrasting, *rasas*. These *rasas* or prescribed emotions such as erotic love and anger (perhaps the two most common characterizations of miniaturists) skillfully built up, expanded, and compared were the primary objectives of expression. Passions might be expressed obliquely, so that it was left for intuition to comprehend them, but musicians, poets, and miniaturists all worked at creating intense emotional flavors or moods.

The eight *nayikas* (or heroines, who were especially popular subjects in the Pahari region) exemplify something of the emotional range of passion aroused by a lover. The women in the Cleveland drawing [122] expressing simultaneous desire, coldness, anger, pride, and weakening of stubborn resolve show the complexity of alternating emotions in such scenes. In addition, types of poetry combine the *nayika's* moods with other *rasa*-associated subjects such as the intensity of love in separation or the moods of the seasons [124]. The literature of lovers' quarrels and predicaments (often with the word "*rasa*" forming part of the title) is structured to allow varying mood to predominate. The *Rasamanjari*, seldom illustrated in Rajasthani art (see [90]), was represented several times by Pahari rulers [103, 136]. A Sanskrit text on the classification of lovers at different levels of experience who face situations causing them to express strong emotions, it is thus much like the Hindi *Rasikapriya*, which was immensely popular in Rajasthan.

The easily comprehensible *Ramayana* epic—the subject of Mughal, Popular Mughal, and Rajasthani manuscripts—was done with great warmth and affection by Pahari painters. Rama, an incarnation of Vishnu, embodies all the moral virtues associated with this preserver and restorer of order. Deprived of his right to the succession of his father's throne through the manipulation of his stepmother, he selflessly relinquishes his position, retiring to the forest with his wife Sita and his brother Laksmana. In this idyllic setting away from the intrigue of the court, his real destiny as a destroyer of the demonic forces then plaguing earth emerges. In the course of one of these encounters with evil forces, however, Rama's wife Sita—who represents courageous wifely loyalty—is abducted by the demon king Ravana and taken to his capital of (Sri) Lanka [70]. Through the kinship that links creatures in the forest, Rama allies himself with the monkey-leader Sugriva [102], whose energetic followers agree to search for Sita. Although the unhappy Sita is subjected to Ravana's attentions, she is eventually rescued by Rama with the help of the monkey and bear armies [113].

Like the Krishna legend, the *Ramayana* as done in the Pahari states shows the artists' sympathetic affinity for animals and elements of landscape. The monkey and bear armies, imbued with human traits but also retaining their own typical qualities, are rendered with painterly humor and insight. The landscapes in the early paintings are symbolic; scale is meaningless, and all features such as the large trees rendered like exploding flowers are ecstatic conceptions. In general, the early painting is far more expressionistic than the later, quiet lyrical miniatures developed in Guler or Kangra that evolved naturalistically and then became decorative by the beginning of the nineteenth century.

1. Archer, 1973, I: 372–73, Mankot 1, 2, 3.
2. Archer and Binney, no. 63; W. G. Archer, 1973, II: 169–71, Bilaspur 1, 3, 4.
3. Ibid., I: 383.
4. Ibid., II: 303, compare Nurpur 6 with [29].
5. Ibid., I: 227.
6. Ibid., II: 169, Bilaspur 1.
7. Ibid., I: 131, 144.
8. Ibid., 286–96.
9. Eastman, pp. 15–16; W. G. Archer, 1973, I: 300.

Page from a *Rasamanjari*, Pahari, Basohli, ca. 1660–70, 17.5 × 26 cm, 23.4 × 32.4 cm with border. Water stain concentrated along left edge of border extends outward, especially along bottom border; flowers scraped from border of rug and architecture; paint loss across wall of pavilion; right pillar of pavilion scraped, roof towers have chunks of silver paint missing; blue of Krishna's upper body heavily flaked, and gold worn off his *dhoti,* leaving yellow underlay (this loss of gold can also be seen on architectural details); outer parts of yellow border wrinkled; hole in paper at edge of curtain on right side of pavilion. Inscriptions: (on left border) number *135;* (above) *sakshat darshana*—"Seeing the lover face to face"; (reverse) Sanskrit text—see W. G. Archer, 1973, 1: 39.

Purchase, Edward L. Whittemore Fund

Ex collection: Kramrisch.

Published: V. Dwivedi, 1969, pp. 262–69; Spink, fig. 86.

Comparative Material: (A) *The Approach of Krishna,* by Devidasa, page from a *Rasamanjari,* Pahari, Basohli, dated 1695; Randhawa and Bhambri, no. 81, or V. Dwivedi, 1969, fig. 5 (as *Sakshat Darshana*). (B) *Krishna Brings an Orange,* page from a *Rasamanjari,* Pahari, Basohli, ca. 1660–70; Coomaraswamy, 1926, pt. 5: pl. XCV. (C) *The Courtesan Estranged,* page from a *Rasamanjari,* Pahari, Basohli, ca. 1660–70; Randhawa and Bhambri, no. 35. (D) *The Rake,* a page from a *Rasamanjari,* Pahari, Basohli, ca. 1660–70; Randhawa and Bhambri, no. 69.

In this miniature Krishna plays the heroic lover who is causing the woman he faces to feel faint as she glimpses him. It is probably no accident, therefore, that the shape of the god's full face and his eye are emphasized by the swelling lotus in his hand—a long-recognized symbol of beauty. The god wears a large crown glistening with applied beetle wings and is draped in a scarf once gracefully ornamented with flowers. The waiting woman also sparkles with an elegant array of beetle-wing jewelry inside her once-gleaming silver palace.

This leaf is the concluding illustration from the first of three seventeenth-century manuscripts of the *Rasamanjari* done in Basohli. The paintings of this first series are works of such amazing passion that the manuscript has excited more interest than almost any other Rajput work. It represents the height of an extraordinary style; yet few of its predecessors were known until very recently. A slightly earlier Devi series that has now appeared demonstrates that the artists of this first *Rasamanjari* united the savage style, apparently current in the state, with sophistication. The result was a paradox of refinement balanced with primitive energy startling in its effect, since the figures and settings are courtly but also savagely intense.

In the scenes of this series, shapes, colors, and patterns expressing the passion of the poetry are substituted for action. Though other miniatures of the set (B, C, D) have compositions similar to the Cleveland painting, the individual colors and patterns in each scene raise the pictures to high expressionistic levels characterizing the imagined nature of the various love relationships.

The painters have skillfully arranged tense confrontations in the compositions by juxtaposing busy patterns that shock the visual senses. Decorated surfaces seem capable of exploding and are kept from doing so only by rigid boundary lines segregating each area. The figures, compressed into thin vertical shapes, have bulging eyes, as if from the strain of this metamorphosis. Both males and females, lit by glittering masses of jewelry, seem to be generating intense emotional electricity.

It is unfortunate that the damage suffered by the Cleveland miniature obscures some of its impact. The raised pigment of the boldly emblazoned flowers on the border of the rug, and also of the architectural cornice, has been badly scraped. Furthermore, the architectural framework of the pavilion, once silver, is now tarnished, and paint loss is extensive. Strangely, the beetle wings, applied as jewelry in many Basohli paintings, remain unharmed. Colors, where the painted surface is intact, are typically deep-hued: dark green contrasts with strong red, which in turn is warmed by yellow and metallic gold. Since the figures are only slightly rubbed, one can sense in their apparel and postures the controlled passion characteristic of the series that was once consciously enhanced by both textiles and vivid colors.

In the Cleveland scene, the closing one of the series, the shy heroine appeals to her eyes to remain open and her mind to be steady so that she can apprehend the vision of Krishna. This is one of eleven verses throughout the poem specifically mentioning Krishna by name.[1] It has been conjectured that this last verse may have been crucial in causing the patron and artist to associate all the illustrations with the blue god.[2] Since Krishna does not play the central role in the two later Basohli *Rasamanjaris,* some circumstance must have been different when this manuscript was illustrated. However, it seems probable that the elevation of Krishna was simply a whim of the raja patron's, arising from his desire to magnify the comparatively novel god-hero, and did not stem from the literary work itself. The insertion of Krishna into the *Rasamanjari* tale is so awkward that it indicates an arbitrary decision.

The Cleveland leaf demonstrates that the artist was either unaware of or unconcerned with the specifics of this poetic verse, thus lessening the possibility that its meaning affected his concept of the poem. The same closing scene from the third Basohli version of the *Rasamanjari* done in 1695 (A) compositionally resembles the Cleveland painting, but the artist has followed the specific description of the poetic stanza, which states that the lord wears a peacock feather, carries a flute, and has a lotus behind his ear. The heroine in this case stands with her head raised in rapt devotion as Krishna approaches, conveying the awe and adoration implicit in the poetry. In the Cleveland scene, Krishna lacks the described accessories, and the seated heroine is casually in command of the situation rather than suppliant.

Many paintings from the set are similarly composed, with the lover outside the lady's open pavilion pictured on the right side of the page, and it appears as though the artist illustrated verses with only a generalized idea of their meaning. The Takri inscription on the front of each page summarizes the full Sanskrit verse on the back of the paintings; thus the patron of the set, probably Raja Sangram Pal (r. 1635–ca. 1673),[3] may have had only a general familiarity with the full Sanskrit work.

Because it was the last illustration of the manuscript, this page was severely battered in comparison with others. Since almost all the other pages have entered collections in large groups,[4] it may have become separated from the remainder of the leaves at some time. Because water damage is evident here and on other pages, however, the manuscript as a whole must have been poorly stored at some date.[5]

1. Randhawa and Bhambri, p. 3.

2. W. G. Archer, 1973, 1: 39.

3. Archer previously assigned this set to the later (ca. 1678–93) reign of Kirpal Pal (Archer and Binney, p. 70), but with the appearance of more paintings in this style has reassessed the series to a period earlier than the divergent 1695 *Rasamanjari* by Devidasa.

4. The largest groups are owned by Dogra Art Gallery, Jammu (35 paintings); Victoria and Albert Museum (12 paintings); Museum of Fine Arts, Boston (7 paintings). Comparatively few miniatures exist apart from these; for other sources, see Randhawa and Bhambri, pp. 4–5; *Sotheby*, 28 April 1981, lot 165; *Sotheby*, 29 March 1982, lot 169; *Sotheby*, 15 Oct. 1984, lot 122.

5. A leaf in a private collection illustrating a verse near the beginning of the *Rasamanjari* is also damaged along the left side (Welch and Beach, no. 21).

FURTHER READING: Randhawa and Bhambri.

Figure 103.

Figure 104.

104 *Shiva and Devi on Gajasura's Hide* 52.587

Figure 104, detail.

Pahari, Basohli, ca. 1675–80, 23.5 × 16.2 cm. Painting has been cut down, probably on all sides, but certainly along verticals. Paint scraped in sections, completely removed in areas at top.

Purchase, Edward L. Whittemore Fund

Ex collection: Heeramaneck.

Published: W. G. Archer, 1973, 2: 25, Basohli no. 7; Kramrisch, p. 189; Lee, 1960, no. 58; and 1973, color pl. 19.

Comparative Material: (A) *Radha and Krishna in the Forest*, Pahari, Basohli, ca. 1680; Khandalavala, 1958, color pl. 20.

Although the figures in this miniature with their huge eyes conform to the Basohli idiom, other elements are more singular—the gray and red coloring, for example, is subdued in comparison with that of most Basohli miniatures, and the artist has accentuated the soft, shifting atmospheric effects as opposed to the hard background forms that appear in other early Basohli scenes. This painter was given the unusual theme of Shiva and Parvati sitting in the clouds on the skin of the vanquished elephant demon; he was forced to face his task with originality apparently because there was no extant prototype. The infrequently used story concerns Parvati's fear that because of Shiva's ascetic vows the two would have to endure the coming monsoon without shelter; but the rains started, Shiva floated his wife, seated on the skin that he usually wears, up into the clouds above the storm to an atmosphere of tranquility.[1]

The consideration of the god and the reverence of his wife are echoed in the gentle beauty of the landscape, which is unusually naturalistic despite the artist's use of common conventions for the trees. Most landscape passages in Basohli miniatures impose the painter's own emotions on the natural world, whereas this artist has tried to observe and transmit nature directly. The swirling air currents and the maplike bands of river and earth convey surprising depth, even compared with later Basohli miniatures in more naturalistic styles. The technique of using loose transparent spirals to depict ethereal elements such as smoke occurs in various Pahari paintings, but here seems to reflect the painter's desire to describe a real monsoon. The particularly sensitive motif of the birds rising over the land in response to the falling rain also seems to come from the artist's observation.

The vertical format of this miniature is somewhat unusual; another vertical painting also showing a god and his consort in a natural setting (A) is one of the few examples related to this miniature.

1. Kramrisch, p. 188.

Figure 104, detail.

105 *Markandeya Viewing Krishna in*   67.241
the Cosmic Ocean

Pahari, Basohli, ca. 1680, 15.2 × 10 cm, 20.5 × 15 cm
with border. Slight split across bottom.
Gift of Dr. and Mrs. Sherman E. Lee
Published: Spink, fig. 119.

This tiny painting depicts the ancient sage Markandeya reverencing Vishnu, who is seen in his form of Krishna floating on a pipal leaf in the cosmic sea. Markandeya is a legendary figure credited with reciting part of a *purana*, or scriptural discourse, which is named after him, in answer to the questions of a disciple. In this story Markandeya had been wandering in the worldly dream contained with the sleeping Vishnu when he fell out of the god's mouth into the infinite ocean. The baby Krishna then ironically addressed the sage without titles or formality, calling him "child"; Markandeya, angered, was led to realize the primeval existence of this baby, which belittled his own venerable life span of several hundred years.[1]

The point of the myth—the unimportance of any being viewed in relation to the awesome cosmic order—is well expressed by the simplicity and small size of the Cleveland miniature whose two figures on pipal leaves are truly diminutive. The treatment of the ocean in weblike patterns is unusual but has some similarity to a few other works.[2] The tale of Krishna and Markandeya is repeated in other Pahari paintings, but these scenes have no stylistic association with this miniature.[3]

1. Zimmer, pp. 42–44.
2. See W. G. Archer, 1973, 2: 179, Bilaspur no. 31(i).
3. Philadelphia Museum, 55-11-1.

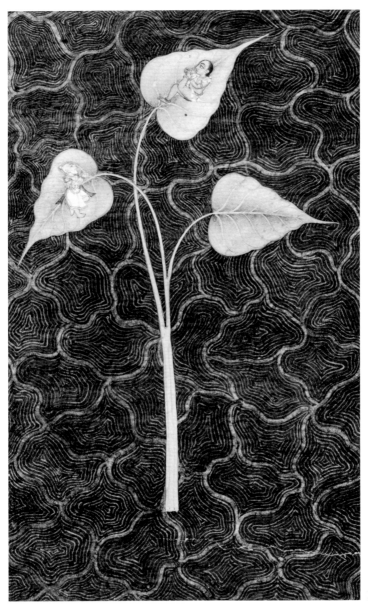

Figure 105.

106 *Four Leaves from the Large Basohli Bhagavata Purana*

Pahari, Basohli, ca. 1760–65

This large *Bhagavata Purana* set, represented by four leaves in the Cleveland collection, is one of at least two *Bhagavata Purana* series done in Basohli during the period when artistic ideas brought from other states, notably Guler, were transforming the Basohli idiom.[1] Although figure styles changed, the most significant alterations in Basohli painting were probably those of decoration. Basohli miniatures of the seventeenth century are remarkably florid, with a great deal of emphasis on strongly colored, contrasting patterns [103]; but in 1730 a series mainly done by the painter Manaku from Guler showed that a much quieter type of painting had begun appealing to patrons.[2] Manaku created scenes that have simple outlines and wide, open areas that differ radically from the tightly rhythmic kind of Basohli work. Manaku, however, was not an inventor; most aspects of his designs are attributable to his family background and training in Guler. For example, the dense, dark green trees and boxlike architecture used throughout the 1730 Basohli manuscript are characteristic of the near-contemporary Guler *Siege of Lanka* series.[3]

Painting in the state of Guler was linked with that of the Mughal court from its inception. Both the early portraits and the few remaining illustrations of epics are quite naturalistic.[4] Guler was the central base of Manaku's exceptionally talented, artistically influential family, and Manaku, the oldest son of the patriarch Pandit Seu, received thorough training in skills that were a heritage of both state and family.

After the more open Guler style was introduced into Basohli in 1730, the tense, decorative manner used in early manuscripts was virtually abandoned. Two *Bhagavata Purana* sets—a small one and this larger series—must have been among the most extensive and important commissions for works in the Guler-influenced style. These later manuscripts are far less stylized than Manaku's 1730 *Gita Govinda* and represent the general trend toward naturalism developing all over the Pahari region from about 1740 to 1760.

When this ca.-1760 *Bhagavata Purana* set, which had been preserved in a British collection, was dispersed at auction, its significance as a nearly complete manuscript was overlooked. Unfortunately the pictures were widely scattered following the sale, and no adequate photographic record of the sequence now exists.[5] At the time, the important transitional era between early Basohli and later Guler/Kangra painting was to some degree ignored. Scholars and collectors seemed to concentrate either on the paintings of the late seventeenth and early eighteenth centuries or on the miniatures done in the latter part of the eighteenth century, thus leaving a sort of vacuum in between. Many of the individual miniatures of the *Bhagavata Purana* set were admired, but the fact that the manuscript represented one of several logical stages between early Pa-

hari painting and the Kangra school type appears to have been imperfectly appreciated until some time after the dispersal of pages. This *Bhagavat* also provided crucial evidence of the manner in which members of artist-families cooperated in the hill area.

Some of the simpler compositions and figures are clearly derived from Manaku's 1730 *Gita Govinda*.[6] Although by 1760 Manaku himself may have retired or died, the resemblance of this *Bhagavata Purana* series to his earlier work is strong. But there are also many scenes with more naturalistic figures that contrast sharply and are characteristic of Manaku's younger brother Nainsukh. The manuscript was done during the latter part of Nainsukh's career, just prior to the death of his major patron, Balwant Singh of Jammu, in 1763. By this time Nainsukh's grasp of the Muhammad-Shah-style imperial painting and his ability to experiment with figural positions must have made his work extremely influential in the Pahari area. Members of his family seem to have had access to his sketches, since this *Bhagavata Purana* has many figures that are typical of his inventiveness and skill. Unfortunately, because of the dispersal of the manuscript, it is difficult to assess precisely in what ways the more old-fashioned style of the older brother was combined with the newer type of painting perhaps employed by younger members of the family who had been inspired by Nainsukh. Without the entire manuscript, it is difficult to judge the relative prominence of the Manaku and Nainsukh styles and to ascertain whether both styles occurred throughout the manuscript.

The smaller *Bhagavata Purana* mentioned above has similar mixed traits, but its naturalistic elements do not seem to be so complex or so specifically related to Nainsukh. Because of its simplicity and more limited compositions, the small set appears to be the earlier one, although this assessment has been challenged.[7]

The conservative compositions of the large *Bhagavata Purana* appear to have been produced by Manaku or an assistant who had learned Manaku's style. The most innovative compositions were done by a skilled artist whom W. G. Archer tentatively identifies as Manaku's son, Fattu, a logical assumption, not only because of the hereditary artistic system but also because the designs incorporated features employed by both Fattu's father and uncle.[8] Certain compositions depend rather specifically on Nainsukh's unique skill in handling frontal and back views or turning poses (cf. poses of men with turned heads in miniatures 160*ii* B and C). If Fattu indeed worked on this series, however, he was unwilling or unable to completely dispense with conventions learned from his father, Manaku, and his style is consequently not as fresh as Nainsukh's.

The *Bhagavat* manuscript originally had long sequences of illustrations that follow each narrative episode of the text fairly exactly and seem to have been done by various artists, since style is sometimes but not always consistent. For example, the miniatures depicting the story of Brahma and the cowherds seem to be by different hands (106*i* and 106*i* A).

Figure 106*i*.

One of the most distinctive characteristics of this series is that the artists have generally composed the large pages using only a few forms. The backgrounds are treated as vast flat spaces in varying dramatic colors. These large expanses of space could have been built up suggestively with clouds, and so on, but in 1760 the painters were too inexperienced to handle such panoramas imaginatively. Slightly later, painters who worked on the *Bhagavata Purana* done in Kangra for Sansar Chand (including some from the Pandit Seu family) were able to depict airy skies or more specific landscapes confidently. Surprisingly, although the Basohli set is assumed to have been unified, its borders vary between blue and red, as noted below.

1. For a discussion of the other *Bhagavata Purana*, which is smaller, see W. G. Archer, 1973, 1: 51; Beach, 1965, pp. 168–77; Goswamy, 1968, figs. 23 and 24.

2. W. G. Archer, 1973, 2: 33–34, Basohli no. 18.

3. Ibid.: 98, Guler no. 9(ii).

4. Ibid.: 95–96, 99, Guler nos. 1–3, 14.

5. *Sotheby*, 1 Feb. 1960, lots 1–63.

6. Chester Beatty Ms. 68.14; W. G. Archer, 1973, 2: 36–37, Basohli nos. 22(i, iii, v).

7. Beach and Goswamy give an earlier date for this manuscript, but W. G. Archer (1973, 1: 51) dates it as later than the large *Bhagavata Purana*.

8. Ibid., 50–51; Archer and Binney, pp. 70–71.

FURTHER READING: Goswamy, pp. 17–57.

106i *Brahma Hides the Cowherds and the Calves in the Cave*   65.335

23 × 33.2 cm, 29.2 × 40.8 cm with border. Red border.
Gift of Mr. and Mrs. Edward B. Meyer

Comparative Material: (A) *The Submission of Brahma before Krishna*, leaf from the large Basohli *Bhagavata Purana*, Pahari, Basohli, ca. 1760–65; Spink, fig. 31.

The story of Brahma acknowledging Krishna's superiority—an important incident in the *Bhagavata Purana* text—was usually elaborately treated by painters. This leaf shows Brahma flying away on his goose after imprisoning Krishna's friends, the cowherds, in a cave as a prank. The boys remained safely asleep in the cave for a year; Krishna meanwhile created duplicate cowherds so that they would not be missed, and Brahma's trick was turned upon himself.

The fantastic rock formations here in shades of pink and orange were used in other Pahari miniatures[1] but are now multiplied so as to cover almost the entire page. In the final episode of this tale showing Brahma bowing to Krishna (A, illus.), the mountain cave surrounded by rocks is done in a totally different manner. While the cave in the Cleveland miniature looks remote and moonlike, the cave in the other miniature is set into a smooth, grassy hill with tree-covered slopes—a setting much like the scenery of the Pahari area. The two concepts are so strikingly different that the miniatures seem as if they must have been done by two painters who were trained to use the same general type of figure but who visualized the myth in different ways.

1. W. G. Archer, 1973, 2: 309, Nurpur no. 14(vi); p. 310, Nurpur no. 17(ii).

106ii *Akrura Rides Toward Dwarka*   71.94

27.5 × 37.8 cm, 30.6 × 40.2 cm with border. Two lines of text on reverse; folio numbered 229. Red border.
Purchase, Andrew R. and Martha Holden Jennings Fund
Ex collection: MacDonald.
Published (with photograph of text on reverse): Goswamy, pl. 26.

Comparative Material: (A) *Prithu Chases the Earth Cow*, leaf from the small Basohli *Bhagavata Purana*, Pahari, Basohli, ca. 1740–50; Beach, 1965, fig. 1. (B) *Mian Mukund Dev on a Riding Picnic*, by Nainsukh, Pahari, Jammu, ca. 1775; W. G. Archer, 1973, 2: 149, Jammu no. 48. (C) *Akrura Returns the Jewel*, leaf from the large Basohli *Bhagavata Purana*, Pahari, Basohli, ca. 1760–65; W. G. Archer, 1973, 2: 39, Basohli no. 22(xii).

This incident is part of the narrative concerning the Syamantaka jewel. This jewel was a gift to mankind that brought freedom from famine or oppression to its righteous owners but misadventure to the unworthy. A long chain of ownership is described in the *Bhagavata Purana*, which culminates in the theft of the jewel by a man who is forced to pass it to the sage Akrura because he is being pursued by Krishna. Krishna kills the thief but does not recover the gem, which is finally brought back to Dwarka by Krishna's uncle when he discovers its source.

In the Cleveland miniature Akrura and his companion ride through a lush green landscape made fruitful by the presence of the jewel. A high hill rises in successive arcs above the two men; trees and bushes are arranged in rows across it. This type of hill formation derives from the back-

Figure 106i(A). *The Submission of Brahma before Krishna*, leaf from the large Basohli *Bhagavata Purana*. Edwin Binney 3rd Collection.

grounds of eighteenth-century Mughal painting, but the artist has here created an encompassing panorama that captures the freshness of his native region. The trees have been skillfully constructed of soft blots of paint without outlining to make their forms appear airy. By contrast, the horses and men are precisely drawn with crisp outlines and fine details of costume emphasized.

Krishna's uncle Akrura had recognized his nephew's divinity and remained devoted to Krishna from young manhood. As pictured in a miniature following the Cleveland episode, Akrura attempted to return the Syamantaka jewel when he reached Dwarka (C, illus.). However, in consideration of Akrura's character, Krishna decreed that his uncle should retain the gem, which subsequently brought good fortune to the surrounding countryside.[1]

A miniature from the smaller copy of the *Bhagavata Purana* illustrated in Basohli depicts a similar but less complex landscape (A, illus.), but the Cleveland painter is both freer and more skilled at evoking his native landscape. If this painter was Fattu, his landscapes are more stylized, however, than those of his uncle Nainsukh and more dependent on previously evolved conventions. A comparison of the Cleveland miniature with a landscape by Nainsukh (B, illus.) indicates that Fattu learned from his uncle's method of figure drawing but that the landscape itself is much more tightly controlled and abstract.

1. Dowson, p. 315.

Figure 106*ii*.

Figure 106*ii*, detail.

Top
Figure 106*ii*(A). *Prithu Chases the Earth Cow*, leaf from the small Basohli *Bhagavata Purana*. Courtesy, Museum of Fine Arts, Boston; Bequest of Helen S. Coolidge, John Gardner Coolidge Fund, 63.145 (titled: *Archer in Pursuit of a Cow*).

Center
Figure 106*ii*(B). *Mian Mukund Dev on a Riding Picnic*. Victoria & Albert Museum, London.

Bottom
Figure 106*ii*(C). *Akrura Returns the Jewel*, leaf from the large Basohli *Bhagavata Purana*. Mildred Archer, London. Photograph courtesy of the Victoria & Albert Museum, London.

263

106iii   *Pradyumna and Sambara*   60.184
         Fight with Maces

28 × 38.3 cm, 30.2 × 41 cm with border. Numbered
226.

Gift of the Mundane Club

Comparative Material: (A) *Sambara Receives the Fish*,
leaf from the large Basohli *Bhagavata Purana*, Pahari,
Basohli, ca. 1760–65; W. G. Archer, 1973, 2: 38, Basohli
no. 22(xi).

This leaf from the large Basohli *Bhagavata Purana* illustrates a portion of the Pradyumna story. Pradyumna was the
son of Krishna and Rukmini. After he was born, a demon
named Sambara learned that the child, when grown, would
destroy him. The demon therefore stole the baby from the
nursery and cast him into the ocean, where he was certain
the infant would drown or be eaten by fish. Pradyumna was,
however, swallowed unharmed by a fish who was shortly
caught and delivered to Sambara's own kitchen. The baby

was saved by Sambara's wife Maya and, after reaching maturity, fought the demon and his forces.[1] The Cleveland miniature shows one of the duels fought by the two antagonists
that resulted in the eventual annihilation of Sambara.

Another miniature of the sequence depicts the fish that
had swallowed Pradyumna being brought to Sambara's palace (A). The two works contrast in mood: the scene of Sambara's palace is relatively naturalistic, while the Cleveland
miniature depicts the duelists in an abstract landscape with
a vivid orange sky. The latter setting emphasizes the mythological nature of the struggle between the young boy and
the spotted, horned demon.

Although these two miniatures are both from the large
Bhagavata Purana series, they are among the few examples
with dark blue rather than red borders. This alteration appears to be arbitrary. The following leaf in this sequence
[106iv] has the more usual red border.

1. Garrett, pp. 461–63.

Figure 106*iii*.

106iv *Pradyumna and Maya Fly to Dwarka* 71.93

28.1 × 38.5 cm, 30.5 × 41.2 cm with border. Narrow red border.

Purchase, Andrew R. and Martha Holden Jennings Fund

Ex collections: MacDonald.

Published: Goswamy, 1968, pl. 27.

This scene completes the sequence of Pradyumna's struggles with Sambara. When Maya acknowledges her love for Pradyumna—whom she had raised but who had vanquished her husband—Pradyumna marries her. The two are shown flying to Dwarka, Pradyumna's true home, to be reunited with his parents, Krishna and Rukmini.[1]

Like many paintings in this set, this miniature has a stark, dramatic background, which the artist has handled from the unusual perspective of the treetops. As exemplified by the previous leaf, many of the *Bhagavata Purana* miniatures have a dominant color for the entire background. In this painting the ground is a rich chartreuse, against which the embracing Maya and Pradyumna are silhouetted. Voluminous rolling clouds are a characteristic feature of this set (see [106i]), whose landscapes are both stylized and relatively naturalistic.

1. Garrett, pp. 461–63.

Figure 106*iv*.

Figure 107.

107 *Raja Dalip Singh of Guler on a Dais* 60.49

Pahari, Bilaspur, ca. 1720, 22.7 × 15.3 cm,
27.1 × 19.8 cm with border. Slightly rubbed. Red border,
worn and paint flaking. Inscription on reverse in Takri:
"Shri Dalip Singh."

Purchase, Mr. and Mrs. William H. Marlatt Fund

Published: Lee, 1960, no. 65.

Comparative Material: (A) *Raja Dalip Singh of Guler,*
Pahari, Mankot, ca. 1720; W. G. Archer, 1973, 2: 294,
Mankot no. 31. (B) *Raja Dalip Singh of Guler Playing
Polo,* Pahari, Guler, ca. 1730; W. G. Archer, 1973, 2: 100,
Guler no. 10. (C) *The Gopis Look for Krishna,* leaf from a
Krishna Lila, Pahari, Bilaspur, ca. 1710; E. Waldschmidt,
"Illustrations de la Krishna-lila," *RAA* 6 (1929/30): pl.
LIIIa.

This portrait of a raja seated on a dais is inscribed on the
reverse, in Takri, "Shri Dalip Singh," which is repeated in
English. The Takri identification is likely to be reliable, and
the man's features correspond with those of the Guler raja
Dalip Singh, who had a prominent curved nose (A). The
paper held by Dalip is unfortunately not meant to be legible, and therefore adds no further information.

Dalip Singh, influential ruler of Guler, succeeded at the
age of eight, in 1695, and died in 1741.[1] This painting of him
is not in the clear, evenly rhythmic style of native Guler
artists but is done in a more delicate, detailed fashion with
vegetational elements characteristic of Bilaspur. Since
Dalip was an influential ruler, portraits have been discovered in several styles other than those associated with
Guler.[2] Guler and Bilaspur were not neighbors, but
they were on the same trade route and had a friendly
relationship.[3]

The Guler portraits of Dalip Singh are ultimately derived
from Mughal types (B). In the Cleveland painting, for instance, the formal pose as well as the treatment of the figure
recall Mughal portraits, and the artist has adapted a basically Mughal conception of garment folds. It seems probable, therefore, that the Cleveland scene was based on a
Guler depiction of Dalip Singh. Since Bilaspur bordered on
the plains, it was a state open to some artistic influences
from the Mughal court, but its painters commonly did less
sophisticated scenes than this one.[4] Judging both stylistically and by the age of Dalip Singh, the Cleveland miniature should date to around 1700.

The artist has varied his naturalistic work with graceful
Bilaspur conventions. The feathery willow branches, the
tree trunks with holes and knots, the dark green masses of
foliage, and the curling flowers are repeated in many other
Bilaspur pictures (C). The squareness of Raja Dalip's face is
also typical of the Bilaspur style.

The Cleveland miniature was created by a sensitive hand,
probably accustomed to drawing more stylized traditional
forms (C). Details are lightly done with both care and spontaneity, and the colors of the portrait—chartreuse ground,
yellow *jama,* and pink rug—are fresh and original. The
insects and the four birds show the artist's gentle refinement
as well as his delight in his work. Compositionally, the
Cleveland picture is related to another Bilaspur portrait
showing a seated raja framed by drooping tree branches.[5]

1. W. G. Archer, 1973, 1: 127.
2. Ibid., 2: 133, Jammu no. 7, or p. 288, Mankot no. 19.
3. Ibid., 1: 131.
4. The early Bilaspur portrait of Raja Dip Chand (ibid., 2: 169,
Bilaspur, no. 1) has features derived from Mughal painting that
were also carried into other Bilaspur works.
5. Sharma, cat. no. 83, pl. 96.

Figure 107, detail.

Figure 108.

108 *Rama and Laksmana Fighting*   53.357
Ravana

Pahari, Bilaspur, ca. 1750, 21.2 × 15.8 cm,
26.8 × 19.4 cm with border. Long tear across upper
right through mule head. Red border. Inscription on
reverse identifying subject.

Purchase, Edward L. Whittemore Fund

Ex collection: Heeramaneck.

Comparative Material (A) *Vamana, the Dwarf Avatar,
Asking a Boon from Bali*, Pahari, Bilaspur, ca. 1750;
W. G. Archer, 1973, 2: 181, Bilaspur no. 35; or Sharma,
cat. no. 81, pl. 85. (B) *Churning the Sea of Milk (the
Tortoise Avatar)*, Pahari, Bilaspur, ca. 1750; H. Trubner
et al., *Asiatic Art in the Seattle Art Museum* (Seattle,
1973), no. 47. (C) *Boar Avatar of Vishnu*, Pahari,
Bilaspur, ca. 1750; Brooklyn Museum, 41.1026,
unpublished. (D) *Balarama Diverting the Jumna*, Pahari,
Bilaspur, ca. 1750; Archer and Binney, no. 74.
(E) *Balarama Pausing in Diverting the Jumna to Converse
with Krishna*, Pahari, Bilaspur; Coomaraswamy, 1926,
pt. 5: pl. LXIX.

These Vishnu *avatara* paintings all seem to come from the
same set, with the exception of one in Boston (E) that dupli-
cates the Balarama scene in the Binney collection (D). The
Boston miniature, apparently the sole example from a further set of *avatara* miniatures, would indicate that the two
groups were nearly identical.[1] During the mid-eighteenth
century, painters of the state were producing many series,
especially *ragamalas*, that were closely related. The remaining leaves listed here depict five *avatars* of Vishnu;
missing subjects are the fish Matsya, the man-lion Nara-
simha, the horse Kalkin, Parasurama, and Krishna. The
incarnations of Vishnu were popular in Pahari painting, and
partial sets can be attributed to several hill states.[2]

This group of *avatara* miniatures includes formations like
the stiffly curved, flowering branches and bands of puffy
clouds, which are near-trademarks of the Bilaspur tradition.
The series is from one of several widely used contemporary strains of Bilaspur painting, each related by different
features to other groups; for example, certain Bilaspur
paintings have the same dark backgrounds as the *avatara*
examples but vary in figure type.[3] Thus, elements of style
were not universally employed—the Bilaspur painters
chose selectively from a fairly broad, though conventionalized, vocabulary.

The rich black backgrounds of the *avatara* miniatures,
which are neither land nor sky, have great visual impact.
The series combines refinements such as the contrast between darkness and bright detail with strong folkish sim-
plifications. In the Cleveland and other miniatures of the
series (C, illus.), figures are powerfully though awkwardly
drawn.

The theme of this leaf is treated more symbolically than
as a true confrontation. Rama and his brother Laksmana are
pressed closely against their enemy the demon Ravana by
the border of the miniature. Rama is in the process of shoot-

ing at a row of attacking bees flying from the ass head that
tops Ravana's numerous human heads. The ass head is a
symbol of malevolence repeated in other portrayals of Ravana (see [52]). Ravana's car is supposedly driven by asses
whose braying denotes evil. Some members of the demon's
family also have ass heads.[4]

1. Since all the paintings are approximately the same size, discrimination is difficult; however, the Boston painting (E), acquired
before the others, is in a very damaged state. The remainder are
in good condition. It seems likely, therefore, that D can be
grouped with miniatures A through C plus the Cleveland painting,
but that E is from another series.
2. See Archer and Binney, nos. 53b, 82, and Czuma, no. 103. For
other Bilaspur *avatara* sets, see W. G. Archer, 1973, 2: 178, Bilaspur no. 25, and p. 182, no. 37.
3. Ebeling, no. 374.
4. E. W. Hopkins, *Epic Mythology* (Varanasi: Indological Book
House, 1968), p. 42.

Figure 108(C). *Boar Avatar of Vishnu*. The Brooklyn Museum,
Brooklyn, New York, 41.1026.

Figure 109.

109 *The Lovelorn Heroine* 71.86

Leaf from a *Sat Sai* of Bihari, Pahari, Garhwal, ca. 1780–90, 19.3 × 14.2 cm (oval), 26.5 × 21.1 with borders. Some paint flaking. Oval set in red rectangular border with dark blue outer border.

Purchase, Andrew R. and Martha Holden Jennings Fund

Ex collection: MacDonald.

Comparative Material: (A) *Krishna Talking to a Milkmaid*, leaf from a *Sat Sai* of Bahari, Pahari, Garhwal, ca. 1780–90; Maggs *Bulletin*, no. 5 (April 1963), no. 102. (B) *Krishna and Radha Conversing*, leaf from a *Sat Sai* of Bihari, Pahari, Garhwal, ca. 1780–90; Maggs *Bulletin*, no. 5 (April 1963), no. 103; also Archer and Binney, 1968, no. 89. (C) *Krishna Watching Radha*, leaf from a *Sat Sai* of Bihari, Pahari, Garhwal, ca. 1780–90: Maggs *Bulletin*, no. 5 (April 1963), no. 105. (D) *The Lovelorn Heroine*, drawing from a *Sat Sai* of Bihari, Pahari, Kangra, ca. 1790; Randhawa, 1966, fig. 13. (E) *The Lovelorn Heroine*, leaf from a *Sat Sai* of Bihari, Pahari, Garhwal, ca. 1810–20; *Sotheby*, 11 Oct. 1982, lot 98.

This miniature depicting a heroine sitting pensively under a flowering tree is from one of several sets done in the Pahari area that illustrate the poet Bihari's *Sat Sai*. In this case, the emotion of the poetic verse is nostalgic: the heroine sits lost in thought, brooding on her absent lover, as two women walk by gossiping. The composition was commonly used for this verse and was employed for a roughly contemporary Kangra drawing (D) as well as for a later Garhwal miniature (E).

Though born in the state of Orchha, the poet Bihari moved with his family to Mathura, the traditional center for creative writing on Krishna during his youth.[1] Bihari, who won Shah Jahan's favor, was one of the later poets whose work was illustrated by miniature painters. That he composed for both Mughal and Rajasthani nobles and had his works illustrated at Pahari courts shows the distillation of Indian culture despite increasing Hindu/Muslim exclusiveness. The love verses of the *Sat Sai*, which mainly describe the beauty of women and were composed for the powerful Raja Jai Singh I of Amber (r. 1625–67), were perhaps more frequently illustrated in the Himalayan foothills than in Rajasthan. The romantic Sansar Chand of Kangra appreciated this work, and it was also illustrated several times for the rajas of Garhwal.

Garhwal was an extremely poor, barren hill state not associated with any miniature paintings that date before 1760, when economic conditions seem to have improved somewhat. Since the rajas of the state had close marital ties with the Guler rulers during the second half of the eighteenth century, it is possible that Guler painters migrated to Garhwal. Despite the fact that Kangra miniatures such as the *Sat Sai* drawing (C) parallel Garhwal works, a connection between these two states has been disputed.[2] It seems probable that Guler was the source for Garhwal painting but that there was also an interchange between Kangra and Garhwal during the latter part of the eighteenth century.

Though based on the Guler/Kangra idiom, the Garhwal style is an individual one with several unique traits. The miniatures from this Garhwal *Sat Sai* series (A, B, C) share many of the same characteristics. Among the elements to be noted in this composition are the parallel lines of flowering branches pulled across the upper surface of the painting—a prominent feature in many Garhwal paintings (A). In addition, the small, bare bushes in the background of the Cleveland painting are typical of the Garhwal artist's handling of vegetation.[3] Arbitrary shading is done in horizontal lines across the hills and in lines running down the tree trunk.[4] In general, a thick, slightly coarse line animates Garhwal paintings and causes designs to appear harsher than those of Kangra art. The heavy facial features seen in this miniature are also characteristic of the idiom.

1. Randhawa, 1966, p. 15.
2. Although other writers have mentioned the stylistic closeness of Kangra and Garhwal, W. G. Archer believes that the Garhwal style originates in Guler and that painters from Sansar Chand's wealthy court in Kangra would not have migrated to the poor, culturally deprived state of Garhwal (1973, 1: 101, 108, 111). S. Panwar ("Garhwal Painting—Some Erroneous Impressions Corrected," *LK*, no. 19, pp. 51–56) disagrees that there was the amount of exchange others suggest.
3. W. G. Archer, 1973, 2: 78–79, Garhwal no. 4, 5(i), 5(ii), 6.
4. Ibid., Garhwal no. 5(ii), 6.

Figure 110.

110 *Krishna and the Cowherds* 71.301

Pahari, probably Garhwal, ca. 1830, 22 × 33 cm.

Gift of Mr. and Mrs. John D. MacDonald

Ex collection: MacDonald.

Comparative Material: (A) *Rejoicing at the Birth of Krishna*, Pahari, probably Garhwal, ca. 1830; W. G. Archer, 1973, 2: 127, Hindur no. 8, or 1976, no. 17. (B) *The Road to Krishna*, Pahari, Garhwal, ca. 1775–90; W. G. Archer, *Garhwal Painting* (London: Faber & Faber, 1957), color pl. I, or 1973, 2: 80.

This miniature summarizes some of Krishna's many exploits with the cowherds. The later Pahari schools often use this device of combining many sequential events within one composition. In the background, Brahma, riding on his goose, symbolizes the various competitions in which he tried to engage Krishna at the cowherds' expense. In the upper right is Aghasura, the giant snake who opened his mouth so that the cowherds entered, thinking it a cave; Krishna also went in and, swelling instead, burst the demon. The two scenes in the foreground—also traditional subjects—are contrastingly peaceful rather than heroic. On the left the scene of the picnicking herd boys shows them eating rice on banana leaves, while on the right they drive the cows home.

Many variations of the Kangra style that developed among hill states in the nineteenth century have not been convincingly attributed to specific locations as yet. Miniatures, however, indicate that painters adapted strange idiosyncrasies (for example, the crossed eyes of the figures in this painting and in another that belongs to the same series [A]), which may eventually be traceable to a particular area.

Although this series was termed "of uncertain provenance" when it was published, it was tentatively classified as coming from Hindur. The paintings done in this minor state, whose rulers were allied to Kangra by marriage, are known exclusively from a collection that had been passed down within the raja's family.[1]

From the evidence of these nineteenth-century works, the Hindur atelier seems to have been a small one that only developed at a late date and added a slight decorative originality to the basic style borrowed from Kangra. Although the attribution to this state is possible, on the basis of observation the series more closely resembles works done in Garhwal. Heavy striations across layers of rippling hills capped with small, round bushes are a typical feature of Garhwal landscapes (B), and flowering trees along with bare branches protruding from trees or bushes also characterize the Garhwal style (see [109]). Finally, figures drawn with heavy outlines are seen in many paintings from Garhwal, as they are in this series. In addition to the Cleveland miniature and comparison A, another miniature of this sequence is in the Boston Museum collection.[2]

1. W. G. Archer, 1973, 1: 171–72.
2. Museum of Fine Arts, 61.383.

111 *Four Scenes from an Aniruddha Usha*

Pahari, possibly Garhwal, ca. 1840, each 18.2 × 25.5 cm, 19 × 26.5 cm with borders. All are damaged to some extent and show evidence of varying degrees of water staining. Narrow dark blue borders.

Gift of Mrs. Charles Eisenman

Comparative Material: (A) *Aniruddha Brought to Usha*, Pahari, possibly Garhwal, ca. 1840; Skelton, 1961, pl. 88.

111i *Krishna Vanquishing Vanasura* 34.219
111ii *Shiva Intercedes for Vanasura* 34.218
111iii *Krishna Fighting Vanasura's Sons* 34.216
111iv *Vanasura's Sons Submit to Krishna* 34.217

The *Aniruddha Usha* is another section of the scriptural *purana* also containing the *Devi Mahatmya* (see [114, 116, 131]). The basic story involves the romance between Krishna's grandson Aniruddha, and Usha, the daughter of the demon Vanasura. Aniruddha had been spirited to Usha's palace in his sleep while he dreamed of Usha but was captured by Vanasura. Krishna defeated the demon, and the lovers were married.

These four leaves detail the battle between Krishna and the *asura* accompanied by his sons. In the first scene Vanasura is overcome by Krishna riding on Garuda, and by Balarama. His many arms are hacked off, symbolizing the end of his multiple evil powers. In the second scene he bows in submission before Krishna and Garuda as Shiva intercedes for him and finally leads him away reformed. Krishna then attacks the *asura's* sons in the ocean, where they are surrounded by water monsters and giant fish. They are also forced to bow before the god.

The style of the water in the last two miniatures—freely swirling waves drawn with parallel lines—is very typical of the Garhwal idiom, but by the time these miniatures were done, this technique had also been used in other states.[1] Another miniature, probably from the same series, has also been attributed to Garhwal (A).

1. W. G. Archer, 1973, 2: 78, Garhwal no. 4; Aijazuddin, p. 20.

Figure 111*i*.

Figure 111*ii*.

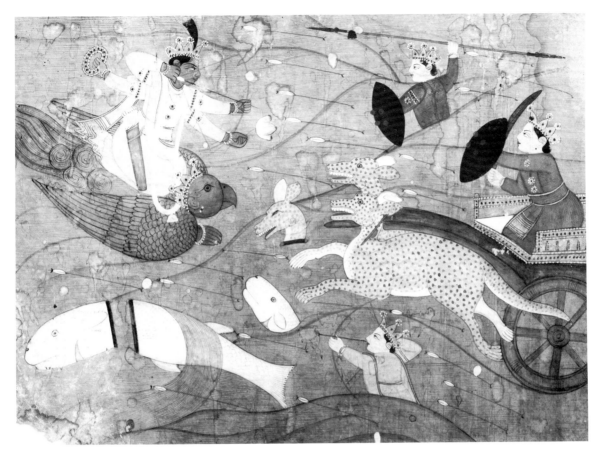

Figure 111*iii*.

Figure 111*iv*.

112 *Portrait of an Aging Man* 68.41

Drawing with traces of white ground. Pahari, Guler, ca. 1700, 18 × 13.3 cm. Staining, fold marks, and extraneous strips of paper pasted to surface.

Purchase, Cornelia Blakemore Warner Fund

Published: V. Dwivedi, 1969, fig. 8.

Comparative Material: (A) *Sital Dev of Mankot Seated*, Pahari, Mankot, ca. 1660–80; W. G. Archer, 1973, 2: 284, Mankot no. 1. (B) *Sital Dev of Mankot Supported by Attendants*, Pahari, Mankot, ca. 1660–80; W. G. Archer, 1973, 2: 284, Mankot no. 3. (C) *Seated Courtier*, Pahari, Guler, ca. 1700–1720; W. G. Archer, 1973, 2: 97, Guler no. 4. (D) *Raja Bikram Singh of Guler Worshipping*, Pahari, Guler, ca. 1700–1720; W. G. Archer, 1973, 2: 97, Guler no. 5.

The subject of this portrait has been thoroughly studied and depicted by the artist in uncompromising but respectful terms. The face is austere and composed, uplifted with Rajput hauteur evident in the head and straightforward pose. The artist further indicates the strength of the personality in the thrust of the face and its firmly outlined features. It appears that the aging noble has some disease of the eyes and may possibly be blind. By concentrating on the fine lines around the eye and the puffing of the lid, the artist has intimated the effects of this infirmity.

The drawing is so detailed that it is almost certainly contemporary with the subject. Though the sitter has been previously identified as Sital Dev, a ruler of Mankot who was blind, this hypothesis has proven incorrect for several reasons. The facts of Sital Dev's life and rule are indefinite, but the dates of his authority in Mankot seem to extend from around 1630 to 1650 or 1660.[1] Despite these early dates, there are fairly well documented portraits of this ruler that show him to be unrelated to the man in the Cleveland drawing.[2]

Sital Dev was painted in a style modeled ultimately on Shah Jahan period portraits although simplified by Pahari painters (A, illus.; B). Apparently Sital Dev's blindness caused his eyes to be completely closed, while the eye of the man in the Cleveland sketch is partially open. As indicated even by the somewhat naive Mankot portraitists, Sital Dev was ill at ease with the exterior world. He has been shown leaning on his attendants or sitting in a contorted position with his head lifted vaguely into the air. This constraint and tension are unlike the knowing poise of the noble in the Cleveland drawing. Furthermore, it seems unlikely that Sital Dev would have been depicted as a comparatively young ruler in portraits painted posthumously had he lived to the age of the subject in the Cleveland drawing. The latter depiction is in a somewhat later style than that of Sital Dev's period.

Figure 112(A). *Sital Dev of Mankot Seated*. After W. G. Archer, *Indian Paintings from the Punjab Hills*, 2 vols. (London & New York: Sotheby Parke Bernet, 1973), 2:284, pl. 1.

Figure 112, detail.

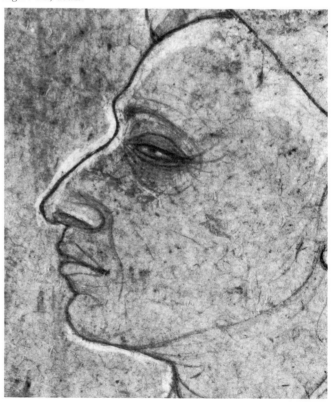

While his Pahari background is indicated by the simplified curves of the body that communicate a feeling for abstract design, the artist of the Cleveland drawing was fluently conversant with the Mughal naturalistic style. The portrait reveals technical skills far beyond those indicated by Mankot portraitists. The naturalism and objectivity of the depiction, which are paralleled in certain Guler works, suggest that the painter was from one of the artist-families of this area; but since Guler artists were widely known in the hill area for producing portraits, the subject might be a courtier of some neighboring state rather than from Guler itself.

1. W. G. Archer, 1973, 1: 368.

2. Archer unequivocally states (1: 33) that this is not Raja Sital Dev.

Figure 112.

113 *Sita in the Garden of Lanka* 66.143

Pahari, Guler, ca. 1725, 55.5 × 79 cm, 56.3 × 81 cm with border. Torn along bottom border, paint gone at upper left and in front of Sita; slight rubbing in other areas. Red border, damaged.

Gift of George P. Bickford

Ex collections: Coomaraswamy, Bickford.

Published: see list in W. G. Archer, 1973, 1: 146.

Comparative Material: (A) *Ravana Produces the False Head of Rama*, Pahari, Guler, ca. 1725; Coomaraswamy, 1926, pt. 5: pl. XII, no. LIX, or Gangoly, 1926, pl. XIVA. (B) *Sita Is Consoled by a Demoness*, Pahari, Guler, ca. 1725; Coomaraswamy, 1926, pt. 5: pl. XII, no. XX. (C) *The Cheated Courtesan*, leaf from a *Rasamanjari*, Pahari, Nurpur, ca. 1710; W. G. Archer, 1973, 2: 308, Nurpur no. 14(iii). (D) *The Abduction of Sita*, leaf from a *Ramayana*, Pahari, Nurpur, ca. 1720–30; W. G. Archer, 1973, 2: 310, Nurpur no. 17(ii). (E) *Muhammad Shah in His Garden*, Mughal, ca. 1735; Welch, 1976, no. 23.

The latter part of the *Ramayana* epic, which describes Sita's captivity in the golden city of Lanka and her eventual rescue by Rama, acquires its moral significance mainly from the description of Sita's resistance to her captor. That the weaker Sita can defy her forceful abductor is explained by a curse laid on the demon following his violation of another woman. Because of this curse, Ravana cannot rape a woman again without precipitating his own destruction. Although he does not really have a chance to seduce the loyal Sita by his offers of marriage to someone with riches, political power, or almost invincible strength, it does appear during the course of the story that Ravana's cruelty and the terrifying environment of his palace may bring Sita to the point of

Figure 113, detail.

death. Throughout this portion of the epic the heroine is alternately cajoled and threatened by Ravana and his wives.

In this Cleveland painting Ravana sits in the *durbar* hall of his golden palace in council with his demons (on the left); on the right, this figure—made large and aggressive by his many heads and arms—seeks out Sita who is kneeling under a tree in his walled garden guarded by fanged demonesses. He urges her to accept his proposal of marriage. The natural setting with fish swimming in the moat and flowering or fruiting trees in the garden appears very peaceful, but the high fortress wall with its narrow archery slits blocking off the lower part of the miniature is somewhat more foreboding.

The well-known *Siege of Lanka* series from which this Cleveland painting comes is today represented by twelve paintings and a greater number of drawings—all from the latter part of the epic.[1] If the series once illustrated the entire *Ramayana* story, it was an extensive one, since most of the painting or drawing compositions follow each other in close sequence, and the artists have often illustrated in two scenes episodes that could have been condensed into one.

As many have noted, the group, which has larger dimensions than any other Pahari set, easily defies the term "miniature." Because of its size, critics have debated whether or not the series may have had some purpose other than enjoyment or religious illustration. A proposal that the scenes were intended as mural cartoons has been countered by the assertion that no others of this type are known and that the set is more elaborate than necessary for a preliminary work.[2] The fact that much of the series is represented by unpainted drawings and that four of the twelve extant paintings are unfinished appears due to some circumstantial accident and does not signify that the works were created casually, or for a temporary purpose.

Even among early Pahari paintings, which are generally notable for skillful artistic abstractions, this series stands out for its carefully measured, formal compositions. The restrained style effectively conveys the objectivity, universality, and inevitability of order within the *Ramayana* itself. In the illustrations the progressive development of a situation, which often carries great dramatic impact in the story, is suggested by bold color alterations between pages more than by marked action or emotional differences in the characters. Dominating the illustrations, the varying backgrounds of this large series carry the epic drama forward and in this way resemble theatrical settings. It is a stylized type of theater in which the facial or positional changes of a given character are subordinate to the general abstract structure.

In this painting from the Cleveland collection, the demon king Ravana presses his marriage proposal on Sita, while in a following scene (A, illus.), he produces a severed replica of Rama's head by hypnosis to force Sita into capitulating out of despair. The restrained portrayal of emotion in the queenly figure of Sita is exquisitely sensitive, yet functions as only a small part of the epic unfoldment. In the Cleveland miniature Sita bows her head, an acquiescent gesture expressing her gentle upbringing and her fate as a prisoner. In the second scene, with her head on her knees, she withdraws into herself, seeking some refuge from Ravana's aggressive hostility. In physical appearance Sita is identical with Ravana's other wives, some of whom stand behind him in the Cleveland picture. Beauty, therefore, is not personalized but is an abstraction harmonizing with the total dramatic conventionalization.

The Cleveland painting and the Boston scene are consistent in format and depend primarily on color for differentiation. As in other paintings of the series, the sky functions as a key element, coinciding with the artist's expressionistic desires rather than defining an actual time of day. In the Cleveland painting it is pale blue, in the Boston scene (A) and other leaves it is fire orange, and in still other scenes it is navy or royal blue. Since each painting involves carefully selected repetitions of the artist's chosen color tones and accents, an impression is given of floodlights

Figure 113, detail.

Figure 113.

Figure 113(A). *Ravana Produces the False Head of Rama.* Courtesy, Museum of Fine Arts, Boston; Ross-Coomaraswamy Collection, 17.2747.

Figure 113, detail.

altering a stage set. Included within this concept of set design are perpetual costume changes that accord with the imagined passage of time. Ravana's clothes alter from leaf to leaf or within a given painting when two actions are portrayed. In the Cleveland painting, for example, he wears dark green during his conference on the left and yellow when he proposes to Sita on the right.

The artist also employs certain arbitrary devices to vary his gigantic maplike stage. Most scenes that include Lanka are split between the palace on the left and the open hill on the right—a basic setting maintained even when, as in the Cleveland leaf, it is not vital to show Ravana in conference on the left. When Rama's forces of good are shown on the hill, the boundary wall wraps closely about the castle, but when both halves of the scene represent Ravana's territory the wall is extended across the same hilly backdrop and redefines the area.

The palace building, like the wall, is infinitely variable—the façade opens and closes, towers rise, and balconies appear. Vivid rugs, draperies, and other changing stage properties focus sudden attention on Ravana's audience hall. In moving from left to right, the artist is aware of unifying or breaking time by compositional devices, as in a comparison of the Cleveland painting and the Boston scene (A). The Cleveland painting, intended as two scenes, is divided (see also B, illus.); in the later episode (A) one of Ravana's demons unifies the central space.

Although Basohli is often considered the fountainhead of pre-Kangra styles, the Guler *Siege of Lanka* series has little relation to the paintings of the state. The strongest stylistic connections are with works from the state of Nurpur, which borders Guler on the east and was allied with Guler. The long faces, particularly evident in the female figures of the Cleveland painting, are like Nurpur prototypes (C, D) and

280

Figure 113(B). *Sita Is Consoled by a Demoness.* Courtesy, Museum of Fine Arts, Boston; Ross-Coomaraswamy Collection, 17.2748.

very unlike the heavy, square heads seen in other Guler paintings. Nurpur compositions arranged in precise geometric grids and only occasionally enlivened with pattern are closely related to the *Siege of Lanka* series (cf. the use of a rug in C with the Cleveland painting). The *Seige of Lanka* paintings have been associated with a Nurpur *Ramayana* (D) that has similar facial types, trees, and architectural drawing.[3]

By 1929 the Lanka series was connected to Guler by Ghose, who obtained drawings of the set from this state, found that Coomaraswamy's paintings had come from Guler, and established that the set had been in the collection of a former Guler ruler.[4] While the Guler provenance of the series has been accepted, it is less difficult to relate the set to Nurpur than to Guler artists—probably due to the scarcity of evidence. The earlier Guler paintings seem to have been mainly portraits with pronounced Mughal traits, whereas Nurpur artists produced epics and poetry in tightly controlled geometric settings. Archer does not associate the Lanka paintings with prior Guler styles in his comprehensive Pahari study but stresses the influence of the set on later Guler art.[5] The feeling for abstraction, clean forms, and precise contours that passes into later Guler art is particularly significant. It is interesting that Guler narrative scenes were conceived differently from portraits, and that even relative naturalism in epic illustrations such as this one post-dates quite naturalistic portrait depictions by several decades.

While the Lanka series does not superficially reveal Mughal influence, it has been conjectured that its scale and spatial openness derive from Muhammad Shah works (E).[6] There is indeed no known Pahari prototype for the great vistas of this set that introduce new objectivity into painting. Because the universe has been depicted on such a vast

scale, human figures occupy more natural proportions than they do in toylike Nurpur scenes (D). The change appears gradual because artists were still preoccupied with symbolic space, time, and emotion; but they were also becoming aware of natural body proportions and facial features. The difference between this and later sets, however, is chiefly that the remarkable human poignancy illustrated here remains elevated on an epic plane, whereas in later decades a comparison of Rama and Sita or Krishna and Radha with ordinary lovers is invited by increased naturalism.

1. The paintings and drawings of the set are found in the following collections:

Museum of Fine Arts, Boston—six paintings (five complete, one half-completed), all published (Coomaraswamy, 1926, pt. 5: pls. X–XIII); five drawings, three published (ibid., pls. XIV–XV).

Cleveland Museum of Art—one painting, published.

Metropolitan Museum of Art—one finished painting, published (J. Jain-Neubauer, *The Ramayana in Pahari Miniature Painting* [Ahmedabad: L. D. Institute of Indology, 1981], fig. 24); one unfinished painting, published (ibid., fig. 34); two drawings, one published (in Craven).

British Museum—one painting, mainly completed, published (Gangoly, 1926, pl. 15, or J. C. French, *Himalayan Art* [Oxford: Oxford University Press, 1931], frontispiece).

Private collections—one painting, published (Czuma, no. 116, or Welch, 1973, no. 41); one painting, mainly complete, unpublished.

Prince of Wales Museum, Bombay—nineteen drawings, published (Jain-Neubauer, 1981 [see above], figs. 35, 37–39, 41, 43–45).

2. W. G. Archer, 1: 147.

3. Ibid., 146.

4. A. Ghose, "The Schools of Rajput Painting," *RL* 1 (1929).

5. W. G. Archer, 1973, 1: 147.

6. Beach, 1965*a*, p. 176.

Figure 114.

Figure 114, detail.

114 *Kali Attacking Nisumbha* 68.44

Pahari, possibly Guler, ca. 1740, 22 × 33 cm,
23.7 × 35.2 cm with border. Paint scraped at bottom.
Plain paper border, apparently meant to be colored.

Purchase, Edward L. Whittemore Fund

Comparative Material: (A) *The Devi with Kali Battles Sumbha and Nisumbha*, three leaves from a *Devi Mahatmya*, Pahari, Guler, dated 1781; Aijazuddin, Guler no. 41(xxiii)–41(xxv).

Although the iconographic details of this miniature are incorrect, the scene apparently illustrates an episode in the myth of the goddess that is described in the *Devi Mahatmya*. The miniature is, however, likely to be a single design rather than part of a manuscript, because the artist seems relatively unfamiliar with the text.

In the illustrations conforming to iconographic tradition, Devi rides the lion/tiger (her traditional vehicle) while Kali moves beside her on foot, lapping the blood of demon forces. In the Cleveland miniature, however, Kali herself rides the tiger astride a crimson and gold saddle. The demon she spears with the enormous *trisula* is Nisumbha, one of two brothers, a many-armed green *asura* who rides in a chariot.[1] The story is that his brother Sumbha, seeing Devi in an alluring form, attempted to woo her by boasting of his own great power. When he was repulsed, he sent his army in anger at her proud retort. Having killed his troops and forced his retreat, the goddess took on Nisumbha, the less important brother, and finally annihilated Sumbha also.[2] A sequence of three miniatures from a later Guler manuscript (A) shows the accepted dramatization of the battle: Devi astride her vehicle is accompanied by Kali as the demon brother Sumbha attacks, but when he falls temporarily, Nisumbha rides up and Devi attacks him alone with her three-pronged spear.

The Cleveland miniature creates a strong impression because of its colors and its refinement—a precision that increases the impact of its eccentric subject matter, since the macabre details delineated so exactly appear horrifically logical. The elegance of the treatment is shown in the relatively unusual employment of gold on such objects as the saddle, the chariot, and the harness of bells. The fact that the painter's perception of reality is somewhat uneven adds another dimension of strangeness to the scene; for example, the horses and the small chariot are elements of naiveté, whereas Kali's figure is fairly developed. The tiger is simultaneously accomplished and savagely primitive.

The miniature has some relationship with later Guler versions of the *Devi Mahatmya*, but these manuscripts have conventional details handled with a less "ferocious" sophistication. The collapsed or cross-eyed horses are a bizarre motif, sometimes seen in Kulu paintings,[3] and it is uncommon to see Kali wearing a necklace of diminutive bodies (rather than skulls) or to be carrying such a large spear.

There is virtually nothing that relates stylistically to this accomplished but savage style; the miniature is far too bru-

Figure 114, detail.

tally austere to derive from the Basohli type of painting, which tends to have florid details. In addition, the golden yellow, crimson, and green color tones are unlike those of Basohli or related schools that mainly employ clear yellow, red, and different shades of green. The graphic ability of the painter may indicate that he came from Guler, but the power and ferocity of the scene are different from the usual Guler picture.

1. Aijazuddin, pp. 31–32.
2. F. E. Pargiter, trans., *The Markandeya Purana* (Calcutta, 1904), pp. 506–9.
3. See Welch, 1973, no. 40, and Archer and Binney, no. 71.

115 *Krishna Awaiting Radha* 36.685

Pahari, Guler, ca. 1750–60, 18.6 × 13.2 cm. Extensively cropped; paint rubbed and flaking.

Purchase, Edward L. Whittemore Fund

Ex collection: Coomaraswamy.

Published: W. G. Archer, 1952, Guler no. 18; Coomaraswamy, 1916, pl. XLIVa; Lee, 1960, no. 76 and 1973, color pl. 21; Spink, fig. 85.

Comparative Material: (A) *Radha and Krishna on a Balcony*, Pahari, Guler, ca. 1760; Czuma, no. 117. (B) *Radha with Krishna*, Pahari, Guler, ca. 1750–60; Coomaraswamy, 1916, pl. XLIII. (C) *Radha and Krishna Listening to Music*, Pahari, Guler, ca. 1760; Philadelphia Museum 17-1964-8, unpublished. (D) *Rama and Sita*

Worshipped by Hanuman and Laksmana, Pahari, Chamba, ca. 1760; *Sotheby*, 11 Dec. 1973, lot 364. (E) *Radha and Krishna Exchanging Pan*, Pahari, Chamba, ca. 1765; W. G. Archer, 1973, 2: 60, Chamba no 28. (F) *Radha and Krishna on Sesshu*, Pahari, Jammu, ca. 1740; W. G. Archer, 1973, 2: 136, Jammu no. 13.

There is a group of miniatures that represents a refreshing adolescent stage of development in Pahari painting and that shares certain stylistic traits, although the works emanate from different states (A–F). Led by artists from Guler, painters from Chamba, Basohli, and a few other states abandoned the early painting styles used to create intense, fantastic mythological worlds and opened themselves to new possibilities. Their styles became simpler and more honest

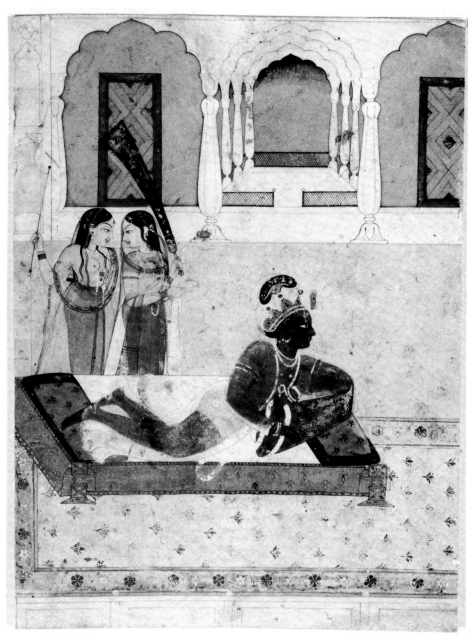

Figure 115.

as they exchanged an emotional intensity that had reached a dead end for a new childlike curiosity about the world around them. Florid details and hot colors were replaced by a more basic interest in forms, particularly those of human figures.

The evidence of this change in attitude is first seen in pictures such as those from the Guler Siege of Lanka series done about 1725 [113]. By 1750, however, the alteration is increasingly evident. Figures in paintings done from 1750–60 are fuller and more naturalistically proportioned (A–F; A and C illus.) than those in earlier miniatures. In contrast with seventeenth-century Basohli or Mankot works, the bodies treated experimentally by artists of this period are soft, with a slightly unformed character. Faces particularly seem to be very broad and rounded, with innocent expressions conveying not only new sweetness but also the painter's pleasure in his own ability to depict such a mood. While not all the subjects of this period are love scenes, they are all inspired by a new romantic idealism. During the eighteenth century the Krishna cult became ever more influential in the Pahari states, and the romantic sensitivity engendered by this worship was progressively intensified in painting. For the first time, Pahari artists developed the facility to illustrate the textual descriptions of a young, appealing Krishna figure.

The Cleveland miniature and others show that the Pahari artist was not yet skilled at manipulating the personal emotions that went with this evolution in romantic painting. Here, for example, Krishna is a dreamy figure whose state of thought is left unresolved. He is not the ardent, very-knowing lover of either earlier or later paintings. In general, the figures of this group are drawn as if they were less consciously aware of themselves than are the figures of later Kangra painting. Most pictures have very simple architectural forms and uncluttered compositions similar to those of the Cleveland miniature. The large areas left open and free of decoration reflect the still-developing artistic imagination. Unfortunately, this stage lasted only a few years before its pleasing hesitancy and spontaneity were lost in conventional repetitions of poses or lines that artists believed had been successful. The youthful dignity of painted figures gave way to a more obvious prettiness.

Although the pensive Krishna stretched on the low divan with servant girls quietly exchanging intimacies behind him was surely meant to be the focal point of the Cleveland miniature, the work is a fragment. It has been cut down somewhat on all edges, as can be discerned from the fan chopped off in the attendant's upraised hand and other details. However, from the appearance of the panel that has been cut in the upper right, this side of the painting was probably quite a bit wider and may have had other figures. The delicate but rather voluptuous women in the Cleveland miniature are shorter than others in Guler paintings of the time, but they have the typical rounded brows, sharp noses and long eyes of the beauties created by the painters of the state.

Figure 115(A). *Radha and Krishna on a Balcony.* George P. Bickford Collection; on loan to The Cleveland Museum of Art.

Figure 115(C). *Radha and Krishna Listening to Music.* Philadelphia Museum of Art, City of Philadelphia Collection, 17-1964-8.

116 *Vishnu Battles Madhu and Kaitabha* 74.46

Leaf from a *Devi Mahatmya*, Pahari, Guler, ca. 1760,
16.7 × 25.8 cm, 20.2 × 29.2 cm with border. Numbered
52 or *62*. Plain paper border.

Purchase, John L. Severance Fund

Comparative Material: (A) *Vishnu Battles Madhu and
Kaitabha*, leaf from a *Devi Mahatmya*, Pahari, Guler,
dated 1781; Aijazuddin, Guler no. 41(iii). (B) *Vishnu
Severs the Heads of Madhu and Kaitabha*, leaf from a
Devi Mahatmya, Pahari, Guler, ca. 1760; Doris Wiener
Gallery, *Indian Miniature Paintings* (New York, 1974),
no. 31.

The composition of this Cleveland painting was reemployed
by Guler artists in successive manuscript illustrations of the
Devi Mahatmya describing the forms and activities of the
goddess, the female counterpart of Shiva. From about 1740
on, the Devi legend was produced repeatedly from the
same basic series of designs possibly passed down by artist
workshop drawings. Not only was the *Devi Mahatmya* a
popular subject in Guler, but a prominent temple to Durga
in Haripur, the capital, shows her influence on everyday
life.[1]

This episode is an interjection into the account of female
supernatural deeds in the *Devi Mahatmya* that describes

Figure 116.

how Vishnu, the preserver of the universe, saved primeval Brahma from destruction by two demons, Madhu and Kaitabha. At this time in the cosmic cycle the universe was entirely fluid and Vishnu was slumbering prior to further creation. Since the nature of Brahma is more quiescent than active, he knew that he could not defend himself when he saw the two demons descending on him. He therefore attempted to wake Vishnu, who finally arose and fought the demons for five thousand years before cutting them to pieces.[2]

In the Cleveland miniature Vishnu is shown twice—in his kinetic being as well as in his potentially powerful form reposing on the serpent Sesshu (Madhu is the light-colored demon and Kaitabha is the darker). The figures are blocked out in simple shapes with clean outlines as is characteristic of Guler painting. Guler artists were boldly imaginative and apparently enjoyed rather than feared treating the vast stretches of open space that bring out the cosmic scope of the drama in this composition. Another of the ocean scenes from the same series as the Cleveland painting is also planned with two sequential episodes of the story in a single frame (B, illus.).

A comparison of the Cleveland miniature of ca. 1760 with the same scene from a series dated 1781 (A) shows the continuity of tradition in the *Devi Mahatmya* designs. The positions of the fighters and of Vishnu resting with one set of hands around his knees are identical in the two works. The only change occurs in the waves, which in the later painting (A) have pronounced spirals usually characteristic of Garhwal.[3]

An unpublished nineteenth-century bound copy of the *Devi Mahatmya* also from Guler (now in the Los Angeles County Museum of Art) shows that there were three compositions in the traditional set of designs that interrupt the main theme of the poem with this oceanic episode of Vishnu's strength. (The Cleveland miniature and comparison B comprise two parts of this sequence.)

1. Aijazuddin, p. 33 (also see Guler no. 27); W. G. Archer, 1973, 2: 101, Guler no 17(i), 17(ii), and p. 117, Guler no. 61(ii); Coomaraswamy, 1926, pt. 5: pl. XLII, for other Guler illustrations of this *purana*.
2. F. E. Pargiter, trans., *Markandeya Purana* (Calcutta: Asiatic Society, 1904), pp. 469–72.
3. Aijazuddin, p. 20.

Figure 116(B). *Vishnu Severs the Heads of Madhu and Kaitabha*, leaf from a *Devi Mahatmya*. After Doris Wiener Gallery, *Indian Miniature Paintings* (New York, 1974), pl. 31.

Figure 116, detail.

117 *Krishna Reaching for the Moon* 71.80

Pahari, Guler, ca. 1820, 24 × 16 cm, 26.5 × 18.7 cm with border. Paint scraped. Dark blue border.

Purchase, Andrew R. and Martha Holden Jennings Fund
Ex collections: Gangoly, MacDonald.
Published: Gangoly, 1926, pl. 37; Khandalavala, 1958, no. 287.
Comparative Material: (A) *Krishna's Bath*, Pahari, Kangra, ca. 1790–1800; Khandalavala, 1958, color pl. I. (B) *Yasoda with Krishna and Balarama*, Pahari, Guler, ca. 1820; W. G. Archer, 1973, 2: 119, Guler no. 70.

This scene of Yasoda preparing to bathe Krishna, who is gesturing toward the moon, has special significance in relation to the baby god, because one of his titles likens him to the moon's bright (auspicious) face.[1] Krishna's reaching for the moon symbolizes not only his aspiration for cosmic heroism but also the equality of the divine baby with all natural forces. The episode is taken from the *Valya-lila* (*Baby Pranks of the Divine Childhood*) by Sur Das; the poetry expresses what his uncomprehending foster mother believes to be a typical child's desire to possess the unattainable.[2] Not realizing his godlike nature, Yasoda gestures toward the reflection in the water symbolizing the simple, pragmatic aspect of life, while the child Krishna identifies himself with cosmic reality. Among the maids standing, one offers a toy and another holds Krishna's brother Balarama.

Another miniature of Krishna in the bath held by Yasoda (A) is a reworking of the same composition, but is without the motif of the moon. A third miniature (B)—stylistically comparable with closely related short, stocky figures—illustrates the popular theme of Yasoda with her young foster children in a similarly intimate way. The broad figures with exaggerated facial features are typical of the nineteenth-century Guler style.

1. Spink, p. 38.
2. Gangoly, 1926, text to pl. 37.

Figure 117.

Color Plate XVII. A Young, Angry Heroine [90].

Color Plate XX. Sita in the Garden of Lanka [113].

Color Plate XXI. Kali Attacking Nisumbha [114].

Color Plate XXIII. Shiva under Trees [120].

118 *A Saddled Horse* 68.106

Drawing, Pahari, Jammu, ca. 1750, 24.5 × 21.5 cm.
Vertical fold mark, staining, and discoloration.
Gift of the Folio Club

Comparative Material: (A) *Raja Dhrub Dev of Jasrota Examining the Points of a Horse*, Pahari, Jammu, ca. 1740–50; W. G. Archer, 1973, 2: 140, Jammu no. 35.
(B) *Mian Mukund Dev on a Riding Picnic*, by Nainsukh, Pahari, Jammu, ca. 1755; W. G. Archer, 1973, 2: 149, Jammu no. 48.

The simplifed line drawing here and the manner in which curves defining the horse's neck, rump, and tail are reduced to rhythmic essentials typify Jammu art and can be compared with various examples of horse portraiture from that state (A, illus.; B illus. as comparison B in [106*ii*]). By eliminating angles and rounding all contours, the Jammu artists have tended to accentuate the fullness of the horses. Not only are these artistic conventions similar, but the stocky

Figure 118(A). *Raja Dhrub Dev of Jasrota Examining the Points of a Horse*. Victoria & Albert Museum, London.

Figure 118.

type of horse with a short neck and small head is also comparable.

Although documentation is difficult, it appears that Jammu was the main source of animal and bird portraiture from the Pahari area. A large number of such works date from the mid-eighteenth century and like this one are quite straightforwardly drawn, with few ornamental details. The artist Nainsukh, who helped to revolutionize painting in the hills, is credited with doing many of the Jammu bird and animal drawings; he had an exceptional feeling for rhythmic line drawing, but other artists who contemporarily worked in Jammu seem to have had a folkish ability to reduce form to its essentials. The artist of the Cleveland drawing is one of the type who was a simple but able draftsman.

119 *Falcon* 68.42

Pahari, probably Jammu, ca. 1770, 27.6 × 16 cm, 31.6 × 19.8 cm with border. Multiple flecked-paper borders.

Purchase, Edward L. Whittemore Fund

Since falcon hunting was a favorite sport of both Mughals and Rajputs, portraits of specific prize birds were frequently produced, even though the treatment might be decorative, as in this Cleveland example. The strong, even line employed here is characteristic of the Jammu school. The feathers and markings are simplified in a bold, abstract design. Usually falcons are shown on perches with jesses around their legs, and in Mughal miniatures the perch is set at an angle to create a spatial illusion. This Pahari artist, however, has conceptually drawn a straight perch parallel to the picture plane so that the bird cannot grasp the bar (as in Mughal examples) but sits atop it.

Figure 119.

120 *Shiva under Trees* 60.48

Pahari, Kangra, ca. 1780, 18.2 × 14 cm. Cropped jaggedly and torn at edges; remains of yellow border at left.

Purchase, Mr. and Mrs. William H. Marlatt Fund

Ex collection: Heeramaneck.

Comparative Material: (A) *The Holy Family,* Pahari, Guler, ca. 1755; W. G. Archer, 1952, no. 29, or 1973, 2: 104, Guler no. 25. (B) *Krishna Bathing with the Gopis,* Pahari, Kangra, ca. 1780; W. G. Archer, 1973, 2: 212, Kangra no. 36(vii); or Randhawa, 1960, color pl. 16.

This miniature fragment of Shiva with his trident epitomizes the early Guler/Kangra style still closely related to the first Guler paintings in which this type of naturalism evolved. The pensive figure is much like that in a Guler painting (A, illus.) done about two decades earlier, in which the figure of Shiva is, however, less full and sensuous, as is typical of the earlier style.

The red ground of this miniature is a feature often associated with Guler, but the scene was probably done by one of the painters who worked on Sansar Chand's *Bhagavata Purana,* since the drawing is very light and refined in contrast

Figure 120.

Figure 120(A). *The Holy Family*. Mildred Archer, London. Photograph courtesy of the Victoria & Albert Museum, London.

Scene from the *Nala-Damayanti* drawings, Kangra, Pahari, ca. 1790–1800, 22.2 × 33.5 cm.

Purchase, Edward L. Whittemore Fund

Ex collection: Coomaraswamy.

Published: Eastman, pl. v.

Comparative Material: (A) *Damayanti's Svayamvara Is Announced*, leaf from the *Nala-Damayanti* painting series, Pahari, Kangra, ca. 1800; Goswamy, 1975, pl. 35.

Kangra artists frequently illustrated the ancient story of *Nala and Damayanti*, recounting the struggles of two yearning lovers, apparently because the narrative (which was rarely produced in other states) appealed to Raja Sansar Chand, who was noted for his romanticism.[1] The successive illustrations of *Nala and Damayanti* commissioned by this raja who molded the Kangra style have been discussed in two publications.[2] This Cleveland leaf belongs to a group of forty-eight drawings acquired before 1910 by the Indian scholar Coomaraswamy and has been published in its correct sequential position within the group, which is now mainly owned by the Museum of Fine Arts, Boston.[3]

The set has been noted for its lyricism and long, sinuous line patterns. Among the most beautiful aspects of the line drawing are the artists' depiction of wide, airy settings and their sensitivity to fluid feminine movement. A series of 110 sketches in the National Museum, New Delhi, is closely linked with Coomaraswamy's group but is more casually prepared.[4] The style of the Coomaraswamy group is controlled—a refinement that is apparently in anticipation of the painting process. (The Cleveland drawing shows the beginning of paint application: washes and some heavier color are applied in the background.) Although the Coomaraswamy drawing series begins only in the middle of the narrative, its relationship with finished works illustrating the first portion of the romance is problematic. A hypothetical reconstruction of the incomplete set beginning with finished paintings followed by drawings has proven controversial.[5] The fact that there are remnants of several painted sets still extant shows how many times Sansar Chand requested the subject within a short time, and it increases the complexity of the issue.

In this scene Bhima, the father of Damayanti, consults astrologers to determine if the signs favor her marriage to Nala. He then announces to his wife and daughter (in the upper left of the picture) that the astrological predictions are positive. The heroine Damayanti has already gone through an unusual ceremony of choosing a husband from among suitors and has selected Nala, who must, however, win final approval. In the lower scene a messenger with his sword over his shoulder goes out to welcome Nala, who is seated in a pavilion at the upper right.[6]

The *Nala-Damayanti* illustrations are interesting as a group because the same idealized figure types reappear throughout. The astrologers in the Cleveland scene, for

to harder, more emphatically outlined Guler works. In addition, the naturalistic, twisted trees with their soft, hazy foliage that expands high in the air are very characteristic of the early Kangra school (B), noted for its development of landscape passages reflecting the freshness of the surrounding Beas Valley.

The sophistication of Sansar Chand's artists is evident in the complexity of Shiva's expression: gentleness, sensuousity, mysticism, and regret seem to mingle on the god's face. This is perhaps the most appealing period of Kangra painting, when artists were genuinely endeavoring to create original and provocative rather than attractive work. For example, Shiva's enigmatic face and delicate hands are compelling but not overly prettified, nor do they convey the feeling of having been created by artistic tricks.

The yellow at the left is unusual for a border color; its wideness seems to indicate that the original painting was fairly large.

example, are identical with painters or secretaries in other scenes; attendants or courtiers are also reused in stock poses (A). King Bhima, the personification of the dignified king, resembles princely figures in a much earlier manuscript done in the state of Guler[7] that illustrates how suitable characterizations of particular types passed from artist to artist through several generations and across state borders.

1. The narrative comes from the twelfth-century poem the *Naishadhacharita* by Sriharsha rather than from the original account in the *Mahabharata;* see W. G. Archer, 1973, 1: 300.

2. Eastman; and Goswamy, 1975.

3. Eastman, pp. 81–82; the Cleveland drawing is inscribed 56 on its upper border, which shows its position in the narrative is fifth in Coomaraswamy's group.

4. Archer, 1973, 2: Guler no. 49.

5. The scholar B. N. Goswamy (1975, p. 4) maintains that the forty-seven paintings illustrating the beginning of the *Nala-Damayanti* tale are stylistically identical with the drawings that illustrate the next part of the story, and that it is thus logical to consider them a single, unfinished series. W. G. Archer (1973, 1: 301), however, believes that the drawings were produced between 1790–1800 and that the paintings date from about 1800–1810.

6. Eastman, p. 81.

7. Archer, 1973, 2: 99, Guler no. 14.

FURTHER READING: Eastman; Goswamy, 1975.

Figure 121, detail

Figure 121.

122 *Radha and Krishna's Reconciliation* 36.682

Drawing with slight color. Pahari, Kangra, ca. 1790–1800, 18.3 × 14 cm. Inscription above top border: "The stubborn heroine, wrathful and recalcitrant, drew the sheet over her head feigning sleep. As her *sakhi* entered, the lover, signalling with his eyes, rose and sat at her feet. Although she knew it was Hari's touch, the heroine dissembled, saying with a smile: 'Come, friend [feminine gender], let us sleep on one bed and spread one sheet [over us].'"[1]

Purchase, Edward L. Whittemore Fund

Ex collection: Coomaraswamy.

This composition was one purchased by the Museum from Coomaraswamy along with [121]. Since the verse had been published in his 1916 work on Rajput painting, the drawing was then already in his collection and was presumably one of the Kangra type he considered to represent classic Rajput sensibilities because of its purity and lyricism. The architectural forms and flowing rhythmic line uniting the three figures in the composition are related to the *Nala-Damayanti* scenes that Coomaraswamy believed represented a high point of Hindu evocative expression (see previous entry).

The theme is one from Sringara literature that deals with the ever-changing emotions of love. The numerous paintings illustrating *Sringara* are designed so that the viewer savors all the variant moods, or *rasas*, in romantic relationships. In this case the miniature illustrates a phase of love in separation caused by the angry or haughty withdrawal of the heroine, Radha—termed "*manini*" from the word "*mana*," meaning coldness and stubbornness.[2] The artist has drawn Radha alone on a bed with Krishna at her feet. In the interpretation of the poetry given by Coomaraswamy, she pretends not to feel Krishna's touch but finally makes an indirect move toward reconciliation through an appeal ostensibly to her *sakhi*.[3]

1. Inscription translated in Coomaraswamy, 1916, 1: 48–49.
2. Randhawa, 1962, p. 170.
3. Coomaraswamy, 1916, 1: 49.

Figure 122.

123 *Couple Playing Chaupar on*   36.683
    a Terrace

Drawing with red ochre underdrawing, Pahari, Kangra,
ca. 1790–1800, 19.4 × 13.2 cm.

Purchase, Edward L. Whittemore Fund

Ex collection: Coomaraswamy.

Published (repr. only): V. C. Ohri, ed., *Arts of Himachal*
(Simla: State Museum, 1975), fig. 58.

This scene, another acquired from Coomaraswamy's collection, consists of a loose red ochre underdrawing with
more graceful black sketch lines over it. Some alterations
have been made in the second version, particularly in hand
gestures. The sustained lines and the stylized figures of
this sketch are similar to those of the *Nala-Damayanti* drawings also admired by Coomaraswamy for their lyricism
(see [121]).

The game of *chaupar*, played with dome-shaped game
pieces and dice on the four-part board or cloth shown here,
was one of the popular leisurely recreations often pictured
in Pahari miniatures.

Figure 123.

124 Krishna and Radha Watching Rain Clouds 73.104

The month of Bhadon from a *Baramasa* series, Pahari, Kangra, ca. 1790, 13 × 9 cm (oval), 20.7 × 15.2 cm with borders. Paint loss across top and bottom of oval. Numbered 7. Verse and title have been cut out and remounted with painting at a late date; oval painting is in floral rectangle surrounded by a yellow border.

Purchase from the J. H. Wade Fund

Comparative Material: (A) *Watching the Approaching Storm*, Pahari, Kangra, ca. 1790; Randhawa, 1962, fig. 75. (B) *Lovers Watching the Clouds*, Pahari, Kangra, ca. 1790; Randhawa, 1962, fig. 76.

This delicate composition from a *Baramasa* series is one that was frequently used to illustrate the mood of lovers during the rainy season.[1] Two other versions from Indian collections also show a couple on a terrace with female attendants watching the approaching storm (A and B). In each miniature the lover gesticulates at the billowing clouds and the flight of white birds across them. In these illustrations, but particularly noticeable in the Cleveland painting, a landscape of low rolling hills continues into the distance— typical of the actual scenery of the state.

The hero and heroine stand in the balcony of a palace with four women in attendance, two of whom are playing music on the terrace. This minature is one of a late eighteenth-century Kangra type that has a tastefully restricted palette of soft colors chosen to enhance the lyricism of the romantic theme. The dark, stormy sky is echoed very gracefully by the gray of the palace and the pale, neutral colors of several of the costumes. The green of the landscape and the saffron of the heroine's dress—used to emphasize her precedence over the other women—are the only bright colors.

The *Baramasa* poems have the dual subjects commonly interrelated in Indian literature of seasonal change and human love. *Baramasa* pictures produced in other states were often symbolically treated, but when done in Kangra by miniaturists who excelled at landscape painting, the illustration of Pahari hillsides is as lyrical and evocative as the accompanying poetry. Love is depicted either in separation when the beauty of nature gives painful reminders of loneliness or when everything about the setting enhances the joy of the united lovers, as in the Cleveland miniature.

The month of Bhadon (August/September) illustrated here is supposed to be especially dedicated to the happiness of love because of its coolness, the fragrance of blooming flowers, and the pasionate nature of the fertilizing thunderstorms.[2]

Figure 124.

1. Randhawa, 1962, pp. 134, 140.
2. Ibid; see pp. 133–34 for list of Kangra *Baramasa* sets.

125 *Krishna Being Dressed in* 33.453
Women's Clothes for Holi

Drawing with patches of slight color. Pahari, Kangra, ca.
1790, 19 × 27.4 cm. Somewhat darkened by dirt.

Purchase, Edward L. Whittemore Fund

Ex collection: Coomaraswamy.

Published: A. K. Coomaraswamy, *Indian Drawings*,
2 vols. (London, 1910–12), 2: pl. XII.

Comparative Material: (A) *Dressing Krishna in Woman's
Clothes for Holi*, Pahari, Kangra, ca. 1785; *Chhavi Jubilee
Volume*, color pl. 5; or Khandalavala, 1958, color pl. 9.

This drawing is a slightly later version of a composition that
occurs in a completed Kangra painting (A). The drawing,
like others from the state, bears notations of the colors to be
applied and has a few preliminary test patches of color.
Themes connected with the popular celebration of Holi are
frequently depicted in Kangra, but in this drawing the subject is more complex than the usual spraying of colored
water or powder for the festival. Holi is a time for rule

breaking, role change, and mischievous pranks. One of the
occurrences that accords with the spirit of the day is Radha
and Krishna's exchange of garments.

In the Cleveland drawing and in comparison A, Krishna
is in the center of the composition, being dressed by the
gopis while Radha holds his crown. Only Krishna has put on
other clothes, but the idea of role exchange is the implied
theme. The rigid social lines of division between the sexes
as well as many other aspects of tradition-bound authority
are confounded in the Krishna worship (*bhakti*) symbolically perceived as the union of Radha, the devotee, and the
god: "The exchange of clothes is merely another manifestation of the lover's sporting . . . and of the intricacy and
intimacy of their identification with each other. In the final
analysis, there can be no distinction between the divine
power which reveals itself in earthly form, and the earthly
form which discovers its inner and ultimate divinity."[1]

1. Spink, p. 87.

Figure 125.

126 *Hindola Raga* 75.9

Pahari, Kangra, ca. 1790–1800, 20.5 × 15.3 cm. Cropped; fragment of red border remains on left side.

Purchase, Edward L. Whittemore Fund

Comparative Material: (A) *Hindola Raga*, Pahari, Kangra, ca. 1790–1800; Randhawa, 1971, pl. VI.

This scene is an unusually joyous version of *Hindola Raga* combined with the Krishna/Radha theme. The spring setting characteristic of the *raga* is accentuated by the yellow background and by the flowering trees along the horizon. Similar arrangements of trees are also found in other Kangra *ragamala* scenes picturing the spring season; such settings apparently symbolize an enclosed, ideal world of beauty and playfulness.

Although the compositions used in Pahari *ragamalas* deviate from the Rajasthani type, *hindol*, meaning "a swing,"

is universally illustrated with this romantic accessory. The iconography is the only one that remains the same in each area where *ragamalas* were produced.[1] Since it is a male melody, however, in the Pahari area *Hindola Raga* is often pictured as a man swinging alone and surrounded by only a few women (A).[2] The Cleveland miniature instead shows a united couple, the more usual subject for Hindola as painted in Rajasthan. The group of male and female musicians in this scene is larger than in other Hindola illustrations and indicates that the artist wished to evoke the idea of universal celebration and festivity. The Kangra style is fresh, simple, and restrained, lacking the mannerisms or exaggerations characteristic of later decades.

1. Ebeling, p. 273.
2. See Ebeling, no. 300, for a similar composition in an earlier Pahari painting.

Figure 126.

127 *Radha's Hair Being Dressed* 69.35

Drawing with touch of red ochre for mirror image. Pahari, Kangra, ca. 1790–1800, 25 × 17 cm (oval), 29.7 × 20.3 cm overall. Oval drawn on plain paper; border also drawn. Torn in several areas; disintegrated around three edges. Partial inscription in lower left no longer legible.

Purchase, Edward L. Whittemore Fund

Published (repr. only): V. C. Ohri, ed., *Arts of Himachal* (Simla: State Museum, 1975), fig. 59.

This drawing, like [129], shows the toilette of Radha, who holds a mirror while some of her attendants raise a cloth to screen her as Krishna overlooks the scene. Krishna's heavy face is treated in a similar manner in both works.

The oval format is charmingly echoed by the artist throughout his composition. A small repetition of the shape is presented at an angle by the mirror. Curved segments of an oval are then created by the women's bending bodies, their veils, and the line of the fan—all of which unify the design. Such contrivance—one of the distinguishing features of the Kangra style—can perhaps be seen more clearly in drawings like this one than in finished works.

Figure 127.

299

128 *Utka Nayika*   32.118

Pahari, Kangra, ca. 1800, 16 × 10.2 cm (oval),
23.8 × 14.8 cm with border. Oval set in white rectangle
surrounded by red border.

Purchase, Edward L. Whittemore Fund

Ex collection: Heeramaneck.

This woman is one of several among the eight classifications
of *nayikas* (heroines) who go out to meet lovers and suffer
fear, disappointment, or frustration, The *nayikas'* actions
and consequent emotional states are intensified by the traditional social background of female dependency and re-
striction; the subject therefore constitutes an important
dramatic theme in Indian painting.

Utka Nayika is a heroine whose lover fails to meet her in
the forest and who consequently undergoes much mental
turmoil during her vigil. Generally she is shown, as in this
miniature, sitting or standing on a bed of leaves that she has
prepared for the assignation. The composition used here
was often employed by both Guler and Kangra artists.[1]

1. W. G. Archer, 1973, 2: 107, Guler no. 30; Randhawa, 1962,
fig. 34.

Figure 128.

129 *Toilette of Radha*　　　　　　　　　　53.245

Pahari, Kangra, ca. 1810–20, 21.1 × 14.5 cm,
24.8 × 18.3 cm with borders. Dark blue floral inner
surround, white outer border.

Purchase, Edward L. Whittemore Fund

Ex collection: Heermaneck.

Published: Randhawa, 1962, fig. 49.

Comparative Material: (A) *Radha*, Pahari, Guler, ca.
1790; Randhawa, 1962, pl. X. (B) *Radha*, Pahari, Guler,
ca. 1810–20; Gangoly, 1926, pl. 38, or W. G. Archer, 1973,
2: 118, Guler no. 68. (C) *Radha*, Pahari, Kangra, ca. 1790;
Khandalavala, 1958, no. 205.

Miniatures A through C are among the many Guler/Kangra
compositions that show Radha bathing, dressing, or being
ornamented. In each of the comparative examples, Radha,
surrounded by maids, gazes at herself in a mirror. The
attraction of each scene lies in its intimacy and informality
as well as in Radha's youthful enjoyment of her own beauty,
here observed by Krishna from an upper window.

The decorative, detailed treatments of clothing and jewelry place this miniature in the early nineteenth century.
The Kangra style is more graphic and less suggestive than
it had been about 1790. Such features as the hemline folds
of saris are now exaggerated in an abstract manner for the
interest inherent in the jagged lines. In addition, a flatness
and conventionalization are apparent in certain figures,
such as that of the woman holding the peacock fan.

Figure 129.

130 *Scenes from the Birth of Krishna*   53.13

Pahari, Kangra, ca. 1840, 25.1 × 34 cm, 29.9 × 38.5 cm
with border. Paint scraped and flaked. Text on reverse.
Gray inner border, pink outer border.

Purchase, Edward L. Whittemore Fund

Ex collection: Heeramaneck.

On the left side of this painting Krishna appears to his
mother at the time of his birth seated on a lotus in his
complete godlike form. The other areas of the painting sum-
marize the exchange of infants that took place to protect the
newborn Krishna from his uncle, the demon Kamsa, eagerly waiting to kill the child prophesied to destroy him. Krishna was carried by his father to the nearby village of Gokula
and substituted for the baby girl born to Yasoda, who thus
became Krishna's foster mother. The composition with
bright colors and flowery patterns contrasted by areas of
white is characteristic of late Pahari painting, as are the
figure and facial types.

Figure 130.

seen from a small remnant of white that once ran along the right side of this page, the picture has been cut down and may have once included a shrine or something similar beside Man Dhata.

Figure 134, detail.

1. S. H. Levitt has written an article on the Cleveland miniature soon to be published in *Lalit Kala*.

2. See also W. G. Archer, 1973, 2: 303, Nurpur no. 6; Khandalavala, 1958, no. 18.

3. W. G. Archer, 1973, 1: 383. K. C. Aryan and B. N. Goswamy, *Marg* XVII (1964): 3, pp. 61–62, believe the paintings are from Daya Dhata's reign or later.

4. W. G. Archer, 1973, 2: 310, Nurpur no. 17(i).

5. A. Mookerjee, *Tantra Asana* (Basel: Ravi Shamar, 1971), pl. 3; idem, *Tantra Magic* (New Delhi: Sanskriti in ass'n with Arnold-Heinemann Publishers, 1977), pl. 4.

6. W. G. Archer, 1973, 2: 311, Nurpur no. 18, or 2: 310, Nurpur no. 17(i).

Figure 134.

135 *Durga Slaying Mahisha*   60.51

Pahari, Nurpur, ca. 1700–1710, 15.5 × 21.2 cm. Slight staining and rubbing; cropped on all sides, but fragment of top border remains.

Purchase, Mr. and Mrs. William H. Marlatt Fund

Ex collection: Heeramaneck.

Published: Lee, 1960, no.66.

Comparative Material: (A) *Durga Slaying Mahisha,* Pahari, Nurpur, ca. 1760; W. G. Archer, 1973, 2: 316, Nurpur no. 35, or 1952, no. 67.

In general, paintings of the Pahari school are characterized by strong rhythmic patterns, and miniatures of Durga killing the buffalo demon Mahisasura are often essays in vital-istic movement produced by the complex interlocking forms. Mahisasura, who defies the authority of the gods and is swollen with pride, represents a blockage in the creative cycle, and his extermination signals a return to the correct balance or flow of events. Thus the very bloody scene is treated with an abandon that reflects the joy inherent in a destruction that is liberating. Durga's tiger leaps forward exuberantly with claws and tongue extended as the two figures with outstretched arms rise into the air like colliding spheres to fight their cosmic battle.

The scene is done in a slightly rough, very direct Pahari style close to that of the previous entry depicting Man Dhata of Nurpur. The artists of Man Dhata and Daya Dhata's ateliers worked with bold abstract shapes, but this

Figure 135.

Figure 135(A). *Durga Slaying Mahisha.*
Victoria & Albert Museum, London.

painter is unusually free, with rapid brush movements epitomized by the swirls of blood flowing from Mahisha's head. His figures give the impression of bursting from the constraining limits of the picture frame, and his sweeping rhythms used to define the two animals are uncommonly powerful. The composition is like that of a later miniature from Nurpur (A, illus.) that also shows the true form of the demon—exposed by Durga's ferocity—rising above the buffalo shape he had assumed and grasping his shield to withstand the goddess's attack on his fully revealed manifestation of evil.

Figure 135, detail.

Figure 135, detail.

Figure 136.

Leaf from a *Rasamanjari*, Pahari, Nurpur, ca. 1710, 17 × 26.8 cm, 20.5 × 28.2 cm with border. Inscription on reverse, with title of verse in Takri—"Madhya Svadhina-patika"—followed by Sanskrit verse and prose summary in Sarada script—"Although I refuse his amorous advances and do not yield myself, my sweetheart continues to attend me. What shall I do, O companion?" [numbered *70* though this is verse *71*].

Gift of Dr. and Mrs. Sherman E. Lee

Published: V. Dwivedi, 1969, fig. 3.

Comparative Material: (A) *The Heroine Who Is Faithfully Loved*, leaf from a *Rasamanjari*, Pahari, Basohli, 1695; Randhawa and Bhambri, fig. 48. (B) *The Confidante Speaks to the Lover*, leaf from a *Rasamanjari*, Pahari, Nurpur, ca. 1710; Barrett and Gray, p. 168. (C) *The Mistress Fears Separation*, leaf from a *Rasamanjari*, Pahari, Nurpur, ca. 1710; Randhawa and Bhambri, no. 57. (D) *The Sarcastic Mistress*, leaf from a *Rasamanjari*, Pahari, Nurpur, ca. 1710; W. G. Archer, 1973, 2: 307, Nurpur no. 14(i), or 1976, no. 72. (E) *The Remorseful Mistress*, leaf from a *Rasamanjari*, Pahari, Nurpur, ca. 1710; W. G. Archer, 1973, 2: 307, Nurpur no. 14(ii), or Randhawa and Bhambri, no. 19. (F) *The Lover Listens*, leaf from a *Rasamanjari*, Pahari, Nurpur, ca. 1710; K. Khandalavala and M. Chandra, "The *Rasamanjari* in Basohli Painting," *LK*, no. 3-4 (1956/57), fig. 9.

The Nurpur *Rasamanjari* is an important series that serves as a bridge between early Pahari styles and those with more naturalistic elements. The Nurpur painters seem to have had associations with both the Basohli/Mankot school and Guler, although the exact nature of the relationship is difficult to document. It looks as if Nurpur painters absorbed elements of the Basohli style, evolving new ideas about design in the process of assimilation, which they then passed on to artists of Guler. The correlation between the style of the Nurpur *Rasamanjari* and that of the crucial Guler *Siege of Lanka* series is very apparent (see [113]).

The importance that is accorded to Basholi painters by scholars has unfortunately overshadowed the considerable significance that the Nurpur style must have had for other Pahari artists in the early seventeenth century. Although the Basohli painters had evolved a remarkably expressive style, they were restricted to its conventions; whereas the Nurpur painters were aware of the most interesting developments in their native area as well as being familiar with a variety of Mughal miniatures. Their free-ranging imaginations assimilated features of Basohli or Mankot painting with Mughal naturalism in ways that inspired other artists.

The number of paintings produced in Nurpur during the late seventeenth- and early eighteenth-century reigns of Man Dhata and his son Daya Dhata was considerable. Both rajas were interested patrons, and their painters can be seen to have grown increasingly capable during the course of their reigns. The Mughal-influenced but folkish style persistent in Man Dhata's era was made more tense and elegant during Daya Dhata's. Although the cleaner, more cohesive compositions may have been initiated by contact with Basohli, the Nurpur style—quieter and more geometrically structured—should be recognized as completely distinct.

The logical source of new ideas brought from Basohli is the Nurpur painter Devidasa, who in 1695 illustrated the last of three successive *Rasamanjari* manuscripts done in that state. The Nurpur *Rasamanjari* illustrations have compositions similar to those employed in the three previous Basohli *Rasamanjari* manuscripts, wherein blocks of architecture break a horizontal format. The Nurpur landscapes with miniature trees and limited space are much like those in the first Basohli *Rasamanjari*. In the Nurpur miniatures, patterns are much less explosive than in this Basohli *Rasamanjari*, but the treatment of rugs and architectural ornament has some relationship. However, Devidasa's style, childlike and somewhat weak, seems unrelated to either the previous Basohli paintings or to the Nurpur conventions that evolved after 1695;[1] it is possible that Devidasa was only the catalyst for change and that he brought back miniatures done by Basohli artists, or that stylizations he had learned in that state were given new vitality by others—probably by one superior painter who was then imitated. Since sketches and techniques were passed down through families, this artist may have been Devidasa's son Golu, whose reputation as a great painter is recorded, but who has not been connected with specific miniatures.[2]

One of the most notable characteristics of the Nurpur *Rasamanjari* is the depiction of its heroes with portrait heads resembling Raja Daya Dhata. This type of substitution had already been employed in one of the Basohli *Rasamanjaris*, and the idea could have been adopted by Nurpur painters.[3] Overly large heads placed on conventionalized *nayaka* bodies are done in many ways throughout the Nurpur mansucript; other miniatures (D, E, and F) in comparison with the Cleveland leaf show some of the possible variations.

From the evidence of the male portraits, it is clear that several artists contributed to the Nurpur *Rasamanjari*; these painters varied in their skills of drawing naturalistic males, but in general they could create similar patterned compositional arrangements and stylized female figures. Since the *nayaka's* profile seems to have been the least familiar part of the formula on which the *Rasamanjari* illustrations are based, it is an element likely to reveal the various artistic hands. A confident blend of portraiture and stylization is found in the Cleveland miniature as well as certain other leaves (B, C) that seem to have been done by the main artist (Golu?). This man's drawing is the most refined, his gestures are the most expressive, and his women are particularly complex, enigmatic types. The other miniatures indicate probably about three assistants or secondary artists.

The style evolved by the master artist was so successful that it played an important role in the transformation of Pahari painting that occurred in Guler. In particular, the combination of abstraction, lyricism, and monumentality in this Nurpur series contributes much to the developments in the large Guler *Siege of Lanka* set (see [113]).

The Nurpur *Rasamanjari* series is one of the most effectively contrived essays on geometry in Indian painting.[4] The Cleveland miniature, typical of the manuscript's pavilion scenes, reveals the master designer's fascination in working with unbroken contours. Like a skater gliding as long as possible on the ice, this artist stretches and lengthens lines, whether in architecture, eyes, arms, or the hero's *jama*. The abstract shapes, formulated to appear precise or pure, emphasize geometric contrasts between curves and rectangles—as demonstrated by the treatment of the pavilion wall in this leaf. While within the first Basohli *Rasamanjari* empty space exists to stress tightly packed spatial compartments, the Nurpur *Rasamanjari* reflects a more harmoniously balanced flow between sparseness and decoration. Its atmosphere is one of thought and order rather than smoldering emotionality.

Throughout the Nurpur *Rasamanjari*, colors are as subtly juxtaposed as are lines and shapes. Clearly planned in a conscious manner by the artist, color in this miniature is surprising and original. The tones of Delft blue, bright yellow, and pale chocolate are contrasted with the red border, red objects, and multi-colored rug. The use of brown with primary colors subdues them and alters their relationships in interesting ways. The transparent blue veils demonstrate the effects of one color pulled across other hues—an experiment that reveals the level of artistic skill and complexity reached by this painter.

While most of the women in the *Rasamanjari* and other works of the type must cope with infidelity or desertion, the heroine in this miniature is in the fortunate position of being loved faithfully and attentively. As the hero approaches, twisting his scarf nervously as if his intense feelings had made him diffident, the heroine with her hand outstretched explains his attitude to her *sakhi*. Since she has modestly refused to yield, and yet her would-be lover continues to press his suit, the young, inexperienced girl has decided to ask her companion what her next move should be.

A similar composition of two women kneeling in a pavilion is used for the earlier Basohli *Rasamanjari* illustration of the same subject (A), although in this case Krishna acts as the hero and stands on the left already within the room. Both the position of the hero and the expressions of the three characters in the Nurpur scene are more intelligently related to the text and show a clearer grasp of narrative progression that seems to be characteristic of this *Rasamanjari* in general.

1. W. G. Archer, 1973, 2: 29–30.
2. Ibid., 1: 395.
3. Ibid., 2: 26, Basohli no. 10(ii); the huge, bearded head is obviously intended as a portrait.
4. See Randhawa and Bhambri, p. 5, and W. G. Archer, 1973, 1: 395, for a list of collections in which these miniatures are found.

FURTHER READING: Randhawa and Bhambri.

137 *Sugriva Challenges Bali* 73.103

Leaf from a *Ramayana*, Pahari, Nurpur, ca. 1720, 16.4 × 26.8 cm, 20.7 × 31 cm with border. Text on reverse (illus.). Red border.
Purchase from the J. H. Wade Fund

Published (repr. only): J. Jain-Neubauer, *The Ramayana in Pahari Miniature Painting* (Ahmedabad: L. D. Institute of Indology, 1981), fig. 11.
Comparative Material: (A) *The Funeral of Bali*, leaf from a *Ramayana*, Pahari, Nurpur, ca. 1720; *Sotheby*, 11 Dec. 1973, lot. 353. (B) *The Funeral of Bali*, leaf from a *Ramayana*, Pahari, Nurpur, ca. 1720; *Sotheby*, 11 Dec. 1973, lot 282. (C) *The Monkeys in the Enchanted Cave*, leaf from a *Ramayana*, Pahari, Nurpur, ca. 1720; W. G. Archer, 1976, no. 65. (D) *Conference between the Monkeys and the Bear King*, leaf from a *Ramayana*, Pahari, Nurpur, ca. 1720; Pal, 1976, no. 4. (E) *The Monkeys and Bears Meet Sampati*, leaf from a *Ramayana*, Pahari, Nurpur, ca. 1720; Spink and Son, no. 163. (F) *Sampati Tells the Monkeys of Sita's Whereabouts*, leaf from a *Ramayana*, Pahari, Nurpur, ca. 1720; W. G. Archer, 1976, no. 66. (G) *The Monkeys Carry Sampati*, leaf from a *Ramayana*, Pahari, Nurpur, ca. 1720; *OA 20*, no. 2 (1974): 130. (H) *Rama's Alliance with Sugriva*, leaf from a *Ramayana*, Pahari, Nurpur, ca. 1720; *Christie*, 6 July 1978, lot. 77. (I) *The Monkeys in the Garden*, leaf from a *Ramayana*, Pahari, Nurpur, ca. 1720; Leach, 1982, no. 390.

This scene from a Pahari *Ramayana* here attributed to Nurpur depicts Sugriva challenging his brother Bali to their tragic fight as Rama, Laksmana, and Hanuman look on.[1] Like the other miniatures of the series (A–I), the event is from the *Kishkindakanda* book of the *Ramayana* and portrays episodes from Rama's association with the monkeys. The many scenes of Bali and Sugriva's quarrel and the monkey's adventures in their search for the abducted Sita show that the set was extensively illustrated, but the beginning and ending portions of the story such as Rama's exile or his final fight with Ravana have apparently been lost or destroyed. The series is known from about thirty to forty scattered leaves, including the published references listed above as well as other examples mainly in private collections.[2]

When W. G. Archer published his two-volume Pahari work, the series had not yet been discovered, but the attribution of this group to Nurpur rests mainly on the comparison of human figures with those from the period of the Nurpur raja Daya Dhata. Daya Dhata (r. ca. 1700–1735) succeeded his father when about twenty and molded the developing atelier in his state into a more sophisticated artist group. When he was young he favored romantic depictions of both himself and his soulful mistresses, and the facial type thus developed persisted throughout the reign. Although this *Ramayana* set (which has proven difficult to classify because of its simple compositions and monkey figures) has also been attributed to Mankot, the human types correspond well with those having square heads and long,

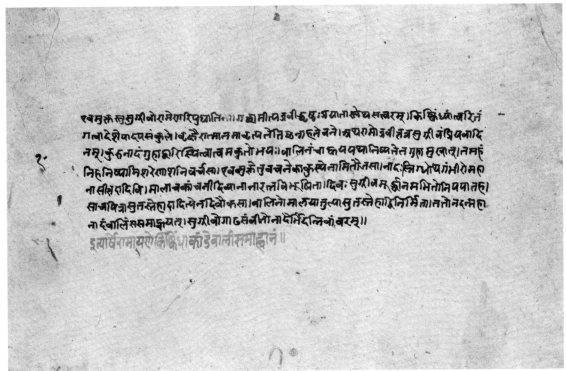

Figure 137, reverse.

Figure 137, obverse.

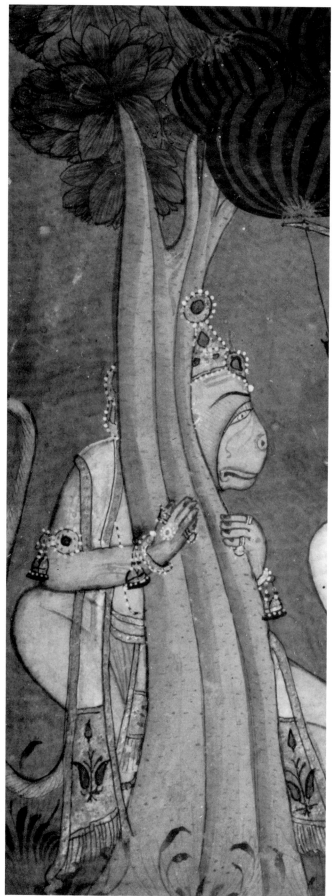

heavy-lidded eyes from Nurpur (cf. the women in A and B).

A slightly later *Ramayana* also attributable to Nurpur has similar figures and was produced by related but different artists who conveyed somewhat more complex views of space and depicted the monkey army with other conventions.[3] By contrast, the artists of the *Ramayana* to which the Cleveland leaf belongs generally portray the monkeys standing in upright poses with near-human proportions, hands, and even facial features, while their consorts are fully human. The master painter of this latter manuscript must therefore have been from another studio, but he was clearly trained to use certain Nurpur conventions.

The most distinctive feature of this earlier set is its restricted orange and olive green color scheme. Unlike Mankot artists who used mainly red, yellow, and blue, the Nurpur artists employed varied colors; but they did not usually work with these particular hues or with such a limited palette. It is surprising to find so many miniatures of a Pahari manuscript with such a repetitive color range. Natural conventions in the *Ramayana* scenes—like those of the flowerlike trees—are common in early eighteenth-century painting, but the sky, executed in loose scrolls of blue wash, is rare in the entire Pahari area and only occasionally is found in other Nurpur pictures.[4]

1. The text on the reverse of the miniature follows H. P. Sastri, trans., *The Ramayana of Valmiki*, 3 vols. (London: Shanti Sadan, 1952–59), 2: 195. The complete, tangled story of the animosity between Bali and Sugriva begins with Bali's entrapment in a cave. Sugriva, who waits at its mouth for a year, is convinced his brother is dead; he thus returns and assumes both Bali's kingship and wife, Tara. When Bali returns, he is enraged and exiles Sugriva and usurps his wife Ruma. Sugriva, knowing himself to be the weaker of the two brothers, narrates his story to Rama and enlists Rama's help to overcome Bali with a ruse in return for help in locating Sita—an unusual portion of the tale that is rationalized to maintain Rama's moral reputation.

2. References to some unpublished leaves are given in Pal, 1976, no. 4. Additional leaves are found in collections such as that of J. P. Goenka, Bombay.

3. Archer, 1973, 2: 310, Nurpur no. 17(ii).

4. Ibid., 312, Nurpur no. 22.

Figure 137, obverse, detail.

138 *Portrait of Raja Gulab Singh* 25.1338
of Jammu (?)

Sikh, ca. 1830–40, 19.8 × 13.8 cm. Slightly scraped.
Gift from J. H. Wade
Ex collection: Coomaraswamy.
Comparative Material: (A) *Raja Gulab Singh of Jammu,*
Sikh, ca. 1840–50; W. G. Archer, 1966, no. 34.

By the end of the seventeenth century, because the Sikh religious sect had become a fairly powerful organized movement, it came into conflict with the Mughal court. Persecution brought about the militancy and separatism that eventually forced the sect to concentrate its headquarters in the Punjab—an area that had relative freedom from Mughal interference. With the eighteenth-century disintegration of Mughal power and the strong leadership of

Ranjit Singh (1780–1837), the Sikhs emerged as a major power in the Pahari hill states as well as in the plains of the Punjab.

A majority of Sikh portraits, like this one, are equestrian scenes demonstrating the military prowess of leaders. This raja is posed in typical fashion under a tasseled umbrella that denotes his status. He and his attendants wear a characteristic type of Sikh turban. The raja portrayed may be Gulab Singh of Jammu (1792–1857), who was depicted numerous times in different conventionalized styles and is therefore difficult to identify.[1] The popularity of this leader's image, however, contributes to the likelihood of the identification. Gulab Singh was the heir of Ranjit Singh's power and a military hero greatly revered by the Sikhs.

This portrayal is an unusually active one: many Sikh paintings are done in a constrained, stylized manner that

Figure 138.

indicates lack of confidence in draftsmanship. Horses often have spidery legs and overly small heads. In this miniature, however, the full-bodied energetic horse springs forward and is hardly contained by the painting's border.

1. W. G. Archer, 1966, pp. 52–56.

FURTHER READING: Aijazuddin, 1977; W. G. Archer, 1966.

139 *Portrait of a Seated Man* 68.43

Drawing, Sikh, ca. 1830–50, 18.4 × 14.6 cm. Drawing has been altered so that other hand and foot positions are visible.

Purchase, Edward L. Whittemore Fund

The Sikhs were not noted for refined or decorative paintings, but their pragmatism and integrity found an outlet in certain portrait-sketches that are among the most original Sikh miniatures. Portraits of well-known leaders tend to be stereotyped, whereas casual sketches of less important subjects can be very poignant, like this drawing of a seated man. Like others depicted in this simple manner, he is probably a figure noted for religious piety.

The intensity of the subject's face is heightened by the fragility of his characteristically tubular body. As in many Sikh portraits, attention is centered on the head, while hands and feet are tiny and limbs are emaciated. Despite some desire for naturalistic effects, the Sikh artists were not trained in either draftsmanship or figure drawing—as can be seen by the alterations made for this portrait.

Figure 139.

Glossary

Anjali—the typical Hindu greeting and accordance of honor with joined palms upraised.

Asana—a position or posture, usually used in reference to yoga; the most common yogic pose is the so-called lotus, or *padma asana*.

Asoka (tree)—(*Saraca indica*) a tree revered by Buddhists but also important in Hinduism; because of Sita's confinement in the *asoka* grove, the species acquired the significance of constancy and purity.

Asura—a titan, an enemy of the gods; from the late Vedic period, a demon.

Avatar—one of ten incarnations of Vishnu that preserve world order in different aeons.

Bhakta—a Hindu devotee.

Bhakti—devotion or emotional worship as opposed to knowledge of scripture, yogic discipline, etc.; the medieval *bhakti* cults were centered on Vishnu's *avatars*, Krishna or Rama.

Bhandar—a library; (plural) the scriptural repositories formed by the Jains to preserve religious texts.

Bhang—(*Cannabis sativa*) a drug prepared for smoking or in a drink; often used by members of religious cults.

Braj Bhasha—the dialect used notably by the medieval Krishna poets whose center was at Mathura.

Cakra—a wheel, a sun symbol, Vishnu's discus; when applied to the human body the word refers to six circles running up the spinal cord believed to be centers of power.

Chakdar jama—a long-sleeved tunic, but in the style of the early Mughal period, with four long points on the hem.

Chauri—a flywhisk, commonly made of horse hair.

Chenar—a plane tree.

Choli—a short bodice worn by Hindu women.

Darshan—the ceremony of viewing an important person; the Mughal emperors had daily *darshans* in which they appeared to the populace from a palace window.

Devanagari—the script used for writing Sanskrit and Prakrit as well as contemporary Hindi and Marathi.

Dhoti—the lower garment of Hindu males, consisting of a piece of cloth draped around the body and between the legs.

Durbar—an audience of the emperor and his nobles or of a raja and retainers generally held in a hall especially built for the purpose.

Firman—an imperial decree.

Gopa—a cowherd-boy; the boys associated with Krishna in his youth.

Gopi—a cowherd girl, a milkmaid; the *gopis* are the village girls enamored of Krishna, of whom Radha is the chief personality.

Hamsa—a goose; the *hamsa* has various roles in literature and mythology, including its use as vehicle for the god Brahma.

Holi—the Hindu festival of spring.

Jali—a pierced window screen.

Jama—a long-sleeved tunic, with the skirt varying from thigh to ankle length during the seventeenth and eighteenth centuries; the *jama*, which was typical court dress, fastened on the left side for Hindus and on the right for Muslims.

Jauhar—the death of members of a Rajput clan in the face of defeat; the men died in battle and women immolated themselves.

Jina—"conqueror"; one of the Jain *tirthankaras* who has succeeded in working out of reincarnation.

Kanphat—a yogic follower of Gorakhnath, recognizable by large round earrings.

Karkhana—factory, workshop, studio; includes painting ateliers.

Katar—a wedge-shaped Rajput dagger.

Kayotsarga—the standing posture for meditation prescribed for Jain monks, with the arms at the sides of the body.

Ksatriya—the warrior caste; this class included royal families and their aristocratic branches.

Kuladhar (turban)—a turban wound around a *kullah*, or cap, to varying heights; it is the distinguishing headgear of pre-Mughal paintings.

Lila—"sport"; used to describe the activity of a god during phases of creation; used also to characterize Krishna's acts as a cowherd and Rama's conquest of the demon king, Ravana.

Mahout—an elephant tamer and handler.

Mansabdar—a basic class of Mughal official who was graded in a standard military ranking but who might have civil or ceremonial court duties.

Mantra—a word or formula repeated because of its supposed supernatural power.

Mudra—a hand gesture, part of a sign language important in religious worship, drama, dance, sculpture, and painting.

Mujaddid—a reformer or redeemer prophesied by Islam.

Mullah—a Muslim elder or pious man.

Muraqqa—an album consisting of calligraphy and/or painting.

Naga—a serpent; the subject of veneration and cult worship in India from ancient times.

317

Nasta'liq—a cursive script used for writing Persian.

Nawab—a Muslim ruler of a princely state during the late Mughal and British periods; the most powerful *nawab*, really a king, was that of Oudh.

Nayaka—a hero.

Nayika—a heroine in love who is classified in one of eight ways according to her aggressive actions or her situation.

Nilgai—(*Boselaphus tragocamelus*), the so-called blue bull; an antelope found only in India which inhabits dry, deciduous, thorny jungle country.

Nim qalam—partial coloration of a drawing.

Odhni—a veil worn by Hindu women, often of transparent muslin.

Om—a sacred syllable; used from early times as a religious formula and incantation because its reverberative sound suggested omnipresence and omnipotence.

Padshah—emperor.

Pan—a betel leaf with pieces of areca nut, lime, and often other substances rolled in it for chewing.

Parakiya—"one belonging to another"; secret romance with one already married, common because of arranged weddings.

Patka—a sash worn over the *jama*, often with expensive, highly decorative borders.

Patua—a Bengali folk-painter.

Pechwai—a cloth that hangs behind the image in a shrine of Vallabhacharya's sect.

Pietra dura—inlay; in India the classic period of *pietra dura* work was the Shah Jahan era when floral patterns were set in marble architecture and were also used for many small decorative objects.

Prana—vital breath; in Indian sculpture the plasticity of *prana* is far more significant than musculature.

Puja—worship in which offerings such as flowers, fruit, and other food are made to a divinity.

Purana—a scriptural account of creational and other mythology often recorded from the oral tradition; although the *puranas* are supposed to be ancient and many in fact date back to the period of AD 300–500, the composition of *puranas* went on until roughly AD 1500.

Purdah—the Islamic practice of cloistering women, also adopted by many Hindus.

Pushti marg—the doctrine of the Vallabhacharya sect of Krishna worshippers that salvation comes through grace, pleasure, and joy.

Raga—a melody personified as a male, commonly one of six in a *ragamala* presiding over six female melodies.

Ragamala—a musical, poetic series generally made up of thirty-six modes, each personifying some facet of love.

Ragini—a female melody classified with others in a *ragamala* under a male heading.

Rasa—sap, essence, flavor; *rasas* are the basis of Hindu aesthetic theory, since drama, poetry, and painitng are organized around the fluctuation and interplay of moods, or flavors.

Sakhi—a female companion, a confidante.

Siddha—"a liberated one"; in Jain belief, one who has succeeded in working out of reincarnation.

Thikana—fief, a small territory.

Tirthankara—"ford-maker"; one of the twenty-four Jain saints who have shown the way out of reincarnation through example.

Trisula—a trident, the emblem of Shiva.

Ulama—the Islamic orthodoxy; Muslims who interpreted the doctrines of the faith, including those associated with jurisprudence, and often created a political role for themselves.

Vasli—the decorative border of a calligraphic or illustrated page in an album.

Vina—a stringed musical instrument with two gourd-resonators.

Wazir—a prime minister.

Yaksa—a type of male vegetational deity originating in the pre-Vedic period; the female counterpart is the *yaksi*.

Yogi—a male ascetic, a practitioner of yoga.

Yogini—a female ascetic.

Zamindar—the function of the *zamindars* varied throughout the Mughal and British periods from hereditary landowning to tax collection, but they continued to be powerful local officials.

Zenana—female apartments.

Select Bibliography

Abbreviations

AA	*Artibus Asiae*
AARP	*Art and Archaeology Research Papers*
Arc	*Archives of Asian Art*
ArsO	*Ars Orientalis*
ArtsA	*Arts Asiatiques*
BMQ	*British Museum Quarterly*
BPWM	*Bulletin of the Prince of Wales Museum, Bombay*
Christie	Sales of Oriental Miniatures and Manuscripts from Christie, Manson, and Woods
CMAB	*Bulletin of The Cleveland Museum of Art*
IC	*Islamic Culture*
JISOA	*Journal of the Indian Society of Oriental Art*
JPHS	*Journal of the Pakistan Historical Society*
LK	*Lalit Kala*
MFAB	*Bulletin of The Museum of Fine Arts, Boston*
OA	*Oriental Art*
RAA	*Revue des Arts Asiatiques*
RL	*Roopa-Lekha*
Sotheby	Sales of Oriental Miniatures and Manuscripts from Sotheby and Co., London
Tooth	Catalogues of Indian Paintings from Arthur Tooth and Sons

Abu'l Fazl. 1927–49. *Ain-i-Akbari*. Translated by H. Blochmann and H. S. Jarrett. 2nd ed. 3 vols. Calcutta: Royal Asiatic Society of Bengal.

Abu'l Fazl. 1907. *Akbar Nama*. Translated by H. Blochmann. Calcutta.

Aijazuddin, F. S. 1971. "The Basohli *Gita Govinda* Set of 1730 A.D.—A Reconstruction." *RL* 41, nos. 1 & 2: 7–34.

Aijazuddin 1977. *Pahari Paintings and Sikh Portraits in the Lahore Museum*. London: Sotheby Parke Bernet.

Alvi, M. A., and Rahman, A. 1968. *Jahangir, The Naturalist*. New Delhi: National Institute of Sciences of India.

Andhare, S. K. 1967. "Painting from the Thikana of Deogarh." *BPWM* 10: 43–53.

Ansari, M. 1957. "Dress of the Great Mughals." *IC* 31: 255–67.

Ansari 1960. "Harem of the Great Mughals." *IC* 34: 107–24.

Archer, M. 1972. *Company Drawings in the India Office Library*. London: Her Majesty's Stationery Office.

Archer, M., and Archer, W. G. 1955. *Indian Painting for the British*. Oxford: Oxford University Press.

Archer, W. G. 1951. "The Problems of Bikaner Paintings." *Marg* 5, no. 1: 9–16.

Archer, W. G. 1952. *Indian Painting in the Punjab Hills*. London: Her Majesty's Stationery Office.

Archer, W. G. 1957*a*. *Indian Paintings from Rajasthan* (The Kanoria Collection). London: Arts Council of Great Britain.

Archer, W. G. 1957*b*. *Loves of Krishna*. London: George Allen and Unwin.

Archer, W. G. 1958. *Central Indian Painting*. London: Faber and Faber.

Archer, W. G. 1959. *Indian Painting in Bundi and Kotah*. London: Victoria and Albert Museum.

Archer, W. G. 1960. *Indian Miniatures*. New York: New York Graphic Society.

Archer, W. G. 1966. *Paintings of the Sikhs*. London: Victoria and Albert Museum.

Archer, W. G. 1973. *Indian Paintings from the Punjab Hills*. 2 vols. London & New York: Sotheby Parke Bernet.

Archer, W. G. 1976. *Visions of Courtly India*. Washington, D.C.: International Exhibitions Foundation.

Archer, W. G., and Binney, E., 3rd. 1968. *Rajput Miniatures from the Collection of Edwin Binney, 3rd*. Portland, Oregon: Portland Art Museum.

Arnold, Sir T. W., and Grohmann, A. 1929. *The Islamic Book*. Paris: Pegasus Press.

Arnold, Sir T. W., and Wilkinson, J. V. S. 1936. *The Library of A. Chester Beatty, A Catalogue of the Indian Miniatures*. 3 vols. London: Private printing at Oxford University Press.

Babur [Babar], Emperor of Hindustan (1483–1530). 1922. *Babarnamah in English*. Translated by A. S. Beveridge. London: Luzac & Co.

Badauni, A. 1884–1925. *Muntakhabu t-tawarikh*. Translated by W. H. Lowe, et al. 3 vols. Calcutta.

Banerji, A. 1956/57. "Illustrations to the *Rasikapriya* from Bundi-Kotah." *LK* no. 3/4: 67ff.

Barrett, D., and Gray, B. 1963. *Painting of India*. Lausanne: Skira.

Beach, M. C. 1965a. "A *Bhagavata Purana* from the Punjab Hills and Related Paintings." *MFAB* 63, no. 333: 168–77.

Beach. 1965b. "The Gulshan Album and Its European Sources." *MFAB* 63: 62–91.

Beach. 1966. "Rajput and Related Paintings." In *The Arts of India and Nepal: The Alice and Nasli Heeramaneck Collection*. Boston: Museum of Fine Arts.

Beach. 1970/71. "Painting at Devgarh." *Arc* no. 24: 23–35.

Beach. 1974. *Rajput Painting at Bundi and Kota*. Ascona: Artibus Asiae.

Beach. 1976. "A European Source for Early Mughal Painting." *OA* 22: 180–88.

Beach. 1978. *The Grand Mogul: Imperial Paintings in India 1600–1660*. Williamstown, Mass.: Sterling and Francine Clark Art Institute.

Beach. 1981. *The Imperial Image: Paintings for the Mughal Court*. Washington, D.C.: Freer Gallery of Art.

Bernier, F. 1914. *Travels in the Mogul Empire*. Translated by V. Smith. Oxford: Clarendon Press.

Bhanu, D. 1954. "The Mughal Libraries." *JPHS* 2, pt. 4: 287–301.

Bhattacharya, S. 1967. *A Dictionary of Indian History*. New York: Braziller.

Binney, E., 3rd. 1972. "Later Mughal Painting." In *Aspects of Indian Art*. Edited by P. Pal. Leiden: E. J. Brill.

Binney. 1973. *Indian Miniature Painting from the Collection of Edwin Binney, 3rd: The Mughal and Deccani Schools*. Portland, Oregon: Portland Art Museum.

Binyon, L., and Arnold, Sir T. W. 1921. *Court Painters of the Grand Moguls*. Oxford: Oxford University Press.

Blochet, E. 1928. "Les peintures orientales de la collection Pozzi." *Bulletin de la société française de reproductions de manuscrits* 12: 5–68.

Blochet. 1930. *Catalogue of an Exhibition of Persian Paintings from the XIIth to the XVIIIth Century Formerly in the Collections of the Shahs of Persia and the Great Mughals*. New York: Demotte.

Bodleian Library. 1953. *Mughal Miniatures of the Earlier Periods*. Oxford: Oxford University Press.

Brown, P. 1924. *Indian Painting under the Mughals*. Oxford: Oxford University Press.

Brown, P. 1932. "An Illustrated History of the Moslem World." *Parnassus* 4: 29ff.

Brown, W. N. 1933. *The Story of Kaloka*. Washington, D.C.: Freer Gallery of Art.

Brown, W. N. 1934. *Miniature Paintings of the Jaina Kalpasutra*. Washington, D.C.: Freer Gallery of Art.

Bussagli, M. 1976. *Indian Miniatures*. New Delhi: Macmillan of India.

Chandra, M. 1949. *The Technique of Mughal Painting*. Lucknow: U. P. Historical Society.

Chandra, M. 1951/52. "An Illustrated Set of the *Amaru Sataku*." *BPWM* 1/2: 1–63.

Chandra, M. 1955/57. "Paintings from an Illustrated Version of the *Ramayana* Painted at Udaipur in A.D. 1649." *BPWM* 5: 33–49.

Chandra, M. 1957. *Mewar Painting*. New Delhi: Lalit Kala Akademi.

Chandra, P. 1949. *Jain Miniature Paintings from Western India*. Ahmedabad: S. M. Nawab.

Chandra, P. 1956/57. "A Ragamala Set of the Mewar School in the National Museum of India." *LK* no. 3/4: 46–74.

Chandra, P. 1959. *Bundi Painting*. New Delhi: Lalit Kala Akademi.

Chandra, P. 1960. "Ustad Salivahana and the Development of Popular Mughal Art." *LK* no. 7/8: 25–46.

Chandra, P. 1971. *Indian Miniature Painting* (The Watson Collection). Madison: University of Wisconsin Press.

Chandra, P. 1976. *Tuti-Nama: Commentarium*. Graz: Akademische Druck.

Clarke, C. S. 1921. *Twelve Mogul Paintings of the School of Humayun Illustrating the Romance of Amir Hamzah*. London: Victoria and Albert Museum.

Clarke. 1922. *Indian Drawings: Thirty Mogul Paintings of the School of Jahangir*. London: Victoria and Albert Museum.

Commissariat, M. S. 1957. *History of Gujarat; with a survey of its monuments and inscriptions*. 2 vols. Bombay: Orient Longman.

Coomaraswamy. A. K. 1916. *Rajput Painting*. 2 vols. Oxford: Oxford University Press.

Coomaraswamy. 1926. *Catalogue of the Indian Collections in the Museum of Fine Arts, Boston*. Pt. 5, *Rajput Painting*. Pt. 6, *Mughal Painting*. Cambridge: Harvard University Press.

Coomaraswamy. 1929. *Les miniatures orientales de la collection Goloubew*. Paris: G. Van Oest.

Craven, R. C. 1966. *Miniatures and Small Sculptures from India*. Gainesville: University of Florida.

Czuma, S. 1975. *Indian Art from the George P. Bickford Collection*. Cleveland: Cleveland Museum of Art.

Das, A. K. 1967. "Mughal Royal Hunt in Miniature Paintings." *Indian Museum Bulletin* 1: 19–23.

Das. 1971. "Bishndas." In *Chhavi, Golden Jubilee Volume*. Banaras: Bharat Kala Bhavan.

Das. 1974. "Ustad Mansur." *LK* no. 17: 32–9.

Devapriam, E. 1972. "The Influence of Western Art on Mughal Painting." Ph.D. dissertation, Case Western Reserve University.

Dickinson, E., and Khandalavala, K. 1959. *Kishangarh Painting*. New Delhi: Lalit Kala Akademi.

Dimock, E. C., et al. 1974. *The Literatures of India*. Chicago: University of Chicago Press.

Doshi, S. 1972. "An Illustrated Manuscript from Aurangabad Dated A.D. 1650." *LK* no. 15: 19–28.

Dowson, J. 1957. *A Classical Dictionary of Hindu Mythology*. London: Routledge and Kegan Paul.

Dutt, M. N., ed. 1895–1905. *A Prose Translation of the Mahabharata*. 18 vols. Calcutta: H. C. Dass.

Dwivedi, R. A. 1966. *A Critical Survey of Hindi Literature*. New Delhi: Motilal Banarsi Dass.

Dwivedi, V. 1968. "Two Kedara Ragini Paintings." *CMAB* 55: 19–27.

Dwivedi, V. 1969. "A *Rasamanjari* Painting from Basohli." *CMAB* 56: 262–69.

Eastman, A. C. 1959. *The Nala-Damayanti Drawings*. Boston: Museum of Fine Arts.

Ebeling, K. 1973. *Ragamala Painting*. Basel: Basilius Presse.

Egger, G. 1974. *Hamza Nama (Facsimile)*. 3 vols. Graz: Akademische Druck.

Ettinghausen, R. 1959. "Abdu's-samad." In *Encyclopedia of World Art* 1: 18.

Ettinghausen. 1961*a*. "The Emperor's Choice." *De Artibus Opuscula* 40: 98–120.

Ettinghausen. 1961*b*. *Paintings of the Sultans and Emperors of India in American Collections*. New Delhi: Lalit Kala Akademi.

Ettinghausen. 1962. *Arab Painting*. Lausanne: Skira.

Falk, S. J. 1976. "Rothschild Collection of Mughal Miniatures." In *Persian and Mughal Art*. London: Lund Humphries.

Falk, T. 1978. "Mughal and Rajput Painting." In *Indian Painting*. London: Calnaghi & Co.

Falk, T., and Archer, M. 1981. *Indian Miniatures in the India Office Library*. London: Sotheby Parke Bernet.

Farooqi, A. (n.d.) "Reassessment on the Commencement of the *Dastan-i-Amir Hamzah*." *RL* 42, nos. 1 & 2: 35–37.

Gangoly, O. C. 1926. *Masterpieces of Rajput Painting*. Calcutta: Rupam.

Gangoly. 1935. *Ragas and Raginis*. Bombay: Nalanda Publications.

Gangoly. 1961. *A Critical Catalogue of Miniature Paintings in the Baroda Museum*. Baroda: Government Press.

Garrett, J. 1973. *A Classical Dictionary of India*. New York: Lenox Hill.

Gascoigne, B. 1971. *The Great Moghuls*. New York: Harper and Row.

Glück, H. 1925. *Die Indischen Miniaturen des Haemzae-Romanes*. Zurich: Amathea-Verlag.

Godard, Y. A. 1936. "Les marges du Murakka Gulshan." *Athar-e Iran* 1: 13–18.

Godard. 1937. "Un album de portraits des princes Timurides de l'Inde." *Athar-e Iran* 2: 179–277.

Goetz, H. 1930. *Bilderatlas zur kulturgeschichte Indiens in der Grossmoghul-zeit*. Berlin: D. Reimer.

Goetz. 1950. *The Art and Architecture of Bikaner State*. Oxford: Bruno Cassirer.

Goetz. 1957. "The First Golden Age of Udaipur." *ArsO* 2: 427–37.

Goetz. 1958. "The Early Muraqqa's of the Mughal Emperor Jahangir." *Marg* 11: 33–41.

Goswamy, B. N. 1961. "The Pahari Artists: A Study." *RL* 32, no. 2: 31–50.

Goswamy. 1965. "The Artist-family of Rajol: New Light on an Old Problem." *RL* 35, nos. 1 & 2: 15–23.

Goswamy. 1966. "The Problem of the Artist 'Nainsukh of Jasrota.'" *AA* 28: 205–10.

Goswamy. 1968. "Pahari Painting: The Family as the Basis of Style." *Marg* 21: 17–62.

Goswamy. 1975. *Pahari Paintings of the Nala-Damayanti Theme*. New Delhi: National Museum.

Gray, B. 1934. "An Early Mughal Illuminated Page." *BMQ* 8, no. 4: 149–51.

Gray. 1950. Section on *Painting*. In *The Art of India and Pakistan*. Edited by Sir L. Ashton. London: Faber and Faber.

Gray. 1951. *Treasures of Indian Miniatures in the Bikaner Palace Collection*. Oxford: Bruno Cassirer.

Gray. 1961. *Persian Painting*. Lausanne: Skira.

Gray, B., and Godard, A. 1956. *Iran: Persian Miniatures, Imperial Library*. Greenwich: New York Graphic Society.

Grube, E. J. 1968. *The Classical Style in Islamic Painting*. New York: Pierpont Morgan Library.

Grube. n.d. *Islamic Paintings from the Eleventh to the Eighteenth Century in the Collection of Hans P. Krauss*. New York: H. P. Krauss.

Haig, W., ed. 1922–37. *The Cambridge History of India*. Vol. 4, *Mughal India*. New York: Macmillan Company.

Hajek, L. 1960. *Indian Miniatures of the Mughal School*. London: Spring Books.

Haldane, D. 1978. *Mamluk Painting*. Warminster: Aris & Phillips.

Hambly, G. 1968. *Cities of Mughal India*. New York: G. P. Putnam's Sons.

Haq, M. M. 1931*a*. "Discovery of a Portion of the Original Manuscript of *Tarikh-i-Alfi*." *IC* 5: 462–71.

Haq. 1931*b*. "The Khan Khanem and His Painters." *IC* 5: 621–27.

Hendley, T. H. 1883. "The *Razm Namah* Manuscript." In *Memorials of the Jeypore Exhibition*. Vol. 4. Jeypore.

Hendley. 1897. *The Rulers of India and the Chiefs of Rajputana*. London: W. Griggs.

Holt, P. M., et al. 1970. *The Cambridge History of Islam*. 2 vols. Cambridge: At the University Press.

Hopkins, T. J. 1968. "The Social Teaching of the *Bhagavata Purana*." In *Krishna: Myths, Rites, and Attitudes*. Edited by M. Singer. Chicago: University of Chicago Press.

Hutchins, F. 1980. *The Young Krishna*. West Franklin, New Hampshire: Amarta Press.

Ikram, S. M. 1964. *Muslim Civilization in India*. New York: Columbia University Press.

Ivanov, A. A., et al. 1962. *Albom indijskihi persidskih miniatur XVI-XVIII v.v.* Moscow: USSR Academy of Sciences.

Jahangir, Emperor of Hindustan (1569–1627). 1968. *The Tuzuk-i-Jahangiri*. Translated by A. Rogers and H. Beveridge. 2nd ed. 2 vols. Delhi: Munshiram Manoharlal.

Jain, J., and Fischer, E. 1978. *Jaina Iconography*. Leiden: E. Brill.

James, D. 1981. *Islamic Masterpieces of the Chester Beatty Library*. London: World of Islam Festival Trust.

Jindel, R. 1976. *Culture of a Sacred Town: A Sociological Study of Nathdwara*. Bombay: Popular Prakashan.

Kanoria, G. K. 1952/53. "An Early Dated Rajasthani Ragamala." *JISOA* 19: 1–10.

Keay, F. E. 1920. *A History of Hindi Literature*. Calcutta: Association Press.

Khan, A. N. 1969. "An Illustrated *Akbarnama* Manuscript in the Victoria and Albert Museum, London." *East and West* 19: 424–29.

Khandalavala, K. 1950. "Leaves from Rajasthan." *Marg* 4, no. 3: 2–24, 49–56.

Khandalavala. 1958. *Pahari Miniature Painting*. Bombay: New Book Co.

Khandalavala, K., and Chandra, M. 1965. *Miniatures and Sculptures from the Collection of the Late Sir Cowasji Jehangir*. Bombay: Board of Trustees of the Prince of Wales Museum.

Khandalavala, K., and Chandra, M. 1969. *New Documents of Indian Painting: A Reappraisal*. Bombay: Board of Trustees of the Prince of Wales Museum.

Khandalavala, K., and Chandra, M. 1974. *An Illustrated Aranyaka Parvan in the Asiatic Society of Bombay*. Bombay: Asiatic Society of Bombay.

Khandalavala, K.; Chandra, M.; and Chandra, P. 1960. *Miniature Painting from the Collection of Sir Motichand Khajanchi*. New Delhi: Lalit Kala Akademi.

Khandalavala, K., and Mittal, J. 1974. "The Bhagavata Manuscripts from Palam and Isarda—A Consideration in Style." *LK* no. 16: 28–32.

Kinsley, D. R. 1979. *The Divine Player*. Delhi: Motilal Banarsi Dass.

Knizkova, H., and Marek, J. 1963. *The Jenghiz Khan Miniatures from the Court of Akbar the Great*. London: Spring Books.

Kramrisch, S. 1981. *Manifestations of Shiva*. Philadelphia: Philadelphia Museum of Art.

Krishna, A. 1963. *Malwa Painting*. Banaras: Bharat Kala Bhavan.

Krishnadasa, R. 1966. "A Fablebook for Akbar." In *Times of India Annual*.

Kuhnel, E. 1923. *Miniaturmalerei im Islamischen Orient*. Berlin: Bruno Cassirer.

Kuhnel, E., and Goetz, H. 1926. *Indian Book Painting from Jahangir's Album in the State Library in Berlin*. London: Kegan Paul.

Leach, L. 1981. "Later Mughal Painting." In *The Arts of India*. Edited by B. Gray. Oxford: Phaidon Press.

Lee, S. E. 1957. "The Decorative and the Super-real: Two Rajasthani Miniatures." *CMAB* 44: 180–83.

Lee. 1960. *Rajput Painting*. New York: Asia House.

Lee. 1964. *A History of Far Eastern Art*. New York: Harry Abrams.

Lee, S. E., and Chandra, P. 1963. "A Newly Discovered Tuti-Nama and the Continuity of the Indian Tradition of Manuscript Painting." *Burlington Magazine* 105: 547–54.

Losty, J. P. 1982. *The Art of the Book in India*. London: British Library.

MacLagan, E. 1932. *The Jesuits and the Great Mogul*. London: Burns, Oates and Washbourne.

Majmudar, M. R. 1965. *Cultural History of Gujerat*. Bombay: Popular Prakashan.

Majmudar. 1968. *Gujerat: Its Art-Heritage*. Bombay: University of Bombay.

Mujumdar, B. 1969. *Krishna in History and Legend*. Calcutta: University of Calcutta.

Majumdar, R. C., ed. 1960. *The History and Culture of the Indian People*. Vol. 6, *The Delhi Sultanate*. Bombay: Bharatiya Vidya Bhavan.

Majumdar, R. C., ed. 1974. *The History and Culture of the Indian People*. Vol. 7, *The Mughal Empire*. Bombay: Bharatiya Vidya Bhavan.

Marg. 1958. Vol. 11, no. 3: "Early Mughal Art"; Vol. 11, no. 4: "Later Mughal Art."

Marg. 1963. Vol. 16, no. 2: "Deccani Kalams."

Marek, J. 1963. "Mughal Miniatures as a Source of History." *JPHS* 11: 195–207.

Marteau, G., and Vever, H. 1913. *Miniatures persanes . . . exposées au Musée des Arts Décoratifs 1912*. Paris: Bibliothèque d'art et d'archéologie.

Martin, F. R. 1912. *The Miniature Painting and Painters of Persia, India, and Turkey*. 2 vols. London: Quaritch.

Meredith-Owens, G. 1967. "The British Museum Manuscript of the *Akbarnameh*." *Burlington Magazine* 109, pt. 1: 94.

Meredith-Owens, G., and Pinder-Wilson, R. 1956. "A Persian Translation of the *Mahabharata*." *BMQ* 20:62–65.

Miller, B. S. 1971. *Phantasies of a Love-Thief*. New York: Columbia University Press.

Nadvi, S. 1945. "Libraries During the Muslim Rule in India." *IC* 19: 329–45.

Naik, C. R. 1966. *Abdur-Rahim Khan-i-Khanan and His Literary Circle*. Ahmedabad: Gujerat University.

Nawab, S. M. 1956. *Masterpieces of Kalpasutra Paintings*. Ahmedabad: S. M. Nawab.

Nizami, A. 1972. "Socio-Religious Outlook of Abu'l Fazl." In *Medieval India, a Miscellany*, vol. 2, pp. 99–151. 3 vols. New York: Asia Publishing House.

Oaten, E. F. 1973. *European Travellers in India*. Lucknow: Pustak Kendra.

Pal, P. 1967. *Ragamala Paintings in the Museum of Fine Arts, Boston*. Boston: Museum of Fine Arts.

Pal. 1976. *The Flute and the Brush*. Los Angeles: Los Angeles County Museum of Art.

Pinder-Wilson, R. 1976. *Paintings from the Muslim Courts of India*. London: World of Islam.

Pinder-Wilson, R., ed. 1969. *Paintings from Islamic Lands*. Oxford: Bruno Cassirer.

Prasad, I. 1956. *The Life and Times of Humayun*. New York: Longmans, Green and Co.

Prasad, I. 1974. *The Mughal Empire*. Allahabad: Chugh Publications.

Prasad, R. C. 1965. *Early English Travellers in India*. New Delhi: Motilal Banarsi Dass.

Randhawa, M. S. 1958. "A Journey to Basohli." *RL* 28, nos. 1 & 2: 14–24.

Randhawa. 1959. *Basohli Painting*. New Delhi: Indian Ministry of Information.

Randhawa. 1960. *Kangra Paintings of the Bhagavata Purana*. New Delhi: National Museum.

Randhawa. 1961. "Maharaja Sansar Chand—The Patron of Kangra Painting." *RL* 32, no. 2: 1–31.

Randhawa. 1962. *Kangra Paintings on Love*. New Delhi: National Museum.

Randhawa. 1971. *Kangra Ragamala Paintings*. New Delhi: National Museum.

Randhawa, M. S. (n.d.). "Paintings of the Babur-Nama." *RL* 42, nos. 1 & 2: 9–16.

Randhawa, M. S., and Bhambri, S. D. 1966. "Basohli Paintings of Bhanudatta's *Rasamanjari*." *RL* 36, nos. 1 & 2: 1–124.

Randhawa, M. S., and Galbraith, J. K. 1968. *Indian Painting: The Scenes, Themes, and Legends*. Boston: Houghton Mifflin.

Robinson, B. 1958. *Descriptive Catalogue of the Persian Paintings in the Bodleian Library*. Oxford: Clarendon Press.

Roychoudhury, M. L. 1941. *The Din-i-Ilahi or the Religion of Akbar*. Calcutta: University of Calcutta.

Santhanam, K. 1969. *An Anthology of Indian Literatures*. New Delhi: Gandhi Peace Foundation.

Sarkar, J. 1912–30. *The Fall of the Mughal Empire*. 4 vols. London.

Sarre, F. P., and Martin, F. R. 1912. *Miesterwerken Muhammedanischer Kunst*. Munich: F. Bruckman.

Sastri, H. P., trans. 1952–59. *The Ramayana of Valmiki*. 3 vols. London: Shanti Sadan.

Schulberg, L. *Historic India*. 1968. New York: Time-Life Books.

Schulz, P. W. 1914. *Die Persisch-islamische miniaturmalerei*. 2 vols. Leipzig: Hiersemann.

Sharma, O. P. 1974. *Indian Miniature Painting*. Brussels: Bibliothèque Royale Albert.

Shiveshwarker, L. 1967. *The Pictures of the Chaurapanchasika, a Sanskrit Love Lyric*. New Delhi: National Museum.

Singer, M., ed. 1959. *Traditional India*. Chicago: American Folklore Society.

Singer, ed. 1966. *Krishna: Myths, Rites, and Attitudes*. Chicago: University of Chicago Press.

Singh, B. S. 1967. *Rahim*. New Delhi: National Book Trust.

Skelton, R. 1961. *Indian Miniatures from the XVth to XIXth Centuries*. Venice: Neri Pozza Editore.

Skelton. 1969. "Two Mughal Lion Hunts." *Victoria and Albert Museum Yearbook* 1: 33–47.

Skelton. 1970. "Mughal Paintings from Harivamśa Manuscript." *Victoria and Albert Museum Yearbook* 2: 41–53.

Skelton. 1972. "A Decorative Motif in Mughal Art." In *Aspects of Indian Art*. Edited by P. Pal. Leiden: E. J. Brill.

Skelton. 1973. *Rajasthani Temple Hanging of the Krishna Cult*. New York: American Federation of Arts.

Skelton. 1976. "Indian Painting of the Mughal Period." In *Islamic Painting and the Arts of the Book*. Edited by B. W. Robinson. London: Faber and Faber.

Smart, E. 1973. "Four Illustrated Mughal *Baburnama* Manuscripts." *AARP* 3: 54–58.

Smart. 1977. "Paintings from the *Baburnama*: A Study of Sixteenth-Century Mughal Historical Manuscript Illustrations." Ph.D. dissertation, London University.

Smart. 1978. "Six Folios from a Dispersed Manuscript of the *Baburnama*." In *Indian Painting*. London: Colnaghi & Co.

Smith, V. A. 1911. *A History of Fine Art in India and Ceylon*. Oxford: Clarendon Press.

Soustiel, J. 1973. *Miniatures Orientales de l'Inde, les écoles et leurs styles*. Paris: Librarie Légueltel.

Soustiel. 1974. *Miniatures Orientales de l'Inde, écoles mogholes, du Deccan, et autres écoles indiennes*. Paris: Librarie Légueltel.

Spear, P. 1951. *Twilight of the Mughals*. Cambridge: At the University Press.

Spear. 1965. *A History of India*. Vol. 2. London: Penguin Books.

Spink, W. 1971. *Krishnamandala*. Ann Arbor: University of Michigan.

Spink & Son. 1976. *Painting for the Royal Courts of India*. London: Spink & Son.

Srivastava, A. L. 1962. *Akbar the Great*. 2 vols. Agra: Shiva Lal Agarwala.

Staude, W. 1928a. "Muskine." *RAA* 5: 169–82.

Staude. 1928b. "Le paysage dans l'*Akbar-namah*." *RAA* 5: 102ff.

Staude. 1934. "Contributions a l'étude de Basawan." *RAA* 8: 1–18.

Staude. 1935. *Moghul-maler der Akbar Zeit*. Vienna: C. Schmeid.

Staude. 1955. "Les artistes de la cour d'Akbar et les illustrations du *Dastan-i-Amir Hamzah*." *AA* 2: 47–65, 83–111.

Staude. 1960. "Basawan." In *Encyclopedia of World Art*. Vol. 2: 386.

Stchoukine, I. 1929a. *Les miniatures indiennes de l'époque des grands Moghols au musée du Louvre*. Paris: E. Leroux.

Stchoukine. 1929b. *La peinture indienne a l'époque des grands Moghols*. Paris: E. Leroux.

Stchoukine. 1929/30. "Portraits Moghuls." *RAA* 6: 212–41.

Stchoukine. 1931. "Quelques images de Jahangir dans un *Divan de Hafiz*." *Gazette des Beaux-Arts*. 6: 160–67.

Stchoukine. 1931/32. "Portraits Moghuls." *RAA* 7: 163–76.

Stchoukine. 1935. "Portraits Moghuls." *RAA* 9: 130ff.

Stchoukine. 1937. "Un *Bustan* de Sadi illustre par des artistes Moghols." *RAA* 9: 69ff.

Stooke, H. J., and Khandalavala, K. 1953. *The Laud Ragamala Miniatures*. Oxford: Bruno Cassirer.

Strzygowski, J., ed. 1933. *Asiatische Miniaturenmalerei*. Klagenfurt: Kollitsch.

Suleiman, H. 1970. *Miniatures of Baburnama*. Tashkent: Fan of Uzbek SSR.

Tagare, G. V., trans. 1978. *The Bhagavata Purana*. Delhi: Motilal Banarsi Dass.

Titley, N. 1975. "Miniature Paintings Illustrating the Works of Amir Khusrau." *Marg* 28, no. 3: 20–52.

Titley, 1977. *Miniatures from Persian Manuscripts*. London: British Library.

Tod, J. 1827–32. *The Annals and Antiquities of Rajasthan*. 2 vols. London: Lund Humphries.

Topsfield, A. 1980. *Paintings from Rajasthan in the National Gallery of Victoria*. Melbourne: The Gallery.

Topsfield. 1981. "Rajput Painting." In *The Arts of India*. Edited by B. Gray. Oxford: Phaidon.

Tyulayev, S. I. 1955. *Indian Art in Soviet Collections*. Moscow: State Fine Arts Publishing House.

Tyulayev. 1958. "Miniatures from a Sixteenth-Century *Babur Nama*." *Marg* 11: 45–52.

Tyulayev, comp. 1960. *Miniatures of Babur Namah*. Moscow: State Fine Arts Publishing House.

Victoria and Albert Museum. 1979. *Arts of Bengal*. London: Her Majesty's Stationery Office.

Victoria and Albert Museum. 1982. *The Indian Heritage: Court Life and Arts under Mughal Rule*. London: Her Majesty's Stationery Office.

Waldschmidt, E., and Waldschmidt, R. L. 1967. *Miniatures of Musical Inspiration in the Collection of the Berlin Museum of Indian Art: Ragamala Pictures from the Western Himalaya Promontory*. Pt. 1. Berlin: Museum für Indische Kunst.

Waldschmidt and Waldschmidt. 1975. *Miniatures of Musical Inspiration in the Collection of the Berlin Museum of Indian Art: Ragamala Pictures from Northern India and the Deccan*. Pt. 2. Berlin: Museum für Indische Kunst.

Welch, S. C. 1958. "Miniatures from a Manuscript of the Diwan-i-Hafiz." *Marg* 11: 56–62.

Welch. 1959. "Early Mughal Miniature Painting from Two Private Collections Shown at the Fogg." *ArsO* 3: 133–46.

Welch. 1960. "The Emperor Akbar's Khamsa of Nizami." *Journal of the Walters Art Gallery* 23: 86–96.

Welch. 1961. "The Paintings of Basawan." *LK* 10: 7–18.

Welch. 1963a. *The Art of Mughal India, Paintings and Precious Objects*. New York: Asia Society.

Welch. 1963b. "Mughal and Deccani Miniature Painting from Private Collections." *ArsO* 5: 221–34.

Welch. 1972. *A King's Book of Kings*. New York: New York Graphic Society.

Welch. 1973. *A Flower from Every Meadow*. New York: Asia Society.

Welch, S. C., and Beach, M. C. 1965. *Gods, Thrones, and Peacocks*. New York: Asia Society.

Wellesz. E. 1952. *Akbar's Religious Thought Reflected in Mughal Painting*. London: George Allen and Unwin.

Wilber, D. N. 1962. *Persian Gardens and Garden Pavilions*. Rutland, Vermont: Charles E. Tuttle.

Wilkinson, J. V. S. 1929. *Lights of Canopus*. London: The Studio.

Wilkinson. 1949. *Mughal Painting*. London: Pitman Publishing.

Wilkinson, J. V. S., and Gray, B. 1935a. "Indian Paintings in a Persian Museum." *Burlington Magazine* 66: 168ff.

Wilkinson and Gray. 1935b. "Mughal Miniatures from the Period of Akbar." *Ostasiatische Zeitscrift* 11: 118–22.

Zafar, M. H. 1955. "Abd-al Rahim Khan Khanan and His Library." *JPHS* 3: 300–310.

Zimmer, H. 1965. *Myths and Symbols in Indian Art and Civilization*. New York: Harper and Row.